DATE DUE

MAY 0 8 2000			

DEMCO 38-297

SUNBELT / SNOWBELT

SUNBELT/SNOWBELT

Urban Development and Regional Restructuring

Edited by

Larry Sawers
AMERICAN UNIVERSITY

William K. Tabb
QUEENS COLLEGE

New York   Oxford
OXFORD UNIVERSITY PRESS
1984

Library of Congress Cataloging in Publication Data

Main entry under title:
Sunbelt/Snowbelt.

 Bibliography: p.
   1. Cities and towns—Sunbelt States—Growth—
Addresses, essays, lectures.   2. Cities and towns—
New England—Growth—Addresses, essays, lectures.
3. Urban policy—United States—Addresses, essays,
lectures.   4. United States—Economic conditions—
1971–   —Addresses, essays, lectures.   5. Regionalism—
United States—Addresses, essays, lectures.
I. Sawers, Larry, 1942–   .   II. Tabb, William K., 1942–
HT371.S89   1983   307.7′64′0973   82–14145
ISBN 0-19-503264-0
ISBN 0-19-503265-9 (pbk.)

Printing (last digit): 9 8 7 6 5 4 3

Printed in the United States of America

Preface

The genesis of this volume was a conference on New Perspectives on the Urban Political Economy at American University, Washington, D.C., on May 22–24, 1981. (A first conference had been held in 1975.) In issuing the call for conference papers, the editors suggested seventeen panels ranging over the very broad field of urban political economy. Much to our surprise, well over half the submissions which we accepted fit the single problematic of uneven regional development. These papers concerning the growth of the Sunbelt, plant closings in the Snowbelt, and the impact of industrial transformation and regional restructuring, while based on independent research by scholars from across the United States, quite remarkably shared a common understanding of economic forces, class formation, and political conflict. Authors tend to see changes in the forces of production (transportation or energy technologies, for example) as intertwined with social relations of production (for example, the organization of work through the wage bargain or the organization of conglomerate corporations able to centralize control even as they decentralize production). The struggle between capital and labor over the fruits of production on the one hand dictates disinvestment in high-wage, high-tax areas and prompts search for new labor pools and tax incentives. On the other hand, workers who have achieved a higher standard of living experience these shifts as a loss of job security. They realize that if they lose their jobs, they are unlikely to find employment at comparable wages. In most of the instances discussed, government action and interaction seem to encourage capital mobility at the expense of workers and communities. Market forces are the reflection of class interests and a political process heavily saturated with class bias.

We believe that over the years between the first and second New

Perspectives on the Urban Political Economy conference, a shared paradigmatic stance has emerged among a wide sector of urbanists, and that this coherence is reflected in this book. There will undoubtedly be a third New Perspectives conference, and we would urge scholars who find the approach taken here a helpful one to stay in touch with us. Any science should be an evolving one, deepening its theory with involvement in policy and testing itself against the background of real world events. The last word will never be said. As a statement of what we know and how we understand the urban political economy, the present volume serves as a guide. Urban growth and restructuring in our view is a process that can be both understood and influenced in a positive way by self-conscious social intervention. Present policy directions are too costly to the American people to be continued. We believe there is need for a dramatically new policy direction and that class analysis is a central tool in understanding what is wrong and how to change matters. We believe that the split between the interests of the majority of working-class Americans and those of unregulated capital lies at the heart of not only our urban crises but our larger economic crisis. We hope that readers of this volume will find it useful in their efforts to work for progressive social change.

New York City   W. K. T.
Washington, D.C.   L. S.
June 1983

Contents

PART THREE. FEDERAL POLICY

PART FOUR. LOCAL POLICY

PART FIVE. WHAT IS TO BE DONE

SUNBELT / SNOWBELT

1

Urban Development and Regional Restructuring, an Overview

WILLIAM K. TABB

Regional restructuring and urban growth, industrial reconstitution and labor market recomposition form the subject of this overview. It deals as well with government responses to such changes. This introductory essay will highlight developments in these areas over recent decades. We start with the suburbanization phenomenon and then discuss the growth of the Sunbelt.

The federal government's post–World War II urban, or rather suburban, policy included highway building under the Federal Interstate and National Defense Act of 1956 and home ownership under FHA, VA, FNMA, HLBB, and other alphabet soups of underwriting agencies. Such dramatic subsidies by taxpayers accelerated the tempo of the urban exodus, giving a lift to the economy and changing the spatial ordering of the American Way of Life.

Suburbanization was the engine of growth for the post–World War II United States economy. Billions of dollars in highway subsidies went to build the costly circumferential routes looping and bisecting older cities. Billions in housing subsidies allowed millions of Americans to acquire suburban homes, generating millions of jobs and billions in profits for construction, earth-moving equipment, building materials, appliances, and autos and gasoline, and indirectly as well for the suppliers of these industries. Suburbanization also set the ground for the subsequent deterioration of the central city. Rising suburban land val-

3

ues (thanks to these federal subsidies) were accompanied, as the process matured, by declining central city property values (and tax yield). The following round of expenditures, from urban renewal and public housing to Model Cities and the Neighborhood Youth Corps, attempted to undo the damage. Growth of suburban America had left central cities with serious problems of a declining tax base and a swelling population of unskilled workers with limited employment opportunities.

Such was the situation when the urban crisis of the 1960s exploded. The problem was seen then primarily as economic decline in central cities in contrast to rapid growth in suburban areas. Nationally between 1958 and 1967, manufacturing employment increased by 7 percent in central cities but by nearly a third in suburbs, and wholesale trade advanced by 11 percent in cities but grew by 90 percent in the suburbs.

A growing rural-suburban majority turned its back on the needs of the central cities. At the ballot box, the votes of the new majority brought the Nixon administration to the White House. The new coalition supported the move away from Great Society programs to a New Federalism under general revenue sharing. The Nixon approach was to redistribute money to *both* poor cities *and* rich suburbs. Not all federal aid was on a no-strings-attached basis, and some program funding was biased in favor of low-income citizens in need of help, but in general mayors of large cities could use the funds as they saw fit without community involvement. Elected officials used this funding to finance central business district development in an effort to shore up the city's dwindling tax base while accommodating real estate and banking interests.

A new city was created in the downtown areas of many older urban jurisdictions. Older cities became smaller. They existed as transaction centers, islands of affluence and activity surrounded by decay, unable to provide enough jobs to sustain their surplus population. Gentrification, or upgrading housing stock for more affluent users, reclaimed some former slum areas. Residents were forced out by high rents or cooperative and condominium conversion. Public resources flowed to the renewal of downtown areas at the expense of the poorer neighborhoods.

While there was an important racial dimension to this urban transformation, the decentralization of manufacturing and population out of the central city was not simply a matter of white flight since the same pattern is found in all older cities regardless of the extent of their black population (although as Sawers and Remy and Squires show in chapters 5 and 6, minority groups have suffered disproportionately from job loss caused by plant closings due to urban displacement). Plants moved to suburbs, to Southern cities and rural areas, and overseas in search of low-wage labor and cheaper land, energy, and taxes. The less-educated workers in the older cities were left with low-wage service jobs—and not enough of them.

The transformation of the older industrial cities to office-convention-tourist centers meant a bimodal job creation pattern: high wages for lawyers, accountants, corporate executives, and advertising and media types, but poorly paid jobs for maintenance personnel and most office workers, keypunch operators, messengers, typists, and clerks. In chapter 3, for example, Bennett Harrison describes how this transformation has taken place in the New England economy.

Many American cities had never been industrial centers and so could more easily meet new functions without going through a painful period of adjustment. So while many older urban giants shrank—between 1970 and 1980, St. Louis lost 28 percent of its population, Detroit 21 percent, and Cleveland 24 percent—newer cities grew as dramatically over the decade: Houston by 26 percent, Phoenix by 34 percent, and San Jose by 36 percent. The regional distribution of growing and declining cities forms a stark contrast. The mid-decade estimate of state populations shows that in the first half of the 1970s, 85 percent of the growth in U.S. population, an increase of ten million people, took place in the South and West. The growth of the Sunbelt and the alleged rise to power and prestige of the "cowboys" stands in sharp contrast to the population loss or exceedingly slow growth in most areas of the Northeast and North Central census regions. (Characteristics and definitions of the Sunbelt will be discussed later. As it suggests, the term refers to the Southern and Western rim of the United States [see table 1.1]).

This second phase of postwar spatial transformation had some things in common with the earlier suburbanization process. The need for unbuilt space and the difficulty of remolding older areas to new purposes were crucial to both phenomena. In addition, politics, economics, environmental amenities, and technology combined in each instance to favor the new direction of spatial growth. Suburbs, as upper income enclaves, allowed the affluent to escape proximity to urban poverty on the one hand, and enjoy the amenities of smaller-scale living in comfortably homogeneous communities on the other. Using their political influence, the suburbs frequently provided a swing vote in conjunction with rural areas against central cities. Economic growth in the suburbs became cumulative as construction generated more em-

Table 1.1. Regions and Geographic Divisions of the United States*

Northeast	North Central	South	West
New England	East North	South Atlantic	Mountain
Connecticut	Central	Delaware	Arizona
Maine	Illinois	District of	Colorado
Massachusetts	Indiana	Columbia	Idaho
New Hamp-	Michigan	Florida	Montana
shire	Ohio	Georgia	Nevada
Rhode Island	Wisconsin	Maryland	New Mexico
Vermont		North	Utah
	West North	Carolina	Wyoming
Middle Atlantic	Central	South	
New Jersey	Iowa	Carolina	Pacific
New York	Kansas	Virginia	Alaska
Pennsylvania	Minnesota	West Virginia	California
	Missouri		Hawaii
	Nebraska	East South	Oregon
	North Dakota	Central	Washington
	South Dakota	Alabama	
		Kentucky	
		Mississippi	
		Tennessee	
		West South	
		Central	
		Arkansas	
		Louisiana	
		Oklahoma	
		Texas	

* The federal government has divided the fifty states into four regions: Northeast, North Central, South, and West. Each of these in turn is divided into two or three geographic divisions. Unless otherwise noted, these are the categories used in this book.

ployment and jobs came to be closer to a growing suburban labor force. Businesses moved to the suburbs to avoid central city congestion and other urban problems. The technology of one-story plants in manufacturing and the need for parking also favored land-intensive suburban industrial parks. The shopping center was the analogous innovation in the consumer realm.

The growth of the Sunbelt also combined technological, political, environmental, and economic forces. Innovations in air travel, information processing, and other forms of communication and the development of air conditioning made major differences in the attractiveness of the South and the West. The federal highway program and water and sewage projects supplied needed infrastructure. The cold war meant military bases and defense plants. The politically more conservative politicians of the area were quick to see the potential of federal funds as an engine of regional growth. Falling transportation costs, attractive climate, and other environmental amenities combined with a low cost of living and available inexpensive land attracted migrants, including large numbers of retired Americans. The increased profitability of the petroleum industry and agribusiness were also important. As the Northeast and North Central regions suffered decline in population growth, tax base, jobs, and credit rating, so the Sunbelt came to be seen as the new frontier of economic development and political power. As costs are evening out, however, movement of people and resources is slowing. Equally important, what at first appeared as a matter of uneven regional growth can now also be seen as a larger industrial restructuring and a general economic crisis affecting the nation as a whole.

While economists tend to talk about consumer sovereignty (expressed by individual decisions to move to the Sunbelt states), we would stress the role of federal expenditures in fostering growth of that part of the country. Researchers comparing the three most populous rim states (California, Texas, and Florida) with the three most populous mid-Atlantic states (New York, Pennsylvania, and New Jersey) in terms of the impact of federal expenditures in the early 1970s found not only the rim states greatly favored, but their advantage greatest in expenditure categories most likely to stimulate future economic growth. They conclude: "If the East is indeed disadvantaged, the reasons for such a disadvantage lie in the recent history of federal allocations." They report that

> in those areas having the greatest multiplier effects on economic development (defense spending, farm subsidies, highway expenditures, and federal civilian employment) the ratios of federal spending favor the rimland states. Only in the areas of housing-urban development and public assistance do the three eastern states have a clear edge. The Nixon freeze on subsidized housing programs and the present reliance on a special revenue sharing to support urban development, however, mean that whatever advantage the eastern states enjoy in these two areas will eventually disappear. (Fainstein and Fainstein, 1976:28.)

In addition to all the missile command, space flight centers, and naval bases, these Sunbelt states are also heavily dependent on corporate contractors for the military—Lockheed and the rest. Ohio, an older

industrial state paying three times as much in federal taxes, has about
the same number of federal military and civilian employees as Alabama. This pattern, noticeable since World War II (when 60 percent
or so of the military budget was spent in the Southern rim states), has
been a major factor in the region's development. Indeed, today retired
military personnel make up a significant proportion of the pensioners
in the area. Payrolls in the region's 140 military installations exceed
those in the rest of the military posts in the United States combined.
Half of the Pentagon's research funding is spent in the Sunbelt. Between grants for social programs, defense contracts, and military bases,
the region is supported by Big Government to a degree far in excess of
other parts of the nation. In 1969 military and civilian federal payrolls
accounted for four times as large a percentage of all personal income
in the five most rapidly growing states as in the five with the largest
outmigration (Anderson et al., 1982; Muller, 1975:7–8).

Between 1950 and 1975, the Northeastern and North Central states
lost 11,500 defense workers while the West gained over 150,000 and
the South more than a third of a million. The Northeast at the end of
that period had less than 10 percent of all military personnel, the West
over a third.

As to the civilian government jobs, in the years of alleged growth
of the federal bureaucracy (1960–1975), nearly a half million new federal civilian jobs were created. Only 16,000 were in the Northeast
while 135,000 were in the West and 270,000 in the South.

One of the major functions of the federal budget (along with
growth and stabilization policies) is to subsidize certain patterns of
growth. Key industries have done well in the post–World War II period. We have noted the growth of the auto industry, aided by hundreds of billions for the interstate highway program; suburban housing
with a boost from FHA, VA, and from federal income tax provision for
deductions of interest and local property taxes; and the military-
industrial complex as a result of the fear of communism and expan-
sionist foreign policy. It is clear that all of the above factors have
worked to dramatically favor the South and West over the North and
that billions upon billions have been involved. The federal role has favored an evening out of interregional per capita income. In 1930 per
capita income in the New England, Mideast, and Far West states was
30–40 percent above the U.S. average while in the Southwest it was
less than two-thirds and in the Southeast half of the national average.
In 1975 the Sunbelt's real disposable income per capita was 99 percent
of the national average and growing at a considerably faster rate

(ACIR, 1980:11; and Peterson, 1977:7). Even without adjusting for cost of living, income was higher in the Sunbelt than the Snowbelt by the eighties.

The transition for both declining and growing areas is not easy. Revenue loss, fiscal deficit, and increasing dependency on federal assistance by blighted, worn-out older cities and towns in the Snowbelt is matched by a surface prosperity in the Sunbelt which masks excessively rapid growth: an infrastructure which is not being built to last, overcrowding, and destruction of amenities. For the Sunbelt the problems of rapid development have been exacerbated by its uneven distribution; a few states account for almost all the growth. Take away Texas, Florida, North Carolina, Arizona and, in the early postwar years, California, and the growth rates look very modest. Further, there are even greater disparities within individual states. Even in fast-growing states such as Texas, it is clear that the prairies are not paved with gold (as Joe Feagin shows in chapter 4).

Other states more closely resemble the declining areas of the Snowbelt. The interior states of the South—Alabama, Arkansas, Mississippi, and Tennessee—are as dependent on old industries (apparel, automobile parts, textiles, wood products) as the older industrial states. Alabama and Michigan are not far apart in economic distress. Old industrial cities in the South are very much like their Northern counterparts. But being smaller, Corinth, Mississippi, or Florence, Alabama, do not get much notice in the national discussion.

Labor costs and labor attitudes are a crucial determinant of the location of economic activity. Bureau of Labor Statistics data show that one in three factory jobs in the South in 1978 was in an industry with hourly earnings below the national average for all production jobs (nonsupervisory workers on nonfarm payrolls). Nationally, only one in four factory workers was in such low-paying jobs. In 1978 half of manufacturing employees nationwide were in industries with average wages above $6.50 an hour, but only a third of Southern workers held such jobs (Rones, 1980:14). Many of these workers are employed in high technology industries producing such products as semiconductors, calculators, and computers. High technology and low pay frequently go together.

Sorting out these trends can be confusing. One important misconception is that *only* low-wage industries are attracted to the South. On the contrary, it has been in the fast-growing, high-wage industries that the South's growth has been most spectacular—expanding at twice the national rate between 1940 and 1960. Over those two decades, 90 percent of the more than one and a half million new Southern manufacturing jobs were in high-wage, faster-growing industries. But this is not of course to say that low wages were *not* a factor. "High"-wage industries paid lower wages in Southern plants, and this has been an important attraction. In some cases low wages have been maintained by violently antilabor employers willing to break the law and/or refuse to accommodate unions as some of the same firms have in the North and Northeast and North Central region labor markets.

The textile industry employs one out of five manufacturing employees in the South. The industry includes companies like J. P. Stevens, the nation's second largest textile firm and a target of a multi-million-dollar AFL-CIO organizing drive, which has been convicted on numerous occasions of violating federal labor laws, and in one case was ordered to pay $1.3 million to harassed or illegally dismissed workers. Among other acts, J. P. Stevens illegally bugged union headquarters. To the company, it is worth stalling through the courts while using whatever means it can find to stave off unionization. Other large firms generally do the same. Since the court of appeals usually has a large backlog, unions, even when they win elections to represent workers, find management unwilling to bargain in good faith although ordered to do so by the courts. After closing a shock absorber plant in Michigan and reopening it in Georgia, GM managed to hold off the United Automobile Workers for over a dozen years, refusing to bargain, appealing on technicalities, and keeping up its fire on union activists. GM has tried to show Southern workers that the union was bad for them. Finally, in early 1977, a union contract for GM workers in Monroe, Louisiana, was achieved, raising average wages from $5.50 an hour to $7.50.

In 1982 the AFL-CIO spent a million dollars on the Houston Organizing Project. Its staff of twenty organizers was there because only 13 percent of the workers in that rapidly growing state were unionized. Texas ranked forty-seventh among the states in the proportion of its work force which is unionized. Texas is a right-to-work state like many others in the Sunbelt. Closed shops, operated under a contractual agreement between union and employer requiring the employment of union members only, are prohibited under right-to-work laws. These laws make it more difficult to organize since under them nonmembers can benefit from union contracts without paying dues.

William Brown, chairman of the Legal Rights and Strategy Committee of the Houston Associated Builders and Contractors, stood ready

to help companies prevent unionization. He said: "Most of the northern states are not right-to-work states and most have a long history of
union domination, corruption, violence, sabotage and mass picketing.
The first step is to control politics. If they can elect all the local sheriffs
and chiefs of police and judges and district attorneys, they can coerce
and compel employers to sign pre-hiring agreements. You don't have
that sort of situation in Houston" (Balz, 1982:A9).

Brown calls attention to a number of items that fall under the
heading of "business climate," and as Storper and Walker demonstrate
in chapter 2, it is just these factors that are important location considerations for industry. The lack of a prounion environment can mean
lower wage costs (and a lower standard of living for workers).

An antiunion environment typically coexists with negative attitudes
toward government regulation. Sunbelt cities (preeminently Houston
as Feagin's discussion in chapter 4 shows) tend to have minimal land
use controls and public service provisions. It is likely that after their
growth spurt is over, their laissez-faire patterns of physical and social
space promise decay and service breakdown on a grand scale, neces-
sitating costly infrastructural investment. Such a future is not yet evident in Texas-style real estate developments, almost self-contained cities which can isolate themselves from lower-income citizens. Sunbelt
cities can build income-segregated communities more effectively than
older urban space can be reshaped for such a purpose.

Competition for jobs is increasingly a source of tension in the Sunbelt, especially as the rate of growth slows down. As job growth in the
expanding parts of the Sunbelt fails to keep pace with inmigration, social tensions grow between older residents and new arrivals. A Michigan license plate may cause a native driver discomfort in Texas although the recent wave of migration in a sense is only the reversal of
the last great rural-to-urban movement. One worker who migrated
from Arkansas to the auto plants of Detroit in 1947 came to seek employment in the booming oil refineries of Houston, ironically noting:
"They called us hillbillies up there; we come down here, and they call
us Yankees" (Stevens, 1981:1). Backmigration is even more prevalent
in the South, which experienced net outmigration until the late 1960s.
A majority of those coming into the South to live in the mid-1970s
cited family reasons, suggesting regional loyalties of return migrants.
Six in ten interstate migrants cited job-related factors as their major
reason for moving (Long and Hansen, 1980). It seems noteworthy
that as many as four in ten interstate migrants did not give job-

related reasons for moving. While companies frequently move based
solely on profitability, quality-of-life issues and family and individual
preferences appear to be quite important in individual location decisions.

As a nation we are shaped by regional loyalties which can obscure
the close relationship between quality of life and economic issues.
Older Northeast and North Central cities undergoing a process of deindustrialization experience rising rates of unemployment, crime, and
social distintegration which "push" people out. Good climate can combine with the perception of job opportunities to "pull" people. Depending on education and work experience, family history and personal ties, people may relocate in complex patterns.

Summing up the diverse currents in population and job movements
is a difficult task. While we title our book *Sunbelt/Snowbelt,* each of
these huge regions contains contrasting and contradictory phenomena.
As has been seen, Sunbelt growth is really a phenomenon of the coastal
states of the South and the West (plus Georgia), and much of the
boom is related to energy and amenities. As production and living
costs rise faster in the South, transportation costs even out, and more
low-income people take up residence in the Sunbelt, urban problems
will look similar across the United States. Indeed, the failure to rebuild
aged and decaying infrastructure—bridges and water tunnels for example—in the Snowbelt states has its counterpart in the shoddily built
infrastructure and housing stock in the Sunbelt. They are aging fast,
and in many areas are not being maintained. As Saxenian's study of
Silicon Valley demonstrates (chapter 7), even rapidly developing
areas may, as a product of their growth, diminish quality of life for
area residents. On the other hand, a rebuilt world corporate city such
as New York is becoming offers a sharp contrast with familiar stereotypes of South Bronx decay (Tabb, 1982:89–106).

Some experts expect the most rapid rates of population growth in
the late 1980s and 1990s to be in the Rocky Mountain states and on
down through the Southwest to the southern Appalachians; this development will occur as high cost of living and rising labor costs slow
down the coastal states of the West and Southeast (Kresge, 1981). In
terms of growth rates, Nevada, Arizona, Wyoming, Utah, and Alaska
are expected to do well, according to the Commerce Department's
Bureau of Economic Analysis projections to the year 2000.

Such a dynamically shifting tableau of regional growth with its
reorganized spatial division of labor and location of industry follows
a logic that has been too complex for social scientists to predict ade-

quately or for government policy makers to understand and respond to successfully.

While manufacturing job decentralization seems to have led the process of Sunbelt growth, decline of older Snowbelt manufacturing is a more complex matter, as Harrison shows in chapter 3. Manufacturing jobs were 50 percent of all growth of nonmetropolitan employment in the 1960s as corporations sought out a low-wage, underemployed, rural, and heavily female labor force with "better" work attitudes (less affected by unionization, less demanding about working conditions, and more willing to take dead end jobs without pension and health benefits). At the same time, those left unemployed or facing deteriorating working conditions in older industrial areas are heavily racial minorities and women, as Remy and Sawers and Squires demonstrate in chapters 5 and 6.

The federal tax structure encourages corporations to write off old plants, counting the cost of relocation as a business expense and allowing generous investment tax credit for plant and equipment, tax policies helping to refinance runaway shops (see Luger, chapter 8). It would be possible for the U.S. government to disallow the tax writeoff on moving expenses and abandonment of old plant and equipment unless workers and communities were properly compensated. Federal norms on local tax and other benefits for locating corporations could also be adopted to reduce or even eliminate the ability of corporations to play one jurisdiction against the other. Relocation permits could be made mandatory and their granting dependent on gains being justified in relation to total social costs generated. It would seem reasonable to charge the firm the social costs of its actions. Now the public sector must pay the private in hope of better treatment. Economic democracy would offer workers the rights to relocation allowances and equal wages at the new plant site. (At present, important policy initiations reverse this priority—see Goldsmith, chapter 13.) Similarly, three to five years of local taxes might be demanded for the abandoned community. Just as stranded workers should be provided with continued health care and other benefits over some appropriate period, so too should the intrastructural and operating needs of the community be provided for by the corporation. The public policy debate on these issues is enjoined by Wilmoth and Wolff in chapters 9 and 10. Lower wages and higher tax levels for working people in all areas result from workers in one area having to compete for jobs with those in another, and of certain jurisdictions encouraging plant location through tax giveaways and free services. In chapters 11 and 12, Luria and Russell and Hill develop this theme. In the concluding essays in this volume, alternative political and economic programs are discussed which draw on the experiences of other capitalist democracies.

In almost all Western European countries, capital's "right" to close down plans and lay off workers is limited by law. In West Germany, plant relocation must be approved by the government as well as the unions. If the work councils do not agree to a move, mediation resolves the dispute, and even if workers approve, the state labor exchange can deny a permit in areas of high unemployment. In France, too, a local exit permit is required before an employer can leave. Companies must provide notice to workers. In Belgium, the Netherlands, and England, government also plays a role in where firms can locate and when they can move. (Kraushaar discusses planning experiences at the local level in England in chapter 14.) There is of course a range of national policies. In Sweden a company is denied investment tax credits if it does not come up to quotas on generating jobs for underemployed and for segments of the population who are the victims of discrimination. Bluestone and Harrison argue in chapter 15 that the United States can learn from these experiences.

In the concluding essay, Tabb places U.S. urban and regional policy within the larger context of global restructuring and draws conclusions for economic policy.

Trained in a variety of disciplines, the authors represented in this book come from many regions of the country. If any single belief unites them, it is probably that leaving our fate to the "free" market is a certain prescription for losing our freedom to choose. In the policy sections of these chapters, one theme recurs: Americans must make their democratic process work so that they may control their economic destinies, and this can only occur by maximizing social benefits, not simply private profit. This book explores the whys and hows of economic democracy.

REFERENCES

Advisory Commission on Intergovernmental Relations. *Regional Growth: Historical Perspective*. Washington, D.C.: ACIR, June 1980.

Anderson, Marion, and associates. *The Empty Pork Barrel: Unemployment and the Pentagon Budget*. Lansing, Mich.: Employment Research Associates, 1982.

Balz, Dan. "Organized Labor Follows the Sun, and Sets Up House in Houston." *Washington Post*, March 7, 1982.

Burks, Edward C. "Northeast and Midwest States Find Irregularities in Defense Outlays." *New York Times,* September 22, 1977.

Fainstein, Susan S., and Fainstein, Norman I. "The Federally Inspired Fiscal Crisis." *Society* (May/June 1976).

Greenberg, Michael R., and Hughes, James W. "Recent Economic Trends in the Major North-eastern Metropolises." In *Post-Industrial America: Metropolitan Decline and Inter-Regional Job Shifts,* edited by George Sternlieb and James W. Hughes. New Brunswick, N.J.: Center for Urban Policy Research, 1975.

Kresge, David I. *Regional Diversity: Growth in the United States 1960–1990.* Cambridge, Mass.: Harvard-MIT Joint Center for Urban Studies, 1981.

Long, Larry H., and Hansen, Kristin. "Americans on Wheels." *Society* (Mar./Apr. 1980).

Muller, Thomas. *Growing and Declining Urban Areas: A Fiscal Comparison.* Washington, D.C.: Urban Institute, November 1975.

Peterson, John E. *Frostbelt vs. Sunbelt.* Part I: *Key Trends of the Seventies.* New York: First Boston Bank Corporation, 1977.

Rones, Phillip L. "Moving to the Sun: Regional Job Growth, 1968 to 1978." *Monthly Labor Review* (March 1980).

Stevens, William K. "New Wave of Jobless Migrants Reverses Old Path from South." *New York Times,* June 3, 1981.

Tabb, William K. *The Long Default: New York City and the Urban Fiscal Crisis.* New York: Monthly Review Press, 1982.

Part One

THEORY

2

The Spatial Division of Labor: Labor and the Location of Industries[1]

MICHAEL STORPER and RICHARD WALKER

Location theory has long been dominated by the precepts of neoclassical economics. That situation has been changing in recent years as more and more of the mainstays of the neoclassical approach to the location of industries have come under fire (Storper, 1981; Walker and Storper, 1981; Walker, 1982). One of the most glaring shortcomings of the traditional approach has been the treatment of labor as just another "factor of production" of little importance to location outside of a few labor-intensive industries. The purpose of this essay is to enrich this impoverished view of labor and in so doing push the "labor factor" to the forefront in the analysis of the modern geography of industrial capitalism.[2]

It is readily apparent to rubber workers that closures of tire plants in Akron at the same time new factories have been constructed in the open shop states of the Sunbelt has had something to do with union contract demands on the industry. The movement of electronic assembly plants to Asia also seems to be based on the almost ten-to-one wage ratio between there and the United States. But attempts to explain industrial shifts in terms of a labor factor measured only by wages and unionization rates have not proved entirely successful. Why, for example, has all manufacturing not been relocated abroad if wages are so much cheaper? Perhaps other cost considerations outweigh labor in determining location patterns, as some large regression studies have

19

purportedly shown. Or perhaps the wrong things have been measured by both those who believe labor is the critical variable and those who do not.

In order to appreciate the role that labor plays in location, it is necessary to rethink quite thoroughly the conventional (neoclassical) notion of labor as a "commodity" possessing certain fixed qualities (skills), exchanged in "labor markets" for a wage, and utilized by industry in such a way as to optimize its "marginal product." To this end we must dissect the labor factor with care, inquiring into such matters as the changing context of global production; the noncommodity character of labor; its geographic availability; the distinctive technological demands on labor in different industries; the functioning of labor markets; the participation of labor in production and labor relations in the workplace; and the contradictory character of employment. We can then reconsider industrial location as a managerial strategy for dealing with labor; the interaction of employment and location over time; and the resulting spatial division of labor.

GLOBAL CAPITALISM AND THE DIMINISHING IMPORTANCE OF NONLABOR FACTORS IN LOCATION

For an increasing proportion of industrial commodities, markets, production, and competition have become worldwide (Caves, 1980; Barnet and Muller, 1974; Frobel et al., 1980; Palloix, 1975; Mandel, 1975). This globalization of capitalist industry has wrought fundamental changes in the circumstances facing a company deciding where to build a plant. A much broader choice of potential sites has been opened up where the basic conditions for profitable production may be met. The modern corporation engages in what Raymond Vernon (1977) refers to as a "global scan" for investment opportunities. This reduction in cost and revenue differentials among industrial sites applies principally to the realm of industrially produced goods, diminishing the locational force of non-labor factors. The principal sources of what may be called the increased "locational capability" of capital today are the following developments in circulation, production, and organization:

Circulation: Transportation and communication improvements have lowered the costs and time of circulation, bringing a wider geographic market within the range of any industrial plant. (Technical progress has simultaneously reduced the weight of most products.)

Market spreading has also advanced through the economic development of peripheral areas and standardization of products across cultures. Similarly, the internationalization of markets and production has opened up new sources of inputs and reduced the level of differentiation in the cost, quality, and availability of most inputs from place to place. These developments not only create new opportunities; they also mean increased competition through the breakdown of protected markets, introduction of new producers, and opening up of new input cost advantages. This forces firms to look farther for new markets and lower cost inputs.

Production: New forms of automation have increased the separability of the constituent parts of production systems. Rigid mechanically integrated systems have been replaced by electronic controls, permitting greater versatility and smaller production facilities (for the same or greater output). This separability frees different workplaces to seek their best location without being bound to other work units with different needs. Where these units are of the materials-processing type, advances in technology, including more use of synthetic materials and more stages of processing, have reduced the use of raw materials, lowered materials costs, and broadened the range of available supplies for many materials (raw materials have traditionally been the most locationally fixed of all inputs). Where production units are linked together in increasingly complex multiple-component assembly systems, it has become difficult to target a single best location with respect to input markets. Multiple sourcing of inputs to assure more stable supplies, a popular managerial strategy today, has the same result, and joint outputs have a similar effect on output markets.

Corporate organization: The large corporation of today is in the best position to take advantage of the advances in circulation and production. Moreover, these corporations have unprecedented power, either directly or via the state, to shape the conditions of production and circulation in any location, opening up previously unprofitable sites in rural areas, abroad, in urban redevelopment zones, and the like. In addition, the organization of far-flung production and marketing systems within giant corporations severs the strict dependence of subsidiary production units on external markets for many inputs and outputs. This frequently allows them greater flexibility in seeking locations. Finally, large corporations are able to pursue the locational search in an increasingly rationalized way, including specialized, technical, and computerized decision making and the careful weighing of relative profits of subsidiary units.

Probably the best-developed example of the above tendencies in a single industry is automobiles. Autos are now sold in virtually every country, and captive national markets are rapidly breaking down in the face of what is essentially global competition. The product is becoming more standardized, led by the so-called world car design. The producers are all giant multinational corporations which, like Ford Motors, may earn more outside their country of origin than within it. Production systems are global with, for example, one company having an axle plant in Spain, an engine plant in Mexico, a transmission plant in the southern United States, and so forth. These parts are brought together in assembly plants which no longer simply serve local markets but assemble particular models for widespread distribution. As a result, the industry has complex and shifting cross-linkages in the movement of materials, trade of the final product, and organizational ties. Textiles, in contrast, are still produced in single processing factories instead of far-flung parts and assembly systems. Trade and competition are essentially global, nonetheless, and competitive advantage has shifted back and forth between nations.

Of course, locational capability is not equal across all industries. The "global scan" is more a tendency than an accomplished fact. In general, however, locational differences in the availability, cost, and quality of nonlabor commodities are diminishing, a vastly larger number of suitable sites are available to industry, and production systems are becoming more dispersed across the nation and around the globe. These developments have not simply freed plants to be located anywhere businessmen please. Rather, they have made it more important than ever that corporate executives focus in on the labor factor as the key to locational competitive advantage.

THE UNIQUE CHARACTER OF LABOR[3]

With the trend toward globalism, labor steps to the forefront because of its continuing high degree of spatial differentiation. Labor's persistent geographic distinctiveness originates in its unique nature as a "factor of production." Labor differs fundamentally from real commodities because it is embodied in living, conscious human beings and because human activity (work) is the irreducible essence of social production and social life (Marx, 1967; Gintis and Bowles, 1981). While this may appear obvious, its significance has been lost on generations of neoclassical economists and location theorists, who have persisted in treating labor in the same terms as real commodity inputs and outputs, that is, reducible to price (wages) and quality (skills).

True commodities can be industrially produced, purchased at a consistent price and standard quality, owned outright, and employed in a strictly technical manner, however and whenever the owner wishes. (This is somewhat less true for plants and animals than inanimate objects.) Their purchase and use can thus approach a standard of performance versus cost, and they are susceptible to a geographic leveling process, as just indicated. Labor, in contrast, remains idiosyncratic and place-bound because none of these conditions hold.

Four dimensions of the pseudo-commodity labor can be distinguished: conditions of purchase, performance capacity, actual performance (control), and reproduction in place.

Conditions of purchase: Labor is purchased on the market, but the capitalist buys only the right to employ the worker for a limited period of time; one does not buy the worker outright, like a slave. The conditions of purchase for labor entail, besides wages, such things as safety and health, security and regularity of employment, prospects for advancement and fringe benefits, and so forth. Such considerations never enter the picture where true commodities, such as forklifts, are concerned; but they often matter more than wages to workers.

Performance capacity: In determining the cost per unit output of a commodity, the purchase price must be weighed against performance, or use-value. But the pseudo-commodity, labor, presents two difficulties as soon as we look more closely. First, performance is a multidimensional and very human capacity which includes technical skill, intensity, adaptability, discipline, sociability, self-direction, stability, and the like. The way in which a worker must apply his or her mind and body to the essentially *creative* process of work cannot be reduced to a technical formula as can the capabilities of a drill press.

Labor control and actual performance: The second difficulty in measuring the performance of labor is that you do not always get what you pay for. Performance capacity is not the same as actual performance because of the worker's ability consciously to limit his or her mental and physical effort. Workers, unlike computers, must willingly engage their capacity for work and have the power to resist their use and exploitation by the capitalist. The level of intensity, continuity, and quality of work that can be elicited from workers, and with what degree of supervision, monitoring, and punishment, is of fundamental importance to the employer. The usual term for the problem of eliciting performance is *labor control.* Control is perhaps a misleading word since it is not enough that the workers follow the employer's orders; they must actively participate in production and their own exploitation. Capitalist production contains a fundamental contradiction between the need for labor control and the need for thinking, capable working people.

Reproduction: The performance capacity, degree of compliance, and purchase price of labor are socially produced. Because workers, unlike true commodities, are free to leave the plant at the day's end, a substantial part of labor's (re)production takes place in the home and community. In other words, workers cannot be industrially produced as are true commodities. Therefore, labor has no objective cost or quality but varies as widely as human culture allows. Chemical workers in Bayonne, New Jersey, and Port Arthur, Texas, are very different people, while the chemicals they produce are indistinguishable.

LABOR SUPPLY DIFFERENCES IN SPACE

The four dimensions of labor just defined form the basis for geographic variations in the supply of labor. Reproduction in place-bound communities is the starting point. A measure of stability is necessary for, and demanded by, workers for their sanity, nurture, and happiness. More is needed where children are concerned. It takes time and spatial propinquity for personal support systems to evolve out of the chance contacts of daily life. Much longer is needed for the central institutions of working-class life—family, church, clubs, schools, language (dialect), sports teams, union locals—to take shape. These outlive the flux of individual migrations to benefit and be sustained by generations. The result is a fabric of distinctive, lasting local "cultures" woven into the landscape of labor, even in the highly mobile environment of the American working class (Fischer, 1976; Warren, 1978; Timms, 1971).

Living standards, militance, work experience, skills, educational levels, and the like thus vary markedly between locales. First, as regards "conditions of purchase," wage differentials are still substantial in the United States, and such things as occupatioanl safety and health standards vary even more (USBEA, 1978). The performance capacity of various work forces also differs markedly among regions (Scoville, 1973). In Britain, for instance, the main pools of skilled manufacturing labor are found in the cities of the Midlands, office professionals are found in London, miners in South Wales, academics in Oxbridge, and so forth. Despite its exclusion from traditional location theory, the control aspect of labor supply has been shown by empirical research to be a basic consideration in location decisions because of wide variations among labor force in levels of absenteeism, turnover, sabotage, union organization, and other forms of militance.

INTRODUCTION TO LABOR DEMAND

The hypothesis that labor is critical to industrial location rests on the continuing differentiation of labor *demand* as well as supply, if industries are to seek out different locales systematically. At its most elemental, the demand for labor rests on three conditions:[4]

1. Workers must carry out certain tasks at an adequate level of performance. This requires a consideration of the *labor process* and production relations.
2. Work must be compensated at a rate that will attract a sufficient number of laborers. This requires consideration of the *labor exchange*.
3. Unit labor costs must be consistent with the economic survival of the firm or workplace under competitive conditions. We must narrow this to consider only the bounds put on production and the labor exchange by the *character of particular sectors*.[5]

These skeletal elements of employment and job content must now be filled out.

INDUSTRIES: SECTORAL DIVERGENCE
AND PRODUCT TECHNOLOGY

In an era in which aggregate statistical analysis is all the rage in economics and diversified corporations freely cross traditional sectoral lines, a call for "industry case studies" has an antiquarian ring to it. Even most Marxist thinkers are prone to emphasize the common forces set in motion by capitalist production relations, such as "labor deskilling" and "centralization of capital," which cut across industries and cause them to converge in their development. But it is important not to confuse the abstraction of underlying, "structural" tendencies with empirical generalization; that is, the same forces acting on different branches of industry may result in quite distinct outcomes, depending on the specific conditions in each sector.[6] Aggregation can hide as much as it reveals.

The importance of disaggregation was borne out in our research into four industries: microprocessors, cotton textiles, aircraft engines, and auto engines. Many industrial geographers hold to the position that industry has become quite universal in its distribution, unlike past concentrations of sectors as steel in Pittsburgh or garments in New York City. We found, however, that wide dispersion was often a statistical illusion of aggregation. For example, "textiles" are found up and down the east coast, but carpets are almost entirely produced in Georgia, cotton cloth in North Carolina, draperies and woolens in New England. The "electronics" industry is similarly dispersed until one looks closer. Semiconductor wafer fabrication is still almost entirely concentrated in Silicon Valley (Santa Clara County), with some satellite areas opening up around California. Semiconductor assembly, on the other hand, has largely moved out of Silicon Valley to Southeast Asia (chiefly Singapore), the Mexican border, and select spots in Texas, Oregon, Idaho, and Colorado. Mainframe computers, which use the microchips, are concentrated almost wholly in Santa Clara County and Route 128 around Boston. Capacitors and resistors, in contrast, are produced mainly in Pennsylvania and New Jersey.

How do we account for such persistent specialization even in the newest sectors? If industries converged, their materials, labor, and marketing needs would be similar, and locational disparities would then have purely idiosyncratic origins.[7] While the element of chance cannot be ignored, an entirely better starting point for an explanation of locational patterns is the obvious differences in the specific physical and social properties of products to be produced, transported, and consumed. The common forces of competition, class struggle, and concentration of capital have led industries down different evolutionary paths because each product sector faces fundamentally different sets of possibilities and limits in marketing, production technology, and organization (Scherer, 1970; Bain, 1966).

Market sizes and growth rates depend on product uses, adaptability, substitutes, durability, innovation, and the like. For example, petrochemicals spawn new variants with new uses by the thousand each year while shoes can change only slightly in style and little in function. Different products also have substantially different production methods with widely divergent potentials for standardization, mechanization, and automation. The kind of continuous flow, automated processing possible in chemicals can only be dreamt of by the garment industry. Market characteristics and production processes are, in turn, essential determinants of the competitive structure of the industry. For example, the massive costs of setting up assembly lines and a distribution network have been a major barrier to entry in the auto industry, making this long the epitome of an oligopolistic industry. Airplane engines are a large, sophisticated, precision product with limited markets among a few captive buyers; this too presents a barrier to competition. Market fluctuations make profits highly volatile, however. Cotton textiles, on the other hand, are standardized and mass produced, like cars, but machinery costs and distribution problems are much less, so competition is strong and profits low.

All three conditions—markets, production technology, and sector organization—may feed on each other in cumulative fashion, so as to propel an industry further along a particular growth path. For example, because textiles cannot be automated much more at this time and the markets are large relative to any one factory's output, there is a continual opening for new competitors entering the field; hence the industry has a low level of concentration which, coupled with steady but unspectacular sales growth, translates into modest profits; these in turn deny it access to financial resources that might be used to spur innovation. In semiconductors, on the other hand, high growth rates and low entry barriers attract new capital and encourage technical innovators to go into business for themselves, whereupon their new products further revolutionize the industry, opening up more markets, continued rapid growth, and so on.

Because sectoral conditions are closely bound to the peculiarities of products, the deal that can be struck with labor in the workplace and in the labor exchange is necessarily limited. Firms can only go so far in their rapprochement with labor and still meet the competition. Thus, industries offer distinctive economic possibilities for creating jobs that are stable or unstable; high or low wage; high or moderate in pacing; dead end or offering advancement; and so on. (We will consider employment conditions in six industry types below.)

THE LABOR EXCHANGE AND
SEGMENTED LABOR MARKETS

In neoclassical economics fair exchange of equal for equal is the rule, whether it takes place in the market for cabbages or in the market for labor. Thus labor economics, particularly "human capital" theory, argues that workers are paid according to their value in production, whether measured by skills, effort, or scarcity value (cost or time of training). Empirical studies, however, have not borne out conventional expectations as to the operation of the labor market. Rewards—including wages, work conditions, stability, advancement, and autonomy—are not consistent with the performance capacity of workers in particular jobs. Rather, there are systematic industry and occupation-specific differences in rewards even when one corrects for skill, training time or cost, and effort. Overall, the spread of wages and conditions is much wider than the spread of performance capacity, and workers are divided into hierarchical "segments" between which there is relatively little movement (Doeringer and Piore, 1971; Edwards, Reich, and Gordon, 1975).

A typical representation of labor market segmentation is the following:

1. An "independent primary" segment features jobs with high wages and full-time and full-year employment, with work usually self-directed or self-controlled. The worker is relatively autonomous and a considerable amount of social status is attached to the occupation. Professionals and skilled craft workers fall into this category.

2. A "subordinate primary" segment sports relatively high wages and full-time and full-year employment. But work is not self-directed, and workers face occasional layoffs and limited mobility prospects. The better manufacturing jobs fall into this segment, such as in petrochemicals or automobile assembly.

3. The "secondary" labor market has low- to moderate-wage jobs, where the typically unskilled worker faces the possibility of several unpleasant circumstances: limited mobility; overt social control on the job; instability; and physical discomfort. An increasing proportion of production and service jobs fall into this category, as in electronic assembly, garments, machine assembly, and banking.

One way of accounting for labor market segmentation is in terms of sectoral conditions. For example, a highly seasonal, technically unsophisticated industry such as canning utilizes a large secondary labor force, usually minority women, to meet summer and fall peak production. But sectoral conditions do not adequately explain conditions of employment by themselves (Dunlop, 1962; Freedman, 1976).

We must therefore introduce a degree of freedom into the labor exchange. Labor and capital can bargain over the distribution of income, within the context set by the nature of the product sector. Given the possibility of bargaining and the pursuit of advantage by each side, one can see that it is in the employer's interest (and often in the interest of favored workers as well) to segment opportunities and discriminate among workers. If women or blacks can be paid less for doing the same job a white man would do, profits can be increased. The evidence for systematic discrimination based on such crude background characteristics as race, sex, and ethnicity is ample (Reich, 1981; Edwards, Reich, and Gordon, 1975).

But employers do not have all the bargaining chips. Otherwise, we would not find such instances of unexpectedly high rewards as complete recreational facilities in some Silicon Valley electronics plants or the high wage and benefit scale of semiskilled automobile workers in Detroit. These cannot be explained simply by the scarcity of particular types of labor. To discover the sources of worker leverage in dealing with employers, we need to delve into the labor process, going beyond mere conditions of exchange—what is paid and what abilities are purchased—to actual performance and worker control on the job. At the same time, the idea of conflict and bargaining must be extended to the terms of the job itself.

LABOR PROCESS AND PRODUCTION RELATIONS

Production rests on an objective basis in the sense that certain operations must be performed on natural materials to produce a particular product. This poses a problem which must be solved through a definite "technology," or organized system of human tasks (detail division of labor), tools (machinery), and natural processes. But the strict objectivity of production ends at the engineer's design table. Machines never run entirely by themselves; they require the constant intervention of workers, who internalize technology in their personal knowledge and activity. Workers remain necessary to all production, no matter how sophisticated and automatic it is, if for no other reason than to deal creatively with the inevitable failures of machines and materials (Burawoy, 1979; Pfeffer, 1979).[8] The designers of the Bay Area Rapid Transit System (BART) in San Francisco found this out to their regret when they tried to produce a subway system without human operators in the trains or the stations. It did not work, and operators had to be put back in. Even the most nominally "unskilled" jobs still require constant problem solving, although the tasks may be chiefly "manual."[9] If they did not, a machine would be used instead.

Because all workers retain an essential measure of control over the conception and execution of work, their active cooperation in the labor process is required (Aronowitz, 1978; Burawoy, 1979; Gordon, 1980). Managers must come to terms with workers if anything is to be accomplished. This gives workers a basis for leverage in bargaining above and beyond their mere scarcity value in the market. Conversely, workers need employment in order to survive and to have the opportunity to exercise their creative powers. Employers and workers are each other's captives in the workplace; their relationship is characterized by mutual interdependency.

Technology incorporates the workers and social relations in another way: production is always a collective process, involving communication, physical interaction, and group effort. Materials may have to be moved to and from work stations, as in machining; workers may be linked in a sequential work process, as in automobile assembly; groups of workers may come together to assemble a large item, as in aircraft assembly; machine operators need to communicate and coordinate functions, as in petrochemicals; or workers may simply be confined together in a small space, as in garment factories. Such social interaction is based on the specific patterns of technical interdependency in each industry. The quality of the interaction varies, moreover, depending on such things as work pace, noise, the need for mutual aid, and conjunction of work goals. Even nonworktime socializing in lunchrooms or bars will be affected by the opportunities provided by shift schedules, common experiences at work, and exhaustion. Social interaction, it must be emphasized, frequently involves as much creativity and problem solving as individual work tasks.

The combined result of the individual and collective activity of work is not only the production of commodities. Workers create a social life, from which collective strength may be drawn, and a social consciousness, from which a sense of worth and opposition to the employers may arise. Industrial sociologists have frequently pointed out that the organization of work—job autonomy, worker interaction, group segmentation, and so forth—powerfully influences whether workers come to understand the employer's dependence on them and translate this into demands for higher rewards (Burawoy, 1979; Gordon, 1980). Thus worker militance, like individual skill requirements, rests on the character of production processes in different sectors.

Textiles and auto assembly both involve mechanized, routine, semiskilled labor, yet workers in the latter are more often unionized and better paid. Their greater militance rests in part on the distinctive organization of work, which helps generate solidarity: the common status of the workers, the common pace of the assembly line (which it is in everyone's interest to slow down), stationary positions from which it is possible to talk to others nearby, frequently close coordination of several tasks, and the common practice of helping out the next worker in the line. In textile factories, on the other hand, workers are divided by the extreme noise, higher work pace, shifting work position (moving among machines), and competition among workers with tasks having very different pacing. As a result, the work force is sharply segmented along the distinctions between tasks: weavers, machine fixers, doffers, and slashers (not to mention the wholly separate work groups in carding and dyeing). Not surprisingly, racism and sexism are rampant (Burawoy, 1979; Pfeffer, 1979). Similarly divisive relations have been reported for machining and paper cup production. Conversely, longshoring before the age of the container ships involved gang work with a great deal of mutual aid, on which strong feelings of solidarity have been built (Mills, 1979).

Given the potential power of workers over production and leverage in bargaining, employers must create (or take advantage of) counteracting means of control. These occur both within and outside production, mediated by the labor exchange. The former include the personal power of the foreman, bureaucratic regulation and reward systems, and the reorganization of work (technical control), as described by Edwards (1979), as well as union cooptation, internal labor market segmentation, work pace, absence of breaks, specific antisocializing rules (such as no talking), and the like. At the same time, some of the strongest means of control lie outside the workplace, in the condition of the labor force hired, such as race, sex, excess supply, and lack of other job opportunities. For example, electronics assembly factories tend to hire only young women, who are notoriously exploitable because of patriarchical socialization and familial obligations. The exchange bargain can also be used for labor control, by paying workers more than they can get in alternative local employment, in comparable jobs elsewhere, or through unionization. Managerial control mechanisms fundamentally modify the kinds of social relations that might otherwise arise in the workplace and even affect the technologies on which production is based.[10]

One should not see "control" simply as the result of direct employer interventions, however. The nature of the production problem plays its role. More important, so do the workers. Workers and managers together participate in social worlds in miniature in the workplace which no one creates by direct intention. Capitalists and laborers become so ensnared in these relations, or social "games," that the class nature of production and sometimes even the productive goal itself may be lost from sight (Burawoy, 1979). Ironically, then, workers often energetically cooperate in their own exploitation.

In short, the social relations of the workplace, or what Burawoy (1981) calls "relations-*in*-production," mediate the effect of objective tasks and task systems on worker performance and job rewards.

THE EMPLOYMENT RELATION AND ITS CONTRADICTORY DEMANDS

Production relations and the labor exchange together constitute the "employment relation" between labor and capital. Here the two classes come together in a way that is at once a market transaction, a labor process, a site of struggle, and a scene of daily life. The employment relation is a site both of conflict and cooperation. Employers and workers are captives of each other and of the production project they must carry out. Neither side is free to get all it wants from the employment bargain, though the capitalists are in a dominant position. Labor depends on capital to invest, purchase the means of production, and set production in motion; its demands must be within the limits set by the successful reproduction of the unit of capital (firm, factory) on which it depends. If the outcome of the employment bargain in terms of productivity, technical progress, and general managerial control is too favorable to labor, the firm or the sector will fade from the scene. Conversely, capitalists need workers who will participate actively in the labor process, perform at a level of proficiency, and settle for rewards sufficient to create a profit while returning another day to work again; they are limited in their demands by the standards of work and living conditions labor can and will tolerate. Both together must successfully produce a saleable product.

Within these bounds, a variety of technical, economic, and social outcomes are possible. "Labor demand" is therefore not a given set of jobs with set skills and rewards, determined by either technology or the pure logic of the capitalist economy. It is, rather, the indeterminate result of human agency, including individual decisions and group social relations in the workplace and in the labor exchange. But the technical possibilities of the product, the economic conditions of the sector (and firm), and the commanding power of the capitalist give it shape.

Employment in capitalist industry necessarily contains a contradiction between worker cooperation and worker control. Management must keep rewards within the bounds of profitability, productivity, and technology in line with competitors, and it must keep general managerial prerogatives intact. But it must do so without suppressing performance too greatly. Employers therefore "demand" a labor force that can perform the tasks involved in producing useful commodities without unduly exercising its subjective powers to make its own demands for rewards, work conditions, and control over working lives. Firms must continually secure a labor supply that confines the contradiction between cooperation and control in employment relations within the economic bounds of the sector.

If, for example, the firm's competitive status depends on product quality or reliable delivery, as in the computer industry, concessions in areas of worker-employer antagonism are required to secure satisfactory task performance. These concessions affect both rewards in the labor exchange and work rules inside the factory. But if the employer has little or no latitude to make such concessions, and the product is standardized and/or technically unsophisticated, as in cotton textiles, worker bargaining power must be curbed. We must be sensitive, however, to the degree of freedom in labor demand despite apparently fixed production "requirements." In southern California's lemon industry, for example, the end of cheap bracero labor resulted in a drastic reorganization of work despite the absence of breakthroughs in mechanization. The harvest period was simply extended (lemons do not ripen all at once or overripen rapidly), and harvest workers were trained for nonharvest tasks, such as pruning. Furthermore, the switch to year-round employment, coupled with improved wages, secured the loyalty of workers against inroads by the United Farm Workers (De Janvry, LeVeen, and Runsten, 1980).

SIX TYPES OF PRODUCTION PROCESSES
AND LABOR DEMAND

The fulcrum of employment in every industry is the production process. We have investigated six major types of industries, based on their production processes (Storper, 1982). These manifest distinctive labor demands representing different balances between performance (ca-

pacity plus cooperation) and control (in the workplace and through
the labor exchange). These balances are bound, in turn, by sectoral
conditions of competition and profit that are, as previously indicated,
also strongly correlated with the nature of the product and production in that industry. The six production process types are classified
in terms of their dominant technology, although all real production
systems are composites of several discrete labor processes with varying specific technologies. Technologies can be characterized in two
dimensions: conversion (action on the material) and transfer (movement of the material from one work process to another). The former
can be rated on a scale from manual to machine-aided to fully automatic, and the latter on a scale from hand transfer to moving line to
continuous flow.[11] When known manufacturing technologies are plotted
on these two axes, they cluster into nine discrete combinations, of
which the following six are probably the most common. This scheme
obviously simplifies both real production processes and the range of
possible employment relations that may arise on the basis of any technology type. Nonetheless, it offers a helpful first approximation to the
study of industrial labor demands that represents a significant advance over conventional alternative schemes such as capital-intensive
versus labor-intensive industries, monopolistic versus competitive firms,
or the tripartite labor market segmentation model.

1. *Craft-type batch production:* Production runs are short, and
product is customized or changes frequently. Workers may come together in groups to work on a stationary, often large, product. The
work requires high technical skills, as in machining or carpentry, and
adaptability to changing tasks, although each production batch may be
quite routine. Workers are in a strong bargaining position because of
performance requirements, group work activity, and a strong sense of
individual worth and occupational status. But management normally
exercises effective control by promoting the divisive effects of job
hierarchy and occupational status. Profits are higher the more customized the product, but the versatility of limited, specialized markets
creates rather unstable conditions. Labor demand therefore emphasizes
performance capacity more than control, and high wages if workers
can tolerate employment instability. The aircraft and construction industries generally fit this type.

2. *Continuous processing:* Production is continuous flow and highly
automated. Specific technical skills are needed less than general cogni-
tive abilities, which are transformed into plant-specific skills through
on-the-job training. Work is nonroutine and requires a high degree of

responsibility, alertness, and adaptability to minimize down time and deal with unforeseen circumstances. Recruitment is chiefly by such generalized criteria as years of education. The high cost of production technology (combined with securing large continuous sources of raw materials and market outlets) forms a barrier to competition. Some measure of control is achieved through bureaucratic organization and labor market segmentation—ordinary construction and maintenance is often subcontracted to entirely different labor forces. But the principal mechanism of control is to give wages and working conditions better than would be expected for the level of skill involved. This is made possible by good profits and necessary by the need for worker cooperation and trust in protecting and fully exploiting huge capital investments. Petrochemicals and refining exemplify this type of production.

3. *Automated processing:* As in type 2 industries, workers must watch over delicate, integrated machine systems and are expected to minimize down time; they are "polyvalent" machine tenders. But because processing is not as completely machine-contained and automated, there are more workers required and jobs are more physical, work more routine, and conditions less attractive. Sectoral conditions also tend to be more competitive and less favorable for the exchange bargain, although relatively stable. Managerial control is based less on high wages than internal systems of bureaucratic evaluation and promotion. Labor demand emphasizes general performance characteristics rather than rewards or external control. Examples of this type of production are pulp and paper mills and standardized metalworking, such as ball-bearing manufacturing.

4. *Mechanized assembly:* Jobs in this kind of production process require generally modest technical skills. (The mean skill level lies between types 1 and 3 and types 5 and 6, but the variation is wide.) The work is maddeningly repetitive, and the pace can be hard, although it is more moderate than in industries 5 and 6. Because of strong task interdependency on the assembly line, management wants people who are steady at their work and in coming to work each day (absenteeism runs high). On the other hand, the same task relations tend to generate a cohesive and well-organized work force that can stop the entire production process. Stable demand and high entry barriers, similar to industry type 2, have traditionally protected profits, allowing some leeway in labor bargaining (though this is changing, as discussed below). The employment bargain of the last thirty years has therefore involved rewards higher than skills, or scarcity value, and a measure of power over work rules in exchange for greater worker

cooperation, enforced through collective bargaining and the unions. Home appliance and automobile assembly are typical of this type of production process.

5. *Mechanized processing:* Technology is less advanced than in the type 2 and 3 processing industries. Though the jobs may still involve running large machines, they require more manual setting up, feeding, and tending. Specific technical skills are quickly learned although the tasks often require considerable agility, concentration, or strength. There is some range of skills given the separateness of labor processes involved. Work is hard, the pace rapid, and the tasks repetitive. Because of the accessibility of the technology and markets to new entrants, competition is considerable, and profits leave little room for maneuver. Given the prospects of low pay and grueling work conditions, the jobs are not attractive. Turnover is likely to be high. The separability and disjunction of tasks form the basis for managerial control through internal labor market segmentation (which can be compounded by race and sex differences). Management therefore needs a labor force with a low standard of living, little tradition of independence, and few alternatives for employment. The textile industry is the exemplar of this sort of production.

6. *Manual assembly:* This type of production is similar to type 5 in its low job attractiveness. Work is relatively unskilled, repetitive, and fast-paced. It usually needs less strength than agility and patience. Because of low task interdependence, it does not even require particularly low turnover. Competition is high, wages poor, and employment likely to be unstable because of nonstandardized markets and low technical barriers to entry. In other words, any labor force willing to take these jobs is likely to come from marginal members of the working class, usually immigrants or women. Management is likely to enjoy a strong measure of control over such people. But there is a potential for solidarity in the sameness of all jobs and the common plight of workers. Therefore management tries to enforce the isolation of workers, given the individual nature of their tasks. Extreme workplace control is also needed to elicit the necessary hard work. Electronics assembly and garment work are examples of this type of production.

EMPLOYMENT IN SPACE: INDUSTRIAL LOCATION AS A MANAGERIAL STRATEGY

Industrial location plays a fundamental role in the social dynamics of capitalist development. This role derives above all from the inherent tension and instability of the employment relation. Employment must allow for the mutual participation of classes in production while at the same time preventing workers from using their power over production and their leverage over the exchange bargain to threaten capitalist reproduction. Location is one strategy among several available to management for overcoming the potential contradictions of employing human labor to make a profit. Others include internal systems of labor control, recruitment policies, and direct interventions in working-class communities (for example, the creation of company towns). Every industry and every firm has a particular "labor problem" it must solve. Location and relocation offer one vital avenue to a solution. We may imagine, for simplicity's sake, that they have in their minds an "ideal" demand for labor to suit the particular needs of their industry, which they hope to match with a real labor force through a correct choice of location.[12]

As the labor problem varies among industries, so does the location problem. For example, if the production process tends to create cohesion among workers, management will be especially attuned to traditions of organized militancy in communities where it might locate a factory. If labor skills are the outstanding consideration, management will look to the work experience, education, or training level and complementary skilled-work opportunities in a labor market area. If low wages are the key issue, an area with a historically low standard of living will be attractive. Most often, location and choice of labor force will be a matter of juggling opposing considerations and hoping to find just the right mix in the local labor force.

Some examples are instructive. Their locations satisfy the labor-demand/employment-relation considerations previously outlined.

The jet engine industry (in type 1 production process, above) is located principally in southern New England, which has a long machining tradition, generating a supply of highly skilled metal trade-workers. The area also fits the industry's particular "control" problem, given a very unstable product demand. The industry so dominates the region that there are not enough other job opportunities to absorb workers when it goes into a downturn. Workers are faced with the prospect of moving or waiting for the next aircraft boom. The traditional social structure also reduces exits from the region. Workers are thus more stable and lower paid than one would expect for a similarly skilled labor force in a big city labor market.

The cotton textile industry (a type 5 production process) is located principally in North Carolina, drawing workers from captive labor markets in rural areas and small towns that are socially traditional and economically marginal. These conditions have made for a particularly docile, stable, and modestly paid labor force. Alternative employment opportunities are nil, traditions of militance poor, standards of living low, and the people prone to division by racism and sexism. Lack of skills and education are not a problem.

Semiconductor plants (type 6) have been assembled in large numbers in Mexican border towns in the last decade. There they employ only women, also newly arrived in the burgeoning barrios of towns such as Juarez. These women are a highly captive work force in both the physical and social sense. They have no experience of resistance from prior industrial work or their gender training in a patriarchal society. They have no time or energy for resistance given long working hours, long journeys to work by bus, and familial obligations before and after work. They cannot afford to lose their jobs, given the lack of alternative employment and their role as principal wage earner in the family. Their families are poorly integrated into city life and services, further restricting their experience, sense of the possibilities, and class solidarity. And they are, on top of this, closely controlled at work. This is an ideal low-wage, unmilitant labor force (Christopherson, 1982).

TIME AND SPACE: LOCATION AND REPRODUCTION

Location is not, of course, simply a "strategy" in the hands of management, to be manipulated as it sees fit to find the perfect labor supply. Nor is it a one-time decision, in which a new plant is built and an "ideal" labor force sought out afresh. It is necessary to consider the process over time. It has, for instance, been frequently pointed out that relocation occurs chiefly through rechanneling investments, a continuous process in which plant openings and closings are only dramatic moments (Walker and Storper, 1981). Employment needs to be seen in a similar light.[13] The "ideal" of labor demand in the mind of management is extinguished as soon as production begins and the real-life interplay of workers, management, and technique is set in motion. Social relations in production are brought into being which have a life of their own that extends beyond the constant coming and going of individual workers and managers. Employment is not, therefore, a single act of confrontation, cooperation, or bargaining between labor and capital but an ongoing part of their existence. To reiterate, labor is not simply cabbages, which may be exchanged in a single act in a "marketplace"; it is the living substance of the labor process, embodied in a human life.

Breaking out of a static conception of employment means rethinking industrial location. Location is more than matching plant labor demands to appropriate labor forces scattered about the landscape. It is entwined in the reproduction of capital, labor, and the pattern of industrial geography.

Employment, location, and sectoral development: Employment opportunities are not derived from sectoral conditions and technology that are wholly determined by external forces. On the contrary, the ability of management to cope successfully with labor under particular existing sectoral conditions at any period, whether through location or another strategy, is fundamental to the subsequent development path of the sector, firm, or work unit. For example, the securing of a suitably captive labor force may stall further impetus for technological change, as in the case of many California agricultural crops during the bracero period. Social relations that elicit great cooperation from workers and thus prove functional to management in the short run may also involve pride of work or a sense of traditional ways of doing things that hamper management's ability to alter technology in the long run to stay competitive. Postwar collective bargaining has had just such an effect in many cases; on the one hand, it has been a great pacifier of labor militance, but on the other, it has created a welter of protective work rules that are difficult to modify in industries such as autos, agricultural machinery, and rubber. Conversely, an overly demanding work force may cut into the profits available for research and development or enforce work rules that hamper management's ability to introduce new forms of work organization.

Employment, location, and community development: Industry does not often confront precapitalist labor forces in the advanced capitalist countries. Working-class communities have been constituted through their interaction with industries in the past and are reproduced and reshaped through their continuing encounter with capital (Anderson, 1971; Bott, 1971; Joyce, 1980). Employment is the most profound influence on most people's lives. It imparts occupational skills, social contacts, work discipline and militance, money for a certain standard of living, and the like. Coal-mining communities in South Wales are profoundly different from London stockbroker suburbs chiefly because of their disparate employment histories. Industrial history is written in the lives of a nation's peoples as clearly as in its legacy of factories, railroads, or houses (Massey, 1978b). The mixing of industries in some regions and in many workers' lifetime experience complicates matters, of course. But that sort of "cosmopolitan" mix may be exactly the characteristic distinguishing one labor force from another. Baltimore, for example, is known for its variety of skilled laborers coming out of many small enterprises, rather than its specialization in one or two basic industries, as is Pittsburgh.

Employment stability and regional development: The stability of an area's industrial base and of its local labor force is of great significance in maintaining a compatible employment relation and in reproducing labor and capital successfully. It is not by chance that industries and communities so often grow, mature, and decline in tandem. Examples can be drawn from every age of industrial capitalism: the textile and shoe towns of New England; the Motor City, Detroit; the Steel City, Pittsburgh. One can find the same phenomenon occurring within labor submarkets of big metropolitan areas, as in the aircraft industry of the west side of the Los Angeles area or the electronics industry of the Santa Clara Valley (San Francisco Bay area).[14] Employers understand the phenomenon of community stability and frequently seek to exploit it. A good example is the bitter resistance of some small town Southern firms enjoying a captive labor market to the intrusion of Northern companies, with their very different and potentially disruptive wage structures. Conversely, community instability may be in the interest of some industries. For example, California growers steadfastly avoided the use of "domestic" (that is, settled) labor instead of migrants for years because of the former's greater leverage and commitment to higher wages (Galarza, 1977). In a similar way, a firm moving its plant to a "greenfield site," or one that systematically recruits workers (especially immigrants) from outside the locale, is not showing disregard for the importance of labor in location. On the contrary, management is well aware of its power to create a certain kind of community and labor force in the area. The ultimate attempt to stage-manage community formation is the company town, such as Pullman, Illinois (Buder, 1967).

Stable solutions to the dilemmas of the employment relation are possible for a time but cannot be maintained forever. Eventually the contradictions break through. The pressure may come from the side of the workers, for whom stability of employment also means long experience with an industry's control systems, growing seniority, strong community support networks, rising expectations, and so forth; these can translate into increasingly militant demands on employers. On the other hand, it may come from the company, which needs to alter product lines or raise productivity to stay competitive. A stable employment relation can be a real barrier to technical change. Or it may come from the macroeconomy, when a depression forces even prosperous industries to retrench by cutting wages or reorganizing work patterns for greater productivity. Disequilibrating forces of this kind have been hard at work in recent years. The result has been profound upheavals in the geography of industry as companies use locational shifts to reshape employment relations and reorganize their capital (Massey, 1978a; Massey and Meegan, 1978).

A good example of such dislocation is the auto industry today. For years the industry could absorb the costs of relative labor peace and worker cooperation bought by favorable union contracts while remaining concentrated in its traditional center around Detroit. Faced with the treble pressures of economic slump, rising gas costs, and foreign competition, the companies have been building more plants away from the Midwest—in the Sunbelt and overseas—in search of a more compliant, lower-paid work force. The need to innovate to stay competitive has added an extra interest in finding workers without allegiance to existing work patterns and rules.[15] Even foreign entrants to U.S. production have sought out nontraditional locations, as in the case of Datsun's new plant in Tennessee.

In sum, location and relocation are essential means of shaping and changing the employment relation in a continuing effort by management to remain competitive and contain class struggle in the workplace. Mobility in space is not a luxury for capital, but a necessity. Over time the intersection of labor and capital in space, as a critical dimension of employment, feeds back into the fortunes of capital, the evolution of technology, and, of course, the history of working-class communities. Industrial geography is thus both effect and cause of capitalist development or, rather, part of the weave in the fabric of history—not a topic apart of interest only to geographers.

CONCLUSION: THE SPATIAL DIVISION OF LABOR

The matching of labor demands from divergent industries and labor supplies from divergent communities results in what may be called a *spatial division of labor*. The patterns of the industrial landscape are not as large as the conventional idea of a "region," such as the "South" or the "Sunbelt." It fractures along much finer lines of disaggregated industries and particular spatial labor markets, defined roughly by commuting fields, which are rarely larger than a few counties and can be as small as neighborhoods of cities. The fine pattern of industrial location creates what may be called a "mosaic of unevenness" (Walker, 1978). That mosaic is in continual flux, moreover, thanks to the inherent instability of the employment relation.[16]

The spatial division of labor has profound implication for the prospects facing class movements and human welfare in modern capitalist societies. Industrial location projects labor market segmentation and the persistent fragmentation of the working class into space. The spatial division of labor is a spatial division *within* labor that is forever created and recreated by the flux of capitalist development. In addition, with the inevitable divergence among industries and their labor demand, the locational mosaic means a persistent unevenness in local fortunes, even within the advanced "industrial" countries. Given this variegated reality, one should not be surprised that working people perceive genuine differences between themselves and other workers in other places as readily as they grasp common bonds within their class. With the increasing locational capability of corporations, moreover, management is becoming even more adept at playing off workers in one place against those in another (Bluestone and Harrison, 1980).

One should not, however, altogether despair for the prospects of class mobilization and social change, as have so many prophets of working-class immobilization by embourgeoisement, external and internal colonialism, one-dimensional capitalist ideology, and other structural-functionalist theories of an unyielding capitalism. The problem for political theory, as for the industrial workers who toil in their multitude of workplaces and communities, is to build on the particular—the experiences and social bonds and visions of a great variety of people. Intellectual radicals have often been too quick to make sweeping analyses, judgments, and plans of and for everybody else. While it is essential for political change that we try to grasp the general outlines, or underlying logic, of capitalism and promote a thoroughly different socialist order, it is not enough. People must also find in themselves the need for change. History has never yet moved by the grinding of structural gears or the pulling of the self-appointed vanguard. The creation of a more truly humane world, in which the mass of people are more in command of production and social life, will certainly not appear without the participation of those people. The problem for left research, then, is to discover the links between the general and the particular, or structure and agency, in capitalist life, so as to help others see the sources of their plight and discover a way out. And an essential place to begin that search is in the intersection between industry, labor, and geography.

NOTES

1. Research for this paper was carried out under a grant from the National Science Foundation. Much of the background evidence and literature can be found in Storper, 1982. See also Storper and Walker, 1983.
2. Three points of clarification: labor is not the most important factor in every industry or plant location decision; the movements of capital must also be pushed to the forefront of locational analysis, as we have argued elsewhere; with some modification, the basic thesis established here for manufacturing could be extended to office location. See Walker and Storper, 1981.
3. Given the clash between marxist and nonmarxist terminology, we adopt these conventions: labor, workers, laborforce and workforce refer to people; work, production, work process and labor process refer to the activity of those people.
4. The first two correspond to characteristics of labor already mentioned. The first combines performance capacity and actual performance (control). The second combines conditions of purchase and reproduction. The third introduces the reproduction of the unit of capital, i.e. investment, profitability, and accumulation.
5. In so doing we ignore questions of aggregate dynamics of the economy and the internal organization of the modern corporation, both critical but beyond the range of this paper. See Walker and Storper, 1981.
6. For a defense of this "structural-realist" approach see Bhaskar, 1975, and Sayer, 1979.
7. Although they would be compounded over time by agglomeration economies. One of the chief advantages of spatial concentration, however, is sharing a labor pool. Silicon Valley electronics are a clear example of this phenomenon (Saxenien, 1981).
8. Machines are still remarkably stupid by human standards, despite the exaggerated claims of the media about robotics. There are, of course, plenty of cases where people are so cheap they are used in jobs requiring only brute strength or simple repetitive motions. This does not overturn the centrality of labor; it merely shows the inverted values of some societies (Marx, 1967). People are still, in general, one jump ahead of the machines. There have as yet been no reports of a machine building a person.
9. We disagree with the "Braverman school" and its rather one-sided portrayal of capitalist power and the implications of "deskilling" for labor. Undoubtedly capitalists systematically attack the power of certain workers over the organization and pace of production, as well as reducing their scarcity value, through work rationalization, mechanization, and automation (Braverman, 1974; Stone, 1974; Montgomery, 1979). But this tendency is countered in three ways: (1) New jobs are created (chiefly in office work) that have the characteristics of the former "master workman" in manufacturing. Even the low-paid secretary develops

a fund of personal knowledge about his/her job that cannot easily be replaced by a machine or even another person; (2) Increased automation may reduce the worker to a "machine tender," but one with considerable responsibility for the smooth operation of the machinery and a need for a wide range of learned tasks ("polyvalent skills"); (3) Even unskilled workers must often undertake non-routine tasks, deal with unforeseen problems (materials design, equipment failures, etc.) and interact socially in collective work situations. Auto workers and machinists constantly cope with awkward tasks because parts or materials are not right; (4) The term "skill" inadequately captures the many dimensions of individual jobs and workers, such as autonomy, adaptability, endurance, strength, agility, received wisdom, invention and patience.

10. There are few cases of pure control-induced technologies, however. One example is the short-handled hoe (Murray, 1982).

11. We used a scale of 1–8 for each dimension of technology; most of the 64 cells did not correspond to real technologies and the remaining cells could be grouped into nine clusters. Four of the six most common types were chosen for case studies. For each sample industry we used detailed job data gathered by the Bureau of Labor Statistics to corroborate the hypothesis that they could be characterized in terms of a dominant technology or technologies. Three of the four had single peak distributions of job technologies. The semiconductor industry, on the other hand, had a distinctly bimodal distribution. This is not a rare occurrence. Hence the number of production process types in the economy must be greater than the nine basis technologies (Storper, 1982).

12. Location as "matching" labor demand to labor supply is only a first approximation to the dynamic process of employment in space, however. See text below.

13. So does technology. Management does not have a simple choice of pre-designed technologies. Operating production systems undergo modification as they are put into use, thanks to the imperfect design and construction of machinery and the inevitable worker input of technical know-how into machine operation and their own work.

14. Some good studies of the integrated development of an industry and a town or region are Saxenian, 1981; Dawley, 1976; Walkowitz, 1978; and Cumbler, 1979.

15. As a result, one repeatedly finds an inversion of expected center and periphery relations in which more technologically advanced plants are found in previously unindustrialized areas. This is not a new phenomenon, but it does seem to be more widespread today than ever before.

16. This flux should be seen in connection with "waves of investment" in regional and urban development, as discussed by Massey, 1978b and Walker, 1981. See also the comments on spatial disequilibrium in Harvey, 1981.

REFERENCES

Anderson, Michael. *Family Structure in 19th Century Lancastershire.* Cambridge: Cambridge University Press, 1971.
Aronowitz, Stanley. 1978. "Marx, Braverman and the Logic of Capital." *Insurgent Sociologist* 8:2 and 3 (Fall) 26–46.

Bain, Joe. *Industrial Organization*. New York: John Wiley, 1966.

Barnet, Richard, and Muller, Ronald. *Global Reach*. New York: Simon and Schuster, 1974.

Bhaskar, Roy. *A Realist Theory of Science*. Sussex: Harvester Press, 1975.

Bluestone, Barry, and Harrison, Bennett. *Capital and Communities*. Washington, D.C.: The Progressive Alliance, 1980.

Bott, Elizabeth. *Family and Social Networks*. New York: Free Press, 1971.

Braverman, Harry. *Labor and Monopoly Capital*. New York: Monthly Review Press, 1974.

Buder, Stanley. *Pullman*. New York: Oxford University Press, 1974.

Burawoy, Michael. *Manufacturing Consent*. Chicago: University of Chicago Press, 1979.

Burawoy, Michael. "Terrains of Contest: factory and state under capitalism and socialism." *Socialist Review* 58 (July–August 1981) 83–125.

Caves, Richard. "Changes in the Structure of the U.S. Economy, 1947–1980." Paper, presented at conference on changes in the structure of the Postwar Economy. Cambridge: National Bureau of Economic Research, 1980.

Christopherson, Susan. Family and Class in a New Industrial City. Unpublished Ph.D. dissertation. University of California, Berkeley, 1982.

Cumbler, John. *Working Class Community in Industrial America*. Westport, Conn.: Greenwood Press, 1979.

Dawley, Alan. *Class and Community*. Cambridge: Harvard University Press, 1976.

DeJanvry, Alain; LeVeen, E. Philip; and Runsten, David. "Mechanization in California Agriculture: The Case of Canning Tomatoes." Berkeley: Department of Agricultural and Resource Economics. Unpublished report, 1980.

Doeringer, Peter, and Piore, Michael. *Internal Labor Markets and Manpower Analyses*. Lexington, Mass.: Lexington Books, 1971.

Dunlop, John. *Automation and Technological Change*. Englewood Cliffs, N.J.: Prentice-Hall, 1962.

Edwards, Richard. *Contested Terrain*. New York: Basic Books, 1979.

Edwards, Richard; Reich, Michael; and Gordon, David. eds. *Labor Market Segmentation*. Lexington, Mass.: D. C. Heath, 1975.

Fischer, Claude. *The Urban Experience*. New York: Harcourt Brace Jovanovich, 1976.

Freedman, Marcia. *Labor Markets*. Montclair, N.J.: Allenheld, Osmun, 1976.

Froebel, F.; Henrichs, J.; and Kreyer, D. *The New International Division of Labor*. Cambridge: Cambridge University Press, 1980.

Galarza, Ernesto. *Farm Workers and Agribusiness in California* 1947–1960. South Bend, Ind.: University of Notre Dame Press, 1977.

Gintis, Herbert, and Bowles, Samuel. "Structure and Practice in the Labor Theory of Value." *Review of Radical Political Economics* 12:4, Winter 1981, 1–25.

Gordon, David. "The Best Defense Is a Good Offense: Toward a Marxian Theory of Labor Union Structure and Behavior." In M. Carter and W. Leahy, eds., *New Direction in Labor Economics*. South Bend: University of Notre Dame Press, 1980.

Harvey, David. "The Space-Economy of Capitalist Production: A Marxian Interpretation." Paper presented at a conference on New Perspectives on the Urban Political Economy, American University, Washington, D.C. May 22–24, 1981.

Joyce, Patrick. *Work, Society and Politics*. Sussex: Harvester Press, 1980.

Low-Beer, John. *Protest and Participation*. Cambridge and Cambridge University Press, 1978.

Mandel, Ernst. *Late Capitalism*. London: New Left Books, 1975.

Marx, Karl. *Capital* (3 volumes). New York: International Publishers Edition, 1967 (rpt).

Massey, Doreen. "Capital and locational change: the U.K. electrical engineering and electronics industry." *Review of Radical Political Economics*, 10:3, (1978) 39–54. *a*

Massey, Doreen. "Regionalism: some current issues." *Capital and Class*, 6, (1978) 106–125. *b*

Massey, Doreen, and Meegan, Richard. "Industrial Restructuring versus the Cities." *Urban Studies*, 15, (1978) 273–288.

Mills, Herb. "The San Francisco Waterfront: The Social Consequences of Industrial Modernization." In A. Zimbalist, ed., *Case Studies on the Labor Process*. New York: Monthly Review Press, 1979.

Montgomery, David. *Workers' Control in America*. New York: Cambridge University Press, 1979.

Murray, Douglas. "The Abolition of El Cortito, the Short Handle Hoe." *Social Problems* (forthcoming).

Palloix, Christian. *L'Internationalisation du Capital*. Paris: Maspero, 1975.

Pfeffer, Richard. *Working for Capitalism*. New York: Columbia University Press, 1979.

Reich, Michael. *Racial Inequality*. Princeton: Princeton University Press, 1981.

Sayer, Andrew. "Theory and Empirical Research in Urban and Regional Political Economy." *Working Paper* 14. Sussex: University of Sussex, Urban and Regional Studies, 1979.

Saxenian, Annalee. "Silicon Chips and Spatial Structure: The Industrial Basis of Urbanization in Santa Clara County, California." Unpublished M.A. Thesis. Berkeley: University of California, 1981.

Scherer, Frederic. *Industrial Market Structure and Economic Performance*. Chicago: Rand McNally, 1970.

Scoville, James. *The Job Content of the U.S. Economy, 1940–1970*. New York: McGraw-Hill, 1973.

Stone, Katherine. "The Origins of Job Structures in the Steel Industry." *Review of Radical Political Economics*, 6 (Summer 1979) 113–73.

Storper, Michael. "Toward a Structural Theory of Industrial Location." In J. Rees, H. Stafford, and G. Hewings, eds. *Industrial Location and Regional Systems*. New York: Bergin, 1981.

Storper, Michael. "Technology, the Labor Process and the Location of Industries." Unpublished Ph.D. dissertation. Berkeley: University of California, 1982.

Storper, Michael, and Walker, Richard. "The Labor Theory of Location." *International Journal of Urban and Regional Research* (forthcoming)

Timms, D. W. G. *The Urban Mosaic*. Cambridge: Cambridge University Press, 1971.

U.S. Bureau of Economic Analysis. *Occupational Pay Comparisons*. Washington, D.C.: U.S. Government Printing Office, 1978.

Vernon, Raymond. *Storm Over the Multinationals*. Cambridge: Harvard University Press, 1977.

Walker, Richard. "Two Sources of Uneven Development under Advanced Capitalism." *Review of Radical Political Economics* 10:3, (1978) 28–39.

Walker, Richard. "Industrial Location Policy: False Premises, False Conclusions." *Built Environment*, 6:2, (1982) 105–113.

Walker, Richard. "A Theory of Suburbanization." In M. Dear and A. Scott, eds., *Urbanization and Urban Planning in Capitalist Society*. New York: McThuen, 1981.

Walker, Richard, and Storper, Michael. "Capital and Industrial Location." *Progress in Human Geography*, 5:4, (1981) 473–509.

Walkowitz, Daniel. *Worker City, Company Town*. Urbana: University of Illinois Press, 1978.

Warren, R. *The Community in America*. Chicago: Rand McNally, 1978.

3

Regional Restructuring and "Good Business Climates": The Economic Transformation of New England Since World War II

BENNETT HARRISON

On the eve of World War II, New England's economic structure still retained the basic characteristics that had so long distinguished this region from the rest of the country. In 1940, two out of every five persons in the labor force were still employed in those industries which had for a hundred years formed the economic base, manufacturing consumption goods like textiles and shoes and such basic capital goods as machine tools. Production was typically located in old mill buildings scattered throughout the countryside or concentrated in the region's many small cities ("mill towns"). The share of these industries in all employment nationally was only half as great, according to the 1940 census. And largely because of this industry mix, almost 36 percent of the region's workers were employed as craftspersons or machine operatives, in contrast to fewer than 30 percent in the country as a whole.

This traditional mix of activities was not to last for much longer. Some tendencies toward far-reaching structural change had in fact been manifest long before the war, such as expansion of the textile industry into the South, accompanied (eventually) by mill closures in New England. Other changes grew out of the war itself, such as massive government investment in Sunbelt infrastructure (which prepared the way for subsequent private investment) and the development of the computer industry in New York, Pennsylvania, and Massachusetts.

In the twenty-five-year period following the war, the United States became the industrial, political, and military center of an increasingly interdependent international capitalist economic system. This situation created opportunities for the export of new forms of New England producers' goods: computers, jet engines, and all manner of scientific and military instrumentation. Building on that manufacturing base, capitalists invested heavily in a great variety of export-oriented services, selling education and medical care to everyone from foreign dignitaries to the children of Midwestern farmers. Specialized business services were also developed, selling to both domestic and foreign corporations (and governments).

Throughout the country, the combined forces of rapidly expanding international markets and, by the 1960s, the explicit application by the federal government of Keynesian macroeconomic demand management policies greatly increased the discretionary incomes of working families. This provided business with the opportunity to develop and market a wide range of new consumer goods and services. The postwar suburbanization of middle-class households, itself an aspect of this explosive consumerism, reinforced the conditions within which shopping centers, supermarkets, and public facilities proliferated, especially after 1960. From the beginning, the New England region led the country in many of these developments. For example, the discount department store was "invented" in Rhode Island.[1]

As a result of these profound changes in economic activity, by 1977 mill-based employment in New England had fallen to only a tenth of all jobs in the region. Even metalworking and electronics had declined in relative importance. Aircraft engine manufacturers had emerged as the single most important goods producers, and hospitals as the single largest service employer. Taken together, the private services (along with the trade sector) now employed over half of all New Englanders.[2] This extraordinary transformation produced an equally dramatic shift in the region's occupational mix. The "white-collar" occupations, which had employed only a third of the labor force in 1940, accounted by 1978 for over 51 percent of all workers—precisely the same ratio as in the country as a whole.

An economy based on the production of durable capital equipment and nondurable consumer goods—mostly bound for export to other parts of the country—had been transformed into one with a much smaller and far more highly specialized manufacturing base, many of whose products were now exported worldwide, perched atop an enormous low-wage service sector. In a sense, the middle had dropped out of the regional economy. The industries which had paid the best wages for blue-collar workers were almost gone, and within the remaining (as well as the new) industries, jobs were being reorganized in such a way as to substantially reduce employers' need for the mid-range of skills. Thus, even though the overall economy was growing, wages and job opportunities were becoming more unequally distributed over time. Society in the "new" New England was becoming increasingly polarized.

The purpose of this essay is to analyze the transformation of the industrial structure of New England since World War II. The evidence shows that the very process of long-term industrial decline in a region brings into existence the conditions within which a new wave of economic growth may occur. If private reinvestment (or "reindustrialization") *does* begin again, the future development of the newly emerging economic base depends on the interplay between the forces of competition among firms on the one hand, and the antagonism between managers and workers (both inside the workplace and in the community) on the other, all mediated by the policies and regulations of governments at the local, state, and especially the federal level.

This essay begins with a consideration of the process by which the old industrial structure began to break down in the years preceding the Second World War. This will be followed by an analysis of the impact of the war itself on the dissolution of the old structure, and of the conditions which brought into being a new wave of economic development in the region. In the next two sections, I investigate the properties of this new industrial structure and then assess the impact of the transformation on employment, earnings, and the organization of work. The essay will end with a summary of the principal arguments about the process of regional deindustrialization and subsequent restructuring, and will offer speculations about some of the political factors that are likely to affect the region's course of development in the remaining years of the twentieth century.

THE RESTRUCTURING OF NEW ENGLAND
INDUSTRY PRIOR TO WORLD WAR II

The decline of the traditional mill industries of New England began long before the Second World War. The details vary from one industry to another. Thus, for example, the decline of textiles is best understood in terms of the gradual expansion of the industry outside the region of its origin, especially through flows of finance capital, whereas the local production of shoes was severely eroded by the phenomenon of the runaway shop. Nevertheless, in both cases, and with private disinvestment in New England industry generally, there are important underlying commonalities: capital's continuing search for cheaper, more tractable labor power; the capacity of certain kinds of technological change to *facilitate* geographic expansion or relocation (which is not the same thing as *causing* that expansion); and the struggles of working people to improve their living conditions through direct action, unions, and participation in electoral politics.

Consider the restructuring of textiles. During the first half of the nineteenth century, the machinery employed in textile production was largely custom built and then rebuilt for individual mills. The industry was also highly competitive so that producers were continually modifying the designs of their products. As a result, the complex of toolmakers, financiers, and mill operators clustered closely in their original centers of production in eastern Massachusetts. With the introduction of standardized, interchangeable tools and parts, first undertaken for New England's munitions industry around the time of the Civil War, there came a revolution in the design and manufacture of textile machinery. The intimate locational connection betwen the toolmakers and tool users thus became uncoupled. It was then a small step after standardization to the automation of the spinning and weaving processes. Once freed of their traditional dependence on skilled New England labor, textile manufacturers found irresistible the benefits to be gained by expanding into the low-wage Southeast.[3]

Although standardization of parts and automation of the labor process made it possible for firms to decentralize the production of goods that were susceptible to product standardization, and although the low level of conventional wages and absence of industrially experienced (and therefore better organized) workers made the Southeast attractive, the process of geographic restructuring was quite gradual. The South had had a small indigenous textile industry even before the Civil War. In the period following 1865, new Southern mills were founded by itinerant New England weaver-entrepreneurs, often purchasing used equipment from established mills in the North. Later, the big New England and British textile machinery firms began to invest directly in Southern plants. Only after 1880, when these first ventures proved to be profitable, did New England textile combines such as the

Merrimack, Massachusetts, and Appleton companies build or acquire mills in the South. Even then, the Northern textile machinery manufacturers and New York commission houses were more important than the New England millowners per se in financing Southern development.[4]

Considering the general antiunion animus of New England companies, it is both interesting and amusing to observe how those New England textile manufacturers who did not "go South" reacted to the new competition. Between 1895 and 1900, the leading New England millowners were publicly encouraging Southern unionization! As the *Boston Commercial Bulletin* put it: "We cannot level Massachusetts down; let the labor unions raise the other states up."[5]

In any case, New England's textile industry began to decline in earnest after 1924. According to Solomon Barkin, former research director of the Textile Workers Union of America:

> In 1929, the number of establishments shrank from 357 (in 1919) to 259, and ten years later there were only 161 mills. Spindles fell to 5 million and looms to 90 thousand. Woven fabric production declined to 1.2 billion square yards. Prices and mill margins slumped. Losses on financial statements became common. Bankruptcies increased. Many companies skipped dividends and those that paid them had often to dig into surplusses for funds.
>
> Special developments accelerated the degree of collapse of New England mills. . . . Double-shift operations, introduced during World War I, expanded in the South, so that at the end of the twenties, they represented prevailing practice, further aggravating the over-capacity. . . . The demand for industrial fabrics, particularly that originating in the automobile industry, gravitated to the South.
>
> The dominant Borden interests announced in 1924 that they were closing a Fall River mill and moving its operations to Kingsport, Tennessee. The Beacon Mfg. Co. of New Bedford moved all but its difficult weaves to its Southern plant in 1933. The Appleton Co. of Lowell moved to Alabama. . . . In passing, let us note that neither the financial help from the [Depression-era] Reconstruction Finance Corp. nor employee wage "contributions" kept these mills alive.[6]

The boot and shoe industry was even more highly concentrated in the New England area in the 1930s than textiles, but it was very differently organized. Apart from a small number of large companies, this was (and remains today) the classic competitive industry with thousands of small producers. Market entry was facilitated (especially in the segment making women's and children's shoes) by continual style changes and by the practice of such giant machinery firms as

United Shoe Machine of Brockton, Massachusetts, of leasing rather than selling their equipment (a practice later emulated by IBM and Xerox). Thus it is not surprising that even before the Great Depression, the industry was experiencing chronic excess capacity. With equipment easy to rent, and fixed capital assets therefore held to a minimum, footwear manufacturers found it comparatively easy to literally pick up and relocate. Because of competitive pressure to exploit this capability in order to cut costs, the industry was furiously decentralizing, geographically, by the eve of World War II.[7] Most plant relocations involved short-distance moves away from the major production centers in eastern Massachusetts into the New England periphery—western Massachusetts and southern Vermont, New Hampshire, and Maine. Long-distance shifts tended to be westward, following the population. Between 1930 and 1938, seventy-nine firms are known to have moved out of Massachusetts.

Of course, most of the economic trauma experienced during the 1930s resulted from outright business failures associated with the worldwide Depression rather than from plant relocation per se. Between 1930 and 1940, as textile and shoe and leather employment in New England dropped precipitously, whole communities such as Lawrence, Massachusetts, and Manchester, New Hampshire, were devastated. The general business collapse made it virtually impossible for those laid off by the mill and shop shutdowns to find sufficient work to replace their lost family incomes. Not even the legal restrictions against immigration from Southern Europe or the child labor laws were enough to protect experienced factory workers (themselves often recent immigrants) from massive displacement.

The region's workers had never been passive when faced with structural changes in the industries where they had made their living. Sustained by a long tradition of militancy, in the four decades preceding World War II working people organized unions, demanded (and frequently struck for) better wages and working conditions, and brought electoral pressure to bear on public officials to increase the standard of living through the passage of a broad program of social legislation. Had the extraordinarily profitable conditions created by the war not intervened, the militant labor "climate" of the 1930s would undoubtedly have hastened the pace of private disinvestment in the New England region.

The militant environment of the 1930s had roots going far back into New England history. The earliest national unions with a New England base were the International Typographical Union and the

Knights of St. Crispin (shoemakers).[8] In the last quarter of the nineteenth century, the Knights of Labor began organizing in the textile mills of the region, especially in Manchester and Lawrence. Long after the Knights had ceased to be an influential force, these cities continued to be important centers of labor conflict, including the famous Bread and Roses strike of 1912 in Lawrence.[9] Textile workers went out again in 1919, in 1922 in a general strike throughout New England, in 1933 in Manchester, and finally in 1934, when mills across the North were struck in response to wage cuts and shutdowns.[10]

From their earliest years until the mid-1950s, elements of the regional labor movement were deeply involved in radical politics, especially at the state and municipal levels. In the smaller industrial cities and mining towns of the late nineteenth century, labor radicals were sometimes numerous enough to influence the actions of mayors, sheriffs, and even judges. The Socialist party elected officials in Lynn, Massachusetts, and Norwalk, Connecticut, as early as 1886.[11] During the First World War, Socialists elected to local governments by members of the International Association of Machinists in turn led or supported machinists' strikes all over the Northeast, including the armaments and munitions plants in Bridgeport and Lynn.[12] During the first four decades of the twentieth century, Haverhill, Massachusetts, and Bridgeport, Connecticut, had Socialist mayors and city council members at one time or another.[13]

Out of these electoral victories came a series of public programs to protect workers and to underwrite their social security. Nearly all of the legislation that makes up this "social wage" (or, as it is coming to be called, the "social safety net") was first written and implemented at the state and municipal levels (especially in the populist Midwest) and only subsequently institutionalized by the federal government under presidents Wilson and Roosevelt. The first workmen's compensation law was passed in 1909 by the state of Montana. Unemployment insurance was pioneered in Massachusetts in 1916, although the first bill actually to pass a state legislature was drafted in the early 1930s in Wisconsin. (The national program was not institutionalized until 1935, as a provision of the Social Security Act.) The first state welfare board was elected in Massachusetts in 1853 to oversee local relief charities, but it was not until 1917 that a modern state department of public welfare was created, in Illinois. (Massachusetts followed suit in 1919.) By 1926, five states including Massachusetts had aid programs for widowed mothers with children. This was nine years before the federal government created a national minimum in what later became the Aid to

Families with Dependent Children program. Those Northern industrial states which pioneered in the development of social benefits for workers and their families and which actively raised taxes to finance these benefits are precisely the ones currently under attack for having a "poor business climate" or for being "antibusiness."

Not surprisingly, owners and managers fought bitterly against organized labor. The millowners, by accusing unions of being "foreign" or "un-American," helped to fan "red scare" hysteria. When strikes occurred, they routinely called upon the police to help break picket lines. During every era, going all the way back to the Civil War, we can find evidence that employers' attacks on the labor movement could involve government. Melvin Dubofsky writes: "Trade unionists had learned during the many brutal labor conflicts of the nineteenth century that the state was generally the enemy of workers. Federal and state troops had consistently broken strikes, and members of the judiciary had regularly enjoined workers from striking."[14] In Lynn, Massachusetts, as far back as 1868,

> The Lynn shoe workers had established a union—the Unity Lodge of the Knights of St. Crispin—and, in 1879, they struck against the owners' attempts to enforce a large wage reduction. The following period saw many more conflicts in the Lynn shoe industry over wages and hours, including a lock-out in 1872, six wage disputes in 1875, and two very bitter violent strikes over wages in 1877 and 1878. In this latter struggle, intervention by the state—in the form of police protection for the strike-breakers—helped to force the union into defeat.[15]

Later, during World War I, the federal government launched attacks on the International Workers of the World (the IWW, or "Wobblies"). It was soon after the war that the raids on labor radicals by Attorney General Palmer were ordered, while the prosecution of Sacco and Vanzetti in Massachusetts took place in the hysterical political atmosphere of the early 1920s.

Militant New England trade unionists continued to experience harassment into the 1930s. For example, in 1934 the Chamber of Commerce of Seabrook, New Hampshire, posted a $5,000 bond as a guarantee against "labor troubles" should union organizers attempt to "interfere" with the Barr and Bloomfield Shoe Manufacturing Company, which had just moved up from Lynn. When a carload of organizers did indeed attempt to cross the border from Massachusetts, they were turned back by Seabrook's chief of police.[16] During the same period, Joseph Kamp—identified by U.S. Senator Robert LaFollette's investigating committee as one of the most active "union-busters" in the shoe industry—maintained the headquarters of his government-sanctioned Constitutional Education League in New Haven, Connecticut.[17]

There is strong evidence that by the 1930s, the militant climate in labor relations that had been developing since the late nineteenth century had become an important factor contributing to the shifting of capital out of New England.[18] One survey of the boot and shoe industry in Massachusetts, consisting of interviews with owners, concluded that the "agitation of organized labor has been given in many instances as the reason for the removal or liquidation of our shoe factories. . . . In many of the labor contracts are to be found clauses prohibiting the employment of current practices developed as part of modern scientific management and applied to job analysis and wage setting."[19] Another researcher found a strong positive correlation between the incidence of unionization and the relative decline in shoe production in a large sample of American cities.[20] As we shall see in the next section, in the years since World War II, American corporations have continued systematically to place their new investments in states and localities exhibiting a "good business climate" in general, and a strong antiunion posture in particular.

WORLD WAR II AND THE POSTWAR RESTRUCTURING OF THE OLD INDUSTRIAL BASE

Without question, the Second World War was the most momentous event in the modern history of New England. Policies of the national government during the war created new industrial competitors in other sections of the country. Wholly new industries cropped up within New England while existing minor industries catapulted into major prominence under government procurement policies. Perhaps most important of all, the war and its aftermath set the parameters for a new international economic order dominated for two decades by the American military and American business.

Production for military use has always been central to the economic fortunes of New England. In the eighteenth century, the major centers for arms manufacture for the colonies were all located here: in Middletown and Hartford, Connecticut; in Springfield and Bridgewater, Massachusetts; and in North Providence, Rhode Island. In 1794 the new national government selected Springfield as the site for the first federal armory.[21] During the first half of the nineteenth century, in order to facilitate the repair of guns used in remote areas of the continent, the federal government let contracts to New England toolmakers to perfect the development of interchangeable parts. The new machine tools were among New England's most important exports from the time of the Civil War on.[22]

During the years immediately preceding World War I, with the European powers furiously arming themselves, American machine shops were able to sell aircraft, guns, and ammunition to both sides (a pattern that was to be repeated in the 1930s, when U.S. companies sold arms to both the Allies and the Axis countries). With the entry of the United States into World War I, government contracts provided an enormous boost to the development of the fledgling aircraft industry. In 1914 the sixteen aircraft manufacturers listed by the U.S. census turned out only forty-nine planes; by 1918 the output of this infant industry was over fourteen thousand.[23] During the 1920s and 1930s, while the major manufacturers of airframes settled down in southern (and later northern) California, a complex of companies was formed in New England around the Pratt and Whitney Tool Company of East Hartford, Connecticut, to manufacture aircraft engines. Later, at the request of the government during World War II, General Electric began producing engines and parts at its Lynn and Pittsfield plants in Massachusetts. Over the course of the 1930s, two-thirds of total sales by the seven largest companies in the country were to the U.S. army and navy.

Arms sales—and the derivative demand for new machine tools and dies—increased enormously with America's entry into World War II. In order to meet its requirements, the federal government, after experimenting with various procurement arrangements, created the Defense Plant Corporation as a subsidiary of the Reconstruction Finance Corporation to build new facilities and lease them to private contractors. The metalworking machinery industry received some $70 million worth of new plant and equipment in this way, and much of the privately financed $91 million which industry received during the war came as advances on government procurement contracts.[24] The aircraft program was even larger. Under its auspices, General Electric received new publicly constructed plants in Lynn, Everett, and Pittsfield, Massachusetts. Similarly, the federal government built new plants for Pratt and Whitney in Southbridge and Willimantic, Connecticut, and rehabilitated old mills for Hamilton-Standard (later to join P&W as part of the United Technologies conglomerate) in Pawtucket, Rhode Island, and in New London, Connecticut.[25] By the end of the war, aircraft as a whole had become the largest manufacturing employer in the United States while the aircraft engine segment of the industry went on to become the single most important employer of production workers in New England in the postwar period.

Government military orders directly stimulated production in other industries which were either already important to the region (such as textiles in Nashua, New Hampshire, and shipbuilding in Bath, Maine; Quincy, Massachusetts; and New London, Connecticut) or which would soon become so. For example, "the 'communications equipment' industry . . . was a weak and infant industry in 1939, but during the war years it almost trebled in size, laying the foundations for one of the most important new developments of the post-war years, the growth of electronic product manufacture."[26] The development of the computer industry (at first electromechanical, later electronic) grew out of the wartime military demand for precise calculations of shell trajectories and in connection with the Manhattan Project which produced the first atomic bomb.[27]

At the end of the war, Congress passed the Surplus Property Act to facilitate the disposal of these properties so as to discourage monopolistic practices. The disposal agencies in the executive branch paid no attention to the law. In later years, Congress voted to restrict the extent to which the companies with cheap surplus war plants could use the subsidized capital to compete for government contracts (as opposed to sole-source procurements) to produce commodities for private sale. However, Congress never created any enforcement mechanism.[28]

According to John Blair, for many years the chief economist of the Antitrust Committee of the U.S. Senate, $26 billion worth of new plant and equipment was constructed by the government during the war, increasing the nation's productive capacity by half over the space of six years. Fourteen billion dollars were expended on new plants, $4.2 billion for expansion of prewar plants, and $7.8 billion for conversion of prewar plants to wartime uses. By the end of 1946, most of this plant and equipment had been sold or was being leased to the two hundred fifty largest corporations in the country, at prices based on costs which the companies themselves computed for the government. Eighty-seven corporations purchased or leased fully 65 percent of all disposals.

> Just as the three largest steel corporations acquired the great bulk of the government surplus steel facilities, so also did General Electric and Westinghouse account for most of the disposals of electrical machinery facilities. In terms of number of plants acquired, General Electric led all other corporations, having bought fourteen and leased two, at a total

cost of $35.8 million. Westinghouse, with $23.6 million worth of surplus plants, was not far behind.[29]

General Electric was for many years the largest industrial employer in New England.

Industrial development policies pursued during the war also had an indirect impact on New England by creating competitive "growth poles" in such Sunbelt cities as Mobile, Alabama; Dallas, Texas; Wichita, Kansas; Denver, Colorado; and San Diego, California. In each location, the federal government financed streets, sewers, electric lines, and airports as support systems for the new military bases and armaments factories. These public investments created the preconditions for massive expenditure of private industrial capital in the South as soon as the war was over. Most of this new development consisted of locally owned businesses (although financing often came via national capital markets, which then—as now—received substantial funding through financial transfers from banks and insurance companies based in the North). Still, an important component of the new postwar Southern growth consisted of runaway shops (especially in textiles, apparel, and furniture) and, in the later years, new branch plants of major Northern-based corporations. The extraordinary tax breaks offered immediately after the war by states like Mississippi and Alabama may also have been a relevant factor in this initial wave of relocations.[30]

In the small towns of the postwar South, for those firms that could make use of them, there were still large pools of predominantly rural workers with little or no industrial experience. Many of these people continued for years to engage in farming for part of the year or to receive support from farm families. Thus, firms did not need to pay very high wages to attract labor. Then, too, the state and local governments of the region often took explicitly antilabor positions, including the enforcement of "right-to-work" laws that effectively prohibited unions from requiring dues payments of all the workers in a plant even when a majority had voted for union representation. The reservation of such power to the states, and the prohibition against secondary boycotts (which made it difficult for Northern-based unions to bring sanctions against runaway shops), were among the most significant provisions of the Taft-Hartley Act. This law had been passed by Congress in 1947 precisely in order to halt the momentum that industrial union organizing drives had built up over the preceding ten years.

The effects of right-to-work laws extended beyond the reduction of production costs for companies. They were (and continue to be) a

symbol of the general attitude of state governments toward workers'
claims on regional income and social services. As we have seen, unions
have historically been effective lobbyists for social programs whose
benefits extend beyond the union's own membership. Even today, on a
wide variety of indicators—from average wages to taxes on business to
the existence of equal pay laws for women—the twenty Southern and
border states having right-to-work laws show up with *much* lower
scores than the thirty states that do not have such laws.[31]

Small businesses unable to continue operating with aging plant
or obsolete products, runaways to areas with a labor climate more
favorable to business, corporations branching out of the region, and
conglomerate acquisition and subsequent milking and divestiture of
established enterprises all contributed to the wave of plant and shop
shutdowns that swept New England after World War II. Still another
source of closings, especially noticeable in the shoe business after 1970,
was the practice by smaller manufacturers of shifting into the distribution of imports, thus getting out of the production end of the business
altogether.

In this restructuring of the old industrial base, an increasingly
important agency for the transfer of capital across space and among
sectors was the conglomerate. Among the more internationally important conglomerates with headquarters in New England are the Con-
necticut-based United Technologies Corporation and W. R. Grace,
Inc. Providence-based Textron, Inc. is one of the earliest of the conglomerates. Established during the war by Royal Little, a legendary
New England entrepreneur, Textron bought up old mills all over
northern New England. As soon as profits began to soften, or when
speculation in raw goods made the selling off of stockpiles more profitable than continued processing, Textron would shut the mills down
and transfer operations to its facilities in the South. In the ensuing
years, Textron moved into more than a hundred mostly unrelated product lines.[32] Such restructuring was not a new phenomenon in American
industry; what *was* new was the speed with which such highly centralized management was able to make these often sizeable transfers
of capital.

Data on the various forms of capital transfer are for the most part
unavailable except through laborious case-by-case investigations. One
source of information on business closings or shutdowns *not* leading to
relocation is Dun and Bradstreet, Inc., which regularly tracks business
failures among different regions of the country.[33] Figure 3.1 shows
that in every year since 1955 (the earliest for which these data exist),

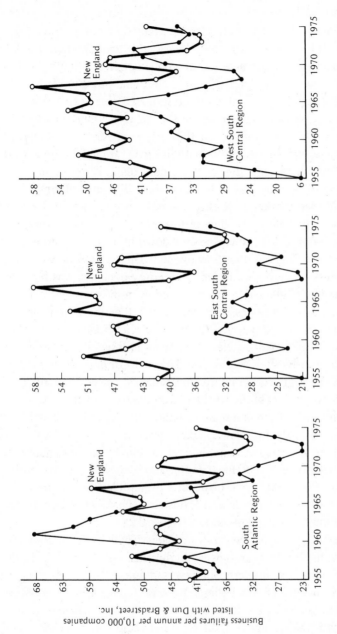

FIGURE 3.1. Annual Business Failures, 1955–1975: New England Compared with the Three Southern Regions. See note 33 for definition of business "failure." (Source: Business Economics Division, Dun and Bradstreet, Inc., *The Business Failure Record*, 1977.)

Business failures per annum per 10,000 companies listed with Dun & Bradstreet, Inc.

business closings through actual failure have been greater in New England than in the East South Central states (including Mississippi, Alabama, and Tennessee). In almost every year, New England has had a higher incidence of business failures than either the South Atlantic region (containing Maryland, Virginia, Georgia, and Florida) or the West Central region (dominated by the state of Texas).

Systematic empirical evidence on the relative impact of conglomerate mergers on New England for the early postwar years is unavailable. However, we do have information—again, from Dun and Bradstreet—on "establishment," that is, individual plant, shop, or store (as distinct from parent firm or enterprise) openings and closings from 1969 to 1976 (see chapter 15 in this volume). In the wake of the burst of merger activity that took place in the mid- to late-1960s, conglomerates in nine out of ten industries shut down more plants, stores, and facilities in New England than they opened. The tradeoff between jobs destroyed through closures and jobs created by openings was far more extreme among conglomerates than among even independently owned (generally small) businesses.[34] Of course, whether these findings pertain as well to the earlier years of the postwar era is unknown.

In sum, employment in New England's mill-based industries declined precipitously after World War II, partly through business failures, partly through corporate reallocations of activity among their plants in different parts of the world, and to some extent through actual physical relocations from one region to another. Capacity utilization in the mills that remained in New England was also cut back ("rationalized"), as many owners became reluctant to reinvest in these generally older facilities. Together, rationalization and geographic restructuring contributed to a vicious cycle of decline exemplified by the trends in the apparel, shoe, and paper mill industries. That decline continued unabated throughout the postwar era (figure 3.2).

As a result, unemployment rates in New England in the three decades following World War II were higher in most years than in the rest of the country, a pattern not reversed until 1978. According to Robert Eisenmenger of the Federal Reserve Bank of Boston, "Every New England state had a total unemployment rate which was well above the national average in 1950. No other region of the country had such serious unemployment during this prosperous period."[35] The census of that year shows an unemployment rate for the region of 6.3 percent, compared to the national rate of only 4.9 percent. By 1960 the relative position of New England had improved vis-à-vis the nation, but from 1965 through the end of 1977, the gap widened again.

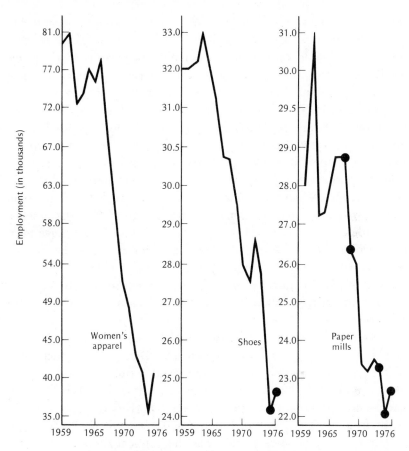

FIGURE 3.2. Annual Employment in Women's Apparel, Shoes, and Paper Mills in New England, 1959–1976. Black dots indicate that observations for some of the New England states were not available that year and had to be interpolated. The details of this procedure are available on request. (Source: Calculations by Lynn B. Ware, Denise DiPasquale, and Barry Bluestone, Social Welfare Research Institute, Boston College, using data from U.S. Dept. of Commerce, *County Business Patterns*.)

DEVELOPMENT OF THE CONDITIONS LEADING TOWARD A NEW WAVE OF ECONOMIC GROWTH IN NEW ENGLAND

In order for a declining area to become attractive to capital again, certain conditions which obtained during earlier periods of growth must somehow be reconstituted. Although the precise features of an earlier era are never literally reproduced,[36] there are certain generic conditions, the establishment of which make profitable growth possible (although certainly not inevitable). First is the recreation of a large supply of "tractable" labor: a pool of potential workers ready to accept the newly emerging kinds of jobs with their particular work rules and wage levels. Second is the availability of financial capital for initiating a new generation of businesses. Third is the provision by the national government of the means for developing the basic infrastructure required by the new generation of industry, such as roads and airports. Fourth is support by local governments for this new economic development, through policies ranging from the preparation of the environment for the new industrial and commercial uses, such as urban renewal, to the active promotion of business interests through the selective application of taxes and regulations. The other factors have been discussed at length elsewhere.[37] Moreover, I honestly believe that the "labor factor" is of paramount importance—precisely because it is so much more than a "factor of production." Therefore, in this chapter I focus on the first condition for economic revitalization: the supply of labor power.

The process by which the new regional labor force was created in New England contained several elements. One was the increasing labor force participation of other household members in the face of the generation-long high unemployment of adult mill workers. Another was the immigration of new groups of poor workers from abroad, primarily from the Third World. A third factor, which contributed to the relative passivity of these groups, was the political suppression of activists who attempted to organize the new workers into a class-conscious political force. Still another element was the destabilization of the older and traditionally coherent working-class communities, caused by chronic long-term unemployment of their residents and exacerbated by the entry of the new immigrants.

The contextual importance of the long history of high unemployment in New England can hardly be exaggerated. For one thing, the presence of a large and continually replenished labor reserve forces wages down and holds them down. The relative bargaining power of even skilled workers is weakened. Writing about the crucial transitional decade of the 1950s, Eisenmenger observes:

> Some skilled male manufacturing workers (such as machine-tool operators, millwrights, and sheetmetal workers) receive lower wages in New England than in any other region of the country. . . . Semiskilled male manufacturing workers are paid lower wages in New England than in

the Middle Atlantic, North Central, or Western states, . . . wage levels
are considerably lower in the metalworking industries in cities in New
England than in cities throughout the country. For example, the average
wage in metropolitan Boston is usually 5 to 20 percent lower than in
other metropolitan areas throughout the country.[38]

High long-term unemployment also increases the dependence of those
workers who do have jobs on their present employers. Thus, a 1954
study by the National Planning Association found that "New England
workers transfer from one job to another less frequently than workers
in other regions . . . this [is] a significant advantage for New England firms."[39]

Eisenmenger further observed a pattern that subsequently spread
to the region's new service industries: wage rates for women office
workers in New England manufacturing firms during the 1950s were
"well below the national average" and even "below those prevailing in
Southern states."[40] Women had always been an important component
of the region's industrial work force, from the earliest development of
the textile industry in the nineteenth century.[41] On the eve of World
War II, while women made up less than a quarter of all workers in the
country aged fourteen and older, their share was over 30 percent in
New England. Here, as elsewhere, many women worked during the
war in defense plants and shipyards. Ever since 1945 they have constituted a larger share of the labor force in New England than in the
country as a whole. The proportion of women who work (or who are
actively searching for work, as measured by the labor force participation rate) has also been relatively higher in this region. The relative
and absolute growth of the female labor supply in New England has
accompanied a steady fall in the male labor force participation rate,
relative to the rest of the country. This is probably due (at least in
part) to structural displacement. That is, along with the national cultural transformation that has validated greater women's participation
in the paid labor force over the last thirty years, working-class mothers
and daughters may to some extent have been *forced* into the labor
force in New England by their husbands' and fathers' loss of their
former mill jobs.

Another growing source of labor power in the region has been
young people under the age of twenty-five. In 1950 the labor force
participation of this group was actually lower in New England than
in the United States as a whole. By 1960 intense competition in the
predominantly Northern mass consumer service industries was forcing

managers to try to hold down labor costs and to operate with maximum flexibility in terms of the scheduling and control of work by bringing large numbers of young people into New England's wage labor force. Their absolute and relative participation rates further increased through the next decade. In Massachusetts by 1976, the labor force participation rate of people under twenty-five was fully ten percentage points above the national rate for the same age group.[42]

The inclusion of new immigrants in the emerging labor pool further enhanced the opportunities for business to undertake profitable operations in New England. During and immediately after World War II, the aircraft companies and their machine shop subcontractors actively recruited machinists from Eastern Europe, many of whom were met on the docks by the Polish cardinal of Hartford, Connecticut. First Puerto Ricans and then other Hispanic workers from the Caribbean were recruited by New England firms to labor in the tobacco fields of Connecticut and (later) in the garment trade in southeastern Massachusetts. A substantial share of the work force in the women's apparel industry in such southern New England centers as New Bedford, Massachusetts, are Puerto Ricans and Portuguese-speaking blacks from the Cape Verde Islands off the coast of Africa.

Mass unemployment created a demoralizing atmosphere, especially in the older mill towns. In that climate, there were always radical activists in the population, both inside and outside the unions, who continued to engage in the "political education" of their fellow workers. With the onset of the ideology of the cold war in the years following World War II, these labor militants were subjected to increasing harassment and repression by agencies of the federal government, led by the House Committee on Un-American Activities (HUAC) and the Senate Investigating Committee of U.S. Senator Joseph McCarthy. Activists were purged from the major unions, and organizers were explicitly blacklisted by companies. Rank-and-file workers' willingness to entertain, let alone to support, radical positions was undermined by their fear that such support would lead to further plant shutdowns, lockouts, and blacklisting. This anxiety was reinforced by the barrage of anti-Soviet propaganda imposed upon the American public by its own government in the postwar years.

A particularly dramatic example of the suppression of labor activism during this period is the experience of the United Electrical Workers (UE).[43] This was the second largest union in the country at the end of World War II. Its militant organizing activity was effectively halted by investigations conducted by HUAC in Bridgeport,

Connecticut, and in other cities and then by the new Atomic Energy Commission's order to General Electric not to permit UE to represent its workers in the new nuclear facility in Schenectady, New York. Armed troops carried UE organizers out of the South Philadelphia Westinghouse plant. President Truman insisted that workers in plants engaged in production vital to the national security take loyalty oaths. When the UE refused, it was ejected from the Congress of Industrial Organizations (CIO), and a new union, the International Union of Electrical Workers, was created to take its place.

Eventually, organized labor acceded to these challenges to its further expansion in return for the institutionalization, through the collective bargaining system, of some of the more important benefits which the unions had been able to win for their members during the struggles of the 1930s. This social contract between industry and big labor was to last for a quarter of a century before what Jack Metzgar has called the "system of negotiated class struggle" was rejected by industry itself during the late 1970s.[44]

The rapid postwar decline of the most highly unionized industries obviously weakened the main blue-collar unions. Because the region's employers were unusually dependent upon military procurement relative to the rest of the country, antiunion government purges such as those initiated by HUAC had especially frequent opportunities to intervene (in the name of "national security") in the affairs of the remaining workplaces. The new service sector jobs were either difficult for the younger unions to organize or—in the case of the public sector—off limits by law.[45]

The reaction by business against the inroads that had been made by organized labor was highly successful in New England, according to a number of indicators. In 1939 only 15 percent of the nonagricultural labor force of Massachusetts belonged to labor unions. Wartime and immediate postwar CIO organizing doubled that rate to 30 percent by 1953. After that, through a combination of political suppression of organizers, the relocation of the industries that had been the most highly unionized, and the growth of the new computer and service industries which tended to employ people who had never been members of a union before, the incidence of unionization fell steadily, to a rate of 24 percent by the mid-1970s.[46]

By the mid-1950s, New England businessmen were describing their workers as more "cooperative" than those in other places.[47] The average number of days lost to work stoppages (strikes, sit-downs, boycotts, and lockouts) as a percentage of all working days fell to less than half the national average. The proportion was only a fourth of the rates in rapidly industrializing Sunbelt states such as Alabama and Arizona and only barely above the rate in Georgia.[48]

Data from the National Labor Relations Board (NLRB) show that in 1950 unions in New England won nearly 70 percent of the elections in which they sought to represent workers. By the 1970s, their success rate had been cut in half.[49] This record compares most unfavorably with that of many other areas of the country. Moreover, the process of erosion of relative trade union power in New England from the early 1950s continues to the present day. In 1979 union success rates in certification elections in manufacturing establishments were lower in New England than in any other region in the country—including the Deep South. With respect to their degree of success in resisting efforts to decertify a successful election—efforts usually initiated or backed by the employer—in the late 1970s, New England unions did no better than average, vis-à-vis the other regions.[50]

The migration flows discussed earlier played an important role in undermining the solidarity of established working-class communities already facing the devolution of the union's power. Mass unemployment and then the very policies effected by local governments in the pursuit of reindustrialization threatened traditional blue-collar cultural values and social networks. The environment became highly combustible and was made even more so by new, predominantly nonwhite immigrants who crowded into (or near) neighborhoods previously occupied by white workers. Organizations trying to bring all of these disparate groups together have had to cope with such obstacles as language barriers, racism, and the ability of charismatic local political leaders to play off one group against another.[51]

In sum, by the 1960s a substantially new labor force had been created in New England: more multiracial, more female, younger, disciplined by the experience of long-term unemployment in the immediate family or among neighbors, not particularly interested in unions (if not actively antiunion), and "flexible" in terms of the number of hours of work, days of the week, work rules, and wages it was prepared to accept. Superimposed on the remnants of the more traditional work force, this heterogeneous population provided the region's emerging entrepreneurs and corporate managers with a large and—at least for the time being—tractable supply of labor power.[52] The most important condition was now in place for a new wave of economic growth in the region.

THE NEW INDUSTRIAL STRUCTURE

By the late 1970s, private industry—provided with new sources of labor power, finance capital, publicly subsidized infrastructure, and a generally supportive tax and regulatory environment—had clearly undertaken investment projects that radically transformed the economic base of New England. The service sector emerges as clearly dominant, with hospitals being the single largest employer in the region. In manufacturing, the aircraft engine–metalworking machinery complex retains its postwar position as the area's most important employer of production workers, although this trend masks a pattern of extreme volatility: the military cycle of "boom and bust." Despite its continuous decline, the shoe industry still reflects its New England tradition even at this late date in its history; on average, between 1959 and 1976 a third of all leather footwear workers in America were employed in establishments located in New England. And of course the manufacture of computers emerges as a growing source of jobs. Over this eighteen-year period, only two of the region's top twenty industries had declining employment trends. This is a powerful indicator of the extent to which the transformation to the new economic base—the "shakeout" of the older industries, in popular jargon—had progressed by the mid-1970s.

The new industrial structure consists of four sectors: the surviving mill-based industries producing mainly consumption goods; the industries manufacturing capital goods for domestic and foreign producers; the so-called high-tech industries fabricating the newest generation of producers' goods (computers and peripheral equipment) and all manner of scientific and military instruments; and that most heterogeneous of all categories, the "service" sector. Let us look first at what has happened to manufacturing operations, and then at these service activities, old and new.

The Mill-Based Manufacturing Industries

By 1977 the traditional mill-based consumption goods industries such as food processing, textiles, apparel, shoes, furniture, paper, printing, and lumber were employing only a tenth of all workers in New England. Wide-scale bankruptcies of small firms had wiped out many jobs, as had the continued shift of some operations to the Sunbelt and, after the early 1960s, to Mexico, the Caribbean, Southern Europe, and the Far East. Federal tax and tariff regulations encouraging "offshore" assembly of standardized products for sale inside the United States facilitated this dispersion of operations.[53]

Within New England, the migration of small shops from the south of the region to its northern periphery continued as manufacturers in Connecticut, Rhode Island, and Massachusetts sought to engage in cheap, simple operations such as the stitching of clothing parts or the batch production of printed matter in the small towns of Vermont, New Hampshire, and Maine.

A significant number of the plant closings in the late 1960s and 1970s in these industries seems to have been associated with corporate and especially conglomerate acquisition policies. Profitable independent (often family-owned) businesses were bought up, operated for a short time, milked of their cash flow, and then sold off or shut down.[54] Companies remaining in business in the region have survived through extreme product specialization—for example, in specialty high-quality papers, women's high-fashion sportswear, or athletic footwear directed toward supplying the jogging fad—or through further mechanization of the production process. The labor redundancies made possible by technical innovations such as computerized typesetting and laser beams to cut large bundles of fabric have been concentrated most heavily on the mid-range of skills, significantly cutting labor costs and increasing the productivity of the remaining workers.

The Traditional Capital Goods Industries

Firms manufacturing metal parts, metalworking machinery, and other producers' equipment—especially engines and power generators—continue to be important to New England. Sales to Washington and to foreign governments and exports to private firms throughout the world provide jobs for many members of the machinists', electrical workers', steelworkers', and auto workers' unions. But this sector, too, has undergone secular employment losses through the heightening of international competition and managements' responses to these pressures.

In some cases, the introduction of automated machine tools has deskilled, if not totally displaced, some specialized machinists (although in other situations we observed, small shopowners and their most experienced machinists were cooperating in phasing in the new equipment). Other local producers have chosen to meet the competition from firms operating out of Taiwan, Singapore, Spain, and Japan—many of them American branch plants or foreign companies partly financed by U.S. firms or banks—by relocating or branching into these areas themselves. Moreover, to sell highly profitable equipment such as jet engines to foreign airlines, which are typically government-owned, General Electric and Pratt and Whitney sometimes have to engage in "co-production," "offset," or "local content" agreements that allocate a share of the production work to firms in the country buying the engines. Even when such deals are not explicitly demanded by customers, the larger American corporations are increasingly shifting much of their subcontracting components to suppliers located in low-wage areas in Europe, such as Spain and Ireland, and in the Third World. The cultivation of multiple sources for parts manufacture seems to be an effort to protect the prime contractors from interruptions in production due to strikes or other expressions of labor unrest anywhere along their supply lines.[55]

The High-Technology Industries

The current fascination with so-called high technology in New England is appropriate; these companies do constitute the region's most rapidly growing source of manufactured exports. There is no formal definition of high-tech, but the term usually refers to small computers, semi-conductors, microprocessors ("computers on a chip"), word processors (themselves small computers), scientific and environmental sensing instruments, medical and laboratory equipment, and all manner of electronic control systems for military use.

Massachusetts is the high-tech capital of the region (and, along with California's Silicon Valley, the high-tech capital of the United States). The state employment agency has constructed an operational definition for the high-tech sector, consisting of fifteen specific manu-facturing and six specific service industries. The growth rates of these industries in Massachusetts during the late 1970s (the latest years for which complete data are available) were indeed impressive, as shown in table 3.1. Still, for all the attention it has commanded, the high-tech sector has not yet achieved the dominance once held by the mill indus-tries. In Massachusetts the twenty-one high-tech industries employed only an eighth of the total state work force in 1978. Within the group, computer hardware and software and computer programming services were particularly important in terms of both level and growth of em-ployment. Even so, their 1978 share of total employment in Massa-chusetts was still only 62 percent. By the early 1980s, these propor-tions were certainly much higher, although final data are not yet available.

Table 3.1. Recent Employment Trends in Massachusetts High-Technology Industries

		Employment		
SIC	Industry	4th qtr. 1976	4th qtr. 1978	Pct. change
281	Industrial chemicals	1,213	1,272	4.9
282	Plastic materials	5,136	5,582	8.7
283	Drugs	2,199	2,463	12.0
351	Engines & turbines	6,783	5,817	−16.6
357	Office machines & computers	22,677	32,430	43.0
361	Electrical distribution	13,702	11,891	−13.2
362	Elec. ind. apparatus	2,767	3,112	12.5
366	Communication equipment	24,723	27,609	11.3
367	Electronic components	32,345	40,555	25.4
372	Aircraft & parts	7,785	9,229	18.5
376	Space vehicles & guided missiles	11,118	12,438	11.9
381	Engineering & scientific instruments	1,939	3,308	70.6
382	Measuring & control instruments	14,637	19,325	32.0
383	Optical instruments	4,786	6,435	34.5
386	Photographic equipment	12,391	17,866	44.2
737	Computer programming services	6,252	10,259	64.3
7391	Commercial R&D labs	8,163	8,677	6.3
7392	Bus. mgmt. & consulting services	8,470	9,003	6.3
891	Engineering & arch. services	18,695	24,688	32.1
892	Nonprofit educ., scient., & research orgs.	6,274	7,723	23.1
Total—High-tech		212,055	259,582	22.4
Total—All Mass. private employment		1,929,150	2,132,695	10.6

Source: Robert Vinson and Paul Harrington, "Defining 'High Technology' Industries in Massachusetts," Policy and Evaluation Division, Department of Manpower Development, Commonwealth of Massachusetts, September 1979, p. 12; based on Employment Service ES-202 reports.

The *growth* of computer manufacturing employment has certainly been quite rapid in the entire region, especially since 1970. Four of the industry's leading producers of "mini" computers, aimed especially at the small and medium-sized business market, are based here: Digital, Data General, Wang, and Prime. The Minneapolis-based Honeywell Corporation maintains major production facilities in and around Boston. Outside Burlington, Vermont, the New York–based IBM operates one of the world's largest and most highly automated semiconductor manufacturing plants.

With both hardware and software undergoing continual redesign in the face of new demands from industrial, commercial, and government users (notably the military), there has so far been a strong tendency for the computer manufacturers in particular and for the high-tech companies in general to keep their testing and much of their production activity close to their research facilities, located within a short distance of Boston's university and business service complex. On the other hand, chips and other subassemblies are increasingly procured from sources located outside New England, often in such low-wage Third World countries as Mexico and Malaysia. However, as the tendency toward greater centralization and concentration of control proceeds in the computer industry (reflected, for example, in the current wave of mergers), the usual pressures to standardize products in order to achieve greater economies of scale are likely to set in. Just such an expectation has already led at least one respected analyst to forecast increasing geographic dispersal of some segments of the New England computer industry over the next decade.[56]

The Service Sector

By the late 1970s, two-thirds of the labor force of New England worked in trade and in the various public and private services (including government and the utilities). The comparable proportion in 1940 had been 50 percent. Moreover, the composition of the sector, always highly heterogeneous, has become even more complex over time.

Service production falls into five categories. First are the infrastructure services, including mainly transportation, communications, and public utilities. Second are distributive services—wholesale and retail trade—which facilitate the sale of commodities, mostly to local workers and their families. Third are services primarily directed to other businesses. The region's largest cities (especially Boston and Hartford) have become major centers for this segment, providing

everything from accounting to financial and legal assistance.[57] Local
users and firms from all over the world buy these services. A fourth
class of services consists of a broad array of recreational and repair
activities sold mainly to workers and their families whether residents
of or visitors to the region. The variety is enormous, from motion pic-
tures, theaters, and restaurants to hairdressers and auto repair shops.
The fifth segment includes the "reproductive" services: health and
education.

Government provides services that fall into all five of these categories. It operates at least some bus or rail transport companies in
most cities and provides many services intended directly or indirectly
for private industry—police protection of commercial property is but
one example. Government even distributes privately produced commodities, such as liquor in New Hampshire, as a way of earning
revenue. Government also provides recreation services, exemplified by
publicly constructed and maintained parks. And, of course, federal,
state, or local governments directly run most schools and many hospitals. New England governments seem always to have been relatively
smaller than their counterparts in the nation as a whole. In 1940 when
one out of eight workers in the United States was employed by some
level of government, the corresponding proportion in New England
was only 4 percent. By 1977 the incidence of national public employment had risen to 16.7 percent, while in New England, the corresponding share of government in all employment was still only 15 percent.[58]

EMPLOYMENT, EARNINGS, AND THE
ORGANIZATION OF WORK IN THE NEW STRUCTURE

What sorts of wages and working conditions do the people of the
region confront in the "new" economy of New England? In other
words, how has the transformation from the old mill- and electromechanical capital goods–based structure to the new mix dominated by
high-tech and services affected the ability of the region's workers to
earn a living?

It is possible to draw five conclusions about the effects of this economic transformation on New England's labor force:

1. Wage levels have fallen, relative to other regions (including the
South) and especially in terms of purchasing power. This is true even
for people who work year-round, and for skilled systems analysts as
well as for factory workers.

2. Employment in the region is highly unstable in several respects: there is a growing incidence of part-time or part-year jobs; the degree of employee attachment to the companies for which they work is lowest in precisely those industries which are growing most rapidly; service-intensive regional economies such as New England have shown themselves not to be recession-proof (as was widely believed); and the region's highest-paying manufacturing companies—the aircraft and metalworking industries—are subject to sharp "boom-bust" swings in employment.

3. There are significant barriers to upward mobility for many of the region's workers, notably those who were employed at one time in the old mill industries and women and minorities employed in the service sector.

4. The developmental tendencies toward intensification of work, rationalization of productive capacity, automation, and geographic restructuring, all of which contributed to the erosion of the old economic base of the region, are still operative, even in the most rapidly growing industries.

5. As a result of all these other structural changes, earned income is becoming more unequally distributed among the region's workers over time, both between and within (most) industries, even among those who work year-round, and within as well as between the sexes.

In a word, although there has been substantial growth and development (especially since about 1970), that development has been profoundly *uneven*. This surely has implications for our expectations about the region's future course of development, especially as that course is shaped by the politics of class within New England.

Detailed quantitative and qualitative analyses of each of these propositions have been published elsewhere.[59] In this section, I will therefore summarize only the main themes and findings.

Low Wage Levels

New England manufacturing wages have been falling relative to the national average for a century. The decline was especially great between 1947 and 1960; in the latter year, New Englanders earned only 92 percent of the national average wage. Relative manufacturing and nonmanufacturing earnings per full-time-equivalent worker dropped sharply again during the 1970s.

This emergence of New England as a relatively low-wage area extends to many high-tech occupations as well (even though employers

continually claim to be experiencing shortages of "skilled labor").
Boston in particular ranks among the lowest-paying areas in the country in a number of these jobs.[60]

While most wages are determined in local markets for labor, the prices which people pay for many of the things they buy are now determined largely at the regional, national, and even international levels. Because their nominal wages are so relatively low, and in the environment of chronic world-wide inflation that has permeated the whole international capitalist system since the early 1970s, New England workers find themselves the *lowest* paid in the United States in terms of purchasing power. To the extent that certain items (such as energy) *are* more expensive in New England, that only makes the relative disadvantage of the region's workers even greater vis-à-vis workers in other regions of the country. As I suggested earlier, this decline in relative wages seems to be a consequence of a generation of unusually high unemployment, the successful recreation of a large and disciplined labor force, and the generally supportive stance of federal, state, and local government policies over the crucial years during which the new economic activities were emerging.

Instability of Employment

Perhaps the most important contribution of the literature of the late 1960s and 1970s on labor market segmentation was the discovery that unstable employment patterns are, to a great extent, associated with the jobs themselves, that is, with the organization of the labor process rather than with "unstable behavior" by workers as such. Some jobs, for example in apparel and food processing, are explicitly *designed* to be seasonal. Workers in these jobs experience periodic and predictable layoffs with recall informally promised by their employers. Many jobs—indeed, an increasing number in industries such as hotels, department stores, and supermarkets—are built around the availability of cheap, part-time labor. Full-time, year-round jobs in these industries are hard to find.

Apart from this growth in the incidence of part-time or part-year jobs in New England, there are three other aspects of job stability which we have been able to measure. First, correlations between the degree of annual employee turnover within an industry and that industry's average earnings and employment trend over the period 1959–1976 reveal that the New England mix is becoming dominated by industries which tend to provide jobs characterized by high turnover and low wages. Second, the shift from a predominantly manufacturing to a mostly service-oriented economic base in New England seems not to have eliminated the sensitivity of the region to national (and international) business cycles, as was widely predicted during the early 1970s.

Third, there is yet another kind of cycle to which the New England economy seems especially sensitive: the boom-and-bust pattern of employment growth and decline in the aircraft-metalworking complex. The rapid Vietnam-induced buildup of employment in the first half of the 1960s was followed by a precipitous retrenchment in the wake of the cessation of war-related orders. In fact, New England's extreme dependence on federal (and foreign) military procurement permeates much of the industrial base, through the derived demand for everything from instruments to paper clips—just as it has ever since the founding of the republic.

Barriers to "Upward Mobility"

The divisions among the region's labor force and the dominance which most employers have had over labor for a generation have strongly influenced the mobility of New England workers in a number of ways. Workers certainly move—across locations, between employers, and even among different kinds of jobs. However, whether that movement leads to "upward" mobility in earnings and status should not be taken for granted.

For instance, what has happened to those workers who eventually left (or were displaced from) the old mill industries? How many were able to find jobs in the new high-tech companies or in the highly unionized, high-paying engineering industries? Or have the shoe, apparel, and textile workers been forced to accept jobs in the predominantly low-wage, more unstable services, where they probably have had to take wage cuts? And finally, how many of the older mill workers moved out of New England altogether, either to look for similar jobs or to retire?

The mirror image of these questions is at least as interesting. Where do the employees in the high-tech growth industries originate? What were they doing before they became "high-technicians"? In particular, to what extent do these firms recruit locally, from the industries whose workers have become redundant, and to what extent do they draw new people into the region from outside?

Consider the cohort of some 833,000 people whose principal activity in 1958 was to work in the mill industries in New England. Sometime after 1958, 674,000 of these workers left the mills. By 1975, only 18,000 of them—fewer than 3 percent—were employed in the high-tech industries of the region. (Another 2,000 had migrated to high-tech jobs outside of New England.) Most went into the service sector (working for private companies or for the federal government), dropped out of the labor force, or had no job at all. Only an eighth of the group had retired by 1975. The picture is almost identical for the youngest cohort taken by itself: the roughly 158,000 mill workers in 1958 who were then under the age of twenty-five. By 1975, eighteen years later, only about 3.8 percent had been hired by the region's high-tech companies, and fewer than 1 percent had found high-tech jobs elsewhere. As with the older members of their cohort, the great majority took private service jobs, went to work for the federal government, dropped out, or were mainly unemployed in 1975.

Then whom *do* New England's high-tech firms employ? They tend to recruit young, inexperienced people out of school or out of the home, especially women. They draw on well-educated professionals from all over the world. They also engage in a spirited "pirating" of the more experienced workers from each other, with these employees moving back and forth among the companies over time. Such movement is sometimes, but by no means always, associated with significant increases in salaries and benefits beyond those received by workers of comparable seniority who do not change employers so frequently.

In short, few of those who leave the generally declining, older mill-based industries of the region are able to move into the relatively good jobs in growth sectors such as high-tech (or even into the still higher-paying jobs in capital goods industries such as aircraft). Relatively few of the mill workers move away from the region, even the youngest and presumably most mobile of them. But in any case, whether they move or not, they tend not to be hired by high-tech companies. The lesson seems clear: the region simply does not create enough new, well-paying jobs in the growth industries to absorb those displaced by industrial disinvestment, and the jobs created in sectors such as high-tech are in any case going to other people, including many recruited from outside the region altogether.

Now consider the mobility problem for an entirely different group of workers: female department store employees.[61] Since 1957 the growth of department store management jobs, nearly all held (in New England, at least) by men, has greatly increased the incomes which more senior men receive. The women's situation is very different.

They used to hold most of the skilled buying and sales positions. They knew the products well and could discuss them intelligently with customers. The growth of television advertising, the advent of the huge one-story, self-service store, and the introduction of automatic data processing point-of-sale computers have enabled managers to substitute even poorly educated, certainly inexperienced teenagers at the minimum wage.

As a result, the earnings opportunities of all but the most senior women employees have worsened. In 1957 the personal earnings distributions of year-round male and female employees in the department store industry were actually quite similar. By 1975 they had diverged to a quite extraordinary degree. The male distribution is now bimodal, reflecting the presence of both part-time low-wage men and full-time highly paid managers. The female distribution continues to display its traditional skew toward low wages.

Even in the nonprofit hospital industry, where wages and opportunities for upward mobility have been somewhat better for New England women than in other pursuits, the gap between men's and women's earnings has not closed over the past two decades. Thomas Barocci has summarized the situation: "Though the figures clearly show real income rising, the ratio of women's (particularly those over 35 years old) to men's earnings has not improved. . . . All interviews confirmed that the majority of new occupational positions in the hospital industry have been filled with males. This is because the areas of greatest growth in employment are related to operation and maintenance of . . . management systems—traditionally male positions."[62] Moreover, Barocci writes, "The doctors, if past is prologue, will resist relinquishing control to nurses while continuing to develop more and more subspecialities to enhance their control over hospital functions even further."[63] Again we see evidence of growing conflict and tension in the workplace.

Some people (especially middle-class youth) may find the rapidly proliferating part-time or seasonal service jobs attractive and helpful. But an important segment of the adult population—and many more young workers than is commonly supposed—find these jobs are basically a dead end. The hotel-motel industry serves to illustrate the problem.[64] It has been one of the region's most rapidly growing industries since the late 1950s, and is currently the focus of much urban economic development policy in New England as elsewhere in the United States. But it is also the industry with the lowest average earnings, even for year-round workers, and with the most unequally distributed earnings.

Worker attachment to a particular job or firm is lower (turnover is higher) than in any other industry in New England. Part of the problem is the seasonality of the tourist-oriented segment of the industry, but low wages and generally bad working conditions characterize all of the industry's segments, including the urban business-oriented hotels which literally lie at the core of so many contemporary central city development plans.

Figure 3.3 shows what happened to a group of workers of all ages who were employed at least part-time in the hotel-motel industry in New England in 1969. After that year, some moved on to jobs in other industries (the "leavers"). Others (the "stayers") continued to work at least part-time in the region's hotels or motels in every year of the period 1970–1975. Although the average annual earnings of the stayers increased as they got older, the rate of increase—the "steepness" of their age-earnings profiles—was far less than that of the leavers, who had typically worked in the industry only for a short time during their youth. Figure 3.3 shows that the relative earnings losses of long-term hotel employees—measured by the difference between the slopes of the two lines in each pair—were considerably greater for the work force in the Boston hotels than for those in the region as a whole. This is important mainly because Boston hotel workers are disproportionately black and Hispanic. Thus, the "career" structure in this industry—and in many other service industries as well—operates to reinforce institutional racism.

Continuing Tendencies Toward Intensification, Rationalization, Automation, and the Geographic Restructuring of Employment

Throughout this history, we have been measuring "structural change" in the New England economy by variations over time in the inter-industry distribution of employment. Orthodox economists and geographers explain these variations mainly in terms of changes in the prices at which commodities, labor, capital goods, land, and finance exchange for one another in various markets.

Marxists, on the other hand, prefer to focus on the processes by which commodities (and labor power) are *produced* rather than on how they are exchanged (or "circulated"). From this perspective, employment change is to be understood as the outcome of a number of interacting tendencies in the process of capitalist production under contemporary conditions of industrial organization—which means under conditions with pervasive elements of monopoly. Following a usage

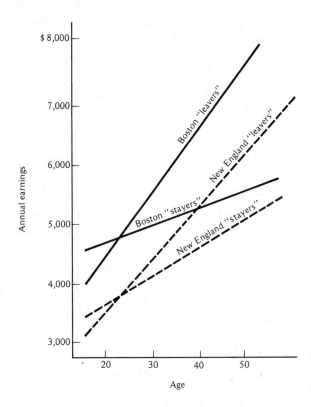

FIGURE 3.3. Age-Earnings Profiles of Workers in New England's Hotel-Motel Industry, 1969. Lines in the figure represent slopes of bivariate pooled cross-section, time-series regressions of earnings as a function of age. "Leavers" worked in the industry in 1969 but never again. "Stayers" remained in the industry after 1969, at least occasionally, through at least 1975. (Source: Daniel Kurtz, "The Hotel-Motel Industry in New England," MCP thesis, Dept. of Urban Studies and Planning, MIT, 1979, figures 6.10 and 6.11.)

developed by Doreen Massey,[65] we may distinguish four such "tendencies."

1. Managers may attempt to rearrange work schedules and physical workplace layouts, or undertake incremental mechanization of various tasks, in order to force existing employees to work harder.[66] This is called *intensification of the labor process.*

2. They may actually disinvest in particular productive capacity—cut it back or close it down altogether—either to reduce profit losses or (of increasing importance in a world of multiproduct,

multinational conglomerate corporations) to free up capital for transfer to other activities or locations. This is *rationalization*.

3. They may attempt to lower their aggregate wage costs, along with their dependence on certain strategically placed skilled workers (such as crafts-persons), by introducing systematically mechanized tools and control devices which reduce the firm's need to have living labor perform skilled tasks. Such "deskilling" of workers is often associated with an *automation* strategy by management. In fact, the underlying process (the so-called Babbage principle, named for its most famous nineteenth-century expositor), does not, strictly speaking, depend on any particular form of mechanization per se but rather on a fundamental reorganization of work tasks. Indeed, the possibility of such reorganization (through product standardization, for example) is often a prerequisite for the cost-effective implementation of the new technology. In any case, since skilled and semiskilled production workers (and their modern service sector equivalents) usually fall into the middle of the range of wages in an establishment, the bias of capitalist technological change toward downgrading or eliminating these sorts of jobs leads to a long-run tendency toward a polarization of earned income as well as skill. In other words, there is a tendency toward increasing *inequality* in earnings as "automation" proceeds.[67]

4. Finally, there is the tendency toward continual spatial reorganization of production, or *geographic restructuring*. Over time, capitalists look to previously peripheral locations, both within the country and beyond its borders, to find new sources of cheap and (at least initially) tractable labor power. As technology simplifies the management of more far-flung operations (especially with respect to transportation and communications), and intensity of competition makes a firm more cost-conscious, capitalists tend to shift certain fragments of the production process itself out of the "home" region. Locational shift can take place either through actual physical relocation or (more commonly) through the establishment of plant or store branches. Another sort of location shift is becoming more common. Corporations are making arrangements to allocate production among their own plants or those of other corporations. These arrangements have given rise to "co-production"

deals, foreign "sourcing," "parallel plant" strategies, and many other institutional innovations that characterize what has been called the new global division of labor. Moreover, the shifting of certain stages of the production process in an industry from one area to another is not neutral with respect to the skill mix. In the process of relocating or branching into low-wage areas, companies disproportionately tend to eliminate the skilled production jobs associated with the manufacturing of standardized products (or the delivery of standardized services). Thus certain technical reorganizations of production, besides transforming the labor process in situ, make it easier for a firm to take advantage of the availability of cheap labor elsewhere.[68]

The format that has been used in this chapter may have made it seem that those tendencies toward intensification, technical change, rationalization, and geographic restructuring are a thing of the past: important in understanding how the contemporary economic structure emerged, perhaps, but of purely historical interest. But this is not so. Capitalist economic development is continually progressing through a dynamic interaction of the reorganization of the labor process (with its associated increases in productivity), further centralization and concentration in the control of capital (which increases the capacity of managers to coordinate production and finance among multiple locations and sectors), and the geographic dispersal of production (and therefore employment) over greater and greater distances, both within and across national borders.

Some of these forces are actually measurable—that is to say, they are sufficiently reflected in standard published data to permit some degree of quantification. Census Bureau records permit the decomposition of employment change over certain periods into the job change associated with variations in (1) the volume of sales (including exports) achieved by New England businesses; (2) the ratio of the actual volume of production undertaken in New England itself to sales, which varies according to the extent to which the industry's firms record their sales (and profits) in New England while engaging in production (or purchasing inputs or components from) elsewhere; (3) labor productivity in the industry in this region; and (4) average hours per worker in the industry in the region. The sales indicator provides a best first guess of by how much employment would be likely to change, holding other factors constant. The second indicator gets at geographic restructuring. The third reflects the result of technical change. And the fourth (very imperfectly) measures intensification. Each of these last three factors will modify the actual employment change which sales increases might otherwise have brought about.

The details of these calculations are available elsewhere.[69] Suffice it to say that an analysis of data on seventy-six New England industries for the early 1970s clearly reveals the instability of the present economic base, that is, the continuing tendencies toward the restructuring and relocation of production and employment. In only three of the seventy-six industries (cleaning materials, building materials, and fabricated metal products) did sales increases produce proportionate increases in employment; these three together accounted for a minuscule share of the region's jobs. In fifteen other industries, the job growth which rising sales would have otherwise created was partly offset by the shift of production or purchasing out of the region, by increased productivity, or by increased hours of work per employee. For example, the increased sales of engines and turbines between 1967 and 1972 might have been expected to have generated a 35-percent increase in employment. However, a declining proportion of the final product actually made (or assembled) within New England, and a substantial increase in productivity, held the actual employment increase to only 4 percent.

In thirty other industries which enjoyed expanding sales, the expected employment was more than offset by some combination of production or purchasing dispersal, higher productivity, or increases in the average number of hours per worker.

The remaining twenty-eight industries in the sample all suffered declining absolute sales during this period. In twenty-four of them, the predictably negative impact of falling sales on jobs was compounded by the shift of production or purchasing out of the region, by higher productivity, or by increased hours of work (in this category, shoes and electrical testing equipment displayed the greatest regional shift). In only four industries was the expected decline in employment mitigated somewhat by increases in the regional content of production or purchasing, by decreasing productivity, or by decreasing average hours per worker.

Increasing Inequality in the Distribution of Earnings

Marxist theorizing leads us to expect that the kinds of changes in the economic structure of New England described here should lead to a worsening of the regional distribution of earned income over time.

Specifically, we should expect to find growing *polarization* of earnings, both within and among industries. Other researchers are presently searching for evidence of polarization per se.[70] In our own studies, we only sought empirical evidence on the presence (and strength) of the tendency toward *inequality* in the distribution of earnings over the period 1957–1975. During these years many businesses in New England significantly increased their utilization of young workers and expanded the number of part-time and part-year (often seasonal) jobs.[71] Each of these factors could by itself contribute to increasing inequality in the distribution of earnings over time, as could the selective erosion of the middle of the skill structure which I have been hypothesizing.

We were able to eliminate at least the effects of seasonality and of casual job attachment of youth by looking only at the earnings of employees who worked all four quarters (although not necessarily full time) in New England, over the nineteen-year period. Using an indicator called the Gini coefficient as a measure of the degree of equality or inequality, we recorded changes in this coefficient over time for each of thirteen specific industries and for the aggregate of all industries in the region. For example, the relative inequality in earnings of workers of both sexes who were employed at some time in each quarter of the year in the production of office machines and computers increased between 1957 and 1975 by 60 percent. Relative inequality in earnings of women working four quarters in commercial banks rose by the same percentage. And men working in all four quarters in the hotel-motel industry experienced a 17-percent increase in relative inequality in their earnings. (This was the industry with the greatest absolute inequality of any we tested.) In nine of the specific industries we studied, and for the aggregate of all industries in the region, earnings have unquestionably become more unequally distributed over time.

Postscript: The "Postindustrial" Society

For a long time, the economic shift from goods production to the production of services was thought by most social scientists to be an inevitable and, what is more, an unquestionably desirable aspect of mature economic growth.[72] Service employers were less likely to discriminate in the hiring of women or minorities. Their activities were environmentally clean, certainly when compared with basic industries such as coal, steel, and chemicals. Moreover, it was often argued, the organization of work in the service sector was somehow more humane. As one author put it,

As the proportion of workers engaged in direct production within industry falls, the proportion of workers in brain work, paper work, people work, and information processing work correspondingly rises. These workers are by all common-sensical notions service workers. They produce intangible ideas, designs, words, data, and customer relations. . . . The salient feature of the post-industrial form of work is a new articulated flexibility between work and the other dimensions of life. . . . People participate in work over the life cycle in a rhythm determined not simply by the requirements of the work setting, but by the development rhythm of their own lives.[73]

Service work has not taken the form, or produced the social benefits, predicted by the philosophers of postindustrialism. Rather, we are coming to realize that many people who work for service sector companies in fact perform essentially manual labor, similar in content to many so-called blue-collar jobs. More importantly, the color of the collar is not a particularly close correlate of the nature of the organization of work. Many white-collar employees—professionals as well as clericals—are now sharing factory workers' experience of loss of autonomy and the boredom associated with extreme fragmentation of tasks, as well as insecurity with respect to the stability of their jobs, and even the presence of serious on-the-job health and safety hazards.[74] What is more, service sector jobs are far more likely than those in manufacturing to pay low wages and to offer inadequate hours of work for the needs of people seeking to support themselves or their families.

SUMMARY, CONCLUSIONS, AND SOME SPECULATIONS ABOUT THE FUTURE

On the eve of World War II, millions of New Englanders worked in the mills and shops of the region, producing mostly nondurable consumption goods for local use and for export. While New England held other kinds of economic activity, it was the mill work which conferred upon the region its most distinctive identity—in architecture and in cultural and social life no less than in economic affairs.

As we enter the 1980s, we find the economy of the New England region profoundly transformed. There are certainly many more jobs. Between 1947 and 1979, a little over 2 million new nonagricultural jobs were added to the regional economy—an increase of 62 percent over the period. Though the national rate of growth was nearly 70 percent higher than this (104 percent between 1947 and 1979), the increase is nonetheless significant in its own right.

However, the true essence of the economic transformation lies in the enormous changes in the industry mix. A high-technology sector, the centerpiece of which consists of the design, manufacture, and programming of computers, now sits amidst a mass of companies providing a wide range of services to other businesses and to worker/consumers living both inside and outside the region. The engineering industries, producing machinery, engines, and transportation equipment, have managed to survive this shift away from blue-collar factory work, but they now employ a far smaller share of the region's work force than they used to. Moreover, these industries, along with what remains of the old textile and shoe operations, continue to be subject to forces that have tended to disproportionately reduce the growth of the demand for semiskilled labor in New England. These forces, or tendencies, have been called intensification, rationalization, automation, and geographic restructuring.

The *timing* of particular instances of rationalization, restructuring, and reorganization of the labor process (and the extent to which these developments proceed in any particular era) depends not only on the competition among firms but also on the antagonism between employers and workers. This antagonism is manifest not only in conflicts over wages and the conditions of work, but also—and in many ways, more profoundly—in the social legislation which governments have been pressed into implementing because of the momentary political power of the working class. Particular instances of this conflict—whether in the form of prolabor legislation or, conversely, of the active suppression of organizers—can have an impact on the course of development in the region lasting long after the moment of their occurrence.

In the case of New England, perhaps the most striking structural characteristic of the transformation from the old to the new economic base is the substantial erosion of both the mid-range of skilled jobs within particular industries (in services as well as in manufacturing) and of whole industries which traditionally employed the largest numbers of skilled and semiskilled blue-collar workers. It is the particular form taken by this transformation—rather than economic change per se—which has created problems for so many thousands of workers in the region, both through this selective elimination of the best blue-collar jobs and through the proliferation of low-wage, seasonal or part-time jobs, primarily in the expanding service sector. What was once a problem of mass unemployment for a generation of New Englanders has been transformed into the far more subtle dilemma of widespread under- (or "sub"-) employment: the lack of an adequate supply of full-time jobs at decent pay.[75] This phenomenon of what might be called the "missing middle" of the industrial structure is also responsible for the gradual worsening of the earnings distribution over time within as well as among so many of the region's industries, and in the New England economy as a whole.

This leads us to the examination of the ways in which class conflict in New England in the years ahead may contribute to the shaping of the future development of the region. At the workplace, all of the objective antagonisms associated with the new structure—full- versus part-time or seasonal work schedules, stable versus unstable product or service demands, unskilled versus skilled job requirements, low versus high wages, upwardly mobile versus immobile career prospects, and of course the presence or absence of labor unions—have exacerbated the divisions among workers of different ages, races, ethnicities, and gender, who experience these structural conditions very differently.

The chilling effect of prior plant, shop, and store shutdowns has further intimidated many workers from acting more forcefully in their own interests in the day-to-day conflict with management over wages, benefits, and work rules. Some new labor organizing is taking place in the region, most notably among women hospital and clerical workers. However, outside the public sector, the labor movement in New England is by and large quiescent and ineffectual, as it has generally been since the political purges of the late 1940s and early 1950s.

Thus, it is outside the workplace—in the neighborhoods, in the suburban tract developments, and in the state capitals—where the antagonism between labor and capital has become most visible in the past twenty years in New England, and where the sharpest conflicts are likely to occur in the next decade. And fragmentation and "false consciousness" within the working class may produce counterproductive political action. For example, facing high prices combined with relatively low wages, working families in New England now find themselves earning the lowest individual real wages in the country. This reduction in their standard of living, both absolutely and relative to those in other areas, may well be the principal factor drawing an increasing number of citizens into taking direct political action, such as the widespread support of the now-famous 1980 Massachusetts property tax cap ("Proposition 2½"). This has contributed to a starving of public services aimed at those very same workers.

These class struggles extend also into the realm of conflict over the land and physical access requirements of many of those very large service enterprises (for example, hotels, urban shopping malls, and corporate office buildings) whose growth has been so loudly celebrated by many as the key to the "revitalization" of the inner city. In fact, either directly or through the indirect effect of land appreciation, many of these developments are displacing (or threatening to displace) the working-class residents of the neighborhoods adjacent to the development sites. In a number of instances, interclass and even multiracial coalitions have grown up initially to resist displacement but have sometimes continued to organize new programs for creating jobs and providing self-help services in the neighboring communities. The outlook for these organizations is certainly anything but sanguine, especially in the Reagan era. Still, that they survive at all is an interesting indication of the depth of the popular concern over—and involvement in—the politics of urban and regional economic development.

Since the late 1970s, a new generation of labor union activists in New England (as elsewhere) has begun to search for new forms of political expression. For the most part, these consist of coalitions made up of rank-and-file members of different unions in the region, including clerical and other service industry workers. But a few of the new coalitions are reaching out beyond the still-dwindling unionized segment of the working class to join forces with community and even statewide groups that are engaged in political struggle over the supply of such public goods as welfare payments and mass transportation, or over the regulation of such critical matters as the price of electricity and runaway shops.

Whether such a revitalized labor movement can succeed in giving organizational expression to the dissatisfactions of workers in the prototypical postindustrial economy that is New England remains to be seen. Certainly the profound divisions *within* the region's working class make such organizing extraordinarily difficult. The future shape of economic development in the region will depend crucially on how contradictions such as these are resolved.

NOTES

Of the many people who have helped me think through the ideas expressed in this paper, I feel especially indebted to Sol Barkin, Barry Bluestone, Gordon Clark, Norman Glickman, Julie Graham, Ned Hill, Maryellen Kelley, Ann Markusen, Bob Ross, Don Shakow, Ed Soja, and Richard Walker. Doreen Massey's work on British industrial restructuring had a major influence on my formulation of the problem. Denise DiPasquale, Alan Matthews, Glynnis Trainer, and Lynn Ware assembled and processed many of the statistics. The research was funded by grants from the U.S. Economic Development Administration, the Employment and Training Administration of the U.S. Department of Labor, and the Work and Mental Health Center of the National Institutes of Mental Health. None of these individuals or organizations is responsible for the particular statements or findings presented in this paper, including the administration and staff of the MIT-Harvard Joint Center for Urban Studies, where the research project was housed. For detailed references and statistical tables and charts, see Bennett Harrison, "Rationalization, Restructuring, and Corporate Reorganization: The Economic Transformation of New England Since World War II," MIT-Harvard Joint Center for Urban Studies, Working Paper No. 72, February 1982.

1. Barry Bluestone, Patricia Hanna, Sarah Kuhn, and Laura Moore, *The Retail Revolution* (Boston: Auburn House, 1981), p. 12.
2. The officially recorded growth of the "service" industries understates the magnitude of the true shift over this period. The Census Bureau classifies the service activities that take place *inside* firms according to the sector associated with that firm's principal output. Thus, a steel company's real estate department is classified under manufacturing, and workers in the data-processing department of the telephone company are counted as employed in the communications industry.
3. "A British observer in 1903 noted, 'At a Georgia mill . . . I was told that probably not 10 percent of the hands had been in a factory before, but this does not seem to be a serious drawback, as they are quick to learn.' This last statement could be changed to read: 'There is not much to learn'" (John Hekman, "The Product Cycle and New England Textiles," *Quarterly Journal of Economics* [June 1980]:712).
4. "Will History Repeat?" *America's Textile Reporter*, December 8, 1966: 27; Hekman, "The Product Cycle"; and Solomon Barkin, "Management and Ownership in the New England Cotton Textile Industry: Their Role in Its Rise and Collapse" (unpublished paper, Department of Economics, University of Massachusetts, Amherst, August 1980), pp. 21–22.
5. Melton Alonza McLanria, *Paternalism and Protest: Southern Cotton Mill Workers and Organized Labor, 1875–1905* (Westport, Conn.: Negro Universities Press, 1971), pp. 129–30.
6. Barkin, "Management and Ownership," pp. 14–17.
7. This discussion is based on Horace B. Davis, *Shoes: The Workers and the Industry* (New York: International, 1940), ch. 1. It is interesting that the book which, more than any other, influenced the extension of orthodox economic theory to the study of spatial relations was concerned with one of the few remaining industries in which monopoly capital was *not* particularly important at the time. See Edgar M. Hoover, Jr., *Location Theory and the Shoe and Leather Industries* (Cambridge, Mass.: Harvard University Press, 1937).
8. Melvyn Dubofsky, *Industrialism and the American Worker, 1865–1920* (Arlington Heights, Ill.: AHM, 1975), p. 51.
9. Sidney Lens, *The Labor Wars* (New York: Doubleday Anchor, 1974), ch. 10. The more radical organizations, such as the International Workingmen's Association and the Industrial Workers of the World, were only sporadically involved in the labor movement in New England throughout this period, although Big Bill Haywood of the IWW eventually became a leader of the 1912 Lawrence textile strike.
10. Tamara K. Hareven and Randolph Langenback, *Amoskeag: Life and Work in an American Factory City* (New York: Pantheon, 1978), p. 24;

and Daniel Creamer and Charles Coulter, *Labor and the Shutdown of the Amoskeag Mills* (Philadelphia: WPA National Research Project, 1939).

11. Dubofsky, *Industrialism*, p. 32.
12. Ronald W. Schatz, "American Electrical Workers: Work, Struggles, Aspirations" (Ph.D. diss., Department of History, University of Pittsburgh, 1977), pp. 229–31.
13. Bruce M. Stave, ed., *Socialism and the Cities* (Port Washington, N.Y.: Kennikat, 1975), p. 5.
14. Dubofsky, *Industrialism*, p. 91.
15. Philip Shapira, "The Uneven Economy and the State in Massachusetts" (MCP thesis, Department of Urban Studies and Planning, MIT, June 1979), p. 35.
16. Davis, *Shoes*, p. 22.
17. Ibid., p. 146.
18. The prevailing view among most contemporary American Marxist scholars studying urban and regional development seems to be that technology and finance make it *possible* for capital to relocate; spatial differentials in the cost of reproduction of labor power dominate capitalists' choice of *destination;* and labor-capital relations in the origin area (together with the state of the business cycle) are the major factors influencing the *timing* of shutdowns and relocations. For some examples, see Barry Bluestone and Bennett Harrison, *The Deindustrialization of America* (New York: Basic Books, 1982); David M. Gordon, "Capitalist Development and the History of American Cities," in *Marxism and the Metropolis,* ed. William K. Tabb and Larry Sawers (New York: Oxford University Press, 1978); and Richard Walker and Michael Storper, "The Spatial Division of Labor," ch. 2 in this volume.
19. Freeland, Bates, and Lawrence, *A Brief Study of Industrial Massachusetts* (Boston: Massachusetts Industrial Commission, 1931); cited by Shapira, "The Uneven Economy," pp. 44–46.
20. Davis, *Shoes*, p. 17.
21. Glynnis A. Trainer, "Metalworking Machinery in New England" (MCP thesis, Department of Urban Studies and Planning, MIT, 1979), p. 27.
22. Ibid., pp. 28–30; and Hekman, "The Product Cycle," p. 709. That war stimulated the production of machine tools in New England in two other ways, apart from the government's need for armaments. Continued prosecution of the war required the rapid expansion of the rail system, and the mass drafting of young men (for both armies) indirectly created a new demand for labor-saving machinery in agriculture.
23. Barry Bluestone, Peter Jordan, Carol Peppin, and Mark Sullivan, *Aircraft Industry Dynamics* (Boston: Auburn House, 1981), p. 20.
24. Trainer, "Metalworking Machinery," p. 39.
25. Bluestone et al., *Aircraft Industry Dynamics*, pp. 31–32.
26. R. C. Estall, *New England: A Study in Industrial Adjustment* (New York: Praeger, 1966), p. 35.
27. Sarah Kuhn, *The Computer Industry in New England* (Cambridge, Mass.: MIT-Harvard Joint Center for Urban Studies, 1982), p. 141.
28. John Blair, *Economic Concentration* (New York: Harcourt, Brace, Jovanovich, 1972), pp. 380–85. Nor did the practice of building defense plants and then leasing them to private companies stop with the end of the war. For example, according to Defense Procurement Agency records, the federal government constructed facilities for the Wyman-

Gordon Company in North Grafton, Massachusetts, in 1946, and for the
Raytheon Corporation in Bedford, Massachusetts, in 1953 and 1958.
Many of these defense plants are still under government ownership today, constituting substantial subsidies to the firms that lease them and
depriving the communities in which they are located of the full tax value
of the property.

29. Ibid., p. 383.

30. Bennett Harrison and Sandra Kanter, "The Political Economy of State
Job-Creation Business Incentives," *Journal of the American Institute of
Planners* (October 1978):424–35. As more and more jurisdictions have
come to emulate one another in offering more or less identical tax and
other business incentives, these policies have come to have no discernible
effect whatever on industrial (re)location. For the latest empirical evidence, see Michael Kischnick, *Taxes and Growth: Business Incentives
and Economic Growth* (Washington, D.C.: Council of State Planning
Agencies, 1981).

31. Harrison, "Rationalization, Restructuring," table 1. Roger Schmenner
(*The Manufacturing Location Decision* [Englewood Cliffs, N.J.:
Prentice-Hall, 1982]) recently completed a massive study of the Fortune
500, consisting of interviews with executives of 60 companies and an
analysis of data on the nearly 18,000 plants of 410 of the largest manufacturers in the country. Among his principal conclusions are those having to do with the relationship between right-to-work laws and industrial
location:

> Giving a union a new workforce that is nearly impossible to organize
> is perhaps the most prized side benefit of a new plant site [as
> opposed to an expansion at the old site]. . . . A good deal of atten-
> tion in plant location is directed to the 20 right-to-work states, most
> of which are located in the Sunbelt and Plains states. . . . while
> only 34% of the [plants in the sample that remained in operation
> throughout the 1970s] were located in right-to-work-states, fully
> one-half of all the new plants were sited in them. These data sup-
> port the contention that the edge for non-unionism in right-to-work
> states has triggered a more-than-proportional degree of plant open-
> ings there. . . . No other public policy carries anywhere near the
> location clout of the right-to-work law.

(The quotation is from a printed summary of findings from the original
MIT-Harvard Joint Center for Urban Studies research project, entitled
"The Location Decisions of Large, Multiplant Companies," 1980, pp. 13,
15, 18.)

32. On the origins of Textron, see U.S. Senate, Subcommittee of the Com-
mittee on Interstate and Foreign Commerce, *Investigation of Closing of
Nashua, New Hampshire, Mills and Operations of Textron, Inc.*, 80th
Congress, 2nd Session (Washington, D.C.: U.S. Government Printing
Office, 1948).

33. D&B defines a "failed" business as one that ceased operations as a company (as distinct from continuing operations at a different location) following assignment of bankruptcy; ceased with loss to creditors; was involved in some court action; or voluntarily compromised with creditors.
If creditors were paid in full, the closing is not counted as a "failure."
This effectively excludes most conglomerate divestitures. Thus, this in-

dicator of business failure undercounts total business discontinuances by an unknown amount.

34. For a much more extensive analysis of these data from Dun and Bradstreet, see Bluestone and Harrison, *The Deindustrialization of America,* ch. 2.

35. Robert Eisenmenger, *The Dynamics of Growth in New England's Economy, 1870–1964* (Middletown, Conn.: Wesleyan University Press, 1967), p. 68.

36. The irreversibility of capitalist technological development forms part of the basis for both Marxist and institutionalist critiques of the ahistorical production theory taught in standard economics. Cf. Thomas Vietorisz and Bennett Harrison, "Labor Market Segmentation: Positive Feedback and Divergent Development," *American Economic Review/Papers and Proceedings* (May 1973):366–76.

37. Concerning the availability of new finance capital, see John Hekman and John Strong, "The Evolution of New England Industry," *New England Economic Review* (March–April 1981) 35–46, where we learn that "the nation's first publicly owned venture capital firm, American Research and Development Corporation, was founded in Boston in 1946" and "the nation's largest publicly owned small business investment company, Narragansett Capital Corporation, was founded in Providence in 1959" (its president, incidentally, is the son of Textron founder Royal Little) (Hekman and Strong, p. 45). Concerning the struggle among different factions of capital to gain influence in state and local government, see Ruth Fincher, "The Local State in the Urban Built Environment: The Case of Boston in Late Capitalism" (Ph.D. diss., Department of Geography, Clark University, June 1980); Sandra Kanter, "Business-Political Relations in the Formation of State Economic Policy [Massachusetts]: 1945–1975" (Ph.D. diss., Department of Urban Studies and Planning, MIT, February 1981); and Shapira, "The Uneven Economy."

38. Eisenmenger, *Dynamics of Growth,* pp. 34, 37.

39. Ibid., p. 23.

40. Ibid., p. 34.

41. Michael S. Folsom and S. Lubar, eds., *The Philosophy of Manufactures: The Early Debates Over Industrialization in the United States* (Cambridge, Mass.: MIT Press, 1980), vol. 1; Hareven and Langenback, *Amoskeag;* and Benita Eisler, ed., *The Lowell Offerings: Writings by New England Mill Women* (Philadelphia: Lippincott, 1977).

42. Harrison, "Rationalization, Restructuring," table 3.

43. Schatz, "American Electrical Workers," ch. 1. See also James J. Matles and James Higgins, *Them and Us: Strategy of a Rank-and-File Union* (Englewood Cliffs, N.J.: Prentice-Hall, 1974).

44. For a brilliant analysis of how this recent historical experience has confused and divided workers who are currently being confronted by a new wave of plant shutdowns and structural unemployment, see Jack Metzgar, "Plant Shutdowns and Worker Response," *Socialist Review* (September–October 1980):9–50.

45. In Massachusetts, for example, the right of unions to collectively bargain over wages with both state and local governments did not become law until 1973. The federal government had achieved this by executive order a decade earlier. William J. Coughlin, ed., *A Guide to the Massachusetts*

Public Employee Collective Bargaining Law, 4th ed. (Boston: Institute for Governmental Services, 1981), p. 6.

46. U.S. Bureau of the Census, *Directory of National Unions and Employee Associations, 1975,* Bulletin 1937, 1977, p. 74. The incidence of unionization in New England has also been falling in relation to the U.S. average, although it is still much higher than the rates in most of the Sunbelt states.

47. Eisenmenger, *Dynamics of Growth,* p. 23.

48. U.S. Department of Commerce, *Statistical Abstract of the United States,* annual (cf. the 1979 edition, p. 247). By the mid-1970s, all of these interstate differentials had closed, due primarily to a general decline in strike activity in most states.

49. *Annual Reports of the National Labor Relations Board* (Washington, D.C.: GPO, 1950, 1955, 1960, 1965, 1970, 1975, 1979), appendix tables.

50. Shervin Freed, with Joseph Lichko, *Measuring Union Climates* (Atlanta: Conway, 1981), appendix J-5.

51. Cf. Fincher, "The Local State in the Urban Built Environment"; and John Mollenkopf, "The Postwar Politics of Urban Development," in Tabb and Sawers, *Marxism and the Metropolis.*

52. These conditions for profitable economic growth are always recreated unevenly, that is, with more or less success, and more or less rapidly, in different sectors and areas. The interregional pattern of postwar development within New England—between cities and suburbs, for example, or among the states—is too big a subject to pursue here, nor was it an explicit concern of the research project on which this paper is based. But see Jeffrey Brown et al., "The Distribution of Employment in New England: Trends, Changes and Prospects, 1962–1977" (Department of City and Regional Planning, Harvard University, May 23, 1980).

53. For example, in 1963 Congress approved the addition of two exemptions to the U.S. tariff schedule (items 806.30 and 807.00) that effectively allowed American firms to export apparel and electronics components to foreign locations for assembly and reimport back into the United States. The companies pay duty only on the value added abroad—mostly the cheap labor used in the assembly process (Bluestone and Harrison, *Deindustrialization,* chs. 2 and 5).

54. Ibid., ch. 6.

55. Multiple "sourcing" is an extremely important aspect of the new international division of labor and is discussed in ibid.

56. John Hekman, "The Future of High Technology Industry in New England: A Case Study of Computers," *New England Economic Review* (January-February 1980):5–17. However, it must be reported that as of 1981, the great majority of recent investments by such leading New England–based firms as the Digital Equipment Corporation continue to be located within the region (scattered among all six states).

57. For a primer on the anatomy of the contemporary big-city business services, focusing on New York City, see Thomas Stanback, *Understanding the Service Economy* (Baltimore: Johns Hopkins University Press, 1979).

58. New England data are from U.S. Department of Labor, Bureau of Labor Statistics, *Employment and Earnings in States and Areas, 1939–75,* Bulletin 1370–12, 1977. National data are from U.S. Department of Labor, *1980 Employment and Training Report of the President* (Washington, D.C.: GPO, 1980), p. 248.

59. Harrison, "Rationalization, Restructuring," pp. 67–115.
60. Ibid., tables 8 and 9. In 1979, averaging across all occupations (including blue-collar production workers) in the high-tech industries, Massachusetts ranked sixth among the ten most important high-tech states in terms of average annual earnings, and seventh in terms of percent of change in average earnings between 1975 and 1979 (Job Market Research Division of the Massachusetts Division of Employment Security, "High Technology Employment in Massachusetts and Selected States," *New England Economic Indicators* [March 1981], p. A4).
61. Bluestone et al., *The Retail Revolution.*
62. Thomas Barocci, *Non-Profit Hospitals* (Boston: Auburn House, 1981), p. 145.
63. Ibid., p. 146.
64. Daniel P. Kurtz, "The Lodging Industry in New England" (MCP thesis, Department of Urban Studies and Planning, MIT, 1979).
65. Doreen Massey and Richard Meegan, *The Anatomy of Job Loss* (London: Methuen, 1982). See also Richard Walker and Michael Storper, "Capital and Industrial Location," *Progress in Human Geography* 5 (1981).
66. Formally, managers want to extract more *labor* from the given quantity of *labor power* that they have already hired. Perhaps people are expected to work faster, or the plant layout is changed to reduce the length of time that a particular worker has to wait to receive intermediate "goods-in-process" from another. Alternatively, the number of coffee breaks may be reduced.
67. The tendency toward the progressive deskilling of workers during the course of capitalist development is the central theme of Harry Braverman, *Labor and Monopoly Capital* (New York: Monthly Review Press, 1974). See also Andrew Zimbalist, ed., *Case Studies in the Labor Process* (New York: Monthly Review Press, 1979); and Richard Edwards, *Contested Terrain* (New York: Basic Books, 1979).
68. Bluestone and Harrison, *Deindustrialization;* Folker Frobel, Jurgen Heinrichs, and Otto Kreye, *The New International Division of Labor* (Cambridge, Eng.: Cambridge University Press, 1980); Katherine Gibson et al., "A Theoretical Approach to Capital and Labor Restructuring," in *Capital and Labor Restructuring,* ed. John Carney (London: Croom Helm, forthcoming); Brad Heil, "Sunbelt Migration," in *U.S. Capitalism in Crisis* (New York: Union for Radical Political Economics, 1978); Massey and Meegan, *Anatomy of Job Loss;* and Walker and Storper, "Capital and Industrial Location."
69. Harrison, "Rationalization, Restructuring," pp. 105–13.
70. Pat Walker, untitled Ph.D. diss. in progress, Department of Economics, University of Massachusetts-Amherst.
71. For example, by 1975, 35 percent of the wage earners in the grocery store–supermarket industry were under age twenty, compared with the all-industry regional average of 12 percent (Paul Cournoyer, "The New England Grocery Industry" [Sloan School of Management, MIT, Working Paper No. 1121–80, 1980], p. 52). Local industry sources report that perhaps three-fourths of all department store employees in New England now work part-time (Bluestone et al., *Retail Revolution,* p. 83). And fully two-thirds of those employed in the hotel-motel industry in 1975 worked during only one or two quarters of that year (usually during the summer months) (Kurtz, "Lodging Industry," p. 198).

72. Larry Hirschorn, "The Urban Crisis: A Post-Industrial Perspective," *Journal of Regional Science* (April 1979):111, 115. See also Daniel Bell, *The Coming of Post-Industrial Society* (New York: Basic Books, 1973); and Roger Bolton, "What's Happening to New England?" in *The Economy of New York State,* ed. Benjamin Chinitz (Binghamton, N.Y.: State University of N.Y., Center for Social Analysis, 1977).

73. For example, even in the public sector, among all federal, state, and local employees in 1970, nearly half of the men and 10 percent of the women worked as craftspersons, machine and transportation equipment operators, laborers, custodians, and guards (U.S. Department of Commerce, Bureau of the Census, *1970 Census of Population: Occupation by Industry,* PC (2)–7C, 1972, table 1). In Massachusetts in 1970, the proportions were even higher than these national averages.

74. See the essays by Evelyn Nakano Glenn and Roslyn Feldberg on office work, by Philip Kraft on computer programming, and by Maarten de Kadt on the insurance industry in Zimbalist, ed., *Case Studies in the Labor Process.*

75. Subemployment was first identified more than a decade ago as a major structural characteristic of inner cities—even the youngest Sunbelt cities, let alone the crisis-ridden central cities of the North. See William Spring, Bennett Harrison, and Thomas Vietorisz, "The Crisis of the Subemployed," *New York Times Magazine,* November 4, 1972. That November CBS-TV News ran a nationwide report on the problem. Since then, the very concept has been almost totally ignored, both by the media and in orthodox academic circles. However, two excellent Marxist treatments are Al Watkins and David Perry, "People, Profit, and the Rise of the Sunbelt Cities," in *The Rise of the Sunbelt Cities,* ed. Perry and Watkins (Santa Monica, Calif.: Sage, 1978); and David M. Gordon, ed., *Problems in Political Economy: An Urban Perspective,* 2nd ed. (Lexington, Mass.: Heath, 1977), editor's introduction to the section titled "Employment."

Part Two

THE IMPACT
OF REGIONAL
RESTRUCTURING AND
URBAN DECLINE

4

Sunbelt Metropolis and Development Capital: Houston in the Era of Late Capitalism

JOE R. FEAGIN

Houston is the preeminent Sunbelt city. It has been described as boom city, space city, oil capital U.S.A., and the "capital" of the Sunbelt in major articles in national newspapers and newsmagazines. A 1978 issue of *U.S. News & World Report* commented on Houston's dynamic growth in typical fashion: "This is not a city. It's a phenomenon—an explosive, churning, roaring urban juggernaut that's shattering tradition as it expands outward and upward with an energy that stuns even its residents."[1] For two decades architectural and real estate journals have touted Houston's booming real estate market for investors, its hundreds of major office towers, and its huge shopping malls. Corporations specializing in industrial-location counseling and their corporate clients have raved about Houston's "good business climate." And thousands of local newspaper articles in Northern towns and cities have heralded Houston's economy to troubled Northerners.

This media and scholarly attention has been generated by the capital flowing to Houston from other regions of the country, a flow expressed in the physical form of new industrial and urban development. Greater Houston is a transparent window through which one can look to see modern capitalism in operation. Industrial capitalists, finance capitalists, and development capitalists are the driving forces behind this "roaring urban juggernaut" which is daily expanding horizontally and vertically and which now sprawls over more than one thousand square miles of the Texas Gulf Coast. Their decisions and actions are the primary determinants of the scale, character, and impact of Houston's growth, and within the limits they set ordinary workers and consumers can exercise only limited choices with regard to jobs, housing, transport, recreation, and quality of life. It is the purpose of this essay to provide an analytical overview of key features of Houston's growth and development, with a particular focus on the scale of its recent urban development, the role of government, and the negative impact of rapid development on the lives of workers and consumers.

PETROLEUM INDUSTRY EXPANSION AND HOUSTON'S DEVELOPMENT

Corporate decisions about where to invest surplus profits and other capital—and thus where to locate plants, offices, and other corporate facilities—have had a fundamental shaping impact on American cities, North and South. Cities such as Houston are constructed, and reconstructed, in response to the fundamental physical and spatial requirements of commercial and industrial corporations.[2]

In the heart of the Gulf Coast industrial belt, Houston is the world's oil and petrochemical center; thirty-four of the nation's thirty-five largest oil companies have located major administrative, research, and production facilities in the greater Houston metropolitan area. In addition to these corporate giants, there are four hundred other oil and gas companies there. Both "old" oil companies—such as Exxon, Shell, and Mobil—and "new" oil and gas giants—such as Tenneco, Occidental Petroleum, and Getty Oil Company—have offices and other facilities in the area. And thousands of smaller oil-related companies have attached themselves to these major petroleum companies. There are thousands of geological firms, petroleum engineering firms, drilling contractors, geophysical contractors, supply and transportation companies, law firms, and accounting firms serving Houston's oil and gas companies. About a quarter of U.S. oil refining capacity and one quarter of the oil-gas transmission companies are located in the Houston–Gulf Coast area. Perhaps most important, one-half of all the petrochemicals made in the United States are manufactured in this area. Petrochemicals are the basis of much modern manufacturing (for example, plastics, synthetic fibers, synthetic rubber) and of agribusiness (for example, fertilizers and pesticides) in the United States. The expanded flow of profits to the oil-petrochemical industrial sector over the last decade or two has provided the direct capital and borrowing capacity for other capital which lie behind much of Houston's industrial and real estate (spatial) growth. The enhanced economic position of the oil-petrochemical industry in the Houston–Gulf Coast area has generated a propulsive dynamism that has attracted not only non–oil-manufacturing corporations but also capital from banks and insurance companies, foreign and domestic, to projects in the area. This reinvigorated inflow of investment capital has been channeled in part to hundreds of large-scale development projects, such as office towers and multiple-use projects, in the Houston area.[3]

Since 1970 more than two hundred corporations have invested in major facilities in Houston, moving headquarters or major divisions there. Many have been non-oil corporations, ranging from electrical manufacturing companies to investment banking corporations. In 1978 Houston was ranked as the fourth largest manufacturing center in the United States, behind Chicago, Detroit, and Los Angeles, in value of manufacturing shipments, and it was first in capital expenditures in manufacturing. Altogether, more than nine hundred major (million-dollar or more) corporations are located in the Houston area; Houston is not only the world's oil and gas center but also an important national setting for other types of manufacturing, for forest products, for agribusiness enterprises, and for banking.

At the heart of investment decision making by these companies is the business leaders' concern for a "good business climate," a codeword for an area with lower wages, weak unions, lower taxes, and a conservative political climate. Companies that function as locators, such as the Fantus Company, have advertised Houston as having one of the best business climates in the United States, and groups such as the National Urban Policy Roundtable have rated Houston as having the healthiest economy in the nation because of its energy and related industries and because of its good business climate. The growth of Houston is partially due, on the one hand, to its cheaper production costs (for example, weak unions, lower wages) and its weaker physical and structural barriers to new development (for example, no aged industrial foundation) and, on the other, to the tremendous federal expenditures for infrastructure facilities, such as highways, and for high-technology defense industries.[4]

EARLY DEVELOPMENT AND BOOSTERISM

The First Houston Developers

Houston began as a land development scheme. In 1836 the Allen brothers (J. K. and A. C. Allen) bought sixty-six hundred acres of land for a little over a dollar an acre, named the area for Sam Houston (a Texas military hero), laid out the city in a gridiron pattern (considered the most profitable layout), and marketed the land to outsiders, including capitalists and settlers from the East and elsewhere who were unaware that the area was marshy, mosquito-infested, very humid, and extraordinarily hot in the summer. An 1836 advertisement by the Allens in one newspaper proclaimed the following: "The town of Houston is located at the point on the river which must ever command the trade of the largest and richest portion of Texas. . . . [It] will warrant the employment of at least *One Million Dollars* of capital, and when the rich lands of this country shall be settled, a trade will flow to it, making it, beyond all doubt, the great interior commercial emporium of Texas."[5] These land developers offered the land to commercial capitalists and ordinary settlers with the hope that Houston would become the regional center of commercial capitalism and of the government of the new Texas republic, and thus make them rich. The Allen brothers succeeded in attracting the new republic's government there, but because of the bad weather, sickness, and competition from other land speculators, the state government was moved within a few years. Still the area grew, with trade and manufacturing slowly expanding, and by 1900 Houston was a regional transportation center, with several railroads and port facilities. Houston was becoming a city "on the move," aggressively advertised by its business elite.[6]

Boosterism

By the early decades of the twentieth century, major industry was moving into the Sunbelt, including Houston, in part because of the local and federal government-subsidized infrastructure being provided for industrial development there. Texas real estate and other business entrepreneurs worked hard to keep the new oil industry from moving elsewhere. Widening and deepening the Port of Houston channel was an important part of the process of providing the necessary facilities to retain existing industries and add new ones. Local capitalists got the federal government to pay for development of the city's port facilities, particularly the ship channel in the southeast sector. In 1909 the federal government provided $1.25 million in aid for a channel-dredging proj-

ect. From the beginning, local capitalists—merchants, developers, lum-
bermen, oilmen—actually ran the city government. Not surprisingly
then, the city government was busy putting up expanded sewer and
water systems and providing the other facilities these leaders saw as
necessary for making Houston an industrial center.[7]

Aggressive efforts to advertise Houston north and east have been
made by local capitalists since the early 1900s. In 1909 the *New York
Times* ran an article on "Cities That Advertise" in which that paper
praised the city fathers of Houston for offering inducements to business investors and homeseekers. One early Houston advertisement
included the following: Houston's "city hall is a *business* house. She
has no wards, no ward politicians, no graft."[8] About the same time,
Houston's superintendent of public schools wrote an article praising
the school board as composed of "a high type of business man" and
noting that Houston's success was the "result of business methods
applied to public affairs."[9] The business of Houston was, even at this
time, business.

Recent Population Growth

Nonetheless, Houston was still a small city in the first two decades of
this century. In April 1909 the Houston police arrested seventeen people for violating a new city ordinance prohibiting horses from standing
hitched for more than thirty minutes on Main Street. The population of
Houston was only 78,000 in 1910, but it grew to 385,000 by 1940. But
this modest size was not to last much longer. Since World War II, the
population growth has been spectacular. In the 1980 census, the population of the city reached 1.7 million, with a million more people in the
greater Houston metropolitan area (SMSA). Among the largest fifteen
SMSAs, Houston was by far the fastest-growing between 1970 and
1980, growing by 40 percent in that period, from 2.0 million in 1970 to
2.9 million in 1980. Moreover, the greater Houston area is projected
to grow by one-third in the 1980s, to a population of 3.9 million by
1990 and 5 million by the twenty-first century. The oil and gas capital
of the world is also one of the world's fastest-growing cities, both in
terms of population and in terms of building construction.[10]

MEGASTRUCTURES AND DEVELOPERS

Houston is today a decentralized city, with builders and developers
active in seven major business activity centers: the downtown area, the

airport area (north), three business centers in the southwest corridor moving out from the center, and two centers in the northwest area. Commercial and industrial corporations have commissioned or leased a vast array of megastructures such as industrial parks, shopping malls, multiple-use projects, and office towers built in all these business centers. Extensive development and construction activity are focused here. Scattered between and beyond these business centers are residential areas, including condominium apartment buildings and sprawling suburban subdivisions, some of which are twenty-five or more miles from downtown. Linking and supporting these private development projects are public works projects, including convention centers, water and sewer projects, flood drainage projects, and highways.

Development Capital

A distinctive type of capitalist, the developer-capitalist, can be clearly seen operating in cities such as Houston. These developers see themselves as the conceptualizers, organizers, and supervisors of real estate development projects. They package the process, pulling together the land, the financing, the construction, the planning, and the leasing or sale of the project; and they coordinate governmental inputs if those are relevant. Developers, notes Lorimer

> look for sites to erect a profitable apartment building or shopping center or suburb, they assemble the site, draw up some kind of plan for the project, get the necessary approvals from governments and public bodies, line up tenants if this is appropriate, line up mortgage lenders to lend them the bulk of the cost of the project once it's built, get the architectural plans for the scheme drawn up, hire the contractors to do the construction, and arrange to rent or sell the building once it's finished.[11]

Many developers diversify their operations into a variety of projects, such as apartment buildings, office towers, and suburban development, in order to maximize profits. And today's profits may be invested in tomorrow's apartment buildings, office buildings, and shopping centers. Developers organize and build projects, but they also own projects, income-producing properties which they develop with the assistance of financial leveraging, and which create profits.

In the last two decades, very large corporations have moved substantially into real estate development. The development industry was once dominated by relatively small capitalist entrepreneurs and corporations, but by the 1960s smaller firms merged to form larger ones, or large firms bought up the smaller ones. Large development companies, such as U.S. Home and Cadillac Fairview, have grown rapidly by acquiring other companies, including builders and building supply firms. Large companies, with greater access to capital sources, have shoved aside or taken over smaller firms, and thus large companies have become even more important in real estate development.

There are various building and development specialities: construction itself; manufacturing prefab houses or parts of houses and other buildings; packaging and subdividing land; and managing ongoing-income properties such as office towers and shopping malls. Numerous real estate development companies incorporate some or all of these functions within one company. Many of the largest development corporations active in North American real estate are unknown to the general public. For example, the North American company of Cadillac Fairview Corporation is one of the largest and most diversified development companies operating in American cities, including Houston. This corporation was created by the merger of several smaller corporations. Typical of the large developers, Cadillac Fairview engages in several categories of projects: (1) *corporate rental projects,* including the development and operation of office buildings, shopping centers, apartment buildings, and industrial plants; (2) *residential projects,* including the development and selling of single-family homes and multi-family housing; and (3) *land development projects,* including development and sale of land for housing and commercial projects. In 1981 the company controlled thirty-three office towers and multiple-use projects, forty-four shopping centers, ninety-four industrial buildings, and fifty residential properties. These projects are located in cities from New York and Philadelphia to Atlanta and Houston. Nonetheless, size is no longer a guarantee of easy times; the recession of the 1980s forced large developers such as Cadillac Fairview to scale down their operations.[12]

MEGASTRUCTURES AND DEVELOPERS IN HOUSTON

In 1980 and 1981, Houston led the nation with $2 billion annually in construction. A sizeable portion of that development was made up of office buildings or multiple-use developments that combine office buildings with other facilities such as shopping centers and apartment complexes. Some of the nation's largest developers have been active in this construction and spatial expansion boom.

Office Towers

Omnipresent office buildings, particularly the skyscraper towers, are clear symbols of who dominates cities such as Houston: the large corporations that build, mortgage, and use such buildings. In industry handbooks, office buildings are sometimes described simply as structures where services are produced or information is processed. But office towers signal far more than this. They signal the growing importance of monopoly corporations, those large multinational corporations which seem to require highly centralized office facilities. Houston's office towers have become the administrative centers where the executive and clerical staffs of oil-gas corporations make and implement the critical decisions affecting their operations around the globe. And clustered in the same or nearby buildings are allied corporations, such as banks and developers, which are closely linked to the capital accumulation dynamism of Houston's energy industry.

The planning and construction of large office buildings (those with more than 100,000 square feet) by industrial capitalists and developers in Houston began slowly between 1930 and 1951; today there are only two dozen large buildings still standing which were built before 1952. But since the early 1950s, there has been a major increase in office construction around the city. As can be seen from the data in table 4.1, three-quarters of Houston's large office buildings have been built since 1970.[13] Increasingly, these structures have been built outside the downtown area. Until 1952 no buildings were built outside the central business district, the first major center of development.

Table 4.1. Houston Office Construction, 1908–1983

Date(s) of completion		Location	Largest building
1908–1951	22	All downtown	681,000 sq. ft.
1951–1970	53	All downtown or southwest	1.6 million sq. ft.
1970–1975	58	All over town, mostly southwest	1.6 million sq. ft.
1976–1980	121	All over town	1.5 million sq. ft.
1981–1983	26	All over town	2.1 million sq. ft.

Between 1951 and 1970, some were built in the southwest corridor as well. But it was not until the 1970s that the office building boom became scattered all over town, in the north as well as the downtown and southwest areas. In one five-year period (1976–1980), 121 major buildings were finished. Many of these are massive structures. The current construction includes the tallest building in the United States outside New York and Chicago (seventy-five stories, 1.7 million square feet), whose developer/owners are Gerald P. Hines Interests and the Texas Commerce Bank, as well as the Allied Bank Plaza (seventy-one stories, 2.1 million square feet), whose developer/owner is the Allen Center Company. These developers are among the nation's largest. Predictions are that in the next fifteen years, the number of office buildings in Houston will again double, if the early-1980 recession ceases.

In 1981 Houston had nearly 100 million square feet of leasable office space, with only a 7-percent vacancy rate (2 percent in downtown buildings). The central business district of Houston is laid out in three hundred square blocks, about one square mile, surrounded on all sides by elevated freeways. In 1981 about 160,000 people worked in that central business district. Downtown Houston has about 40 million square feet of office space, with about 1.5 million added each year. About 60 percent of Houston's office space is now outside the downtown area. It is noteworthy that the office and retail space in just two of these outlying development areas (Post Oak and Greenway) taken together is nearly twice that of downtown areas in major cities such as Baltimore, New Orleans, and Minneapolis. This suggests the unique scale of Houston's office development projects since 1970. Even in the recession at the start of the 1980s, there was demand for office space in Houston. Early in 1981 there were 6 million square feet in (downtown) office buildings being constructed with another 6 million in the planning stage. Half of the space was leased before the buildings were constructed, so most buildings are not really speculative ventures.[14]

A significant feature of modern office building construction is that numerous structures are concentrated in complexes called office parks. In mid-1981 Houston had eighty-two office parks, sixty-six of which had buildings completed.[15] The largest complex has sixty-one buildings and 5.3 million square feet completed on 170 acres.

Multiple-Use Projects

Housing developers have been pioneers in multiple-use developments (called MXDs in developers' publications), the newest type of mega-

structures added to urban development. Developers and allied powerful real estate actors see MXDs as the new wave of urban development,
a wave which is "reshaping much of American life."[16] According to the
Urban Land Institute, the large developers' think tank, an MXD is a
large-scale real estate venture with three (or more) different types of
profit-generating activities integrated into one land-intensive development project.[17] These activities can include office buildings, shopping
malls, apartment buildings, convention centers, and hotels—all as part
of one integrated megastructure complex. There are perhaps one hundred of these huge projects in U.S. cities. Houston's multiple-use projects have been, and are being, built on a huge scale, one that rivals or
exceeds the biggest building projects in all of human history. Three
MXDs—Houston Center, Greenway Plaza, and Galleria—are among the
largest and most influential in the United States, each being built by a
major national developer (called an *investment builder* in trade publications).

    Take, for example, the Houston Center project. In 1968 Texas
Eastern Corporation, a major oil-gas company, bought thirty-three
square blocks (seventy-four acres) on the older east side of downtown
Houston for a price which has been kept secret. Once an expensive
residential neighborhood, at the time of purchase this was a diverse
area of older commercial buildings, small hotels, apartment houses,
and homes. The project has been seen by its developers as remolding
urban life; in their view Houston Center means "the creation of an entirely new city offering fresh approaches to work, recreation and residence. It may well be the prototype of the city of the future. . . . Initial projects will be office buildings, retail stores, hotels, and motels.
The type and mix of tenants have been carefully planned to insure an
economic mix of activities that will generate business for all."[18] Recently an executive connected with the Houston Center project emphasized in a speech that the developer seeks to revitalize the downtown
area so it is more than just a place to work, "to restore a mix of activities by including hotel, retail, residential and leisure-time within the
project."[19] The corporate developers are working with a twenty-year
time frame for completing this city of the future. They even received
permission from the city government to close some streets entirely so
as to remake this section of the downtown area.

    As of 1982 Houston Center includes a forty-four-story office tower
and a forty-six-story office tower linked together by an eight-story
street-spanning wing with a landscaped plaza. Two additional blocks
were sold to a major bank, which built another office tower and a

garage. A thirty-story hotel has been constructed as part of the project along with an exclusive athletic and dining club. In the works is a fifty-two-story building (acquired by Gulf Oil) and a two-block shopping mall with eighty stores and twelve stories of office space. By 1983 the Houston Center complex contained twenty thousand workers and residents. Houston Center will eventually provide more than twenty million square feet of megastructures—hotels, office towers, stores, people-mover vehicles, and parking for forty thousand cars—integrated into one complex.[20]

In the mid-1970s, Texas Eastern ran into a problem with its development schedule and sold half interest in major sections of the project to Cadillac Fairview, one of the world's largest development corporations. The developer has also given 4.5 blocks farthest from the center of downtown so that the city of Houston can build a convention center complex, one which will require the use of public tax revenues. Such a convention center will doubtless enhance Houston Center's profitability.[21] This multiblock Houston Center project, when completed, will be the largest single private urban development project in U.S. history. It will dwarf the famous Rockefeller center development in New York.[22]

Greenway Plaza

Other large-scale development projects are located in business activity centers outside the downtown area; some have even been built where large residential subdivisions once existed. Greenway Plaza, just such a major multiple-use development, involved the buying up of three hundred single-family homes in four large residential subdivisions five miles from the downtown area. The developer, Century Development Corporation, hired real estate agents to buy up houses from middle-income residents at above-market prices. Once 100 percent of the homes had been bought, the developer "voted" to change the subdivision deed restrictions from residential to commercial, and the houses were moved off or razed. Apparently there was no organized citizen protest to this particular destruction of residential neighborhoods, although in other cities citizens have protested the large-scale destruction of much-needed residential housing. Greenway Plaza is of such a scale that it required financing from large insurance firms such as Equitable Life and Northwestern Mutual Life.[23]

Construction of Greenway Plaza began in the late 1960s and is projected to be finished in the mid-1980s, at a total cost of about $1 billion. This megastructure project encompasses 127 acres of central city land, about the size of ninety downtown blocks. In its first two phases, nearly four million square feet of office space were constructed. Greenway Plaza includes a thirty-two-story Conoco Tower, an eleven-story Union Carbide building, a nine-story Dow Center complex, a twenty-two-story Kellogg building, the Richmond and Buffalo towers, a chemical company building, a luxury hotel, high-rise apartment buildings, a huge parking garage, a heliport, and a major sports arena. Twelve thousand office workers are employed in the first eight office towers constructed. This MXD development has had several planned phases; the last is projected to include office buildings and a mass transit center on the other side of a major freeway which the project now straddles. Century Development Corporation's central capitalist entrepreneur, Kenneth L. Schnitzer, got his start in a family-owned Texas business, the Magnolia Paper Company. He moved capital into development projects and has become famous as one of the nation's biggest developers.[24]

Gerald Hines Interests

There are only five or six major U.S. corporations which have development projects in many cities. According to *Fortune*, one Houston developer is the nation's largest, with assets of more than $1.5 billion. Gerald D. Hines started in and is still based in Houston. Since 1957 this developer has built 273 projects, with two dozen more nearing completion, altogether occupying about fifty-five million square feet of space. His major projects can be found in Miami, Denver, San Francisco, Seattle, Cincinnati, Minneapolis, and Montreal. His most famous projects are the nine-hundred-thousand-square-foot Galleria shopping mall, City Post Oak (twenty-four office buildings and hotels), the trapezoidal Pennzoil Place towers, and the Texas Commerce Tower (the nation's sixth tallest building) in Houston. Hines's company has built office towers, manufacturing facilities, warehouses, shopping malls, and some residential housing.[25]

Hines's construction projects dominate one of the business centers of Houston, modestly called City Post Oak. On the west side of Houston, this area includes a famous three-story regional shopping mall on two hundred acres (the Galleria), a twenty-two-story Post Oak Tower, a four-hundred-room hotel, a twenty-two-story CDC building, a twenty-five-story Transco Tower, and many other high-rise office towers, hotels, and apartment buildings.[26]

Hines has become nationally famous for hiring prominent architects to design some of his office towers, sometimes resulting in unique and expensive construction projects. But, as a *Fortune* story notes, he "did so because he thought well-designed buildings would make more money for him and his partners."[27] Monumental construction by architects such as Philip Johnson and I. M. Pei was generally shunned by developers until Hines decided these projects could be undertaken at reasonable cost and good profitability. And he has been right in his judgment. Hines has brought high-powered marketing techniques to the selling of his office buildings. Prospective tenants get a grand tour, called the "processional" in the firm, during which they are presented with huge models of the building under construction, a slide-show extravaganza on fifteen screens, and a lot of words to the effect that this architecture is the cutting edge of Western civilization. *Fortune* magazine quoted a Chicago real estate man: "Gerald Hines is the role model for young developers today."[28]

PLANNED SATELLITE CITIES

Moving farther out from the center of Houston, we come to a number of huge satellite city projects. One of the largest in the nation is called The Woodlands development project, with twenty-three-thousand acres of construction twenty-seven miles from downtown. The project is the brainchild of a Texas oil capitalist, George P. Mitchell, who has moved some of his capital and other resources into the building of a $5-billion satellite city of his own design. Built by Woodlands Development Corporation, a subsidiary of Mitchell's oil company, the "planned unit development" currently houses 13,000 residents and two hundred businesses. By the time its thirty-six-year master plan is completed in the twenty-first century, however, it will have 160,000 residents and twenty-five million square feet of office space. Schools, shopping malls, condominiums, apartments, single-family homes, churches, recreational facilities, and transportation lines will be provided.[29]

Mitchell's view of what he is doing is distinctive. Public relations brochures for Woodlands speak of it as follows: "The hometown idea is refreshingly simple. You'll sense it during your first visit here."[30] But his view of this "hometown" is broader and more idealistic than that of most major urban developers. Mitchell speaks of lower- and moderate-income housing as being a part of The Woodlands, although not much of that type of housing has yet been built. He has insisted that The Woodlands be annexed by the city of Houston so it will not become just another white upper-middle-income enclave feeding off a more nonwhite central city. The Woodlands represents Mitchell's vision of how current urban problems are to be solved. He clearly sees his corporate philosophy as providing a better quality of life by moving money from oil to satellite city development. To quote Mitchell himself:

> Energy is a very fast moving business on pay-out. I have to drill a well every seven years because the well's gone by then, produced out. But if I build a building, it has a slow pay-out of maybe 10 years, but it has a 40-year life. The longterm economics are what make it look interesting.
>
> If we do this well and build human resources and make a profit, then other people will have to do the same to compete with us.[31]

The Woodlands, Mitchell further notes, is "not Utopia, but it's a step better than anything done in the past."[32]

Mitchell's vision of a satellite city where the poor and the rich mingle in one planned suburban development will probably not be fulfilled. The profit logic of modern capitalism is such that new low- and moderate-income housing, in other than token amounts, is practically beyond the pale, for it generates little or no profit. So in effect Mitchell's oil capital will likely create another upper-middle-income residential suburb of Houston, but one with its own careful (private) planning, and with industrial parks, shopping centers, and recreational facilities. It is interesting too that Mitchell recognizes that such huge satellite suburbs require big companies, both development corporations and financial institutions, to provide the capital.

A significant feature of these large-scale planned unit developments, in many cities across the nation, is the role of the state. Federal government loan guarantees have been provided for $50 million in loans for The Woodlands project. The state provides essential startup support for developments which generate privately appropriated profits. But this is not all.[33] In addition, federal funds of $16.1 million were given to the developer as matching grants for community improvements, and another $9.7 million in federal money went to local governments and other organizations for projects in The Woodlands area. Here again capital accumulation receives government assistance.[34]

THE GRAVITATIONAL EFFECTS OF THIS LARGE-SCALE DEVELOPMENT

Large-scale urban development has many effects on U.S. cities. Certain positive effects, such as the creation of employment and an expanded tax base, have received the greatest attention in the mass media and scholarly analyses. But there are other important effects as well. One is the increasing centralization and concentration of development capital. In Houston there has been some tendency for the big fish to eat the small fish. Smaller developers and builders have been gobbled up or driven out of business by larger corporations. But this is not the dominant picture. It is more common for smaller developers to go into joint ventures with larger ones. So far in the 1970s and 1980s, there has been too much development in Houston for many of the smaller companies to go under, although this picture may change in the troubled 1980s.

A critical feature of large-scale developments in cities such as Houston is that they have a gravitational effect. The large development projects set the pattern within which much smaller-scale development takes place. For example, apartment buildings built by smaller developers are constructed near office towers and office parks. Many of these are high-rise apartment buildings with apartments sold as condominiums for the affluent. Older apartment buildings may be converted into condominiums so as to service higher-paid white-collar employees working in the large development projects. This can mean large-scale gentrification of nearby residential areas, which entails the replacement of low-income and moderate-income renters and homeowners by better-off professional, managerial, and technical workers employed in the office towers and other megastructures.[35]

With seven major business activity centers scattered to the north and west, each with major development projects, Houston's physical face is multicentered. And each of these centers has its own centrifugal and centripetal forces affecting large areas surrounding them, destroying residential housing, creating traffic congestion, generating large-scale apartment construction, and forcing major government-funded services projects. We will return to these issues later.

FINANCING URBAN DEVELOPMENT

In Houston as elsewhere, development corporations rely heavily on finance capital in building projects such as office towers, shopping malls, and suburban subdivisions. The financing of large-scale urban projects such as major office towers is usually complicated. A commercial bank may provide the short-term construction financing, while a real estate investment trust, foreign investor, or insurance company may provide the long-term mortgage financing. A developer will often go in with a bank or insurance company as a major partner. Banks and insurance companies once were silent financial sources for large development projects. Today such companies wish to own a piece of the buildings they help to finance. Indeed, many financing corporations will provide long-term financing only if they get the usual mortgage interest plus a portion of the project's equity ownership.

Insurance companies have become very important in financing large-scale projects in American cities. For example, Prudential Insurance and its PIC Realty subsidiary hold $2 billion in real estate assets in Houston alone. Prudential is involved in a number of office buildings. According to an article in the *Houston Business Journal,* Prudential now emphasizes shorter (ten-to-fifteen-year) commercial loans and equity participation.[36] Insurance companies have large amounts of other people's money for investing and thus have great influence over development projects. Indeed, a number of major developers have expressed the view that they are becoming too heavily dependent on financial institutions such as Prudential; they fear that developers may become extinct as finance capitalists organized development subsidiaries under their immediate control.[37]

The power of financial corporations over developers can be seen in other ways as well. For example, many banks and insurance companies are beginning to require certain development restrictions, which create in effect a type of private zoning or planning. When one large Houston developer went to his financial backers to see about expanding a multiple-use project by another three million square feet, he was told the backers would only finance another one million square feet unless there was some type of public mass transit system provided to relieve severe traffic congestion around the project. Concerned with their own profit, finance capitalists are thereby imposing a type of private urban planning on developers in Houston, developers who are accustomed to operating freely without such planning requirements. Note too that mass transit—funded out of taxpayer revenues—has become necessary from finance capital's point of view in a city such as Houston with its extreme traffic congestion.[38]

Foreign investors' money in cities such as Houston has for the most part gone into the office building and multiple-use developments. Foreign banking corporations and other foreign investors have banked surplus profits in Houston real estate. An estimated one-fifth of all new investment money for development has come from foreign sources, much of it kept secret and hidden from public view. Numerous recent Houston development projects have involved a joint venture between a Texas company and a foreign investor. Thirty percent of one major downtown building was reportedly sold to German investors, and Canadian, French, German, Saudi Arabian, and Iranian (the former shah's family) money have been important in Houston's development projects.[39] Foreign and other non-Texas investment activity has been one factor helping to drive land prices sky high in many central city areas.

GOVERNMENT SUPPORT FOR HOUSTON DEVELOPMENT

Houston's business and government officials, as well as national mass media reports, often portray this dramatically growing city as solely the creation of private enterprise. Much is made of the fact that Houston has no government-imposed zoning laws and that what government exists is rather limited and conservative.

But there is a serious flaw in this portrait. Not only is Houston's growth and that of the region substantially indebted to the federal treasury, but Houston's development has also required the routine intervention of conservative government officials at the local level.

The Federal Role

Several researchers have documented the point that federal expenditures for defense and electronics industries and for infrastructure assistance for highways, ports, and utilities helped provide the "opportunity for the emergence of a new phase of capital accumulation and its concomitant new wave of urbanization" in the Sunbelt.[40] This has certainly been true for Houston, with its major NASA facility, the Manned Spacecraft Center, and with its federal aid for port and freeway expansion. Federal assistance also lies behind Houston's growing dependence on nuclear power for its electric utilities. This federal largesse paved the way for construction of large-scale development projects such as industrial parks, office towers, shopping malls, and convention centers—all designed to accommodate the industrial and retail corporations moving operations to, or expanding operations in, Houston.

Local Government

As we noted earlier, the business of Houston's government has from the very beginning been business. For many years Houston's mayors, city councils, and planning commissions have been closely tied to business interests, including real estate and development. Thus Oscar Holcombe, a land dealer and developer, was mayor for twenty-two of the years between 1921 and 1957. Mayor from 1964 to 1974, Louie Welch was a businessman who moved out of the mayor's office to become head of the chamber of commerce.[41] In 1981 the mayor was a real estate developer; many earlier mayors have also had ties to real estate development. In 1981 one-third of the city council was in real estate or in fields closely related to it; most of the planning commission was composed of developers, builders, and other people tied in one way or another to the local real estate industry. As a recent local book on Houston puts it, the "Houston City Hall, then, was an extension, a working area, of the Houston Chamber of Commerce."[42]

The impact of this business-oriented government can be seen in at least three areas: the provision of services needed by the business community, the direct impact of government expenditures, and the lack of government regulation. City budgets in the 1970s were in the $200–$400 million range, with two-thirds of that going for employees. These expenditures help support local business.[43]

But more important than the direct government expenditures have been the services provided. Over many decades the city government of Houston has paid for hundreds of millions of dollars of public construction—bridges, streets, storm and sanitary sewers, water and sewage treatment facilities. This support for the infrastructure of services critical to urban development, large and small, has been provided out of general tax revenues and by using the borrowing capability of the city government. Both citizens and developers have benefitted.

With regard to regulations, the local government has generally responded to the wishes of developers and other business interests. Property taxes have been kept relatively low; Houston has a history of special tax exemptions and underassessment for various types of business enterprises. Into the 1970s Houston had one of the weaker building codes among American cities.[44] Perhaps most conspicuous is the total absence of zoning regulations. There have been several political campaigns to bring zoning to Houston, but all of them have been unsuccessful. There is no zoning commission. As a result, there is relatively modest government planning in the day-to-day life of Houston development. According to a top planning official I interviewed there, large development projects are planned by developers with little or no input from city departments and agencies. As he put it, "In Houston the project just happens." There is often an aspect of mystery to the large developments, as far as the public and planners are concerned. The lack of zoning in Houston has meant that developers often have relatively shorter development times. In a city with stricter zoning and planning, it might take a year or two to get a plan for a megastructure project approved and finished. In Houston it takes six months. Zoning tends to slow down development because of the periodic need to rezone areas for new development projects. The emphasis in Houston is on the private local market. What primarily controls development and land use is this private land sales market. The lack of zoning has also permitted seven major business activity centers to develop more easily, for a developer can purchase a block of residential land and "rezone" it commercial the next day. A zoned city probably would have had fewer business centers because of the inertia often involved in getting planning commission or zoning commission approval.[45]

Deed restrictions on property in Houston provide some development controls, but only 60 percent of the residential areas have deed restrictions. The elite inner suburb, the River Oaks area, pioneered with stiff deed restrictions in the 1920s and 1930s. Deed restrictions have serious limitations, however. According to planning officials, in some areas developers ignore them and go ahead and build anyway. Once the new buildings are started, it is usually too late to force major changes. In addition, in major projects developers can buy out local homeowners, acquire title, and "vote" to change deed restrictions from residential to commercial.

Thus, in spite of tremendous business and residential development, Houston's city planning department did not grow significantly in the last decade or so. There was a little growth in other types of government planning agencies (for example, at the county level). There has been no significant increase in pressure for more city planning or for government involvement in controlling city growth from the business community. Houston has not had any federal urban renewal programs to assist private developers although the city government did get involved in the Model Cities program. One Houston planning official has been quoted as saying that "we plan for Houston's future like weathermen planning for the next weekend." In effect, planning means trying to anticipate what the developers will do next. What city planning exists in Houston is short-range planning.[46]

Houston has had powerful advocates for more planning, as well as for zoning. The wealthy Hogg brothers built up the exclusive River Oaks residential section, and they were vigorous advocates of zoning for the city. Newer citizens coming into Houston from other areas are often amazed that Houston has no zoning controls, so there has been increasing discussion of zoning over the last decade. Yet both planning and zoning remain very controversial issues in Houston. A recent study done for the chamber of commerce recommended more long-range government planning for water problems. Even this recommendation brought heated opposition from some business leaders. However, by the late 1970s and early 1980s, there was at least increased talk about the need for more planning in dealing with Houston's growth and development.[47]

The lack of zoning in Houston has had two major effects on its overall land use patterns. There is commercial business strip development on more major streets than in many other cities. And there are numerous contradictory land use patterns which are less common in zoned cities, such as a cement factory next to a residential subdivision and a small office building next to an adult pornography bookstore. But when we look at Houston as a whole, the broad land use patterns are very similar to those of other cities. In Houston land costs themselves do much zoning and grouping of land uses.

PROBLEMS IN EDEN

"Progrowthism" is the dominant ideology in Houston's influential business community and among most political officials. It is also publicly defended in the city's major newspapers, the *Post* and the *Chronicle*, which are very closely integrated at the top into Houston's capitalist elite. For this reason ordinary Houstonians have gotten a steady diet of progrowthism for many decades, with very few antigrowth advocates rising to public visibility. Even researchers have picked up some of this progrowth philosophy. For example, in an article on Houston's demography, Roberto Marchesini and Joanne Austin have recently argued that

> Houstonians measure progress in terms of population increase, surface area extension, numbers of new buildings erected, and the continual attraction of business to the area. They take great pride in Houston's rise to fifth largest city in the nation from fourteenth in 1950. They view the benefits of growth not only monetarily but also as a means of developing the arts, education, and medicine. In short, growth brings the good life, and, from the Houstonians' point of view, the good life keeps Houston growing.[48]

Even in the minds of social science researchers, Houston's growth is seen as favorable for the quality of life in the city. Here Houstonians as a group are seen as measuring their progress, in money and quality of life, in terms of growth and development.

But in reality Houston is not the utopia these views suggest. In the first place, it has a huge poor and moderate-income population which has yet to see the promised "good life" signaled by the glittering Galleria-type shopping malls with their chic shops for the nouveau riche or the mirrored-glass office towers shining golden in the sun. In the second place, even for the more affluent middle- and upper-income Houstonians, there are severe problems resulting from massive urban growth, from both the huge projects and from the smaller-scale ones. In the 1980s there does seem to be a slowly growing groundswell of public protest, albeit atomized and unorganized for the most part, which is targeting a broad range of problems from traffic and sewage disposal, to air pollution and cancer, to poverty and racism.

The roaring juggernaut of Houston has created many problems as it has rolled on seeking ever-increasing capital accumulation and expansion for its dominant business elite. Take, for example, the mundane problems of sewage disposal and safe water supplies. Houston has a very serious sewage problem. In 1981 three-quarters of the city was under a sewer moratorium, that is, there was not enough sewage treatment plant capacity in many areas to permit any more sewer connections. So developers have had to scramble, trading sewer rights with other developers, using permits they got before the moratorium, and switching permits from one area to another. And some developers have built temporary sewage plants of their own, an expensive burden which the city government will eventually have to shoulder. This has become particularly problematical in the scattered suburban development just beyond the city limits where there is sometimes a very heavy sewage discharge. One such outlying area, a small extraterritorial jurisdiction, has a hundred different waste facilities dumping sewage into a single watershed. Observers fear that excessive sewage outflow in some areas is beginning to contaminate sources of drinking water. There is great pressure on government to spend more for sewage facilities.[49]

One of the unusual consequences of development in Houston is subsidence, the gradual sinking of the city. Houston is only fifty feet above sea level, and the heavy use of underground water weakens the supporting soil structure. Together with oil and gas extraction and the

weight of all the new development construction, the dewatering of
the soil has led to a drop in land elevation of several feet over the last
seven decades. Numerous areas in central Houston are today four or
five feet lower than they were in the early 1900s. Today it is estimated
that most areas are sinking at a rate of one foot every five to six years.
In twenty-five years, this subsidence will mean a drop of five or more
feet for most areas of the city. Subsidence creates serious flooding, construction, and structural problems.[50]

To the visitor the most obvious problem of Houston's vigorous development is traffic congestion. Houston has been famous for its 210-
mile freeway system, often reputed to be one of the largest in the
world. Billions in planned freeway construction will eventually bring
that up to 406 miles of eleven different freeways. According to a brochure put out by the Houston Chamber of Commerce, "any point in
Houston can be reached within one hour" using this freeway system.[51]
Reading chamber of commerce and other business advertising such as
this might lead one to think Houston has little or no transportation
problem. But the city has developed severe traffic problems, particularly on its freeways and suburban roads. By the late 1970s, these roads
were heavily congested all day long. Many commuters drive one and
one half to two hours, one way. The city and county governments have
been unable to provide enough roads to keep up with rapid development. Moreover, noise levels along the major roads have reached levels that are potentially dangerous to human hearing and are already
contributing to the frustration and anxiety of many Houstonians, especially auto commuters. Because of a weak mass transit system, Houstonians are more heavily dependent on automobiles than are residents of
most cities. And the city's architecture reflects this dependence. As a
recent analysis by the U.S. Department of Transportation put it, "The
visual character of Houston is dominated by an expansive mixture of
commercial and residential elements that cater to the automobile, the
principal mode of travel. . . . [There is] the visual confusion that results from conflicts between building design, vehicle control mechanisms, vehicle movement, advertising and other elements of an active
commercial society."[52]

The traffic congestion has even begun to affect the projects and
profits of developers. We have already noted the role of financial institutions in persuading at least one major developer to seriously consider
supporting mass transit studies and programs. To take another example, the developer of a large multiple-use project did not anticipate the
massive traffic jams that his development created. As a result, the cor-

porate officials became very concerned, even to the point of asking city government agencies to help. But some city officials pointed out that the same developer did not want government planning assistance in the beginning. Not surprisingly then, many of Houston's corporate executives are now looking closely at mass transit rail proposals. Although "free-enterprise" advocates, they are hoping that publicly subsidized mass transit will alleviate some congestion caused by their privately planned developments.[53]

There is a great deal of land speculation in the Houston area. New corporations and old Houston oil families have bought up large areas of land in and around the city, just as they buy gold, with the hope that the land will appreciate in value. Foreign corporations, from Germany to Canada, have done the same. Land speculation has become big business. Banks, syndicates of doctors, real estate people, and large corporations have bought and held land, waiting for its rapid appreciation. This has taken place in central areas and on the suburban fringe, where it has helped create a leapfrogging pattern of suburban development. That pattern can be seen as developers jump over some speculator's land to lower-priced land farther out. The pattern has contributed to Houston's higher-than-average commuting distances, now eleven to twelve miles.[54]

Houston's middle- and upper-income residents have so far not become greatly agitated about their urban problems in general. For the most part, those who do organize, a small minority at this time, focus on problems only as they immediately affect them, such as a specific traffic problem. In recent years Houston has seen a few citizens' groups pressing for cleaner air, more parks, and better transportation. (Houston is one-hundred-forty-sixth among cities in park acreage but is fifth in population size.) Today more people are at least talking about quality of life in Houston. Yet the dominant condition is still one of lack of organized effort to analyze and correct the problems.

Houston's low- and moderate-income residents can pay a heavy displacement price for urban development. If homeowners refuse to sell, developers can use a variety of tactics. They may start bulldozing the homes which they have title to, put up a several-story building, and watch the homeowners who refuse to sell suffer from the shade of the building, the traffic flow, and the noise. Eventually, these pressures force most people to sell. And the most stubborn homeowners may simply see a development project built around them. One hotel development was actually built around the home of a couple who refused to sell; then hotel residents can watch clothes drying on the line![55]

Houston's low-income and minority homeowners and tenants have suffered the most from market-oriented growth. The central city is within the "loop," a major circumferential highway. That area, which is heavily black and Chicano with low- and moderate-income families, is under heavy pressure from developers. Many areas of this central city have suffered from gentrification, the replacement of poorer families with better-off professional, technical, and managerial families who wish to live near their jobs in the office towers and office/medical parks. Gentrification has displaced residents of minority areas as well as elderly whites in the Heights area in the north part of the loop. In the west end there is also considerable gentrification. In some areas land speculators are even buying up the oil leasing rights; soon there may be condominiums and oil wells next to one another in the inner city.

The Fourth Ward is one of Houston's oldest black communities with the misfortune of being near the central business district. The area is populated by predominantly black tenants living in single-family dwellings and in a major public housing project. Because of its nearness to downtown, developers are eagerly eyeing the ward. A number of prominent consultant reports have suggested that the area should be redeveloped. While the consultant studies have noted the housing plight of the black tenants, they offer no real solutions. Much of the Fourth Ward is owned by a dozen or so absentee landlords, who are currently asking prices too high for the developers. But the area will soon be redeveloped. In general, Houston has serious housing problems for low-income and middle-income families, minority and white. There are not enough houses or multifamily units at reasonable rents to adequately house the burgeoning population.[56]

Houston will not be able to employ all those flooding the city from the North seeking employment because they have heard Houston is a boom town. And the gap between the poor and the affluent is dramatic. Unemployment is very high, 20 percent, in numerous black and Chicano neighborhoods. And underemployment—part-time and low-wage jobs—is an even more serious problem. One community activist has pointed out, "We have people supporting families with full-time jobs which, when job expenses are deducted, pay less than the minimum wage."

A fifth of Houstonians live near or below the federal poverty line. Yet Houston has only five thousand units of public housing, and developers show no interest in such construction. In 1980 there were forty-five hundred families and individuals on a waiting list for this housing.

Joe Sepeda, a Housing Authority planner, told a reporter that he sees a lot of people "living in cars," particularly near the public housing projects.[57] But many powerful local officials scoff at the idea that Houston's poverty is of great consequence. Former mayor and chamber of commerce head Louie Welch put it this way in an interview with the *New York Times:* "The free market place has functioned in Houston like no other place in America. It has a method of purging itself of slums. No city is without poor people, but the opportunity not to be poor is greater than in most cities. The work ethic, and the opportunities, are strong here."[58]

Houston has a serious problem in its inferior government services. The bus system is inadequate, and many poor and moderate-income Houstonians must rely on it. The city officials and corporate leaders put much emphasis on Houston's relatively low taxes, but low taxes usually mean poor services. And that is indeed often the case. Water pressure has been very low in many parts of the city; numerous low-income and minority neighborhoods regularly face serious flooding and drainage problems, from which the city government does not protect them as well as better-off (white) areas. Moreover, high utility costs can be a problem in extremely hot summers. Some poor people died in the summer of 1980 because they could not afford to pay their electric bills and thus could not run their fans (if, indeed, they could afford fans). In a recent interview, an ACORN (Association of Community Organizations for Reform Now) activist noted that in Houston there has been little commitment to using federal grants to make life better for the poor except near election time, when city politicians will sometimes provide some money for selected low-income and minority groups in an attempt to coopt and control local civic leaders.[59]

In the last few years, the city government has funded studies of mass transit possibilities for Houston. As seen by some minority leaders, the proposed mass transit plans look as though they will lock minority Houstonians into the central city areas. The high fares proposed will keep minority people from making much use of the planned rail system. A bus system is seen as the alternative for minority areas, but the streets in many such neighborhoods do not have the capacity to handle a large number of additional vehicles.[60]

Houston has seen some organization among its low- and moderate-income citizens. It has had an active ACORN organization, with eighteen neighborhood groups and two thousand members. Citizens' groups such as ACORN have been able to force some concessions from Houston's powerful ruling elite. They have forced drainage and street repairs, revising tax exemptions and tax reform, and changes in bus routes. Campaigns directed at factory dust and pollution and housing abandonment have also been conducted. A continuing concern has been local taxes. Downtown office buildings in Houston are dramatically underassessed, some at only 10 percent of what they should be. The big industrial and development corporations do not pay their fair share of taxes, and poor peoples' movements such as ACORN have been pressing forward with research on and organization around issues such as this.[61]

CONCLUSION

Just how this capital of the Sunbelt is doing depends on one's class perspective. From a corporate capitalist and managerial point of view, Houston's market-oriented growth and development looks extremely good. Centered on the oil and gas industry, and assisted by major retail business successes, Houston's economy must look prosperous to those with wealth and resources. Recessions force some cutbacks, but the oil-gas corporations continue to expand, and the larger developers remain active in building megastructure projects. There is still a good business climate in Houston, with no state or local income taxes, few or weak unions, and a business-oriented city government.

But from the working-class point of view, the shining buckle of the Sunbelt has its tarnished side, with its air pollution, congestion, lack of housing, poor mass transit, and nonunionized, low-wage jobs. Houston is indeed a transparent window through which one can look to see the details of urban growth and development in this era of late capitalism. In Houston this era is characterized not so much by Big Government as by Big Business, which takes the form of large-scale development projects and expanding industrial and commercial operations. And it is the centrifugal and centripetal effects of this large-scale development that ordinary Houstonians must bear, as their job opportunities, transportation systems, working conditions, and residential choices are limited significantly by the prior decisions of industrial, development, and finance capital. Moreover, even in Houston recessions inflict a heavy burden on unemployed and underemployed workers, and in good times and bad, Houston's huge poor and minority populations must limp along as the invisible victims of this socially costly pattern of private profitability.

NOTES

1. "A Texas City That's Busting Out All Over," *U.S. News & World Report*, November 27, 1978, p. 47. This booster-type article is distributed by the Houston Chamber of Commerce.
2. Richard A. Walker, "A Theory of Suburbanization: Capitalism and Construction of Urban Space in the United States," in *Urbanization and Urban Planning in Capitalist Society*, ed. M. Dear and A. J. Scott (London: Methuen, 1981), pp. 385ff.
3. Houston Chamber of Commerce, "Houston Data Sketch," 1981 data sheet in author's files; Jack Donahue et al., *Big Town, Big Money* (Houston: Cordovan, 1973), pp. 48–50.
4. Cf. Alfred J. Watkins and David C. Perry, "Regional Change and the Impact of Uneven Urban Development," in *The Rise of the Sunbelt Cities*, ed. Perry and Watkins (Beverly Hills, Calif.: Sage, 1977), pp. 19–54.
5. Quoted in David G. McComb, *Houston: A History* (Austin: University of Texas Press, 1981), p. 9.
6. Ibid., pp. 15–17.
7. "Houston, the Greatest Lumber City," *Progressive Houston* 1 (February 1910):1–2; cf. also McComb, *Houston*, pp. 16–68. Large city budgets for sewers, water, streets, and other services are presented in the 1909–1919 issue of *Progressive Houston*.
8. "New York Times Praises Houston," *Progressive Houston* 1 (April 1909):9.
9. P. W. Horn, superintendent of Houston public schools, quoted in *Progressive Houston* 1 (June 1909):1–2.
10. Houston Chamber of Commerce, "Houston Facts '80," research brochure in author's files, pp. 1–2; Houston Chamber of Commerce, "Houston Data Sketch," in author's files.
11. James Lorimer, *The Developers* (Toronto: Lorimer, 1978), pp. 61–62.
12. Henry Aubin, *City for Sale* (Toronto: Lorimer, 1977), pp. 63–65; Cadillac Fairview Corporation, *Annual Report*, 1981.
13. These data are highly condensed from a detailed analysis by Property Research and Investment Consultants and the Houston Chamber of Commerce, reported in "Buildings of 100,000 Square Feet or More," *Houston* 52 (February 1981): 32–37.
14. Barbara Stokes, "Office Development: A Moderating Market," *Houston* 52 (February 1981):4–12; U.S. Department of Transportation, and Metropolitan Transit Authority of Harris County, draft *Environmental Impact Statement: Southwest/Westpark Corridor*, Houston, Texas, September, 1980, pp. I–10, IV–124.
15. "Office Parks," *Houston* 52 (February 1981):31.
16. Robert E. Witherspoon, Jon P. Abbett, and Robert M. Gladstone, *Mixed-Use Developments: New Ways of Land Use* (Washington, D.C.: Urban Land Institute, 1976), p. 3.
17. Ibid., p. 6.
18. Quoted in Bernard H. Siegan, *Land Use Without Zoning* (Lexington, Mass.: Lexington, 1972), p. 70; the data cited in this paragraph are on pp. 69–71.
19. From a speech by a Texas Eastern executive to a group of hotel managers, July 17, 1981, p. 3, in the author's files.
20. Ibid., pp. 5–6; Donahue et al., *Big Town, Big Money*, p. 102.

21. Houston Center Corporation, "Houston Center," Information brochure, p. 1.
22. Siegan, *Land Use Without Zoning*, p. 70.
23. Century Development Corporation, Greenway Plaza brochures and fact sheets, in author's files; some material in this paragraph is drawn from an interview with a senior research official at the Rice Center research facility in Greenway Plaza, Houston, Texas, May 1981.
24. Donahue et al., *Big Town, Big Money*, pp. 101–02; and Century Development Corporation, Greenway Plaza newsletters and brochures, in author's files.
25. Alexander Stuart, "Texas Gerald Hines Is Tall in the Skyline," *Fortune 101* (January 28, 1980): 101. Gerald D. Hines Interests news release, in author's files.
26. Gerald D. Hines Interests news release and brochures, in author's files; Donahue et al., *Big Town, Big Money*, pp. 102–03.
27. Stuart, "Gerald Hines," p. 102.
28. Ibid., p. 109.
29. The Woodlands Development Corporation, fact sheet in author's files.
30. The Woodlands Development Corporation, "The Woodlands," brochure in author's files.
31. Interview with George H. Mitchell, originally published by Ginger H. Jester in *Houston North Magazine*, November 1980, revised and published as a brochure for The Woodlands, p. 5.
32. Ibid., p. 5.
33. Ibid., pp. 5–6.
34. Mitchell Energy and Development Corporation, *Annual Report*, Houston, January 31, 1981, p. 43.
35. Interview with senior planning official, city hall, Houston, May 1981; Phillip L. Clay, *Neighborhood Renewal* (Lexington, Mass.: Lexington, 1978), pp. 11–32.
36. The *Houston Business Journal*, a fifty-to-seventy-page weekly newspaper, signals in its detailed, data-oriented stories the scale of business development in Houston. It is a major data source for those interested in studying Sunbelt cities.
37. "Prudential Subsidiary to Expand $2 Billion Houston Asset Base," *Houston Business Journal*, November 17, 1980, Section 2, pp. 2–3.
38. Interview with senior research official, Rice Center, Greenway Plaza, Houston, May 1981.
39. Interview with Patricia Cronkright, reporter for *Houston Business Journal*, Houston, May 1981; and Patricia Cronkright, "North Loop: Forgotten Freeway Becomes Development Playground," *Houston Business Journal*, March 23, 1981, Section 1, p. 21.
40. Watkins and Perry, "Regional Change," p. 47.
41. Donahue et al., *Big Town, Big Money*, pp. 27–28; McComb, *Houston*, pp. 113–17 and appendix B; Chandler Davidson, "Houston: The City Where the Business of Government Is Business" (unpublished paper, Department of Sociology, Rice University, Houston, 1981).
42. Donahue et al., *Big Town, Big Money*, p. 28.
43. Ibid., pp. 28–29.
44. Ibid., pp. 33–34.
45. Interview with senior planning official, city hall, Houston, May 1981.
46. Interview with senior research official, Rice Center, Greenway Plaza, Houston, May 1981.

47. Ibid.
48. Roberto Marchesini and Joanne Austin, "Houston: Growth Center of the Southwest," *Texas Business Review* 52 (August 1978):164.
49. Patricia Cronkright, "Houston's Sewer Moratorium: Putting the Squeeze on Growth," *Houston Business Journal*, December 18, 1980, p. 1.
50. U.S. Department of Transportation, *Environmental Impact Statement* (September 1980):III–56.
51. Houston Chamber of Commerce, "Houston Data Sketch," 1981 data sheet, in author's files.
52. U.S. Department of Transportation, *Environmental Impact Statement* (September 1980):III–58.
53. Interview with senior research official, Rice Center, Greenway Plaza, Houston, May 1981.
54. Ibid.; Cronkright, "North Loop," pp. 21–22.
55. Interview with Patricia Cronkright, reporter for *Houston Business Journal*, Houston, May 1981.
56. Interview with Judy Graves, ACORN official, Houston, May 1981; interview with senior research official, Rice Center, Greenway Plaza, Houston, May 1981.
57. Quoted in Davidson, "Houston," n.p.
58. Quoted in ibid.
59. Interview with Judy Graves, ACORN official, Houston, May 1981.
60. Interview with Naomi Lede, Urban Institute, Texas Southern University, Houston, May 1981.
61. Interview with Judy Graves, ACORN official, Houston, May, 1981.

5

Urban Industrial Decline and the Dynamics of Sexual and Racial Oppression

DOROTHY REMY and LARRY SAWERS

The last two decades have witnessed a dramatic technological and geographic restructuring of the meat-packing industry in the United States. The smaller independent producers left behind in the march to the South and West have experienced considerable difficulties, and many have gone bankrupt or sold out. The workers in the distressed firms that hang on have found their economic position steadily eroding, and women and blacks have borne a disproportionate share of the burden. This has occurred despite the presence of militant, progressive union pressure and vigorous government intervention which forced the industry to grant formal equality to minorities and women. The tensions which this process has fostered have weakened the union, leaving it a less effective instrument for protecting the economic position of all workers, white or black, male or female.

We reached these conclusions through an intensive investigation of a single meat-packing plant in a large, industrial city in the northeastern United States. This investigation included observations within the plant, interviews with numerous workers, union officials, and managers, and a statistical analysis of data drawn from the firm's personnel department files. Our goal was to examine the internal workings of the firm, which we call the Square Deal Packing Company, in order to analyze racial and sexual discrimination. Our intentions were clearly stated and announced. The immediate response of the workers when they learned of our mission was that "the women's libbers, pencil-pushers in Washington who don't know the donkey's work of a factory," were responsible for women being pushed out of their jobs and out of the plant. Wherever we turned, to the workers, union officials, or lower management, we were given the same explanation. Much of what we have done in this study is not research in the sense of discovering that which was unknown but is rather a documenting of that which the actors in this drama already knew. We have listened to what the people involved have said and attempted to report it in a way that is understandable to the reader unfamiliar with the meat-packing industry.

Our information was obtained in a variety of ways. The senior author of this essay was experienced in anthropological techniques of observing work environments and spent two months in the plant. While she did not have a paid job, she was there daily standing near the production line, observing the work process, talking with people as they worked, and gradually becoming accepted. She had access to all parts of the plant and, with the union's general steward, observed disciplinary cases involving all levels of management. In addition, she and a black woman field assistant administered a formal questionnaire to about twenty workers. These interviews, which often lasted several hours, were conducted in the workers' homes. Most of those involved with the research project also attended at least one union meeting. The union allowed us to examine its records and freely answered our questions.

The firm also granted us free access to personnel department files. There was found information on race, sex, wage rates, promotions, demotions, and layoffs—in short, everything that the personnel department recorded about its employees. The information was recorded beginning with the date of hire (1928 for the most senior worker) and ending in December 1977, when the study was carried out. All of this information was coded and punched onto computer cards. After these data were collected, the junior author of this paper, an economist, carried out the statistical analysis.

We made considerable efforts to corroborate what we learned from the workers, their leaders, and the records by a careful review of the history of the meat-packing industry, focusing on both the role of technological change and the effects of racial and sexual segmentation of the work force. Sources for this survey are academic studies of the industry, including early field reports from the Women's Bureau of the U.S. Department of Labor. The international office of the Amalgamated

Meat Cutters and Butcher Workmen of North America (now merged with the Retail Clerks Union) also provided help in the form of published reports and answers to our questions. Local union files containing old contracts, letters, minutes of meetings, and clippings from area newspapers rounded out the picture.

What has emerged from our study of all these sources is an extraordinarily consistent picture. From our vantage point outside the factory and with access to the entire spectrum of people involved, we have been able to fill in many details of a process of which most of the participants were probably unaware. Furthermore, the particular theoretical perspective with which we begin allows us to draw conclusions that might not have occurred to many of the people we interviewed.

Before World War II, the firm which we studied openly discriminated against women by paying them lower wages than men and against blacks by refusing outright to hire them. In 1942 the union arrived with its demands that the company move toward equal pay for equal work. Almost simultaneously, the federal government refused to buy meat for its soldiers unless suppliers agreed to hire blacks.

By the end of the following decade, starting wages for men and women had been equalized. Up until this point, the firm had hired only a handful of black workers. After the late 1950s, however, it virtually ceased hiring women and instead hired black men. The effect has been to pit black men against white women, with both groups feeling betrayed by their allies among white men. How could this have happened when both white women and black men were protected by a progressive union, a seniority system, and civil rights legislation? The following account offers an answer to this question.

THE RESTRUCTURING OF
THE MEAT-PACKING INDUSTRY

The upsurge in industrial unions in meat packing in the 1930s led to a profound geographical and technological restructuring of the industry. Management attempted to move the industry geographically in order to produce in regions where unions were weaker and to simplify the production process in order to use ever more unskilled workers. These efforts undercut the economic position of the organized workers.

In the 1930s the major companies built their own yards to make themselves less vulnerable to strikes in the city-wide stockyards such as those that had plagued the industry during and immediately after

World War I. Of far greater significance, however, were shifts in the industry that occurred after World War II. In the North Central region—traditionally the center of the meat industry—production shifted from the eastern to the western part. There was a decline in production in Ohio, Indiana, Illinois, Michigan, and Wisconsin, and an increase in production in Minnesota, Iowa, Missouri, North and South Dakota, Nebraska, and Kansas. The second shift occurred in the South. Prior to 1947–1948, hogs produced in the South were shipped North for slaughter. By 1960–1962, hogs produced in the North Central states were sent South for slaughter.[1] Both of these shifts allowed packers to reduce their labor costs by moving into areas where workers were not effectively organized.

Mechanization and reorganization of production in the industry at large and at Square Deal in particular began in the early 1950s. Major innovations followed the general pattern of reducing the skill level required of workers. One important change was replacing the heavy cleavers used to crack the breastbone of the cattle with an electric saw. A second change was the use of on-the-rail processes in the cattle kill. Killing and skinning the animals became a less physically demanding and skilled job. These changes increased productivity by as much as 50 to 60 percent. Other changes involved the introduction of new equipment and production processes in meat processing, sausage manufacturing, ham curing, and bacon slicing.[2]

These innovations are important in terms of their general impact on employment and also in terms of their specific consequences for women and minorities. The overall result was a decline in total employment in the meat industry and at Square Deal, even though output rose, but the declines were not evenly spread through the labor force. The new equipment and processes were concentrated in the jobs held by women and blacks.

By 1960 the Department of Labor estimated that "at current production levels, new equipment and new technology have been eliminating about 7,000 meat packing jobs a year."[3] A breakdown of the sex and race composition of the work force in the departments where mechanization was most advanced indicates that they were also departments with the highest concentration of black and female workers. Splitting cattle breastbones with the heavy cleaver, for example, had been a "black job." Blacks have also been concentrated in the ham-curing department where injection of curing solution by machines replaced the delicate and highly skilled job of injecting the solution with a hypodermic needle into the main arteries. Sausage manufacturing and bacon slicing have been traditional "women's jobs." New machines fed sausage into artificial casings and tied the links, both jobs previously done by hand by women. New machines did not necessarily increase the speed with which bacon was packed, but they did eliminate the need to train and retain the skilled packers. (Meat processing and the cattle kill, areas where mechanization also changed production processes, are less readily identified with a particular race and sex.) Women's jobs were rapidly mechanized as the union forced the elimination of sex differences in wages.

Black workers appear to have been disproportionately hurt by plant closings. Union studies of the effects of plant closings on employment concluded that workers were not being reabsorbed into the labor force. The new jobs created by mechanization were not being filled by former meat packers. The effects of plant closings, which often accompanied mechanization, varied from city to city, with black workers in predominantly black cities being the least likely to be rehired.[4]

In the 1960s and 1970s, the winds of change that buffeted the industry were not primarily geographic or technological, but rather had to do with the reorganization of the market for which the industry produced, and the implications this had for the nature of competition within the industry. There were three major transformations in the industry. First, major chain stores began buying, slaughtering, and processing their own meat products. Chain store control over both production and distribution enabled them to undercut the major packers. Second, the major packers themselves were bought out by conglomerates who saw investment possibilities in the food industry. Third, traditional forms of beef production and distribution were transformed by innovators within the industry. In highly mechanized plants located near feedlots, beef was prepared for direct retail sale in supermarkets and shipped in boxes, thereby eliminating any butchering within the retail store itself.

The economic transformation of the industry in the 1960s challenged the domination and control of the major packers. The proportion of red meat produced by the major packers declined from 40 percent in 1947 to 29 percent in 1967. The big food chains took a major share of their markets as well as some of their profits. In 1960, for example, the chains had a 12 percent profit rate as compared with 7 percent for the big packers.[5] The supermarket chains had great economic leverage through their control of access to customers, the buying power of their billions of dollars, and their own distribution networks.

In addition, there was an incursion of major conglomerates into the food industry. Wilson and Company was taken over by LTV, a Texas-owned corporation whose earlier specialization had been in aerospace equipment and electronic gear. The fourth largest packer was bought by AMK and then subsequently sold to the United Fruit Company. Now all three are covered by a single corporate umbrella called United Brands, Inc. Armour and Company, itself a conglomerate, was eventually taken over by the huge multinational corporation Greyhound, Inc.[6] As Harrison has argued earlier in this volume, the flexibility of conglomerates allows an acceleration of the restructuring process.

The third new force in the meat industry, Iowa Beef Packers, Inc. (now known as Iowa Beef Processors, Inc.), began in Denison, Iowa, in 1960. By 1969 it had become the largest slaughterer and processor of beef in the world. IBP has been joined by Missouri Beef and American Beef. All three companies have plants adjacent to cattle feedlots. They have large, single-story plants (in contrast to Square Deal's seven-story plant) with the most modern equipment. Some have built airstrips nearby to facilitate shipments of the boxed beef throughout the country. They hire a disproportionately large number of minority women as production workers. These new beef-processing firms have adamantly refused to agree to the terms of the master contracts between the major packers and the union. They argue that the work is less skilled and therefore should be remunerated at a lower rate.

The challenge of these three structural changes in the meat industry is made to both packers and organized workers. We will look at the response of each in turn and then examine the effects of these changes on independent packers, such as Square Deal, and their workers.

The major packers have responded by internal reorganization of production along lines similar to those developed by the beef processors. The process of reorganization began in the early 1960s. In 1961 for example, the packers spent $95 million for new plants and equipment.[7] Single-level plants designed to facilitate the uninterrupted flow of products from one stage of processing to another replaced the multistory factories of the earlier periods. The new plants, located near centers of animal production, attract workers for whom the largely unskilled work represents a steady source of income, not the loss of status it would be for workers with a history in the industry. The major packers have also been increasingly resistant to wage increases and other proposals submitted by the union in contract negotiation.

The unions have responded with three mutually reinforcing responses. The various unions representing packing-house workers have merged, and that union in turn merged with the Retail Clerks Union. There has also been considerable strike activity, and many of these stoppages have been protracted. A third response has been the attempt to organize presently unorganized workers.

The small independent packers left in the older industrial cities experience enormous pressures. Competition from boxed beef, the chain stores, and the traditional giants of the industry now owned by conglomerates threatens profits and, frequently, the continued existence of the firms. Their labor force has long been accustomed to influencing wages and conditions of employment. Both companies and the union feel pressure to adjust to new demands by the federal government for compliance with health and safety regulations, sanitation inspection laws, and affirmative action legislation. The situation for the independent packers is fraught with uncertainty. All concerned feel victimized to a greater or lesser extent by external forces over which they perceive they have little control.

Square Deal Packing is now the last firm in its city that both slaughters and processes pork. Square Deal eliminated its beef-slaughtering operation because it could not compete with the major packers or the new beef-processing firms which now sell boxed beef to local grocery stores in the city. Other operations have been eliminated, and technological innovation and speedup have reduced the work force still further. This drastic decline in the demand for its product has caused a rather substantial drop in the Square Deal work force, from a peak of over eighteen hundred in the 1960s to about one thousand today.

THE IMPACT OF RETRENCHMENT
AT SQUARE DEAL

The dramatic deterioration in Square Deal's market position that led to a nearly 50-percent drop in the number of employees has hurt all categories of workers. Nevertheless, it is generally believed among the remaining workers in the plant—and our research has confirmed this belief—that the women have borne the brunt of the firm's retrenchment. This section explains why the women were pushed out of the plant.

Women at Square Deal first received the same starting wages as men in 1959. The company had made it clear the year before that "with the equalization of male and female rates, separate male and female seniorities had been abolished."[8] The union opposed the abolition of sexual job designations, and its view prevailed, at least for a time. The Civil Rights Act of 1964, however, outlawed dual seniority provisions, and the men's and women's seniority lists were merged in 1967.

The push to reduce the discrepancy between the starting wage of men and women began when the union first organized Square Deal in 1942. The company and the union had a series of meetings in 1958 to clarify the subject of male and female seniority. In the first meeting, the union president said, "In September when male and female rates are equalized in the plant, it is rumored that the company is planning to eliminate females whenever they can." The company replied, "Some jobs that are presently filled by girls will be given to men should the present occupants leave the employ of the company. In the case of layoffs the company would not resort to subterfuge to eliminate girls but neither would they be given preference because of their sex."

Why was the management of Square Deal so interested in eliminating women from its work force? In a word, the greater physical strength of men makes them capable of performing a greater variety of jobs than women, and this attribute is highly valued by management in a period when many workers must be laid off. In order to explain this fully, we must examine the workings of the seniority system.

After an initial thirty-day probationary period, a worker's access to jobs, to work in other departments, and to promotions is determined by seniority. In the event of reduction in the labor force, the person with the least seniority is the first laid off and is the last to be recalled. These general principles of seniority serve both management and workers, but in somewhat different ways. From the workers' perspective, use of seniority as the primary allocating mechanism for jobs, promotions, and some benefits inhibits arbitrary behavior on the part of employers. The employer benefits to the extent that seniority creates a stable and, it is hoped, loyal work force. At Square Deal (as well as at other packing plants and most other establishments with a seniority system) there is a combination of departmental and plant seniority. After thirty days a person acquires seniority in a department, but only after a year does he or she acquire plantwide seniority. A worker maintains departmental seniority until such time as written confirmation of transfer to another department is filed. Thus, a person may work on a temporary basis in one department while maintaining seniority in his or her original department. Job openings within departments are filled on the basis of departmental seniority.

For the purposes of this essay, the significance of these regulations is that once a worker has acquired plantwide seniority, he or she has the right to displace workers in other departments with less seniority when there are layoffs. Plantwide seniority provides protection against "going on the street," but not against forced transfer to another department. Within departments, however, the hierarchy of skills and degree of unpleasantness of the different jobs are ordered by departmental, not plantwide seniority. The job that the senior worker takes when he or she bumps a junior employee out of a department is thus normally at the bottom of the department's skill hierarchy.

This combination of plant and departmental seniority provides strong incentives for workers to remain in their original departments. Even if a worker has many years of plant seniority, his or her ability to bid on the better jobs within the department, as well as a host of lesser privileges (such as choice of vacation times and even who gets to punch out first at closing time), depends on departmental seniority. From the perspective of management, departmental seniority encourages the development of a labor force experienced in the operations of a particular unit of the company and familiar with its machinery and tools. Indeed, a seniority system without some form of departmental seniority would create havoc for management. With every layoff, the most junior worker would leave while the remaining workers engaged in an enormous game of musical chairs, with seniority determining who got the best seats. With the entire work force reshuffled every time there was a layoff, the plant would be in chaos.

The nature of the seniority system has a number of implications for the status of women and minorities at Square Deal. For example, even though the contractual seniority agreements apply equally to men and women, white and minority, the departmental system reinforces and perpetuates any discriminatory effect of initial job placement by discouraging transfers between departments. A department may offer little room for advancement or may have unpleasant or unhealthy working conditions for all its workers. But remaining within the department with much seniority may still be preferable to moving to another department where one will necessarily have the least seniority. Thus, women and blacks become locked into their original departments even if they have undesirable jobs.

Of far greater significance, however, is that these rules have motivated management to cease hiring women. This is because when layoffs occur, senior workers end up with the worst jobs in their new departments, for it is these jobs which the most junior workers, who are being bumped, have held. The worst jobs are also most often the most physically demanding. The women were either physically unable to perform these arduous tasks or did so only with grave risk of injuring themselves. The typical man was stronger than the typical woman and thus could perform a greater range of activities. This flexibility is especially valued in a production system such as the one at Square Deal, in which there is great variation on a daily, monthly, and seasonal basis in both product and quantity produced. But flexibility becomes of paramount importance in bad times because of the continuous re-shuffling of jobs that accompanies any layoff, even where departmental seniority cushions the worst of this effect. Given the fact that women were paid the same wage as men for the same job, and given the fact that the seniority system could not give management enough flexibility to place women in jobs where their lesser physical strength was appropriate, management felt it had no choice but to virtually cease hiring women.

Half of the white male production workers in the plant in 1978 were hired after 1957, and two-thirds of their black counterparts were hired after that date. In contrast, only 5 percent of the white female production workers were hired after 1957. Of the workers hired between 1943 and 1952, 29 percent were women. If women had been hired and retained on the payroll subsequent to 1953 in the same proportion as they were in the ten previous years, there would now be 128 women workers (black and white) at Square Deal hired since 1957. Instead, there are 18. There "should" be 2.3 times as many women workers at the company as there now are.

Some of the women attempted to fight back by petitioning the union and the government for redress. Four filed grievances through the union but were told that they did not have a grievance because none of the contract provisions had been violated. At the union's suggestion, these four visited lawyers at a women's legal rights clinic in the city. They were told that the union should fight for them. The general steward went with the four to city- and state-level conferences on women's rights, but to no avail—no law had been broken, and the contract had not been violated.

The women forced out of Square Deal's labor force in the 1960s and 1970s most likely found themselves in difficult economic straits. Our study examined only the workers still at the factory in 1978, and thus we have only indirect evidence about those severed from the firm's payroll. Square Deal was located within the central city of its metropolitan area and, like central cities throughout the North, it has experienced slow growth, loss of jobs to the suburbs and the Sunbelt, and rising unemployment. The typical Square Deal worker clings to his or her ethnic neighborhood with its tight-knit social structure. Finding a job within a reasonable commuting distance was thus not easy.

The difficult employment situation of the laid-off women was compounded by the fact that by 1978, Square Deal was the only packing house left in the metropolitan area. Branch plants of the major packers as well as other independent packers had all closed their doors in the 1960s and 1970s. A few grocery stores still employed their own butchers, but this was of little help in finding a job: those laid off from Square Deal were not journeyman butchers. Thus, layoff from Square Deal meant entering a labor market with a high level of unemployment where one's skills were not valued. Older women in their forties and fifties faced a bleak prospect indeed.

THE COSTS OF LAYOFF

The reduction in the size of Square Deal's labor force came about through permanent severance of workers from the company's payroll and failure to replace normal attrition, and also through a substantial increase in temporary layoffs of workers who continued in the firm's employ. These temporary layoffs were very unevenly distributed among different sex and race categories for the same reasons that permanent separation was disproportionately experienced by women. Since we have no direct information about those who have left the firm permanently, we can only make qualified guesses about the impact of the firm's cutbacks on them. But for those whose layoffs were only temporary and are still with the firm, we can estimate the costs of those layoffs with some precision.

Table 5.1 shows the average number of layoffs by race, sex, and seniority of production workers on the payroll in January 1978. At every seniority level except the last period, when only two women were hired, white women averaged more layoffs per worker than white men. For instance, for every ten white males hired in the mid-1950s, one has been laid off once during his career at Square Deal. By contrast, the average white woman hired during the same period has been laid off more than twice, and thus is twenty times more likely to have been laid off as a comparable white man. The one white woman hired in the late 1950s has been laid off six times. The few black women hired in the early 1970s have also suffered many layoffs—altogether, the four of them experienced ten layoffs. The contrasts between black and white men are much smaller than the differences between men and women; black men are slightly more likely to have been laid off than white men. Of the men hired since 1942 (when the first black was hired), whites averaged 0.56 layoffs and blacks, 0.82.

Women, and to a lesser extent, blacks, experienced not merely more layoffs but also longer ones. We have measured the length of the workers' layoffs and the wages that they would have earned had they remained in the company's employ.[9] Table 5.1 shows that losses from layoffs and demotions vary widely according to seniority and confirms our perceptions of the differential impact of the firm's retrenchment on its workers. The average white women's losses from layoffs were larger than the average white men's at every seniority level except the most recent (when only two women were hired). White men hired before 1973 averaged only $31 per person in wages lost from layoffs during their entire career at Square Deal. The white women, however, had a dramatically different experience. For those hired before 1952, career losses were quite small—$35 or less depending on seniority. But for women hired in the mid-1950s, losses from layoffs were much larger, nearly $3,600 per worker. The one white woman hired between 1963 and 1973 lost over $4,000. We have argued earlier that in 1958, since men's and women's wages were about to be equalized, management decided to stop hiring women and not to protect the jobs of women remaining in the plant when retrenchment occurred. Women hired before 1953 apparently had enough seniority to protect their jobs by the time the layoffs started in earnest in the 1960s. But the newer women workers did not, as the data forcefully show. The losses of the four black women hired between 1968 and 1972 were substantially greater than those of men with the same seniority. The black women's career losses amounted to $625 while the men's averaged $95. Black men's losses were roughly the same as white men's except in the most recent period.

The figures for losses from demotions also offer some interesting comparisons. Because of the discrimination in placement within the plant, the women were rarely promoted into the higher-grade, better-paying jobs. When the firm's reverses began, they did not have as far to fall down the job hierarchy as the white men who held the better jobs. Except for those hired in the mid-1950s, white women's losses from demotion were smaller than comparable white men's. The white men hired in the 1940s and early 1950s suffered losses in the vicinity of $300, but those hired later experienced much smaller losses. (Some of these relatively high losses for white males hired before 1952 are probably "voluntary." As their physical strength declined, older work-

Table 5.1. Average Number of Layoffs and Average Monetary Losses from
Layoffs and Demotions for Production Workers, January 1978

Seniority (first hired)	Number of workers	Layoffs per worker	Loss per worker (average)		
			All economic reverses	Layoff	Demotion
1928–1937					
White Males	10	.40	$ 101.00	0	$ 83.18
Females	3	1.67	0	0	0
Black Males	0	—	—	—	—
Females	0	—	—	—	—
1938–1942					
White Males	31	.09	368.10	0	260.78
Females	8	.37	170.65	$ 9.97	160.68
Black Males	1	0	30.68	0	30.68
Females	0	—	—	—	—
1943–1947					
White Males	44	.26	357.00	29.62	296.58
Females	24	.42	242.95	35.23	207.73
Black Males	13	.50	511.82	4.92	499.40
Females	0	—	—	—	—
1948–1952					
White Males	75	.09	417.21	2.65	366.92
Females	32	.50	197.91	12.59	165.96
Black Males	7	0	582.14	0	537.38
Females	0	—	—	—	—
1953–1957					
White Males	71	.11	268.26	13.10	151.52
Females	10	2.27	3865.60	3595.60	269.80
Black Males	28	.04	223.61	0.53	223.09
Females	0	—	—	—	—
1958–1962					
White Males	46	.83	406.30	71.55	119.20
Females	1	4.00	1024.70	625.62	399.07
Black Males	11	1.08	286.63	131.67	154.96
Females	0	—	—	—	—
1963–1967					
White Males	54	.66	371.93	18.13	286.42
Females	0	—	—	—	—
Black Males	27	.65	290.82	28.03	232.10
Females	0	—	—	—	—
1968–1972					
White Males	73	.66	461.86	119.29	190.26
Females	1	6.00	4670.90	4670.90	0
Black Males	38	.62	368.85	49.98	250.28
Females	4	2.50	730.17	625.46	104.71

Table 5.1. (*continued*)

Seniority (first hired)	Number of workers	Layoffs per worker	Loss per worker (average)		
			All economic reverses	Layoff	Demotion
1973–1977					
White Males	57	1.53	1660.30	1385.10	10.09
Females	2	1.00	389.13	163.69	225.44
Black Males	24	2.54	2196.30	2112.10	51.50
Females	0	—	—	—	—
F Statistic			12.45	19.56	1.98
Significance			.0000	.0000	.004

ers frequently bid for lower-paid but less strenuous assignments.) Black males as a whole suffered the largest losses from demotion of any group. Black men who had the greatest loss were hired around 1950, and their losses averaged about $20 per year since they were hired.

The data presented here support and clarify the analysis presented earlier. We have argued that the burdens of Square Deal's retrenchment have fallen unevenly on the different race and sex groups. All of the workers have been hurt by Square Deal's economic reverses, but the women, especially the older white women, have suffered most. The men and women hired before 1952 have emerged relatively unscathed in the process we have been describing. They have experiencd little loss from layoff and only moderate losses from demotions. For example, the white men hired between 1938 and 1942 have averaged about $10 per year in losses from both sources since they began working at Square Deal. After 1952 the picture changes remarkably. Women's economic losses mounted dramatically, mostly because of layoffs.

These calculations do not pretend to be a complete estimate of the cost to the workers of the firm's retrenchment. For example, if the firm had not been experiencing economic reverses, it is likely that many workers would have received a promotion instead of a demotion. In addition, the local union acceded to management's demands for across-the-board wage increases below those mandated by the national contract because of the distressed situation of the firm. Indeed, these negotiated "give-backs" have continued, occurring during the winter of 1982. And furthermore, these calculations include only straight-time wages, not fringe benefits.

A few remarks are appropriate to place these calculations of monetary losses or retrenchment in perspective. The white women hired in the mid-1950s averaged nearly $4,000 in losses from layoffs and demotions since they were hired. Most of these losses were incurred between 1968, when the egg-candling department was closed, and 1973, when the night sausage department was closed. Four thousand dollars spread over two decades would have been considerably less worrisome than that amount concentrated in one or a few years. An interesting contrast can be drawn between the losses from layoff and demotion and the benefits from the equalization of wage rates that the union brought to the women. In 1942, when the union arrived at Square Deal, the women's starting wage was 73 percent of the men's. If women had continued to earn 73 percent as much as men between 1959 (when parity was reached) and 1978, the average full-time woman worker would have earned nearly $40,000 less than she actually did. The equalization of wage rates played a prominent role in the process which led to women's bearing the brunt of the firm's retrenchment. This equalization brought *gains* to the women who were able to remain in the plant. In monetary terms, these gains far exceeded the losses incurred by the women which resulted from the way in which management responded to sexual parity in wage rates. Of course, from the women's (and our) point of view, they deserved both wage parity and continuous employment.

NONMONETARY COSTS OF RETRENCHMENT

So far we have dwelt on the more obvious consequences of Square Deal's retrenchment, the permanent or temporary layoff of workers. There are, however, a variety of other costs to the worker that normally escape the researcher's attention. Because of the nature of our research design, we were able to investigate these other costs. As with the monetary costs of the firm's retrenchment, these are spread very unevenly among the different sex and race groups.

In order to survive in the competitive environment of the 1960s and 1970s, Square Deal closed unprofitable operations, mechanized others, increased the pace of work (speedup), and reorganized the production process. These measures allowed the company to reduce its labor force by nearly one-half. As the firm contracted, workers with lesser plant seniority were discharged, and workers who remained were frequently squeezed out of their home departments to find work wherever possible within the plant. The forced departure from job and department has had a number of consequences for the workers. Since women and to a lesser extent black men were concentrated in departments which were closed or in jobs which were abolished, they have disproportionately borne these costs of internally restructuring the firm. These costs are as follows.

First, various perquisites associated with departmental seniority were lost. Departmental seniority gives the worker a variety of advantages. Not only can the most senior worker bid on a preferred job within the department, but he or she also has other advantages, the most important of which is choice of vacation time.

Second, the change of job and department frequently results in injury or stress-related disease. Most of these are simple muscle strains which come from performing the new task. Others are from knife cuts which result almost inevitably as new operations are learned. Still other medical problems are associated with the stress of changing one's job and the effect this has on preexisting arthritic or hypertensive conditions that are common among the firm's workers. Considerable physical stress comes from moving between departments with very different temperature and humidity conditions: some butchering operations are carried out in what amounts to giant refrigerators while many others are performed in a hot and steamy room where the newly slaughtered carcasses are scalded.

The most severe injuries associated with the change in work assignments happened to women who attempted to do heavy laborers' jobs beyond their physical strength. The cases of particular women are known among the female employees and were frequently raised with the investigator during the time she spent in the plant. Women who attempted to lift heavy loads unassisted injured their backs. Several were injured severely enough to require months away from work. These injuries or the threat of injury forced many of the women to accept temporary or even permanent layoffs.

Third, there are psychological effects to forced changes in work assignments. Externally imposed, comprehensive changes in work environment affect the way people think about themselves. There are immediate stresses and tribulations of adjusting to a new work environment. As jobs were eliminated or mechanized, old skills were devalued, threatening a loss in self-esteem. Movement to a new department or new shift meant that old friendships and work relationships were disrupted or lost. More stress is felt by those men and women who spend lengthy periods without a job or even a department that is permanently theirs. There are workers from the 1973 closing of the night manufacturing department who had not signed into a new department five years later, when our field work was conducted. No sooner had a worker adjusted to a new department when he or she was bumped yet again into another department, continuing the odyssey about the plant. Such workers can never set down their roots, build new relationships, and hone new skills.

THE SUBTLETIES OF SEXUAL AND RACIAL OPPRESSION

So far our presentation has been straightforward. The message is that the convergence of competitive pressures and of contractual and legal obligations, administered fairly by both union and management, resulted in the disproportionate costs borne by women and blacks as the firm struggled to keep its head above water. But we would now like to move the argument beyond this point. Both management and union officials, trapped by their sexism and racism, failed to respond flexibly to the unique conditions of women and blacks, thereby exacerbating an already bad situation. It is clear that managers and labor leaders alike believed themselves to be bending over backwards to fulfill their obligations to women and blacks. Indeed, if the company had suspected that any of its managers were discriminating in any way, it would not have permitted us to enter its gates. The insensitive response of both management and union has embittered the women and contributed to a marked decline in the local union's militance. In order to make our case, we will describe three situations in some detail.

June (not her real name) was about fifty-five in 1973 when the night manufacturing department closed. She was physically small—only a little over five feet tall and weighing about one hundred pounds. Her story was told often in the women's locker room to illustrate the unreasonable demands upon displaced women. One job assigned to her on the day shift was to push meat carts weighing over one thousand pounds to be weighed. Another job was to insert gambrels in the hind legs of hogs as they came out of the scald tank. She hurt her back badly attempting this work. At the time of the study, she had a relatively light job of inserting plastic bags of meat into a machine which created a vacuum. The work involves reaching above eye level and removing the hands before the machine lid returns. June found the work difficult and was frustrated by her inability to perform it well;

"I guess I'm too old to learn a new job," she said. "I'm not as fast as before; I must be getting old." "I can't be a spring chick any more." The other women attempted to reassure her, but each effort was met with a reply about her age.

Phil was one of the men incorporated into the consolidated cut-and-kill gang. The slaughtering and initial butchering, performed in extremely hot and humid conditions, is followed by placing the carcasses in a cooler overnight. The next morning the remainder of the butchering operations are carried out in a refrigerated room. Formerly, there was sufficient demand to warrant slaughtering and butchering all day long, thereby allowing two different gangs to specialize. Now the workers are required to work in the cooler in the morning and in the hot, steamy cut room in the afternoon.

Phil was not used to the extreme heat of the cut room, especially when summer weather intensified it. The problem arose when Phil was out of work for four weeks for health reasons. When the doctors authorized his return, Phil failed several times to show up when he said he would. In a meeting with a union steward and the plant superintendent, Phil assured them that medical problems which had caused him to miss work in the past were under control. His hypertension was controlled by medication, and he was participating in a program for alcoholics. The problem was, as the steward explained, "He didn't look forward to coming into the cut—he experienced sick feelings." The company management and the (male) steward agreed that this was a reasonable explanation for his repeated failures to come to work, and that if he returned to the plant he could have a job in another department. The company and the union acknowledged in this meeting and at other times that some other men did not make the transition to the consolidated gang.

The contrast between Jane and Phil strikes us as informative. An alcoholic who complained of "sick feelings" was allowed to transfer to a new department and a new job with union and management approval. Women who were faced with the choice between risk of severe physical injury or layoff were told that the seniority system could not permit them to take a less demanding job.

We have deliberately overdrawn this contrast in order to make our point. In fact, considerable efforts were made to find suitable jobs for the women. Women assigned to strenuous jobs were often assisted by sympathetic men. In one case, two women were told that they might lift boxes together rather than separately (even though this must have lowered their productivity). (Indeed, cooperation of this sort is common in the plant. Younger men often cover for older men nearing retirement age when the work becomes difficult for them. On at least one occasion, a steward criticized a foreman for asking an older man near retirement to work overtime.) In addition, some women apparently refused jobs not because they were physically incapable of performing them, but because the new jobs were not considered "women's work." For example, the two women refused the box-lifting job mentioned above. Their refusal had more to do with culturally reinforced stereotypes of what is proper than with physical capabilities.

Another example relates to the differential way in which the speedup of men's and women's jobs was perceived. A new frankfurter-stuffing machine was set in such a way that twice as many franks were hung on rods (which in turn were placed on metal "trees" to be taken to the smoke room) as with the machine it replaced. The women who lifted the rods of hanging franks as they came back from the smoke room so that the casings could be peeled were accordingly required to lift twice as much weight as formerly. This, of course, greatly increased the stress of the job. One woman's doctor even suggested she take an early retirement rather than continue to strain her back and arms. (This new machine and a sausage-stuffing machine in the same department were now operated by four men, replacing about twenty women who had held the best-paying women's jobs in the plant.) The machine was held responsible for the increased weight per rod by both union officials and management. It was clear, however, that the machine could have been easily reset. This is thus a classic case of speedup.

The women adversely affected by these changes were faced with a situation subtly different from that of the men also affected by management's speedup. For example, the line in the cut-and-kill room used to be set at 300 hogs per hour. At one point it was raised to 426 per hour, but the room became too congested for safe, accurate work. After some experimentation, the rate now rests at 320 hogs per hour. The new rate was determined by negotiations among workers, union officials, and management. None of the individual men in that context were put in the position of publicly affirming physical inability to perform a job when the speed was increased. All could legitimate their objections by reference to very real safety considerations. The situation of the women operating the peeler was different. The peeler operator could object from the beginning to the change in the physical demands of her job, and using the union, negotiate changes in the weight per rod until a satisfactory solution was reached. This very reasonable and probable workable solution, however, must be examined in its social context. One woman working on one machine affirms publicly that she cannot do her job and persuades both the union and management that her objections are legitimate, not just evidence of physical weakness on her part. This is similar to the situation of June, the vacuum-packing–machine operator discussed above, but very different from the situation of the men who could speak as a group concerned with safety. To state the issue very baldly, the women's lesser physical strength was considered to be their own fault, about which little could be done.

An example of the subtle interplay between sexism and racism is found in the case of the worker whom we call Sally. One form of rationalizing production instituted in recent years has entailed use of production workers in quasi-supervisory positions. A leadman or leadlady oversees production procedures, functioning as a kind of "assistant foreman," but does not have the authority to directly order other workers. Leadpersons retain their positions in the union but receive a bonus. The leadperson is regarded as having the most seniority in the department if issues such as bidding on a job, vacation selection, or layoffs arise. Management, of course, feels that it must be able to grant this seniority to the leadman/lady since production would be disrupted if an assistant foreman who happened to be junior was transferred out of the department whenever fluctuations in output occurred. By now the reader should be aware of the crucial importance of seniority to the worker. Management's alteration of the rules of seniority, however well-intentioned, clearly creates a potentially explosive situation. In some departments, notably cut and kill, the lead position, in spite of the inherent tensions, has worked well. But in other situations, a bitter taste has been left in the mouths of the workers. One such incident which we describe illustrates the vulnerability of women and blacks to the negative consequences of automatically assuming they are "the same as" the remainder of the work force.

Square Deal hired its first black women production workers in 1970. White and black workers knew that they were hired in order to comply with the Civil Rights Act. The women were accepted with little incident. One of them, Sally, was assigned to a traditionally women's department, the bacon room. Her white co-workers described her as "a wonderful person to work with," a "good worker." The three black women who had the lowest seniority were the first affected by the 1974 layoffs. They were bumped into other departments and had to do the same work as the men. Sally could not afford a layoff; she had a child to support. She took hard jobs, including pushing carts of sausages weighing up to two and one-half tons to the smoke room. The men would occasionally help, but mostly she did the work herself. Eventually, Sally was able to return to the bacon room. She refused an offer of promotion to foreperson for the same reason other blacks have refused the job—there is too much pressure associated with the foremanship and there is no union protection if the company wants to fire you. Indeed, several black men who had been promoted to foreman in the company's attempts at affirmative action had been laid off and not rehired.

Sally was then offered the job of leadlady in her department, partly because there was a reassignment of foremen in the plant and the regular bacon room foreman was now spending much of his time in another department. According to Sally, he left without teaching her how to use a new computer installed in the department. Sally took the books home with her and taught herself how to service the computer. She also learned to break down and assemble the machines, but here her work was always checked and double-checked by the foreman.

In many ways Sally was placed in a no-win situation: for a variety of reasons, the white women with seniority in the department resented her in her new role as their leadlady. According to the white women, the difference in Sally after her promotion was like that between Dr. Jekyll and Mr. Hyde. She became overbearing and bossy. The more serious problem, from the perspective of the older workers, was that she who had less than five years seniority remained in the department while older women with many more years of seniority were forced to be loaned out to other departments. Sally and the white workers agree that there was a work slowdown and that some attempts were made to discredit her as supervisor by turning out below-standard work. Sally confronted the resentment of the women workers with little or no effective support from management. During the crucial period when she was learning her new responsibilities and assuming a new role in regard to her co-workers, the department foreman was only infrequently present.

The situation reached a crisis. Higher levels of management became aware of what was happening and intervened to reestablish the active role of a foreman in the department. Without the protected seniority of the leadlady position, Sally once again became the person with the least seniority in the department. She soon was transferred out to another department where she, once again, was expected to handle essentially laborer's work. And at least to some of the women workers in the department, the episode with Sally as leadlady has confirmed old convictions that black women are incapable of working in a supervisory capacity and that they can be expected to "take out their anger" on whites if they are put in a position of authority over them.

The difference in perspective between Sally and the white women in the department illustrates the problems of attempting to apply a general guideline (promote more women and minorities to supervisory positions) in isolation from consideration of the social context.

The costs to the workers of the firm's retrenchment are at first blush fairly obvious, foremost being loss of wages. Even the non-quantifiable costs, such as increased risk of injury, are easily evident. But the issue is far more complex than a mere listing of costs suggests. The subtleties of racism and sexism are woven throughout the fabric of our story. Neither a description nor a solution to these problems is simple.

CONCLUSION

By 1960 Square Deal Packing Company ceased openly discriminating against women and minorities. With the merging of men's and women's seniority lists in 1967, both the union and the company gave the appearance of complying with the spirit as well as the letter of the Civil Rights Act of 1964. There were no gender-specific job designations or promotion ladders. The wages of men and women, blacks and whites, with equal seniority were virtually identical. The traditional research methodology would not have found any racial or sexual discrimination. But the in-depth interviews and on-the-scene observation, and the statistical analysis which it inspired, have painted a very different picture. Women, and to a lesser extent blacks, bore a disproportionate share of the burden of the firm's retrenchment.

The frustration and bitterness felt particularly by the women added to the general demoralization which blanketed the factory. The union, in which the women had formerly played a militant and spirited role, was considerably weakened without their enthusiastic support. The women's sense of betrayal goes beyond the factory gates. They believe that it was the bureaucrats from Washington who prevented the union from saving the women's jobs. It is ironic that a contractual provision drafted to protect women's jobs should become illegal under a law intended to advance women's civil rights. But the irony is lost on those women who have lost their jobs. The following are a few of the comments that were heard from the workers in the plant.

I'd like to have Carter send his wife to do our jobs, then he'd change his mind [about civil rights].

Women's lib is for those who have education so they can get the same pay as men, but not for those in factory work. It's for judges who have secretaries to work for them; not for people who have to do heavy work like us.

Now the men have all our easy jobs and the women have the heavy labor jobs. Equal rights, [expletive]!

It should be clear that such views cannot be dismissed as blue-collar conservatism; the strong reaction arises from concrete experience and observation over a long period of time.

This research calls into question the notion of formal equality. It is part of the ideology of capitalism that equity is synonymous with applying rules equally to everyone. For the most part this was done at Square Deal but with severely unequal results. The elimination of sexual and racial oppression thus involves more than the making and implementing of rules. It is particularly true when the economy is undergoing a thorough restructuring which has produced both public and private austerity. This is not to say that liberal reforms are pointless or even counterproductive. The union's commitment to sexual and racial equality was key to its success, and millions have benefited from civil rights legislation. Instead, this research can serve to focus attention on the critical role of the sensitivity to sexual and racial oppression on the part of the leaders of the labor movement, and by implication the movement for social change generally.

NOTES

This research was carried out under the auspices of the U.S. Commission on Civil Rights. The data gathered are used with the permission of the commission, but the analysis presented here is the sole responsibility of the authors.

1. Amalgamated Meat Cutters and Butcher Workmen of North America, "Report on the Packinghouse Industry," unpublished paper, 1961.
2. Amalgamated Meat Cutters, "Meat Industry Collective Bargaining," unpublished paper, 1971.
3. U.S. Department of Labor, Industry Manpower Surveys, *Meat Packing*, No. 101 (September 1961), p. 2.
4. Amalgamated Meat Cutters, "Report on the Packinghouse Industry," 1961, pp. 12–15.
5. Ibid., pp. 5–15.
6. Amalgamated Meat "Meat Industry Collective Bargaining," 1971, pp. 4–5.

7. U.S. Department of Labor, Industry Manpower Surveys, *Meat Packing*, No. 101 (September 1961), p. 2.
8. The issue of merged seniority lists is discussed in minutes from a meeting on November 21, 1958, between representatives of the union and the company.
9. This is not an entirely straightforward calculation. If a laid-off worker has remained on the payroll, he or she would have been granted the annual step increase in wages granted all employees as stipulated in the union contract. Since many of the layoffs were quite lengthy, the failure to include these step increases in the calculations would lead to an underestimation, possibly serious, of the loss in wages.

The calculations are based on straight-time wages and do not reflect fringe benefits, overtime, night bonuses, and so forth. We have also excluded from our calculations of monetary loss any unemployment compensation, public assistance, food stamps, or other transfers received while unemployed. Furthermore, we have not adjusted our data according to the date of layoff. Prices have risen steadily, and thus earlier losses should have carried a greater weight than current ones. Similarly, we have not adjusted these calculations for what economists call the time discount or different preferences for when workers might have had the layoff. This calculation would have taken into account the most people would rather have the layoff later rather than sooner. This implies that the estimates we have made of costs of retrenchment are underestimated, but the relative ranking of the four race-sex groups would probably change little if time discounts were taken into account since the layoffs and demotions were experienced at roughly the same time.

6

Capital Mobility Versus Upward Mobility: The Racially Discriminatory Consequences of Plant Closings and Corporate Relocations

GREGORY D. SQUIRES

In 1964 the Charles Todd Laundries decided to close its inner-city shop and gradually open several suburban facilities. By 1975 the original site was closed, the suburban laundries were operating, and minority employment had been reduced from 75 percent to less than 5 percent of all workers. Officials, clerical workers, and truck drivers (virtually all of whom were white) were offered jobs at one of the new locations. The laundry workers (most of whom were black) were not even informed of the shift. If they wanted to stay with Charles Todd they were told they had to inquire about job opportunities at the individual locations, and if they found jobs, they would not carry over their seniority with the company. The minority laundry workers filed suit (*Braddix* v. *Todd,* No. 74-110-E [SD Ill. May 19, 1979]), charging the company with violating Title VII of the Civil Rights Act of 1964 which prohibits employment discrimination, and they won. In 1979 eighty plaintiffs received a small cash payment and job offers.

This case illustrates four critical characteristics of the American political economy. First, capital mobility can have severe racially discriminatory consequences. Second, at least under certain circumstances, those consequences result from illegal actions, and current civil rights laws can be utilized to obtain some relief. But third, more than effective enforcement of civil rights laws is necessary if equality for minorities is to become a fact of American life. Fourth, despite a long history of racism on the part of organized labor and the working class, racial minorities and labor generally can no longer afford to ignore a common foe, the virtually unchecked power of private capital.

The increasing frequency of shutdowns in all regions of the country, plant relocations, and economic dislocation generally has caused many workers, public officials, and even some corporate executives to reconsider fundamental beliefs about the nature of American society and the rights of various groups within it. Ignored, however, are the racially discriminatory consequences. An understanding of the racial dynamics of capital mobility, however, suggests some new approaches to the problems of dislocation generally and also reveals potentially powerful tactics for more effective civil rights struggles.

CIVIL RIGHTS IN THE 1980s

The adverse impact of economic dislocation on blacks, Hispanics, and other minorities results from a number of direct and indirect factors. During the past few decades, while economic development has been greatest in the Sunbelt states and in suburban communities within metropolitan areas around the country, the minority population has increased faster in the Northeast and Midwest and within central cities (primarily as a result of discriminatory practices in suburban housing markets). Minority workers are concentrated in those industries and within those occupations which have been the hardest hit by shutdowns and relocations. Minority-owned businesses make up a disproportionately small share of U.S. businesses and account for an even smaller share of profits. And holding a disproportionately small share of top-level professional jobs, minorities are less likely to receive relocation or job-hunting assistance when their employers shut down or move.

The most explicit evidence of the discriminatory consequences of capital mobility was recently provided by the Illinois Advisory Committee to the U.S. Commission on Civil Rights (see *Shutdown: Economic Dislocation and Equal Opportunity*), which examined minority employment in Illinois firms which shut down or relocated between

1975 and 1978. The study found that minorities (blacks, Hispanics, Asians, and American Indians) accounted for 20 percent of the total employment in firms which closed down compared to just 14 percent of the statewide labor force. In firms relocating from Illinois to the South, minority employment declined from 23.3 percent to 21.1 percent. Minority employment also declined in firms moving to Illinois from the South, though this decline was just from 29.9 percent to 29.3 percent. Among firms relocating from central city to suburban locations, total employment declined and minorities lost almost 20 percent of the jobs they held compared to less than 10 percent for whites.

In Illinois approximately three-quarters of the minority population is black, and these figures reflect the impact of capital mobility primarily on blacks. For Hispanics, however, the general impact was also negative. Among Illinois firms that shut down, Hispanics accounted for 5.6 percent of all employees compared to 2.9 percent statewide. In firms relocating to the South, Hispanic employment declined from 8.7 percent to 7.6 percent although Hispanics constitute a larger proportion of the work force in the South than in Illinois. Hispanic employment did increase in those firms moving from the South to Illinois from 6.9 percent to 8.4 percent. But it should be noted that the migration to the South accounted for more than twice as many jobs as did the move to the North. Among all companies involved in relocations between Illinois and the South, Hispanic employment declined from 8.3 percent to 7.9 percent.

Not surprisingly, relocation from Illinois to the West increased Hispanic employment (from 6.7 percent to 13.8 percent) and, in terms of net numbers of jobs, more than offset the decline in Hispanic employment (12.9 percent to 11.5 percent) in firms moving to Illinois from the West. Altogether Hispanic employment increased from 7.6 percent to 13.4 percent in firms involved in relocations between Illinois and the West. Surprisingly, Hispanic employment also increased in those companies moving from an Illinois central city to a suburban location, from 3.9 percent to 4.7 percent. Given the far greater number of jobs lost due to shutdowns in Illinois (over 365,000 among firms reporting EEO-1 forms to the Equal Employment Opportunity Commission, which is the data base for this study) compared to the number involved in relocation between central cities and suburbs or between Illinois and all other states (less than 40,000), it is clear that Hispanics were adversely affected by capital mobility, though possibly not to the same extent as blacks.

Many of the forces operating in Illinois are operating elsewhere, of course, so there is reason to believe that this state's experience is not unique. While precisely comparable research has not been conducted elsewhere, other studies have found that plant closings and corporate relocations adversely affect minority workers in states including Michigan, Ohio, New York, New Jersey, Georgia, and Missouri.

The pattern of uneven development which the United States has experienced recently and the discriminatory consequences are not fortuitous occurrences or simply the results of a free market economy. Investment and foreign tax credits induce premature abandonment of viable production facilities in older northern tier and central city locations by discouraging investment in those facilities in favor of opening new plants in other, frequently Sunbelt and foreign, locations. Other provisions of the U.S. tax code have encouraged conglomerate merger activity in the 1960s and 1970s, which has led to shutdowns and increasing concentrations of wealth. Frequently, conglomerates purchase subsidiaries, utilize the profits of those subsidiaries to prop up other operations, and then shut them down after they have been milked dry. According to a Federal Trade Commission (FTC) study, recent merger activities "pose a serious threat to America's democratic and social institutions by creating a degree of centralized private decision-making that is incompatible with a free enterprise system" (FTC, 1979:5). Right-to-work laws in the South constitute another governmentally induced incentive for the Southern exodus. Failure to adequately enforce fair housing laws impedes the ability of minorities to move with their employers in many cases, or forces them to endure higher commuting costs. And according to one EEOC study, one of the factors which encourages some employers to relocate is a desire to avoid minority neighborhoods and minority employees. A former manager of the Automobile Club of Michigan, which recently moved from Detroit to a nearby suburb (and is currently being sued for violating Title VII as a result), asserted that one objective of his former employer was to "escape the obligation of hiring blacks" (Illinois Advisory Commission: 17).

In *Griggs* v. *Duke Power* (401 U.S. 424 [1971]), the U.S. Supreme Court ruled that an employment practice which adversely affects minority employment, regardless of the employer's intent, violates Title VII of the 1964 Civil Rights Act unless that decision is based on a legitimate business necessity (narrowly defined by the court). Following this decision, several civil rights legal experts have argued that relocation from a substantially minority community to a virtually all-white community which reduces minority representation in the current work force or in the pool of workers from which future employees are likely to be recruited is an employment practice which violates Title VII and other federal civil rights requirements. Even if the move can be justified on "business necessity" grounds, it is argued, the employer is obligated to mitigate the adverse impact. Therefore, these authorities maintain, the EEOC and the Office of Federal Contract Compliance Programs (OFCCP) of the Department of Labor should promulgate regulations under Title VII, Executive Order 11246, which establishes affirmative action requirements for federal contractors, and other civil rights statutes, directed at the discriminatory consequences of relocation. Such regulations would require employers contemplating relocation, shift of activities from one site to another, or any movement which substantially affects location of jobs to prepare an employee impact statement to assess the effects on minority employment. If an adverse impact is projected, employers would be required to consider alternative sites, reconsider the move altogether, or implement affirmative programs to mitigate that impact. Programs could include transfer rights for current employees (white as well as nonwhite) with employers paying relocation expenses, housing or transportation services or allowances, pressure on local officials to assure fair housing practices, and affirmative recruitment practices.

The few court decisions on the civil rights implications of corporate relocations have yielded mixed results with plaintiffs faring far better when a series of discriminatory employment practices are proven to be associated with the move, as illustrated by the Todd case. For example, in *Mays* v. *Motorola* (No. 74 C2810 [ND Ill. January 26, 1979]), the Motorola Corporation was found in violation of Title VII because of a number of discriminatory interviewing and recruitment practices it had implemented for several years. Though it was tangential to the decision, the judge noted that the relocation of the company's principal production plant from Chicago to the predominantly white suburb of Schaumberg exacerbated the racial imbalances in the work force. In three other cases, however, (*EEOC* v. *North Hills Passavant Hospital* 466 F. Supp, 783 [WD Pa., Feburary 26, 1979], *Philadelphia* v. *Rumsfeld* No. 76-1090 [ED Pa., April 15, 1976], and *Jacobs* v. *California* No. C-730559 [ND Cal., April 6, 1973]), the court ruled in favor of the defendants on the grounds that while minorities were adversely affected by a relocation, the moves were justified as legitimate business necessities. Despite these mixed findings, there are circumstances where civil rights violations occur in the process of relocating. Promulgation of regulations by the EEOC and OFCCP directed to the discriminatory consequences of capital mobility would constitute an important step in the right direction.

FROM AFFIRMATIVE ACTION
TO ECONOMIC DEMOCRACY

But even these initiatives, which have so far been rejected by the EEOC and the OFCCP and are not likely to be adopted by them in the near future, would fail to address the fundamental cause of economic dislocation and the discriminatory consequences, and therefore would represent only a partial solution.

The fundamental issue is not geographic mobility of capital from one location to another or proportional representation among various segments of the population. The critical problem which racial minorities and workers in general must confront is the unequal ownership and control of the nation's economic resources and the use of those resources for private gain, often at great public expense. As one FTC consultant concluded:

> The private decisions of corporate owners and managers impose costs that affect other businesses, employees, and the community at large. The mental and physical well-being of the community is deleteriously affected; increased stress is placed upon the family; the quality of life in the community can be seriously decreased. Decisions with these wide-ranging effects cannot be viewed solely as private prerogatives; the internal decision-making calculations of the firm do not fully reflect actual costs involved. Public concern and participation is needed to insure that improperly estimated economic gains do not impose major economic costs. (C & R Associates, 1979b:70.)

The solution to the problems created by relocation, however, does not rest with some kind of incentive (for example, tax abatements, industrial revenue bonds, enterprise zones) to induce private corporations to redirect some of their capital investments or even a mandatory geographic capital allocation program. As economists Barry Bluestone and Bennett Harrison concluded:

> Plant closings are real, and the injury to workers and communities when a company closes down is real. But there is much more going on, and far more extensive injury, than "only" what relates explicitly to relocations. . . . The context within which to understand—and resist—plant

closings and relocations is the changing political-economic structure of international capitalism, specifically those changes in law, politics, and technology that have increased the mobility of private capital. Ultimately, unless we are prepared to seize control over these conditions, we will at best only cosmetically treat what is only one part of a much larger problem. (Bluestone and Harrison, 1979:1.)

The beginnings of an adequate response are embodied in a number of proposals which are currently being debated in Congress and in several state legislatures including Illinois, Wisconsin, Rhode Island, Massachusetts, Michigan, Washington, New York, Pennsylvania, Connecticut, Oregon, Maine, and elsewhere. Among the federal proposals are Rep. William D. Ford's (D-Mich.) National Employment Priorities Act; former Sen. Harrison Williams's (D-N.J.) Employee Protection and Community Stabilization Act; Rep. Peter H. Kostmayer (D-Pa.), Stanley Lundine (D-N.Y.), and Matthew F. McHugh's (D-N.Y.) Voluntary Job Preservation and Community Stabilization Act; Sen. Howard Metzenbaum's (D-Oh.) Employee Maintenance Act. These bills call for businesses to notify employees and public officials of any shutdown, relocation, or substantial reduction of facilities in advance (usually two years) of taking such action. Employees are to be offered jobs at the new facility or at other company locations if possible or provided severance pay based on their length of employment. These proposals call for companies to make a one-time payment into a community assistance fund to aid municipalities affected by the action. They also call for job-training and job-seeking assistance for affected workers. The Williams, Kostmayer, Lundine, and McHugh proposals also provide financial and technical assistance for employees to purchase and operate facilities that would otherwise shut down.

The state-level proposals ask for similar action, and some of these bills have been passed into law. Wisconsin has enacted a prenotification law requiring employers of one hundred or more people to advise the state's Department of Labor, Industry, and Human Relations sixty days prior to any merger, liquidation, disposition, relocation, or closing. Maine requires severance pay to affected employees equaling one week's wages for each year employed for those workers with more than three years of service whenever an establishment shuts down or relocates one hundred or more miles away. And Michigan provides financial and other assistance to facilitate employee takeovers.

Similar policies have been implemented through collective bargaining agreements. For example, under the terms of the 1979 contract signed by the United Rubber Workers, Goodyear, Firestone, B. F.

Goodrich, and Uniroyal must provide, among other considerations: six months' advance notice of any shutdown; full pension benefits after twenty-five years of service or five years for those over fifty-five for all workers losing jobs due to shutdowns; preferential hiring at other company plants; and the right to negotiate ways of saving a plant or the manner in which it will be closed if that is necessary.

Several Western European countries have taken more comprehensive action to minimize economic dislocation and the disruption which is created when shutdowns or relocations become necessary. In Sweden, employers must consult with employee representatives before relocating. Irreconcilable issues are referred to a labor court. Similarly, in West Germany no major relocation can occur without the agreement of works councils which are elected by employees. If an agreement cannot be reached, the government has the authority to construct a binding plan. And in England, as well as Sweden and West Germany, a variety of government assistance is provided to help workers relocate or retrain for jobs.

The unifying element of these policies and proposals, including the proposed affirmative action regulations described above, is that they are aimed at striking a balance between public needs and private interests, or achieving what David Smith has called "the public balance sheet." They quite openly call for the public sector and for employees to usurp some of those prerogatives which management has long considered, and still believes to be, its private domain. And the tactics for achieving this objective are based on three principal underlying tenets which distinguish them from conventional approaches to economic development. First, they are geared toward meeting public needs directly rather than through the back door of activities undertaken principally to maximize private profit. Second, they provide more equitable and accountable control over economic goods and services rather than concentration of resources in fewer and frequently more distant hands. And third, they aim for equal results for minorities within more democratic structures rather than equality of opportunity within a system characterized by rigid hierarchy.

Most of these policy initiatives are not generally viewed as civil rights issues. Yet it is becoming increasingly evident that racial and ethnic inequalities cannot be separated out from those inequalities which characterize American society in general. Civil rights and labor organizations both stand to benefit by acting together on these mutual concerns. For civil rights activists to effectively alter the objective conditions of minorities in the United States, they must begin to address these fundamental inequities. Challenging corporate power in general is not a substitute for effective civil rights enforcement and affirmative action. But it represents a dimension to the civil rights struggle which must be addressed if the civil rights challenges of the 1980s are to be met.

REFERENCES

Baron, Harold M. *The Demand for Black Labor*. Cambridge, Mass.: Radical America, 1971.

Bluestone, Barry, and Harrison, Bennett. "Capital Mobility and Economic Dislocation." Outline of paper commissioned by the Progressive Alliance, 1979.

————. *Capital and Communities: The Causes and Consequences of Private Disinvestment*. Washington, D.C.: The Progressive Alliance, 1980.

Blumrosen, Alfred W. "The Duty to Plan for Fair Employment: Plant Location in White Suburbia." *Rutgers Law Review* 25 (Spring 1971): 383–404.

————, and Blair, James H. *Enforcing Equality in Housing and Employment Through State Civil Rights Laws*. Newark, N.J.: Administrative Process Project of Rutgers Law School, 1972.

Boggs, James, and Boggs, Grace. *Racism and the Class Struggle*. New York: Monthly Review Press, 1970.

C & R Associates. *Plant Closing Legislation and Regulation in the United States and Western Europe: A Survey*. Report prepared for the Federal Trade Commission, 1979a.

————. *Measuring the Community Costs of Plant Closings: Overview of Methods and Data Sources*. Report prepared for the Federal Trade Commission, 1979b.

Christian, Charles Melvin. "The Impact of Industrial Relocations from the Black Community of Chicago Upon Job Opportunities and Residential Mobility of the Central City Workforce." Ph.D. diss., University of Illinois, 1975.

Cobb, Sidney, and Kasl, Stanislav V. *Termination: The Consequences of Job Loss*. Washington, D.C.: National Institute for Occupational Safety and Health, U.S. Department of Health, Education and Welfare, 1977.

Federal Trade Commission, *Economic Report on Corporate Mergers*. Washington, D.C.: U.S. Government Printing Office, 1969.

Frieden, Karl. *Workplace Democracy and Productivity*. Washington, D.C.: National Center for Economic Alternatives, 1980.

Geschwender, James A. *Class, Race, and Worker Insurgency*. New York: Cambridge University Press, 1977.

Hill, Herbert. "The AFL-CIO and the Black Worker." *Journal of Intergroup Relations* 10 (Spring 1982):5–79.

Hunnious, Gerry; Garson, David G.; and Case, John, eds. *Workers' Control: A Reader on Labor and Social Change*. New York: Vintage, 1973.

Illinois Advisory Committee to the U.S. Commission on Civil Rights. *Shutdown: Economic Dislocation and Equal Opportunity*. Washington, D.C.: U.S. Commission on Civil Rights, 1981.

Jackson, Samuel C., and Abramowitz, Michael E. "Housing, Transportation and Fair Employment." Paper presented at symposium in observation of the tenth anniversary of the EEOC. Rutgers Law School, 1975.

Kain, John F. *Housing Markets and Racial Discrimination: A Micro-Economic Analysis.* New York: Columbia University Press, 1975.

Kapp, William. *The Social Costs of Private Enterprise.* New York: Schocken, 1975.

Kelly, Edward. *Industrial Exodus.* Washington, D.C.: Conference on Alternative State and Local Policies, 1977.

Lowry, Ritchie P. "A Sociological View of Corporate Mergers." Paper presented at the 29th annual meeting of the Society for the Study of Social Problems, 1979.

McKenzie, Richard B. *Restrictions on Business Mobility: A Study in Political Rhetoric and Economic Reality.* Washington, D.C.: American Enterprise Institute, 1979.

Moberg, David. "Shuttered Factories, Shattered Communities." *In These Times,* June 27–July 3, 1979:11–14.

Nadel, Mark. *Corporations and Public Accountability.* Lexington, Mass.: Heath, 1976.

Nelson, Jack E. "The Impact of Corporate Suburban Relocations on Minority Employment Opportunities." Washington, D.C.: Equal Employment Opportunity Commission, 1974.

Perlo, Victor. *Economics of Racism USA.* New York: International, 1975.

Rifkin, Jeremy, and Barber, Randy. *The North Will Rise Again.* Boston: Beacon, 1978.

Schweke, William. *Plant Closing Strategy Packet.* Washington, D.C.: The Progressive Alliance and the Conference on Alternative State and Local Policies, 1980.

Smith, David, and McGuigan, Patrick. *Towards a Public Balance Sheet.* Washington, D.C.: National Center for Economic Alternatives, 1979.

Stokes, Bruce. *Worker Participation—Productivity and the Quality of Work Life.* Washington, D.C.: Worldwatch Institute, 1978.

Suburban Action Institute. "Petition to the United States Department of Labor for a Ruling That Union Carbide Is in Violation of Federal Contract Compliance Requirements Pursuant to Executive Order 11246." 1977.

Tabb, William K. *The Political Economy of the Black Ghetto.* New York: Norton, 1970.

U.S. Bureau of the Census. *Current Population Reports.* Series P-23, No. 37, "Social and Economic Characteristics of the Population in Metropolitan and Nonmetropolitan Areas: 1970 and 1960." Washington, D.C.: Government Printing Office, 1971.

———. *Current Population Reports.* Special Studies Series P-23, No. 75, "Social and Economic Characteristics of the Metropolitan and Non-metropolitan Population: 1977 and 1970." Washington, D.C.: Government Printing Office, 1978.

———. *Current Population Reports.* Series P-20, No. 334, "Demographic, Social, and Economic Profile of States: Spring 1976." Washington, D.C.: Government Printing Office, 1979.

———. *Current Population Reports.* Special Studies Series P-23, No. 80, "The Social and Economic Status of the Black Population in the United States: An Historical Overview, 1790–1978." Washington, D.C.: Government Printing Office, 1979.

————. *U.S. Census of Population: 1960* Vol. 1. *Characteristics of the Population*. Part 1, United States Summary. Washington, D.C.: Government Printing Office, 1964.

U.S. Commission on Civil Rights. *Equal Opportunity in Suburbia*. Washington, D.C.: U.S. Commission on Civil Rights, 1974.

Vanek, Jaroslav, ed. *Self-Management: Economic Liberation of Man*. Baltimore: Penguin, 1975.

Wilson, Franklin D. *Residential Consumption, Economic Opportunity, and Race*. New York: Academic, 1979.

Zwerdling, Daniel. *Democracy at Work*. Washington, D.C.: Democracy at Work, 1978.

7

The Urban Contradictions of Silicon Valley: Regional Growth and the Restructuring of the Semiconductor Industry

ANNALEE SAXENIAN

If small is beautiful, that mandate is fulfilled not chiefly in windmills and solar cells, but in California's vale of cubistic new factories across the bay from San Francisco—Santa Clara's Silicon Valley, where worlds indeed unfold in grains of sand.

George Gilder's words vividly convey the current mystique surrounding Silicon Valley (Gilder, 1981). The image of a pristine, futuristic seedbed of innovative industry which holds the promise of renewed vigor for America's lagging economy has captured the public imagination. Yet this gilded image bears little relationship to the realities of the California region to which it has been attributed.

The growth of Santa Clara County during the years since World War II has been explosive. It has also been highly contradictory. Prior to World War II, Santa Clara County was a sparsely populated agricultural valley. In the thirty years between 1940 and 1970, the county's population increased by almost one million people, from 174,949 to 1,066,421. Countywide employment doubled itself during each successive decade, resulting in the creation of about 350,000 new jobs. And personal and family incomes rapidly surpassed both state and national averages, with median family income in the county a full 30

163

percent above that of the United States as a whole by 1969. During the seventies, strains began to appear. While job growth accelerated (240,-000 new jobs were created during that decade alone), population growth failed to keep up. By 1975 Silicon Valley was distinguished by unbearably congested freeways, dangerous levels of air and water pollution and a no-growth movement calling for a halt to further industrial expansion. Today the county also boasts among the highest average housing prices in the nation.

The story of Silicon Valley's growth is also the story of the birth and development of a new industry, the semiconductor industry. The electronics-related companies which established operations in the area during the 1940s and 1950s to gain access to war-related markets paved the way for the birth of the first semiconductor companies. The subsequent agglomeration and expansion of this new industry in the valley provided the impetus for its accelerated growth. Almost all of the country's leading semiconductor companies can trace their roots to Santa Clara County. Today, the leaders in this rapidly maturing industry remain headquartered there, surrounded by a dense concentration of smaller electronics-related suppliers and producers. Yet the country's largest semiconductor and electronics companies are no longer expanding production in the region. Plagued by a variety of urban problems, they have started to disperse their manufacturing operations to distant locations.

Regional growth and industrial development have thus been inextricably linked in Silicon Valley. This essay examines the relationship and interactions between these two processes—arguing that neither the region's growth nor the development and spatial patterning of the semiconductor industry can be understood in isolation. For at the same time that the expansion of semiconductor and electronics production generated rapid economic growth, it also transformed the local class structure and influenced the patterns of residential settlement and urban development in Santa Clara County. I argue here that the urban problems which emerged in the region during the seventies—breakdowns of the housing market and transportation systems, along with environmental degradation and the no-growth movement—all are direct outcomes of the evolution of this industrially determined spatial structure. As these urban problems began to raise the costs of production in the region and to threaten already existing activities, they in turn triggered the decentralization of manufacturing operations out of the valley. In short, the young semiconductor firms which brought economic growth to Santa Clara County also shaped the region's urban geography. As the industry developed, the contradictions of this urban form became increasingly pervasive, eventually feeding back into the locational behavior of the very same companies. The current decentralization of production in turn will affect both the nature of growth in Silicon Valley and in the new host regions as well as the future development of the semiconductor industry itself.

After a brief discussion of the theoretical antecedents for this analysis—found primarily in the literature which examines the processes of regional change, but also related to the theory of product cycles and industrial location—this essay is divided into five sections. The first describes the basic characteristics of the young semiconductor industry as it emerged during the 1950s and 1960s in Santa Clara County. This information is then used in the following section to describe the way in which the nature of production and the class structure generated by the industry shaped the county's urban landscape, particularly its patterns of industrial and residential development. In the third section, the urban problems which emerged in Silicon Valley during the 1970s are examined and shown to be a direct outcome of the evolution of this particular spatial structure. The response of the industry to these urban contradictions, and the consequences of this industrial restructuring for future patterns of regional growth, are then discussed in the fourth section. Some concluding comments are proffered in the final section.

THEORETICAL BACKGROUND

As the pace of growth and decline of regions around the world has accelerated, with dramatic changes in the fortunes of particular regions attracting both popular and academic attention, traditional approaches to the study of regional change have been seriously challenged (see, for example, critiques by Holland, 1976; Massey, 1975, 1978; Walker and Storper, 1980). Neoclassical theories of interregional equilibration appear increasingly weak. Empirical evidence casts doubt, for example, on the view that we are not witnessing a convergence of growth rates between the Northeast or Midwest and the Southwest regions of the United States. The related regional growth theories, while each providing insights into certain aspects of the process of regional change, lack comprehensive analytical power. Demand-based approaches, such as export-base theory, isolate external demand for local output as the sole determinant of a region's growth and unrealistically assume that the existing composition of its industrial base remains fixed. On the other hand, supply-based approaches such as growth pole or agglomeration theories explain the fate of a region as a function of the local supply of land, labor, and capital, thus restricting causality to a region's predetermined characteristics. In addition, these theories all neglect the crucial role of macroeconomic forces in regional change, and little if any attention is given to the impact of changing locational strategies of firms on the growth and decline of regions. Location theory, which purports to fill this latter gap, provides insights into the role of comparative costs and revenues influencing a firm's location decision—focusing primarily on the supply of factors of production and the location of markets. Constrained however by its focus on marginal decisions within a static and analytically narrow framework, location theory lacks the capacity to comprehend the forces underlying shifts in the comparative factor costs in a region or changes in behavioral motivations specific to particular firms and industries. Furthermore, social and political factors which significantly influence industrial location decisions are only artificially reflected, if at all, in the cost mechanism.[1]

In recent years a more comprehensive and analytically powerful approach has been developed which identifies industrial restructuring as the key force underlying regional change. This new brand of regional analysis, pioneered by Massey and Meegan (1978), views regions as the outcome of processes of accumulation and industrial development. Industrial behavior both past and present is the object of the analysis. Its method comprises examination of both the evolving characteristics and needs of production in particular industrial sectors and the way in which economic activity responds to geographic variations in the conditions for accumulation. In examining the decline of the old industrial inner cities in Britain, for example, Massey and Meegan demonstrate that technological innovation and cost-cutting reorganizations of the production process in the electrical engineering and electronics industries underlie significant shifts in the regional distribution of employment. They trace this rationalization and industrial restructuring process to the pressure on firms to boost profitability in the face of declining international competitiveness. Similarly, in an analysis of the economic transformation of the New England region in the post–World War II period, Bluestone and Harrison (1980, 1981) use industrial case studies to detail the technological changes and reorganizations of the production processes which allowed the shifting of production tasks out of the region. While stressing the role of changing ownership patterns (which have increased centralization and concentration of control) in facilitating this relocation, their analysis also documents the historical importance of labor militancy in accounting for the timing of these instances of rationalization and industrial dispersion.

In applying this method of regional analysis to Santa Clara County, a new element must be added to our understanding of the process of regional change. Previous researchers have forcefully illustrated the importance of viewing a region's fate within the context of the inter-regional and international division of labor (see also Frobel, 1980); and they have documented the role of shifting industrial strategies, technologies, and ownership structures in regional change. Yet they have failed to examine the impact of production on patterns of urban development *within* a region, and the ways in which this industrially determined spatial structure in turn influences industrial behavior. In this essay, I use the case of Santa Clara County to argue that processes of regional change can only be fully understood by examining the impact of production on the local class structure and urban geography of a region, and the subsequent feedback effects which this particular spatial form has on future industrial behavior.

Santa Clara County provides a rare opportunity to examine the causal links between industry, urban spatial structure, and regional development. The county, which lies at the southern tip of the San Francisco Bay, encompasses a valley flanked by low coastal mountains (see figure 7.1.) Prior to 1940 the valley was devoted entirely to agricultural uses. Today, the electronics industry completely dominates the region, with over one-third of the county's workers employed in electronics-related companies. Many of the remainder are employed in occupations that service or support the electronics complex. Most of the region's recent growth can be attributed to the evolution of this sector alone. Similarly, as there was very little prior urban development, the current organization of space in the county can be traced directly to the characteristics of production in the industry. While these relationships between production, local geography, and regional growth occur everywhere, it is unusual to find a case in which spatial and regional outcomes are so clearly attributable to a single industry.

On a very general level, the spatial behavior of the semiconductor industry in the United States has conformed to the predictions of the product cycle theory of industrial investment associated with R. Vernon (1960, 1966). The theory postulates initial agglomeration in the development of a new product—allowing flexibility and the exploitation of the benefits of communication and external economies. This is followed by a large-scale dispersal of production facilities to lower-cost locations

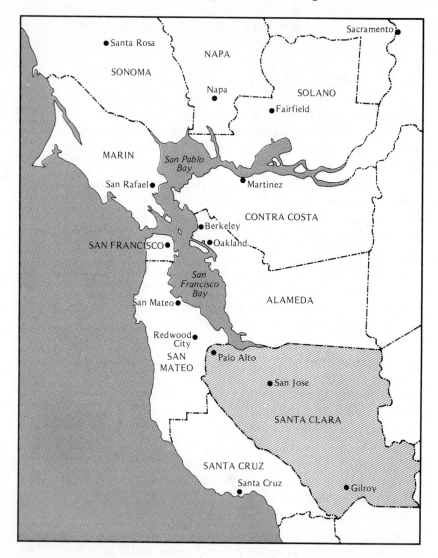

FIGURE 7.1. Santa Clara County in the Context of the San Francisco Bay Area.

as the product is standardized and demand for it grows—enabling the achievement of scale economies through mass output and long production runs. During this process of industrial maturation, new technologies develop which allow the "decomposition" of production processes and their successive transfer outward.[2]

As the material presented here illustrates, Santa Clara County clearly functioned as a seedbed region for the young semiconductor industry, the place where virtually all fledgling firms agglomerated to exploit the benefits of proximity to each other in a new and rapidly changing industry.[3] Furthermore, the subsequent dispersal of production activities out of the valley has indeed coincided with the maturing of the industry. Vernon's observation that movement along the development cycle—involving expanded scale, product standardization, and a declining need for flexibility—renders an industry increasingly footloose is, in this case, a valuable insight. Yet beyond predicting these very general trends, the product cycle approach is of limited value in explaining the locational behavior of the semiconductor industry.[4]

Product cycle analysis provides no explanation of the specific *causes* of the industrial dispersal process, and thus lacks the power to account for the precise timing or destination of these movements as well. Basing its spatial analysis on the simple concept of a decentralization to lower-cost regions, it fails to comprehend the forces underlying both shifting costs within a single region and cost differentials between regions. In the absence of such explanatory power, individual processes of industrial relocation which differ dramatically from case to case are simply homogenized into an overly generalized stage theory. As this paper illustrates, the forces underlying the decentralization of semiconductor manufacturing out of Silicon Valley were not those of the traditionally cited U.S. textile and apparel industries moving south in search of low wage labor. Nor were they the same as those macroeconomic shifts which spurred the locational shifts of the electrical equipment and electronics industries in the United Kingdom. Likewise, while the timing of the technological rationalizations and the dispersal of shoemaking and textiles out of the New England region can be attributed in many cases to upsurges of labor militancy, in the case of Santa Clara County, the timing is related to the growing severity of its urban problems. Only through in-depth analysis of specific industries and regions can the complexities of the industrial location and regional change processes be fully understood.

THE YOUNG SEMICONDUCTOR INDUSTRY

World War II stimulated the emergence of the semiconductor industry and shaped the character of its early development. The industry's birth, generally associated with the invention of the solid state transistor at AT&T's Bell Laboratories in 1948, was spurred by military demand for more versatile components for use in weaponry.[5] Commercial production of transistors began in 1951. During the next two decades, fueled initially by massive defense-related support from the federal government[6] and later through expansion into computer and industrial markets,[7] this new industry literally exploded under the steam of ongoing technological innovation.[8] Its growth was phenomenal: the value of shipments by U.S. firms jumped from $5.1 million in 1954 to over $500 million in 1960, and by 1970 it had reached $1.5 billion.[9]

The young semiconductor industry was characterized by unusually low barriers to entry—resulting from the accelerated pace of technological change, the speedy diffusion of innovations, the absence of economies of scale, and the ready availability of finance capital—which in turn allowed for a proliferation of small, intensely competitive firms. These characteristics also made the spatial clustering of firms highly advantageous. While many large, already established electrical companies and vacuum tube producers began commercial production of transistors during the 1950s,[10] it was the small new firms formed specifically to produce semiconductors which had the flexibility to exploit new innovations in production. By the mid-1960s, they had come to dominate the industry.[11] And it is these new enterprises, formed almost exclusively by scientists and engineers with no prior business experience and extremely limited capital resources, that clustered in Santa Clara County.

World War II also laid the foundation for industrialization of the bucolic agricultural fields of the Santa Clara valley. Hostilities in the Pacific theater greatly stimulated California's economy and generated a massive influx of population into the region for war-related industries such as tank, aircraft, and missile manufacture. The Moffet Field naval air station in the northern part of the county drew in thousands of military personnel for training. Most critical for Santa Clara County, however, was the genesis of a technological watershed at Stanford University, located in the northwesternmost corner of the valley, in the city of Palo Alto. The initial flow of federal funds to Stanford's laboratories for the development of military components and equipment during the war years ballooned into a substantial and ongoing source of support for basic electronics research and development during the years of the Korean War and throughout the ensuing cold war period. In addition, Pentagon contracts for ballistic missiles and other new weapon systems significantly boosted production levels of the west coast aerospace industry, which in turn required large quantities of electronic inputs. During the 1940s and 1950s, a number of large national electrical and electronics companies thus established both manufacturing and research operations in Santa Clara County in order to gain proximity to these sizeable new markets.[12]

While the war stimulated the region's economy and the dramatic growth of government military and aerospace contracts to California-based firms bolstered local electronics-related production and research,[13] Stanford was quick to step up its electrical engineering programs. The number of advanced degrees in engineering awarded annually in the region increased rapidly during these years, as other local educational institutions in turn established special electronics and electrical engineering programs.[14] By the middle of the 1950s, the region was thus distinguished by a rich and supportive technological milieu consisting of high-caliber universities, research institutions, and older technology-based firms, along with an unusually large supply of skilled technical workers. Santa Clara County had become an ideal environment for innovative, science-based industry.

The first semiconductor firm was established in the county in 1955. William Shockley, one of the three inventors of the transistor, left Bell Laboratories and moved to Palo Alto to form the Shockley Transistor Company. He thereby set a precedent for the "spinoff" process, soon commonplace in the valley, whereby engineers and scientists simply left their employers in order to start their own semiconductor companies. In 1957 eight of Shockley's best scientists in turn splintered off and gained financial backing from the local Fairchild Camera and Instrument Company to start their own firm. Fairchild Semiconductor soon became known as the grandfather of the industry, spawning ten new firms by 1965, and almost fifty new semiconductor companies over the next decade and a half. All of these new firms remained in Santa Clara County. While the industry's low barriers to entry and minimal initial capital requirements made this spinoff process possible (many firms were started with only $1 million), the pace of technological innovation and the constant need to remain abreast of new developments ensured this spatial clustering in the valley. By the mid-1960s, this original concentration of production had begun to act as a powerful centripetal force for the continued agglomeration of new semiconductor firms in the region. External economies, including an enlarged supply of both skilled and unskilled workers, specialized inputs and services, and a social, cultural, and educational environment, made the region particularly appropriate for semiconductor production. The proliferation and explosive growth of these new firms in turn fueled the region's economic boom. By 1970 the county was known as Silicon Valley, the worldwide capital of the semiconductor industry and the

densest concentration of high technology and electronics enterprises
in the nation.

As it grew, this new industry shaped the patterns of urban development in Santa Clara County. The key to the region's current spatial
structure lies in the nature of semiconductor production and the unique
class structure which it generates. The semiconductor industry is distinguished by the fact that it is a science-based industry, an industry
which involves ongoing scientific investigation and the application of
scientific knowledge to the process of production (Noble, 1977). Not
only does scientific research contribute to the development of new
technologies and novel applications, but science is also integral to the
production process itself. This becomes evident through examination
of the process of producing semiconductors, a process which has three
phases: (1) product development, (2) wafer fabrication, and (3) assembly and testing.

Product development involves the original conception of a semiconductor device, the extremely complex design and engineering of
circuits to meet given product specifications, the transfer and reduction of the final artwork representation of the circuit design onto miniature glass photomasks, and protoype production runs for adjustment of
both the design and the manufacturing process. This initial phase of
production requires a firm's most highly skilled scientists and design
engineers along with some technical assistance. Wafer fabrication (or
advanced manufacturing) has been described as the most complex
manufacturing technology adaptable to mass production. Basically it
is a batch process with a large number of precise mechanical, chemical, and electrical operations performed in sequence. First the photo-
mask circuit design is transferred onto a thin silicon wafer (ranging
from two to five inches in diameter) through the use of high-intensity
light or electron beams. Selective impurities are then introduced into
the silicon to impart the desired electrical conducting properties. This
begins with ion implantation and other chemical processes inside a
high-temperature furnace and is followed by a series of metalization,
passivation, oxidation, washing, etching, and diffusion processes. Each
step produces irreversible changes in the silicon wafer, so that any
error in the overall sequence means the entire batch must be discarded.
Errors are not uncommon, as uniformity of temperature, extreme clean-
liness, and precise dimensional control (tolerances of up to seventy-five
millionths of an inch are normal) are all essential to the fabrication
process.

Once prepared, the wafers are tested and divided into thousands of identical chips. A yield of under 5 percent usable chips is not unexpected, especially in the early phases of a product's life. The complex and sensitive nature of this phase of production means that semiconductors cannot be produced routinely by production workers under the supervision of a few managers, as can most manufactured products. Skilled engineers and technicians who are versatile with the scientific principles involved must measure and control the variables at each stage, making sure that the overall sequence is in order. While closely controlled by engineers, this process still requires unskilled and semi-skilled production workers to perform routine loading, monitoring, processing, and cleaning tasks. Thus, wafer fabrication has typically required a work force consisting of both skilled technical workers and minimally skilled production workers in a ratio of 1 : 2 or 1 : 3.[15]

The final assembly and testing phase of semiconductor production involves the highly routine process of hand-bonding very fine wire leads or connectors to the chips (under a microscope) and the final sealing of the chips in ceramic, metal, or plastic protective packages. This assembly process is identical for all product lines, varying only in the number of wires to be welded. The final testing and sorting of the chips is a highly capital-intensive, often computerized process. No prior training or education is required to perform these assembly and testing tasks, and the work force thus consists solely of unskilled workers. Furthermore, these tasks form a completely discrete step in the production process which can be physically separated without technical difficulties. As a result, virtually all semiconductor assembly is now being performed outside of the United States, in plants in Asia and Mexico where wage rates are only a fraction of those at home.[16] Most semiconductor facilities in the United States today are thus devoted primarily to either/or both of the first two phases of production, product development and advanced manufacturing operation.

An unusually top-heavy occupational structure reflects the scientific nature of semiconductor production. In fact, the industry has among the highest percentages of nonproduction workers of all industries, with 40 percent of the total U.S. semiconductor work force in 1972 classified as nonproduction workers, compared with 16 percent in the production of motor vehicles and only 13 percent in the apparel industry (Mutlu, 1979). A 1971 occupational survey classified 27 percent of the semiconductor work force in professional and technical positions alone (including engineers and other scientists, skilled technicians, and draftsmen), with another 13 percent in executive, administrative, marketing, and supervisory positions (U.S. Department of Commerce, 1979).

Not only is the employment structure top-heavy, but it is also severely dichotomized. While 40 percent of the industry's 1971 work force was in these managerial and professional positions, 48 percent was in production and maintenance occupations—four-fifths of which are listed as semiskilled or unskilled positions—with the remaining 12 percent in secretarial and clerical occupations. In other words, the industry employs an unusually large proportion of highly educated professional and managerial employees alongside an equally large, but minimally skilled production work force, with very few medium-skilled workers in between.

In Santa Clara County, a region dominated by semiconductor and other electronics-related production, this bifurcated employment structure generated an equally bifurcated class structure, and patterns of residential settlement and urbanization in turn have served to replicate this class structure on the county's urban landscape.

URBAN GEOGRAPHY OF SILICON VALLEY

It was logical that Santa Clara County's first semiconductor enterprises should locate near Stanford University. For these technologically sophisticated but experimental ventures—many of which were started by Ph.D. scientists and engineers leaving academia for the first time—the university environment provided a familiar and supportive intellectual climate. This initial pattern was consolidated with the establishment of the Stanford Industrial Park on 770 acres of land adjoining the university campus in the early 1950s. Leases in the park were granted only to high-technology firms. Seeking spatial proximity in a rapidly changing and highly competitive industry, those firms which failed to find space in the industrial park also located in or around Palo Alto. The adjacent towns of Mountain View and Sunnyvale, and later Cupertino and Santa Clara, soon recognized the tax revenue benefits of a strong industrial base. Following the Stanford model, they too established industrial parks and provided land and financial and infrastructural benefits to attract electronics companies. In this manner new industrial development clustered in the northwest corner of the valley, gradually drifting southward from Palo Alto, city by city. The result is a striking imbalance in the county's land use, with

the electronics industry overwhelmingly concentrated in the five northern cities—the North County (see figure 7.2). By 1970, the ratio of
electronics employment to city population was 1 : 4 in Palo Alto, 1 : 5
in Mountain View, 1 : 9 in Sunnyvale, 1 : 7 in Santa Clara, and only
1 : 50 in San Jose—the county capital, located about twenty miles southeast of Palo Alto (Keller, 1979).

As industry and jobs continued to flow into the North County, San
Jose followed a different route. Explicitly committed to "making San
Jose the Los Angeles of the North," the city's administration—supported
by a coalition of landowners, realtors, contractors, road builders, speculators and bankers—promoted rapid urban expansion and rampant residential and commercial development. The city government rezoned
large tracts of land; provided easy access to credit; aggressively annexed nearby territory; extended sewers, storm drains, and roads to
peripheral areas; and helped to gain access to the freely flowing federal funds for freeways and to FHA mortgage financing which made
tract development of inexpensive, single-family homes highly profitable. San Jose thus grew from an agricultural processing and distribution center of only 17 square miles in 1950 to a sprawling 147-square-
mile metropolis in 1975. Today the city of San Jose alone encompasses
half of the county's total incorporated area and is the home for almost
half of its population.

Immigration swelled the population of Santa Clara County dramatically during the postwar years, generating growth rates that far
surpassed those of both the United States as a whole and even the
booming state of California (see table 7.1). Of the over one million
new residents recorded in the county between 1940 and 1975, a large
majority were in-migrants. (Natural increases, the excess of births over
deaths, accounted for only one-quarter of the annual population growth
during these years.) Coming in a dual stream, these immigrants reflected the electronics industry's unique labor requirements. On the
one hand, an influx of professionals and highly skilled workers responded to the industry's unusually large demand for scientists and
engineers. Close to 50 percent of the adult migrants to the region during the 1950s and 1960s had some college training, so that between
1940 and 1970, the proportion of college-educated adults in the county
doubled from 20 percent to 40 percent (Keller, 1979). At the same
time, the industry's demand for production workers stimulated an
equally large in-migration of unskilled, predominantly minority workers. This included displaced agricultural workers from California and
the Southwest (primarily Chicanos and some Filipino-Americans), for-

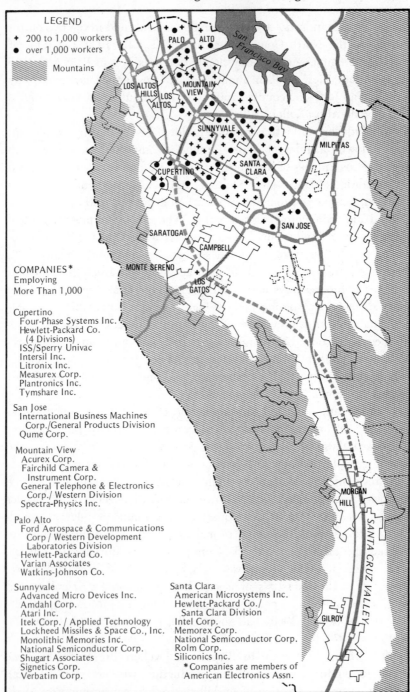

FIGURE 7.2. Location of Electronics Employment in Silicon Valley, 1979.
(Source: *Los Angeles Times,* December 2, 1979.)

Table 7.1. Population Trends: Santa Clara County and Other Geographical Regions

| | Percent increase | | |
Region	1940–1950	1950–1960	1960–1970
United States	14.5%	18.5%	13.3%
Western States*	40.4	38.9	24.1
California	53.0	48.5	27.0
Santa Clara County	66.0	121.1	66.0

* Includes Washington, Oregon, California, Idaho, Nevada, Utah, Arizona, Montana, Wyoming, Colorado, New Mexico, Alaska, and Hawaii.

Source: U.S. Department of Commerce, Bureau of the Census.

eign-born Mexicans and Filipinos, and smaller numbers of U.S. blacks and Native Americans. Chicanos and Mexicans alone accounted for 25 percent of the population increase during the 1960s, and by 1970 minority groups represented approximately 25 percent of the county's total population.

The settlement of this dual stream of immigrants into socially and economically segregated residential communities in turn shaped the urban geography of Santa Clara County. For analytic purposes, the county's fifteen cities can be divided into four homogeneous spatial clusters, each representing a specific social and/or economic function in the county. (These regions are delineated in figure 7.3. City-by-city breakdowns of the socioeconomic indicators used to derive this analysis are presented in table 7.2.)

Santa Clara County's most affluent professionals and executives reside in the Western Foothills (I). The five cities in this cluster are the newest in the county and are solely residential. They were originally settled during the 1950s by electronics industry entrepreneurs and scientists who desired both the spacious natural beauty of the foothills and the proximity to their new workplaces. The residents of these foothill cities earn incomes which dwarf those in the rest of the valley, they have the highest average levels of educational attainment in the county, the majority are in professional or managerial occupations, and virtually all are white.

The five cities of the North County (II) form the heart of the Silicon Valley industrial complex, where virtually all of the county's electronics companies are clustered. Half of the county's jobs are located in these five cities alone. While sharing this common industrial base—which is reflected in municipal property values—the residents of

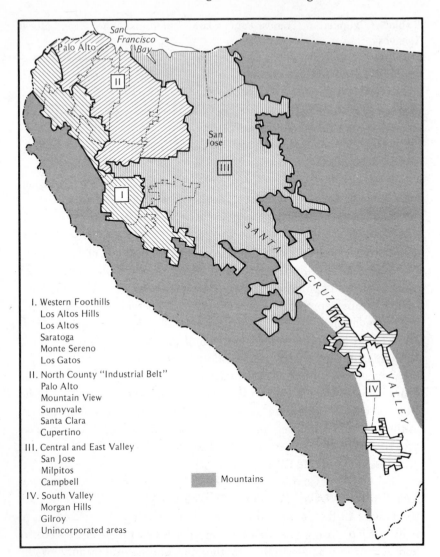

FIGURE 7.3. Social-Residential Segregation in Silicon Valley.

the North County represent an intermediate socioeconomic mix. In
terms of incomes, education levels, occupational status, and racial mix,
Palo Alto clearly belongs with the affluent professional and white
foothill cities, as does the far western city, Cupertino. Moving southward from Palo Alto city-by-city, the socioeconomic level of the local
population declines steadily, the occupational mix becomes increasingly dominated by craftsmen and operatives, and the minority population rises dramatically.

This trend culminates in the three older cities of the Central and East Valley (III), where over half of the county's population resides. Dominated by San Jose (which alone accounts for 47 percent of the population), these rapidly expanding cities served as a landing spot for the influx of unskilled, minority immigrants who were attracted by the electronics boom. With incomes that are below the county average, the residents of these Central and East Valley "bedroom communities" are considerably less well-educated and far more likely to be of minority descent than their neighbors to the north and west.

The cities of the South Valley and the unincorporated areas (IV) are the home of the poorest tenth of the county's population and a disproportionately high percentage of its minority residents. Primarily agricultural and rural, these cities are only marginally connected with the electronics complex.[17]

Silicon Valley's urban landscape has thus come to mimic the semi-conductor industry's bifurcated class structure. The large and affluent professional-managerial strata of the industry's work force are insulated in the north and west—in the foothills, in Palo Alto, and to a lesser extent in the other North County industrial cities—with easy access to the electronics complex. Meanwhile, the industry's large, low-income production work force is concentrated further to the south and east—primarily in San Jose and the adjacent communities. Comparison of a few statistics for Palo Alto and San Jose underscores this social-spatial dichotomy. In 1970, 50 percent of Palo Alto's employed residents were in professional, technical, and managerial occupations, and 42 percent of the city's adults had four or more years of college education, while only 29 percent of San Jose's employed residents were in professional, technical, and managerial occupations, and a mere 15 percent were college-educated. On the other hand, 25 percent of San Jose's employed residents were employed as craftsmen or operatives, and 22 percent of its population was of Spanish-American descent, while only 10 percent of Palo Alto's residents were craftsmen or operatives, and under 6 percent were Spanish-Americans (see appendix).

Severe fiscal imbalances between the cities in the north and south of the county both reflect and in turn reproduce these differences.[18] The vastly different municipal tax bases—the 1974–1975 assessed net valuation per capita in Palo Alto was $7,200, two and one-half times San Jose's—have generated wide disparities in the quality of social services and the nature of both public and private institutions such as schools, parks, libraries, recreation centers, and other social and cultural amenities across the county (Bernstein et al., 1979).

Table 7.2. Socioeconomic Indicators by City: Santa Clara County, California

| | Assessed net valuation per capita, 1974–1975 (in 1000s) | Median family income, 1969 | Median value of owner-occupied houses, 1970 | Occupation of employed persons, 1970 | | Education levels: % persons age 25+ with 4+ yrs. of college, 1970 | Minority population; % Spanish-Americans in total, 1970 |
				Prof., tech., & kindred managers & administrators	Craftsmen and operatives		
North County cities							
Palo Alto	$7,200	$15,036	$33,900	50.6%	10.3%	41.7%	5.7%
Mountain View	4,400	11,830	23,900	37.2	19.1	23.6	14.0
Sunnyvale	4,200	13,078	29,200	34.6	24.0	19.5	13.3
Santa Clara	4,200	12,135	24,100	25.9	27.8	12.6	18.1
Cupertino	5,000	15,122	34,100	45.8	16.3	29.5	6.4
Central and East Valley cities							
San Jose	2,900	11,927	25,400	29.3	24.9	15.0	21.8
Milpitas	3,000	11,865	25,100	22.1	34.7	7.3	18.6
Campbell	3,000	11,543	23,400	26.7	25.0	13.4	10.5
Western Foothill cities							
Los Altos Hills	5,600	25,593	50,000+	63.2	6.3	52.9	n.a.
Los Altos	4,600	18,208	41,600	53.1%	10.2%	38.7%	5.1%
Saratoga	3,900	19,838	46,400	54.0	9.6	37.1	5.3
Monte Sereno	3,200	17,903	44,700	53.4	13.9	34.7	n.a.
Los Gatos	3,600	13,875	33,000	32.8	16.1	26.1	4.9

South Valley cities
& rural areas

Morgan Hill	3,200	10,211	23,200	26.5	22.1	10.9	28.5
Gilroy	2,700	10,131	22,200	21.2	29.9	9.0	46.1
Unincorporated areas	3,500	11,598	24,800	30.0	23.8	18.0	n.a.
County average	$3,600	$12,456	$27,300	33.1%	22.7%	19.5%	17.5%

Sources: Median Income, Occupation, Education and Minority Population from Santa Clara County Planning Office, INFO No. 469 "Socio-Economic Characteristics, Cities, Santa Clara County, April 1, 1970" (November 1972).

Assessed valuations from Santa Clara County Planning Office, INFO No. 565 "Assessed Valuation by City, Select Years, Santa Clara County, 1959–1976" (January 1976).

Home values from Santa Clara County Planning Department "Housing Characteristics, Cities, Santa Clara County, 1970."

Median Income, Occupation, Education and Minority Population from Santa Clara County Planning Office, INFO No. 469 "Socio-Economic Characteristics, Cities, Santa Clara County, April 1, 1970" (November 1972).

CONTRADICTIONS OF THE SPATIAL STRUCTURE

This urban form evolved during the 1950s and 1960s to enable the differential reproduction of the two classes of labor required for electronics production within a single metropolitan area. It did not take long, however, for the contradictions of this spatial structure to manifest themselves. By the 1970s Silicon Valley was plagued with skyrocketing housing prices, overly congested freeways, unhealthy levels of air pollution, and an active no-growth movement—all of which were rooted in the region's distorted pattern of urban development.

Housing

Housing price inflation is a nationwide phenomenon, but the imbalanced social-spatial structure in Silicon Valley has generated housing that is among the costliest in the country.[19] During the 1970s the region's housing supply failed to grow in pace with its accelerated job growth, resulting in price rises which outpaced both national and statewide increases. By 1980 there were over 670,000 jobs but only 480,000 housing units in Santa Clara County, and the average home price had surpassed $100,000—almost double the U.S. average.

This shortage of housing is a direct outcome of the restrictive land use policies and exclusionary planning practices imposed by local governments desiring to preserve the "quality of life"—the differential nature of reproduction—in their jurisdictions. In pursuit of an expanded tax base, each of the already industrializing North County cities chose to rezone extensive tracts of land from residential to industrial usage. Between 1965 and 1975 alone, such rezoning reduced the countywide housing capacity by 43 percent, a loss of 417,000 potential units (Bernstein et al., 1979). Similarly, low-density zoning and residential growth-management policies imposed by the affluent northern and Western Foothill cities in order to preserve the spacious and rural nature of their communities have further limited the county's potential residential land. In 1972, for example, Palo Alto zoned all of its foothill areas exclusively for open space (Greenberg, 1974). Further, virtually all residential construction in the Western Foothills is restricted to single rather than multiple unit housing, and it is generously spread out. There is, on average, only one dwelling unit per acre of residential land in these communities. In the very exclusive city of Los Altos Hills, there are two acres for every home (SCC Manufacturing Group, 1980).

As a result, if all local land use plans were now built out according to their designated uses, there would be 325,000 employed people in the county without the possibility of housing at any cost (SCC Industry Housing Management Task Force, 1980).

In this context the electronics industry's top-heavy employment structure directly fuels housing inflation. Since an unusually large proportion of the new jobs created through an expansion of production are for engineers and scientists or managers, any industrial growth automatically draws more highly paid employees into the county. With incomes that are often ten times those of the industry's production workers, these newcomers have simply asserted their superior buying power in competition for the valley's scarce housing, bidding prices up to levels that only their incomes can bear and often displacing lower-income residents in the process.[20]

This process has a spatial component as well. The concentration of industrial location and expansion in the North County cities has continued, yet virtually all of the remaining land in the county zoned for residential uses is located in east and south San Jose, a long distance from these new jobs.

Although inflationary pressures originated in the socially desirable cities of the Western Foothills and the North County, the limit of this housing supply was rapidly reached. Demand by the higher-income work force thus began to filter into north San Jose and other communities with easy access to the electronics complex. As a result, the least costly homes and apartments in the county—and thus the only residences affordable by the average electronics production worker—are increasingly located in east and south San Jose and the South Valley cities, often as much as fifty miles from the industrial belt. With incomes that have failed to rise in pace with the inflation of housing prices, the county's low-income population is being gradually forced further south, frequently out of the county altogether.

Transportation

The spatial imbalance of jobs and housing location and the sprawling nature of postwar residential development have always meant long commutes for many of Santa Clara County's residents. More than thirty years of sustained population growth have exacerbated the congestion of the county's roadways. But it was not until the 1970s, when the dynamics of the housing market began to force the industry's large pool of production workers to locate (or relocate) yet further from the "jobs belt" in the north, that the transportation problem in Silicon Valley reached crisis proportions.

With no viable mass transit alternatives—municipal buses typically take twice the driving time—local residents are dependent upon private automobiles for transportation. By 1975 over four millon automobile trips were being taken daily in the county. Of these, a large proportion were home-based work trips, and the imbalanced location of jobs and housing meant that most of these commutes were long, slow, and costly. An average ten-mile commute at rush hour now takes thirty minutes, and workers living in the eastern and southern parts of the county face round-trip commutes of over three hours daily (SCC Planning Department, 1979).

According to a transportation study conducted by the Santa Clara County Planning Department (1979), within a decade there will be more than 130,000 cars reaching destinations in the northwest part of the county during morning rush hours—that is, more than ten times the number of vehicles that can be accommodated during a single hour on a six-lane freeway. The study concludes that "as now planned, the land use patterns and growth rates of Santa Clara County will overwhelm the capacity of the major roadways in the urban area by 1990."

The negative effects of congestion and overburdened traffic networks fall most heavily on those who commute from the southern and easternmost reaches of the county—almost exclusively lower-income workers who can least afford the rising fuel costs. However, all commuters now suffer delays and frustrations, and the overflow of traffic onto residential streets has brought noise, accidents, and disruptions to even the more affluent neighborhoods in the North County.

Environment

All of this has taken a toll on the environment of Santa Clara County. Auto emissions have generated the brownish-orange cloud of smog which now hangs over the valley, where one or more federal air quality standards are violated at least 10 percent of the time (SCC Industry Housing Management Task Force, 1979). In the Central and East Valley cities which face severe shortages of tax revenues, improvements in sewers, roads, parks, and other basic public works have failed to keep up with the demands of local population growth and development. Repeated breakdowns of San Jose's sewage treatment plants in recent years have seriously damaged the aquatic life and water quality of the

San Francisco Bay.[21] The fruit orchards and agricultural fields have disappeared. With the exception of the most affluent foothill communities, the entire valley is covered over with strip development, shopping centers, industrial parks, parking lots, and freeways. In 1971 the city of San Jose maintained only eight acres of open space per thousand residents, compared to thirty-five acres in the nearby San Francisco area and twenty-five acres in New York City (Stanford Environmental Law Society, 1971).

No-Growth Movement

As late as 1974, an observer described the environmental and social attractions of Santa Clara County for the electronics industry's professionals as follows:

> It's a particularly pleasant place to live and work—a beautiful landscape of hills and plains, a bounteous garden of nature where fruit trees and wild flowers bloom even in February. . . . Few places on earth so agreeably mix hedonistic delights with the excitement of urbanity. Outdoor sports and recreation are year round attractions. . . . The area boasts 4,000 PhDs. There are also at least 12,000 horses, some kept by those PhDs right on their home acreages, which are often within minutes of work. And within an hour's drive are the shops, restaurants and cultural offerings of San Francisco. (Bylinsky, 1974.)

Yet the qualities of life which once made the valley so desirable an environment for the industry's executives and scientists are rapidly being undermined. Even living in the isolated cities of the Western Foothills no longer provides protection from the region's urban disamenities. The no-growth movement in Santa Clara County, which was mobilized by these well-educated, middle-class professionals, is another manifestation of the urban contradictions generated by the particular form electronics production has taken. It is their response to the environmental degradation and urban problems wrought by the region's distorted spatial development, as these urban problems now threaten the very lifestyles which this spatial form arose to preserve.

This no-growth movement includes local environmentalists, planners, housing activists, women's groups, elected officials, and individual residents. It accumulated strength gradually during the 1970s, as community concern developed over a number of seemingly isolated issues. The work of several studies and countywide task forces examining the region's environmental, transportation, and housing problems culminated in a recognition of their interconnectedness. "Living Within Our Limits: A Framework of Action for the 1980s," a report by the Santa Clara County Industry and Housing Management Task Force (1979), identified uncontrolled job growth as the primary cause of the county's urban and environmental problems. In the interest of preserving the county as "a desirable place to live and work," the task force advocated the imposition of strict governmental controls over the rate, amount, type, and location of further industrial development.

Santa Clara County thus became the first area in the country to legislate public controls over industrial growth. The task force's most sweeping recommendation—for countywide planning of job growth, revenue sharing to redress the fiscal disparities between cities, and taxation of local industry to improve housing and transportation systems in the region—all were defeated at the county level. However, ameliorative measures were enacted by some of the industrial North County cities. In 1980 the Sunnyvale city council rezoned substantial amounts of land from industrial to residential usage, imposed fees on all new industrial development in order to improve the transportation system, and legislated strict regulations on the job density in local plants. Similarly, Palo Alto now requires fees for all industrial development to contribute to a fund for low- and moderate-income housing in the city. And most of the North County cities have imposed strict regulations concerning the environmental impacts and physical appearance of new development.

INDUSTRIAL RESTRUCTURING AND
REGIONAL REALIGNMENT

By the mid-1970s, Silicon Valley's high-technology companies began to feel the strains of these urban contradictions. According to local semiconductor producers, their operations in the region were seriously threatened by two problems.[22] First and foremost, the inflated price of housing had undermined their ability to attract the professionals who are crucial to their operations. With housing costs more than 50 percent above those in other Western states and close to double those in the rest of the United States, even the most prestigious semiconductor firms could not attract experienced engineers and top caliber scientists from outside the region.[23] Second, all suffered from a shortage of production workers and high turnover rates among their production work forces which they attributed to the lack of affordable housing and the increasingly long and expensive commutes to work. As the personnel manager of one firm noted, "We're in trouble with our commuting patterns. Eventually the local labor force isn't going to be able to get here because of the crowded highways." By 1980 there were over ten thousand unfilled jobs at all skill levels in Santa Clara County (SRI International, 1980).

The initial response of local firms was to raise wages, salaries, and benefits. A survey of sixty-eight Silicon Valley companies showed the salaries of engineers rising 15 to 20 percent a year during the late 1970s while benefits were expanded to include everything from stock options, dental insurance, and group legal services to paid sabbaticals and scuba diving lessons in the company pool (Garcia, 1979). Most companies also began to offer "bounties" to their professional employees, paying up to $1,000 per new recruit. In competition for the local labor force, these firms were also forced to raise hourly wage rates and benefits.[24] Some devised gimmicky reward schemes to lure new workers (and keep the old ones).[25] A few companies even began to provide bus tickets or van pool services for their workers.

Relocation, however, soon emerged as the preferred long run solution for these companies. In contrast with past policies of concentrating all manufacturing growth within the valley, by 1980 Silicon Valley's largest semiconductor and electronics companies had started to expand their advanced manufacturing operations in distant locations. As the spokesman for American Microsystems, Inc.—which recently opened a plant in Pocatello, Idaho—commented to the author, "Housing costs here are outlandish compared to elsewhere. You can get an awfully good home for $85,000 in Pocatello. . . . The cost of living is 30 to 40 percent cheaper." National Semiconductor has turned its fifty-five-acre plot in Santa Clara into a park for its employees while dispersing the growth of its wafer fabrication activities to new plants in Tucson, Arizona, and Salt Lake City, Utah. Intel is building a new manufacturing facility in Albuquerque, New Mexico, having recently completed construction of fabrication plants in Aloha, Oregon, and Chandler, Arizona. Signetics is now in Orem, Utah, and Advanced Micro Devices is in Austin, Texas. Hewlett-Packard's most recent expansions have been directed to sites in Idaho, Oregon, Colorado, California, and Washington. None of these companies intend to expand manufacturing operations in Santa Clara County any further.

This sudden dispersion of semiconductor manufacturing activities out of the Santa Clara Valley was thus triggered by the contradictions of the spatial structure which became critical in the late 1970s and which were experienced by local firms as massive shortages of labor and escalating production costs. Yet it is only the simultaneous evolution of the industry itself which allowed firms to undertake this decentralization strategy. While the precise timing of the dispersion can only be explained as an outcome of the urban processes in the region, the consolidation and restructuring of the semiconductor industry—which began during the 1970s—provided the capability for the shift.[26]

Dramatic increases in the technological sophistication of semiconductor devices and the growth of huge new markets for these products have fundamentally altered the nature of competition in the industry.[27] Miniaturization—the process of squeezing more and more electronic components onto a single chip—has raised the effective barriers to entry significantly in recent years. The newest breed of circuits is essentially immune to copying by rival firms,[28] the R&D and design costs required to keep abreast of new technological developments have risen precipitously,[29] and the increased chip complexity demands fabrication equipment which is far more sophisticated and costly than in the past.[30] Driven thus by rapidly escalating capital needs along with the pressures of growing international competition, the small independent semiconductor companies of the past are rapidly being acquired or forced into mergers with larger electronic systems producers or conglomerates.[31] Only the largest, most financially stable, and technologically advanced producers have escaped this amalgamation process. Meanwhile, the emergence of the mass-consumer, automotive and telecommunications markets for semiconductors has enabled these still independent firms to exploit economies of scale in both production (through product standardization, longer production runs, and automation of the fabrication process) and in marketing—thereby further boosting their competitive advantage and reinforcing their positions of dominance. Capital formation, labor productivity, cost minimization, and marketing have thus replaced the former preoccupation with technological advance as the main concern of these leaders in an increasingly concentrated industry.

By the late 1970s, Silicon Valley's major semiconductor firms had thus changed from small, intensely competitive, technology-dominated ventures to large, mature, marketing-oriented corporations. The five leading companies in the valley, all of which rank among the top eight worldwide, now dwarf the remainder of the county's producers in terms of both sales and employment.[32] Their increased size has given them the financial ability to disperse their advanced manufacturing operations, and in conjunction with the changing nature of competition in the industry, has freed them from the need to agglomerate in Silicon Valley. (Meanwhile, numerous smaller firms which lack the scale and financial ability to decentralize their manufacturing activities, and which still remain dependent upon the external economies of the region, are placed at a further disadvantage by the escalating costs of production in the area.)

Yet the industry is not leaving Silicon Valley altogether. Hewlett-Packard recently completed a new international corporate headquarters building in Palo Alto, and Advanced Micro Devices is starting operations at its new Technology Development Center in Sunnyvale. As manufacturing growth is directed elsewhere, the region is gradually being transformed into a high-level control center—the site of corporate headquarters and sophisticated research, design, and development activities. Eventually only the highest-paid professional and top managerial segments of the industry's work force will remain in an increasingly expensive and exclusive white-collar enclave. The region's population growth has already slowed down dramatically. As condominium conversions speed the displacement of the county's low-income population, the urban landscape is being upgraded as well, through newly imposed environmental regulations and other programs to preserve the region's urban and rural amenities.

Ironically, it appears that the no-growth movement in Silicon Valley will thus end up serving the long-run interests of growth. It is now advantageous for the large local firms to follow the exhortations of these no-growth activists—to stop the local growth of manufacturing and to devote ample resources to upgrading the urban environment— in the interest of promoting future growth of a leaner, more elite sort in the region. Meanwhile, expansion of production is proceeding rapidly elsewhere in the country.

New hubs of regional growth are now booming throughout the South and the West as a result of this dispersion of semiconductor and electronics manufacturing. These new production sites are all medium-sized urban areas, with populations in the five hundred thousand to one million range. In contrast to the final highly labor-intensive assembly phase of production—which is now located in low-wage areas of the Third World—this advanced manufacturing phase of semiconductor production still requires a sizeable proportion of engineers and electronic technicians along with an unskilled production work force (in a ratio of at least $1:3$). New locations must thus provide both a sizeable and tractable pool of unskilled workers, and more importantly—since the first is commonly available throughout the Sunbelt in the form of low-wage, often immigrant, female labor—a social and cultural environment that will ensure an adequate supply of engineers and other professionals. Such locational factors as proximity to a university, cultural and social activities, and availability of recreational facilities as well as affordable housing are thus key elements in the locational calculus for a new semiconductor fabrication facility.[33]

One observer has even predicted the emergence of a "silicon desert" in Arizona, a "silicon prairie" in Texas and a "silicon mountain" in Colorado (Marshall, 1980). While it is unlikely that any one region will face the sort of agglomeration that exists today in Santa Clara County, this possibility is not so farfetched. New centers of semiconductor production in Roseville, California, in Phoenix and Tucson, Arizona, in Salt Lake City, Utah, in Austin, Texas, and in Colorado Springs, Colorado, all are experiencing economic booms. All also face dramatic inflation of land and housing values along with increasingly severe transportation congestion and environmental damage. As the industry constitutes its labor force in these new regions, by recruiting professionals and management personnel from afar and by hiring unskilled production workers locally, it is replicating the top-heavy and bifurcated class structure of Santa Clara County. And with it, we can expect familiar urban problems.

CONCLUDING COMMENTS

An entire cycle has thus been completed. We have seen how agglomeration and expansion of the semiconductor industry transformed Santa Clara County from an agricultural community into one of the fastest-growing and most affluent regions in the nation within a few decades. We have also seen the way in which semiconductor production shaped the class structure and the organization of space in the region, and how the contradictions of this spatial form in turn have translated into significant costs which have caused the industry to restructure. As advanced manufacturing is decentralized, we are witnessing the creation of a new interregional division of labor within the semiconductor industry. While Silicon Valley is upgraded as an elite control and research center, new cities throughout the West and South are growing as manufacturing regions for the industry.

The case of Silicon Valley demonstrates that a region's spatial structure, itself a product of the past and present industrial base, can significantly alter the profitability of a particular region for production. It is important to stress here that this dispersion of semiconductor manufacturing out of Santa Clara County is not a response to some abstract or general congestion costs in a city that is too big or has too many people. Nor are its urban problems simply those of misplanning or overly rapid growth. Rather, they are due to the specific class and urban structures produced by the industry and the social and functional contradictions inherent in them. Semiconductor production generated a bifurcated class structure in the county, one which was distinguished by a large proportion of highly skilled engineers and managerial personnel alongside an even larger number of minimally skilled manufacturing and assembly workers. A highly segregated residential pattern evolved to accommodate the vastly different nature of social reproduction required for these two dominant classes of labor power. As the industry expanded, it became increasingly difficult to accommodate and reproduce both segments of this dichotomized work force within the same metropolitan area. Inflation of housing prices, transportation congestion, labor shortages, and the no-growth movement all are manifestations of the limitations of the local spatial structure for accommodating the industry's bifurcated work force. These urban contradictions eventually caused the industry itself to restructure, thus preserving Silicon Valley as a site for headquarters, high-level research, and prototype production activities.

Many residents recall the days, not long ago, when Santa Clara County had clean air, an abundance of affordable housing, and uncongested roads. The whole cycle—the transition from a rural agricultural region to a highly urbanized manufacturing center, and the ensuing emergence of urban contradictions which spurred the industry to restructure and once again transform the nature of the region's growth—took only three decades. The case of Silicon Valley exemplifies the drastic acceleration in the pace of regional change today. As new regions boom through the dispersion of the industry's manufacturing operations, production will once again shape the local class and spatial structures. While it is rarely possible to isolate the effects quite so neatly as in Silicon Valley, similar analyses of the impact of industry on the organization of space—with particular reference to the location of residential communities and jobs—and the eventual feedback effects which this spatial structure has on industrial behavior, will enrich our understanding of the processes of regional change in the future.

NOTES

This paper is based on the author's master's thesis entitled "Silicon Chips and Spatial Structure: The Industrial Basis of Urbanization in Santa Clara County, California" (Department of City and Regional Planning, University of California, Berkeley, 1981).

1. Many elements of the critique outlined here grew out of discussions with the Western Regional Development Collective in Berkeley, California. For a longer version of the argument, see Markusen and Walker, 1980.
2. A more detailed discussion of this product cycle process and an empirical application is presented in Vernon's analysis of the New York Metropolitan Region Study of the 1950s. See *Metropolis, 1985* (Cambridge, Mass.: Harvard University Press, 1960).
3. The only major U.S. semiconductor firms that did not originate in Silicon Valley were Texas Instruments and Motorola, from Texas and Arizona respectively.
4. While it is beyond the scope of this paper, the internationalization of the semiconductor industry provides a dramatic illustration of the shortcomings of the product cycle theory. In the early 1960s, virtually all of Silicon Valley's semiconductor companies relocated their labor-intensive assembly operations to low-wage areas in the Third World (primarily Asia and Mexico). This dispersal began only a short time after the invention of the product—at a time when there was considerable uncertainty in production and major changes in both the product and process technologies were to continue throughout the decade. Further, this relocation was spurred by intensive cost competition, a phenomenon which according to product cycle theory occurs only as the product/industry matures.
5. The first generation of active components, electron tubes, had actually existed since the 1920s, but their size and fragility made them inappropriate for military use.
6. A vast impetus to production and innovation was generated by the combination of a large and profitable defense and aerospace market for semiconductors and by extensive government funding directed toward semiconductor R&D. Production for the defense market grew from $15 million to $294 million between 1955 and 1968, during which time it accounted for between 30 and 50 percent of total industry sales. Meanwhile, various branches of the federal government collectively funded $930 million worth of R&D between 1958 and 1974, nearly equal to the $1.2 billion the semiconductor firms themselves spent for this purpose.
7. Production for the consumer market did not become important until the 1970s, when it rapidly expanded to account for almost 25 percent of total sales.
8. Within its first twenty years alone, the industry completed the full life cycle for three generations of semiconductor products. While a transistor in 1956 contained only a single circuit (and thus a single electronic function), by 1970 thirty thousand circuits were being squeezed onto a single silicon chip. Meanwhile, literally thousands of new products were introduced every year.
9. This explosive growth continues today. Total shipments surpassed $5 billion in 1977 and are now just short of $15 billion. Industry analysts predict that they will reach $30 billion by 1985 (U.S. Census of Manufacturers, 1979; *San Francisco Examiner,* July 26, 1981).

10. Including RCA, Sylvania, General Electric, Raytheon, and Westinghouse.
11. The exceptions, by no means minor, are Texas Instruments, which was a small geophysical services company when it began producing semiconductors, and Motorola, which was already a large diversified electric and electronic equipment producer. These two companies now lead the industry in production for commercial markets, with a combined market share of about 30 percent. IBM has long been the largest producer of semiconductors, but it produces solely for in-house use.
12. This included the manufacturing branch plants of General Electric, Sylvania, Philco, Ford, Westinghouse, Kaiser, and Itel; and R&D laboratories for Lockheed, IBM, IT&T, and Admiral.
13. Military prime contracts awarded to the firms in the Pacific region of the United States grew from 12.3 percent of the total during the Second World War to 17 percent during the early 1960s. California alone received 20 percent of all defense-related prime contracts of $10,000 or more and 44 percent of all National Aeronautics and Space Administration (NASA) subcontract awards during the 1960s. By that time 15–20 percent of the cost of an aircraft and at least 30 percent of missile systems was accounted for by electronic inputs.
14. In the early 1960s, the number of advanced degrees in electrical engineering granted yearly by Stanford University surpassed the number granted by MIT. Since 1960 the University of California at Berkeley and Stanford together have granted twice as many electrical engineering Ph.D.s yearly as MIT (Mutlu, 1979).
15. In the late 1970s, the largest semiconductor companies began to automate their wafer fabrication processes. This will certainly alter the labor force requirements in the future. The irony lies in the fact that this industry, which has done so much to automate other industries, remained highly labor-intensive for so long. The explanation for this lies primarily in the rapid pace of technological change, as any investment in costly machinery would have tied a firm to a technology which was likely to become obsolete before sufficient returns on the investment could be reaped.
16. This internationalization of assembly was clearly a result of the pressure to reduce labor costs in an industry characterized by intense price competition. Fairchild established the firm's offshore assembly operation in Hong Kong in 1961. Soon thereafter, the firm introduced price reductions which allowed a dramatic expansion of market share. In order to simply preserve existing market shares, even the smallest semiconductor firms were soon forced by the competitive pressures to establish assembly plants in low-wage areas. By the early 1970s, every established U.S. semiconductor firm was engaged in some offshore assembly. This rapid internationalization was facilitated because transportation costs for semiconductors are minimal, and because U.S. tariff items 806.7 and 807 allow U.S. manufacturers to export products for assembly abroad and reimport them paying duty only on the value added abroad.
17. The analysis presented here refers to 1970 data concerning the county. While the overall picture has not changed significantly, the status of the South Valley cities is changing as the demands of continued population growth have spread to the most remote reaches of the county. In addition, during the late 1970s, a few electronics firms had located operations in San Jose. These changes have no bearing on the sequence of events described here.

18. Much of the analysis presented in this section, especially with reference to the county's municipal fragmentation and fiscal imbalances, was inspired by the work done at the Pacific Study Center. Its pioneering study "Silicon Valley: Paradise or Paradox?" (Bernstein et al., 1977) is extremely informative and a valuable reference for anyone interested in the region.

19. According to the spring 1981 housing surveys by the Nationwide Relocation Service, which lists the average sales figure for a comparable three-bedroom, two-bath house with a family room and a garage in various cities, Palo Alto prices were the highest in the country, at $292,500. The prices for comparable residences in other cities in California were: San Francisco, $211,500; Los Angeles, $157,500; San Jose, $126,000. Elsewhere in the country, the comparable homes sold for: Dallas, Texas, $88,200; Phoenix, Arizona, $72,000; Boston, Massachusetts, $81,000; New York City, N.Y. (Long Island), $85,500 (*San Francisco Examiner*, July 5, 1981).

20. In 1979 the average wage of a semiconductor production worker was $4.52 an hour, or about $9,000 a year, while an experienced engineer now earns over $100,000 a year. Many of the industry's executives earn more than double that amount.

21. In a giant spill during 1980, the second in two years, more than a billion gallons of partially treated sewage were dumped into the bay. According to a state water-quality biologist, this breakdown of San Jose's sewage treatment plant most seriously affected the aquatic life in bay sloughs, destroying the harvest of a local shrimp fishery (*San Francisco Chronicle*, July 16, 1981).

22. The information presented in this section is based on the responses to a series of interviews conducted with representatives of eleven Silicon Valley semiconductor companies during the spring of 1980.

23. Furthermore, their prime out-of-state competitors, Texas Instruments and Motorola, were located in regions with considerably lower-priced housing (see note 19).

24. In early 1980, for example, Advanced Micro Devices raised its entire wage scale for production workers, instituting a minimum starting wage of $4.00 an hour (previously it paid $3.25). This gave the firm the highest wage scale in the county, with the top hourly pay for experienced fabrication workers of $8.00.

25. AMD's American Dream Contest is typical. In this lottery, one assembler received a $240,000 bonus while others received Cadillacs and televisions.

26. Walker and Storper (1979) provide the terminology and analytical approach to industrial relocation as involving both "push" and "capability" factors.

27. A fascinating and informative discussion of this process is contained in a five-part series by A. L. Robinson in *Science* magazine, 1980.

28. IBM initiated the VLSI (very large-scale integration) generation in 1979 with a chip capable of storing 65,536 bits of information—the 64K random access memory, or 64K RAM. The industry is now on the verge of introducing the VLSI 256K RAM, containing over 250,000 components.

29. The cost of research and design for this new breed of circuits has become prohibitive to all but the largest companies. In 1979 Intel spent about $70 million on R&D alone, more than the total sales for all but

the largest Silicon Valley companies. Furthermore, while the first micro-processor developed at Intel had twenty-three hundred transistors and took four man-years to develop, the representatives of Zilog Company report that their most sophisticated device, with twenty thousand transistors, required a full thirty man-years of development effort (Robinson, June 13, 1980).

30. In 1980 the cost of establishing a new state-of-the-art semiconductor fabrication facility was estimated at $50 million, compared to only $1 million during the 1960s (*Business Week*, July 21, 1981).

31. Of the thirty-six new semiconductor companies that were started up between 1966 and 1979, only seven remained independent in 1980.

32. In declining order of 1980 sales volumes: Intel, National Semiconductor, Fairchild, Signetics, and Advanced Micro Devices.

33. Professionals are the only members of the labor force who are free to select their residential location with the secure knowledge that jobs will follow (Massey, 1980). The costs of selecting an inappropriate location are high. For example, when Hewlett-Packard established a division in Corvallis, Oregon, many key engineers refused to move there. Despite the proximity to Oregon State University, those who did move "found themselves fifty miles short of boredom and defected soon after arriving in Oregon's rainy Willamette Valley." That division reportedly lost manufacturing continuity, product development faltered, and manufacturing lapses slowed delivery so that the division has operated in the red for several years (*Business Week*, March 10, 1980).

REFERENCES

Axelrad, Marcie. "Profile of the Electronics Industry Workforce in the Santa Clara Valley." Mountain View, Calif.: Project on Health and Safety in Electronics, 1979.

Bernstein, Alan; DeGrasse, Bob; Grossman, Rachel; Paine, Chris; and Siegel, Lenny. "Silicon Valley: Paradise or Paradox?" Mountain View, Calif.: Pacific Studies Center, 1977.

Bluestone, Barry, and Harrison, Bennett. Papers from research project, "Private Investment, Public Policy, and the Transformation of Older Regions: An Analysis of the New England Economy." Cambridge, Mass.: Harvard-MIT Joint Urban Studies Center, 1979.

———. *Capital and Communities: The Causes and Consequences of Private Disinvestment*. Washington: Progressive Alliance, 1980.

Business Week. "More Elbowroom for the Electronics Industry." March 10, 1980:94–100.

———. "Rolling with the Recession in Semiconductors." July 21, 1980.

Bylinsky, Gene. "California's Great Breeding Ground for Industry." *Fortune* 89 (June 1974):128–35.

Castells, Manuel. *Sociologie de l'espace industriel*. Paris: Editions Anthropos, 1975.

———. *The Urban Question*. Cambridge, Mass.: MIT Press, 1977.

Frobel, Folker. *The New International Division of Labor*. Cambridge, Eng.: Cambridge University Press, 1980.

Garcia, Art. "Silicon Valley Seen Shifting Its Emphasis." *Journal of Commerce*, January 17, 1979.

Gilder, George. *Wealth and Poverty*. New York: Basic Books, 1981.

Greenberg, Doug. "The Dunbarton Bridge: A Study in Regional Conflict." Unpublished paper, University of California, Berkeley, 1974.

Harrison, Bennett. "Rationalization, Restructuring, and the Industrial Reorganization in Older Regions: The Economic Transformation of the New England Region Since World War II." Cambridge, Mass.: Harvard-MIT Joint Center for Urban Studies, 1981.

Holland, Stuart. *Capital Versus the Regions*. London: Macmillan, 1976.

Keller, Joseph. "Industrialization, Immigration and Community Formation in San Jose, California: Social Processes in the Electronics Industry." Paper delivered at the Rackham Graduate School, University of Michigan, Ann Arbor, November 12, 1979.

LeFaver, Stuart. "Will Success Spoil Silicon Valley?" Unpublished paper, Santa Clara County Planning Department, 1980.

Markusen, Ann, and Walker, Dick. "Causal Forces in Regional Development of the Western United States: A Study of Industrial Structure and Location." Research proposal, Institute of Urban and Regional Development, University of California, Berkeley, 1980.

Marshall, Martin. "Silicon Valley Is Filling Up." *Electronics* 53 (February 28, 1980):98–100.

Massey, Doreen. "Toward a Critique of Industrial Location Theory." In *Radical Geography*, ed. R. Peet. Chicago: Maaroufa, 1975.

———. "Regionalism: Some Current Issues." *Capital and Class* 6 (1978a): 196–225.

———. "Capital and Locational Change: The U.K. Electrical Engineering and Electronics Industry." *Review of Radical Political Economics* 10 (fall 1978b):39–54.

———. "Industrial Restructuring as Class Restructuring: Some Examples of the Implications of Industrial Change for Class Structure." Working paper. London: Centre for Environmental Studies, 1980.

———, and Meegan, Richard. "Industrial Restructuring Versus the Cities." *Urban Studies* 15 (1978):273–388.

Mutlu, Servet. "International and Interregional Mobility of Industrial Capital: The Case of the American Automobile and Electronics Companies." Ph.D. diss., University of California, Berkeley, 1979.

Noble, David. *America by Design*. Oxford: Oxford University Press, 1977.

Robinson, Arthur L. "Giant Corporations from Tiny Chips Grow." *Science* 208 (May 2, 1980):480–84.

———. "Perilous Times for U.S. Microcircuit Makers." *Science* 208 (May 9, 1980):582–86.

———. "New Ways to Make Microcircuits Smaller." *Science* 208 (May 30, 1980):1014–22.

———. "Problems with Ultraminiaturized Transistors." *Science* 208 (June 13, 1980):1246–49.

———. "Are VLSI Microcircuits Too Hard to Design?" *Science* 208 (July 11, 1980):258–62.

Santa Clara County Economic Development–Job Needs Project. *Training and Jobs: Ways to Reduce Unemployment in Santa Clara County*. San Jose: Santa Clara County Planning Department, 1978.

Santa Clara County Housing Task Force. *Housing: A Call for Action*. San Jose: Santa Clara County Planning Department, 1977.

Santa Clara County Industry Housing Management Task Force. *Living*

Within Our Limits: A Framework for Action in the 1980s. San Jose: Santa Clara County Planning Department, 1979.

Santa Clara County Manufacturing Group. *Report on Estimates of Job Growth and Building Expansion of Sixty Santa Clara County Companies, 1979–1985.* N.p.:1979.

———. *Vacant Land in Santa Clara County. Implications for Job Growth and Housing in the 1980s.* N.p.:1980.

Santa Clara County Planning Department. "Assessed Valuation for Selected Fiscal Years, 1959–1971, and Estimated Assessed Valuation per Capita, 1959–1970, by City." Information Fact Sheet 389, November 1970.

———. "Socio-Economic Characteristics of Cities, April 1, 1970." IFS 469, November 1972.

———. "Assessed Valuation by City, Selected Years, 1959–1976." IFS 565, January 1976.

———. "Total Population by Age and Sex: April 1950, 1960, 1970 and 1975." IFS 591, June 1978.

———. Components of Yearly Population Increase, 1950–1979." IFS 660, February 1980.

———. "Transportation/Land Use Planning Within the Present General Plans Structure." 1979.

Saxenian, AnnaLee. "Silicon Chips and Spatial Structure: The Industrial Basis of Urbanization in Santa Clara County, California." Working Paper 345. Berkeley, Calif.: Institute of Urban and Regional Development, University of California, 1981.

Stanford Environmental Law Society. *San Jose: Sprawling City.* Palo Alto, Calif.: Stanford University, 1971.

Stanford Research Institute, International. "The Mid-Peninsula in the 1980s." Palo Alto, Calif.: SRI, 1980.

U.S. Bureau of Labor Statistics. "Industry Wage Survey: Semiconductors." Bulletin 2021. Washington: U.S. Government Printing Office, 1977.

U.S. Department of Commerce, Industry and Trade Administration. "A Report on the U.S. Semiconductor Industry." Washington: U.S. Government Printing Office, 1979.

Vernon, Raymond. *Metropolis 1985.* Cambridge, Mass.: Harvard University Press, 1960.

———. "International Investment and International Trade in the Product Cycle." *Quarterly Journal of Economics* (1966):190–207.

Walker, Richard, and Storper, Michael. "Capital and Industrial Location." *Progress in Human Geography* 3 (1981).

Part Three

FEDERAL POLICY

8

Federal Tax Incentives as Industrial and Urban Policy

MICHAEL I. LUGER

The U.S. government has relied increasingly on the tax system to achieve different policy goals. Since the early 1950s, it has periodically liberalized corporation taxes to stimulate overall economic growth, to assist particular sectors, and to induce businesses to behave in certain desired ways. The tax code, in short, has become the centerpiece of the government's industrial policy. Since the mid-1970s, the tax code has also been proposed as an instrument of urban policy. In 1978 President Carter recommended additional tax credits for firms locating in distressed areas, and in the past two years, President Reagan and members of Congress have proposed packages of tax breaks for businesses locating in urban enterprise zones.

This growing use of the tax system for industrial and urban policy purposes is fraught with problems. First, the intended effects of tax code changes are not always achieved. The 1981 Tax Act is a case in point. So far it has failed to fulfill its promise to invigorate the economy. Second, tax code changes have sizeable unintended consequences for businesses and metropolitan areas. These outcomes are often inconsistent with other stated policy goals. For example, since general business tax incentives tend to help large and growing businesses the most, their increased use calls into question the government's commitment to help new and struggling enterprises. Since those incentives tend to bolster the economies of large and growing metropolitan areas the most, their use casts doubt on the government's commitment to help small or declining places. Finally, since targeted business tax incentives are not likely to provide long-term relief for the segment of the population that needs help the most, their proposed use as redistributive policy can be challenged. For all of these reasons, business tax incentives are a poor substitute for explicit and coherent industrial and urban policy.

Each of these points is developed in this essay. The second section focuses on the relationship between federal tax policy and business outcomes; the third concentrates on the connection betwen the tax system and urban outcomes; and the fourth section suggests some alternatives for industrial and urban policy.

LIMITATIONS AND DEFINITIONS

This study is limited to federal government policies. Clearly, state and local governments also have tax, expenditure, and regulatory programs that affect industrial and urban development. The money for many of these programs, however, originates at the federal level. This illustrates the important intergovernmental dimension that is beyond the scope of this chapter. The existence of numerous state and local incentives with their own sets of objectives and consequences reinforces my conclusions: that industrial and urban policy goals need to be made explicit, and that programs to achieve these goals need to be coordinated.

This study is also limited to the effects of tax policy on corporate businesses. There are certainly important consequences for partnerships and sole proprietors as well. These other forms of ownership have been excluded from consideration since they are affected most by changes in the individual (vs. corporate) tax, thus requiring additional analysis, and since noncorporate businesses account for a relatively small share of economic activity in the United States.

Several terms are used repeatedly in this chapter. *Industrial policy* and *urban policy,* for instance, are used both formally and informally. In the formal sense, the terms refer to specific government pronouncements. For example, the 1972 Housing and Community Development Act required the president to present a "national urban policy" to Congress every other year. Informally, industrial and urban policy includes all programs that are directed at businesses and urban areas, even if they are not part of a coherent plan. In this sense industrial policy includes fiscal policy as well as regulatory policy, international trade policy, and, for the financial sector, much of monetary policy.

Another set of terms that is used repeatedly is borrowed from the public finance and taxation literature. *Tax credits* are credits against taxpayers' income tax liability. If a business owed $1 million in taxes (based on its taxable income and statutory tax rate) in 1982 but bought $10 million worth of machines in that same year, it would have to pay only $100,000 in taxes since the investment tax credit, which is equal to 10 percent of that $10 million investment, can offset up to 90 percent of tax liability in any year. If that business bought $20 million worth of machines in 1982, it would qualify for $2 million in tax credits. Since the investment credit is not "refundable," the government would not pay the company the difference between its tax liability ($1 million) and the calculated tax credit ($2 million). The business could, however, "carry over" the additional tax credit to future years to reduce tax payments, or apply the excess retroactively to past years when taxes were actually paid. "Deductions" reduce the taxable income on which business tax liability is based. Generally, businesses are allowed to deduct the costs they incur while generating revenue. These include advertising, travel and entertainment, maintenance, wages and salaries, and depreciation. The value of machine depreciation is a cost since businesses must set aside an equivalent amount of money to replace the machines when they finally wear out. The accelerated depreciation allowance, which is discussed in the second and third sections, is one of the largest business deductions. It allows firms to reduce their taxable incomes by more than the annual value of their machines' physical depreciation. Tax credits and deductions obviously reduce the amount of tax revenue paid by businesses to the Treasury (at least as long as we ignore the stimulative effect of these tax breaks on businesses). This loss of revenue is referred to as a *tax expenditure*.

A third set of terms used throughout the chapter refers to the degree to which businesses are aggregated. *Plant* and *enterprise* apply to individual factories. *Firm* refers to the business entity which may own several plants. *Industry* is the collection of plants producing a similar good, and *sector* is the collection of industries of a similar type. Chrysler is a firm that includes automotive plants as well as finance and air conditioning enterprises and other types of facilities. Transportation equipment is an industry consisting of the auto plants owned by various firms.[1] Transportation equipment, apparel producers, electrical equipment and supplies, and seventeen other types of industries are aggregated into the manufacturing sector.

Finally, the general term for the public sector widely used in the political economics literature, the *state*, has been eschewed here to

avoid confusion since reference is made to various levels of government including the state (for example, the state of California).

FEDERAL TAX POLICY AND INDUSTRIAL OUTCOMES

This section contains three parts. The first chronicles the progressive
tax liberalization that has occurred, especially over the past thirty
years, and notes some of the rationales for those changes. The second
lists some of the consequences of tax policy changes for the economy
in general and specific industries. The third part of the section evaluates the use of the tax system as industrial policy.

A Brief History of Tax Liberalization

Before World War I, the federal government derived almost all of its
revenues from indirect taxes (for example, excise taxes). Following
legislation in 1909 and the enactment of the Sixteenth Amendment in
1913, an increasing share of the revenue base came from taxes on individual and corporate income. By 1922, 56.8 percent of federal receipts were derived from these direct levies, growing to over 60 percent in 1975 (Musgrave and Musgrave, 1980:327–28).

Until the mid-1940s, the corporation tax provided a larger share
of revenue than its individual tax counterpart. Since that time the ratio of the individual to the corporation tax share has grown so that by
1975 the individual income tax was three times as important (45.2
percent of all revenues vs. 15.0 percent) (ibid.). This change in relative significance reflects two opposite trends: increases in personal tax
rates and progressive corporation tax liberalization.[2]

The decreased relative significance of the corporation tax can be
attributed to periodic reductions in the statutory tax rate and increases
in the deductions, tax credits, and carryover periods described earlier.
Table 8.1 lists a subset of these changes for the 1954–1981 interval.
Since 1929 over fifty such tax code revisions have been passed by
Congress.

Of all general tax incentives used since the early 1950s, the investment tax credit and accelerated depreciation allowance have reduced
business tax liability the most. The tax expenditure associated with the
former was approximately $90 billion between 1962 and 1981 and, even
without the 1981 tax code changes, would have been almost $20 billion
more by the end of 1982. The accelerated depreciation allowance is es-

timated to have accounted for almost $30 billion in tax expenditures between 1954 and 1980. As a consequence of the "10-5-3" provision in the 1981 tax law, the depreciation allowance's tax expenditure may rise to $30 billion *a year* by 1986 (*U.S. Code News*, 1981). This provision allows businesses to deduct the full cost of assets approximately 40 percent more rapidly than before. Structures can be depreciated in fifteen or ten years, machines in five years, and vehicles in three, even though all of these asset types can actually be used for much longer periods by the companies that own them. This and other provisions of the 1981 tax law are so liberal, in fact, that several economists have predicted that an increasingly large number of businesses will escape the corporation tax altogether in coming years. President Reagan, also recognizing this possibility, proposed a minimum tax on large corporations in February 1982.

The general tax incentives just described have been justified for different reasons as economic conditions have changed. Following sluggish periods they were touted as an instrument for growth. During inflationary times they were either transformed into a discretionary stabilization tool or lauded for their contribution to productivity. After years of falling profits, they were extolled as a vehicle to increase profitability. And when unemployment surged, they were praised for their ability to create jobs. President Nixon even renamed the investment tax credit the "job development tax credit."

The investment tax credit was first enacted in 1962 following "seven months of recession, three and a half years of slack, and nine years of falling farm income" (Kennedy, 1961:19). Both President Kennedy and Congress cited this slow growth as the rationale for the legislation. The commitment to use fiscal policy to ensure long-term growth was shared by the Johnson administration. The president told Congress in 1966 that "a high investment, high research, high growth economy . . . is a firm, long-term plan that we intend to carry out. A high level of business investment is indispensable to our prosperity and to our economic growth" (U.S. Congress, 1966).

By the mid-1960s, inflation had replaced growth as the premier economic problem in the United States, in part because the government began running large deficits in order to finance the war in Vietnam. The Johnson administration reluctantly suspended the investment tax credit and accelerated depreciation allowance from 1966 to 1967 "as a temporary step to ameliorate inflation and balance of payments problems" (Fowler, 1966:14). President Nixon repealed the programs in 1969 for similar reasons.

Table 8.1. Selected Changes in Business Tax Provisions, 1954–1981

Date	Legislation	Description
1954	Internal Revenue Code	Set tax rates at: 30% of first $25,000 taxable income, 52% of remainder.
1954	Internal Revenue Code (Accelerated Depreciation Allowance)	Allowed firms to depreciate equipment more quickly than straight-line accounting previously permitted. Gave firms a choice between double declining balance and sum-of-years digits methods of depreciation.
1962	Revenue Act (Assets' service lives)	Reduced Bulletin "F" service-life estimates by 30 to 40%. Reclassified assets formerly categorized by industry into larger "asset-type" groups.
	(Investment Tax Credit)	Allowed 7% basic tax credit for investment outlays for depreciable property used in manufacturing, production, or transportation, excluding buildings. Made up to $50,000 of used equipment purchases eligible for credit. Applied 3% basic rate to investment expenditures by regulated utility companies. Allowed assets with lives ≥8 years to qualify for full credit, assets with lives between 6 and 8 years to receive two-thirds of credits, assets lasting 4 to 6 years to qualify for one-third of the allowable credit; and, assets lasting less than 4 years to qualify for no credit. Permitted firms that have had liability reduced by $25,000 to decrease remaining liability by only 25% using tax credits. Allowed excess credits to be carried back 3 years and forward 5.
	(Long Amendment)	Required firms receiving investment tax credits to reduce the cost of their assets by the amount of credits claimed for their purchase when figuring depreciation.
1964	Revenue Act	Set tax rates at: 22% of first $25,000 of taxable income, 48% of remainder.
1964	Revenue Act (Long Amendment)	Repealed (except for binding contracts).
Oct. 1966	(Investment Tax Credit and Accelerated Depreciation Allowance)	Suspended.

Mar. 1967	(Investment Tax Credit and Accelerated Depreciation Allowance)	Restored. Changes: After first $25,000 in investment tax credits, 50% of further liability can be offset. Carryforward extended to 7 years.
1968	Revenue and Expenditure Control Acts	Set income tax surcharge of 10%.
1969		
Apr. 1969	Tax Reform Act (Investment Tax Credit)	Repealed (except for binding contracts).
	(Amortization of Pollution Control Facilities)	Allowed firms to accelerate depreciation by up to 300% (or five years), using a 15-year service life, for pollution control equipment installed before Jan. 1, 1969.
1970	Tax Reform Act	Set income tax surcharge of 5%.
1971	Revenue Act (Job Development Investment Credit)	Basic format resembles old investment tax credit. Utility companies made eligible for 4% credit. Allowed full credit rate to apply to assets lasting 7 years, two-thirds of the rate to apply to assets lasting from 5 to 7 years, and one-third of the rate to apply to assets lasting at least 3 years. Carryforward extended to 10 years.
	(WIN Tax Credit)	Extended this program begun in 1968. Allowed employers to claim tax credits for up to 20% of the wages paid to workers hired from the welfare rolls.
	(Asset Lives)	Depreciation allowed at a rate 20% faster, on average, than before. Under the Treasury Department's Asset Depreciation Range (ADR) system, taxpayers given more freedom to smooth out the depreciation pattern of assets.
1975	Tax Reduction Act	Set tax rates at: 20% of first $25,000 of taxable income, 22% of next $25,000 of taxable income, 48% of remainder.
1975	Revenue Act (Investment Tax Credit)	Investment tax credit increased to 10% of depreciable equipment expenditures made by all eligible investors, including utilities. 11% investment tax credit granted to companies that contribute to employee stock ownership plan. Until 1977, recipients of the investment tax credit allowed to reduce their tax liability by the full amount for which they qualify, even when reduction exceeds $25,000 limit. Allowed up to $75,000 of used equipment purchases to qualify for credits.

Table 8.1. (*continued*)

Date	Legislation	Description
1977	(WIN)	Liberalized to include more kinds of workers.
	Tax Reduction and Simplification Act (Employment Tax Credit)	Allowed firms to claim as tax credit up to 50% of the wages paid to "incremental workers" (i.e., that number of workers that exceeds 102% of previous year's work force), not to exceed $2,100 per workers, or $100,000 per recipient firm.
1978	Revenue Act	Set tax rates at: 17% of first $25,000 of taxable income, 20% of next $25,000, 30% of next $25,000, 40% of next $25,000, 46% of remainder of taxable income.
1978	Revenue Act (Investment Tax Credit)	10% investment tax credit made permanent. Changes: $100,000 worth of a firm's used property made eligible for investment tax credit. Allowed firms to use additional credits to offset up to 90% of their liability, even above the previous $25,000 ceiling. Extended investment tax credit to cover industrial and commercial buildings that have been in use for at least 20 years.
	(Job and WIN Tax Credits)	Limited job tax credit to eight special categories of workers, including: welfare recipients, Vietnam veterans, handicapped individuals, youths, and convicted felons. Allowed credit for two years per hired workers, up to $3,000 for wages paid in the first year, and $1,500 for wages paid in the second year. Applied same conditions to WIN credit.
	(Energy Investment Credit)	Made firms investing in non-oil or gas-power sources from 1978 to 1982 eligible for an additional 10% credit on that investment (unless conversion was financed with industrial development bonds, in which case the tax credit is just 5%). Allowed credit to offset up to 100% of tax liability. Denied the regular investment tax credit to businesses that have installed oil or gas burners (except where there was air pollution danger from coal use). Made credit refundable for investments in solar and wind equipment.

1981   Economic Recovery Tax Act   Reduced tax rates for first $25,000 of taxable income to 15% and for second $25,000 to 18%. Extended loss carryover to 15 years and investment, job, and WIN tax credit carryforward and carryback provisions to 18 and 15 years. Decreased windfall profits tax on newly discovered oil. Decreased service lives for tax purposes to 15 or 10 years for buildings, 5 years for equipment, and 3 years for vehicles. Allowed some assets to be expensed. Extended coverage of investment tax credit to more rehabilitation expenses and to 100% of assets with service lives ≧5 years and to 60% of assets with service lives between 3 and 5 years. Allowed taxpayers with no income tax liability to sell their investment tax credits. Allowed an additional 25% tax credit for wages paid to research and development personnel.

By 1971 the economy had changed once again. Inflation persisted, but unemployment rose above 6 percent of the civilian labor force as the economy slowed down and the foreign trade deficit widened. President Nixon recognized that business tax incentives were again needed to increase investment, employment, and productivity. In August 1971 he introduced the job development tax credit to the American public, explaining that "the replacement of our productive facilities with new, modern equipment would increase the productivity of our workers, making domestic industries more competitive in domestic and foreign markets . . . provid[ing] additional jobs . . . and a sound basis for future wage increases where productivity has increased, and decreas[ing] inflationary pressures on prices" (Nixon, 1971a:1168–74).

High unemployment continued to plague the economy, even with the job development tax credit, and in 1975 President Ford undertook to liberalize tax incentives further. When he signed the Tax Reduction Act of 1975 into law in March he said, "Jobs . . . are my main concern. Unfortunately, though some other economic signs are improving, the employment picture remains bleak. I want most to help those who want to get back to work in productive jobs. This can be done by temporary tax incentives to charge up our free enterprise system" (Ford, 1975:319).

Another problem was cited when the Tax Reduction Act was proposed: falling profits. We can see in figure 8.1 that the rate of profit fell to a postwar low in 1975. This led Gerald Ford's secretary of the treasury, William Simon, among others, to cite business tax incentives as the panacea for corporate profitability (U.S. Congress, 1975:5).

This concern with profits was not new. President Nixon had also cited low profits as a reason for fiscal policy changes. He said, "All Americans will benefit from more profits. Profits fuel the expansion that creates more jobs" (Nixon, 1971b:18). Moreover, when the dates of major tax liberalization legislation are superimposed on figure 8.1 (as in figure 8.2), we can see that in five out of six cases, the measure was enacted following a trough in the profitability cycle. The slight offset in these cases reflects the time it takes decision makers to recognize economic problems that arise, to decide what to do about them, and to implement the policy chosen. The combined lag of up to eighteen months impairs the effectiveness of tax incentives as a countercyclical device (e.g., Ando et al., 1963; Bischoff, 1971; Mayer, 1960; Jorgenson and Stephenson, 1967).

When Jimmy Carter took office in 1977, unemployment, inflation, and profitability problems were acute. The 1977 Tax Reduction and

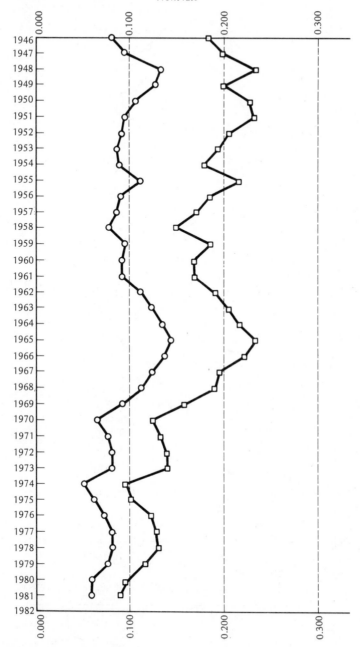

FIGURE 8.1. Before-Tax and After-Tax Profit Rates, All Corporations. Rates are calculated as profits with inventory valuation adjustment and capital consumption allowance divided by value of net capital stock. The after-tax rate is net of tax payments but includes tax credits received. (Source: Data Resources, Inc., U.S. Central Databank.)

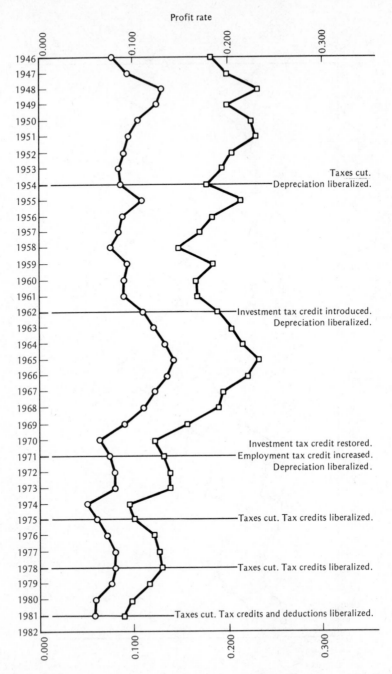

FIGURE 8.2. The Timing of Major Tax Code Changes, 1954–1982. (Sources: Data Resources, Inc., U.S. Central Databank, and Table 8.1.)

Simplification Act was intended to improve the employment picture by subsidizing firms for hiring unemployed workers. And the Revenue Act of 1978 included tax cuts for corporations and liberalization of the investment tax credit. These measures brought only temporary relief from the problems cited above. Consequently, Ronald Reagan was able to win the 1980 election by promising fundamental changes in economic policy.

The Economic Recovery Tax Act of 1981 is the major component of the Reagan administration's program to invigorate the economy. Because of the size of its tax cuts, it has been called "the most significant initiative since the New Deal." The provisions of that act were designed to address three particular problems believed to underlie the economic malaise: the high cost of capital, insufficient private and corporate savings for investment, and uncertainty. In Treasury Secretary Donald Regan's words, "The intent of the President's tax proposal [was] to . . . contribute to substantial increases in savings and investment, to growth and productivity, real wages, and employment" and "to provide a consistent, stable, and rewarding framework for the supply and employment of labor and capital" (U.S. Congress, 1981:6–11).

These quotations from the past six administrations reveal a steadfast belief that tax policy changes can cure all kinds of economic problems from balance-of-trade deficits to the tendency for profit rates to fall. It is in this sense that tax liberalization has become the centerpiece of American industrial policy.

Some Consequences of Tax Liberalization for American Industry

The business consequences of the tax measures just described show up in two types of data. "Macrodata" on the corporate sector in general reveal that the incentives have increased the overall cash flow of businesses, thus inducing some additional investment and stabilizing the economy-wide after-tax rate of profit. "Microdata" on individual industries show that the incentives have benefited some types of businesses more than others.

Macroconsequences

There is general agreement among economists that business tax incentives stabilize after-tax profit rates and induce some new investment in the economy. Figures 8.1 and 8.2 show the first of these effects. While the before-tax profit rate for the nonfinancial corporate business sector has fallen slightly during the postwar period, the after-tax profit rate—while lower—has been relatively stable. This observation has an interesting interpretation: as the tendency for before-tax profit rates to fall has become stronger, the government has had to reduce repeatedly the tax burden on businesses to enable them to maintain a constant after-tax rate of return. Some of the lost revenue has been made up by taxing individual taxpayers more.[3] The rest of the lost business revenue has contributed to the government deficit. Instead of reducing this deficit by curtailing business tax incentives, the Reagan administration has chosen to reduce expenditures on social programs.

While there is a consensus that tax incentives induce some new investment by reducing the cost of capital and increasing business profits, there is considerable disagreement about the size of this stimulus effect. One set of economists concludes that the incentives stimulate a considerably greater volume of investment than they cost in forgone taxes (e.g., Hall and Jorgenson, 1967, 1971). Other researchers are less enthusiastic. They argue that the chief effect of such programs as the investment tax credit and accelerated depreciation allowance is to alter the composition of investment in the economy. The assertion is that business tax incentives induce entrepreneurs to redirect investment to those types of assets that are covered by the legislation more than they stimulate new investment activity (e.g., Auerbach and Summers, 1979; Bradford, 1978; Coen, 1971; Eisner, 1973; Eisner and Nadiri, 1968; Feld, 1979; Harberger, 1971; Sunley, 1973; and Vaughan, 1981).

Microconsequences

In addition to these aggregate economic consequences, tax incentives have particular effects on different kinds of businesses. Some of these "microconsequences" are intentional, but many are inadvertent. The intentional microeffects come from specific provisions in the tax code. The unintentional ones arise because of the differences among businesses in the technical characteristics, organizational structure, and market environment that condition their eligibility for and use of tax incentives.

Since 1975 the tax code has treated small businesses differently than big businesses. In that year, and further in 1978 and 1981, tax rates were graduated so that businesses with less taxable income would pay proportionately less taxes (see table 8.1). It is questionable, however, whether this tax rate gradation offsets the fact that larger corporations are better able to take advantage of tax incentives. In a 1979 study, Alan Feld observed that "the major provisions [of the tax code], although neutral on their face, appear in fact to benefit big corporations" (p. 22).

The tax code also contains provisions that favor particular industries. At various times over the past twenty years, real estate investment trusts, life insurance and movie-making companies, public utilities and extraction firms, and other types of businesses have received special treatment.[4] In some cases these provisions have been made to achieve social goals. In other instances, however, they have been the result of effective lobbying by special interest groups.

These special provisions aside, some firms still benefit more than others from tax incentives. These inadvertently favored firms are generally characterized by (1) growing markets, (2) large-scale operations, (3) capital-intensive production processes, (4) high profits, and (5) flexibility.

Firms with growing markets benefit more than otherwise similar businesses since they typically buy more capital to meet the increase in demand and, consequently, can claim more investment tax credits. The machines operated by businesses in growing markets also tend to be newer, on average, than the machines operated by firms in stagnant or declining markets. Businesses benefit by having newer equipment since they can claim more depreciation deductions. As previously explained, machines can be fully depreciated in just five years under the 1981 tax law. Machines that are more than five years old, then, will generate few tax benefits for the firms that own them.

Big firms having large professional staffs are inadvertently favored by tax incentives since they are generally more likely than smaller firms to know about the incentive programs and take advantage of them. Norman Ture (1967) shows that this has been particularly true for the accelerated depreciation allowance. In 1959 fewer than 60 percent of all eligible firms took advantage of this program.

Businesses that use a relatively large amount of capital to produce their goods especially benefit from tax incentives since they are likely to undertake a greater amount of investment than other businesses that use a relatively large number of workers in production. This inequity arises from the fact that existing tax incentives apply more to the purchase of capital than to the hiring of labor.

Firms with high profits tend to realize greater benefits from tax incentives than other firms for two reasons. First, these businesses face a higher marginal tax rate, so the value of their deductions is higher as well. Table 8.1 shows that a firm having just $25,000 in taxable income is taxed at a 17 percent rate while a firm with several million dollars of taxable income is taxed at a rate close to 46 percent. Every dollar the first of these firms deducts from taxable income, then, is worth 17 cents, while each dollar the second firm deducts is worth 46 cents in taxes saved. The second reason highly profitable firms benefit more from incentives is that they have sizeable tax bills that can be offset. In contrast, less profitable firms that have undertaken a large volume of investment benefit little from existing incentives since tax credits are not refundable. The 1981 Tax Act tried to redress this problem. It allowed firms with little or no tax liability of their own to sell their tax credits to more profitable companies. This provision has helped small and marginally profitable firms, but it has helped Fortune 500 companies at least as much.[5]

Finally, flexible firms benefit more than other companies from tax incentives, all else being equal, since they can change their behavior to take advantage of them. Specifically, they can substitute capital for labor and covered for uncovered types of capital. For example, the 1981 Tax Act favors investment in vehicles more than in machines and investment in machines more than in structures since vehicles can be depreciated in three years, machines in five years, and buildings used for production in ten years. Those companies that can substitute vehicles for other machines, or equipment in general for structures, will be able to take greater advantage of this "10-5-3" provision. Similarly, as shown in table 8.1, the 1981 Tax Act set the investment tax credit rate at 10 percent for equipment kept in production for more than five years, but only at 6 percent for equipment used for three-to-five years. Consequently, companies that can substitute longer-lasting equipment for other machines will come out ahead.

The differential effect that tax incentives have actually had on businesses is revealed in table 8.2. The table shows that in 1975 the receipt of investment tax credits per dollar of net income ranged from $.004 in the food and kindred products industry to $.071 in lumber and wood processing, and that the receipt of depreciation allowances per dollar of net capital ranged from $.074 in paper and allied products to $.491 in petroleum and coal products. While the rankings of favored businesses are different for different years, the range of values is always large. Table 8.2 also shows that the average tobacco company received almost $9,000,000 in tax breaks in 1975 from the investment credit and depreciation allowance alone, compared to approximately $20,000 for the typical apparel company. This is consistent with the

Table 8.2. Investment Tax Credits Received and Depreciation Claimed by Industry, 1975

Industry	Investment tax credits		Depreciation	
	Per active corporation	Per dollar of net income	Per active corporation	Per dollar of net capital
Food and kindred products	$ 18,720	$0.004	$ 197,430	$0.140
Tobacco products	892,510	0.025	7442,030	0.310
Textile mill products	9,470	0.050	162,410	0.091
Apparel and other textile mill products	1,120	0.014	17,950	0.103
Lumber and wood products	6,050	0.071	89,690	0.148
Furniture and fixtures	1,450	0.022	25,860	0.106
Paper and allied products	44,670	0.066	386,570	0.074
Printing and publishing	2,600	0.028	34,650	0.120
Chemicals and allied products	43,050	0.049	389,610	0.101
Petroleum and coal products	313,840	0.029	2559,060	0.491
Rubber and plastics products, etc.	7,760	0.054	117,050	0.087
Leather and related products	2,520	0.016	47,140	0.160
Stone, clay, and glass products	8,830	0.071	124,460	0.112
Primary metal industries	38,750	0.052	719,900	0.097
Fabricated metal products	4,350	0.032	52,520	0.106
Machinery, except electrical	9,590	0.030	137,730	0.173
Electrical equipment and supplies	17,030	0.048	248,670	0.187
Transportation equipment	42,930	0.053	706,280	0.200
Instruments and related products	11,210	0.032	130,010	0.177
Miscellaneous manufacturing	2,150	0.024	35,570	0.209

Sources: All data except net capital are from U.S. Internal Revenue Service, *1975 Statistics of Income: Corporation Returns* (Washington, D.C.: U.S. Government Printing Office, 1979). Net capital stock data are from U.S. Bureau of Labor Statistics, *Capital Stock Estimates for Input-Output Industries: Methods and Data* (Washington, D.C.: U.S. Government Printing Office, 1979).

preceding discussion since tobacco goods production in the United States is divided among a few large and capital-intensive firms while apparel manufacturing is highly competitive and relatively labor-intensive. The other big winners listed in the table—the petroleum and coal products, primary metals, and transportation equipment industries—are similarly dominated by a small number of firms that are rather capital-intensive.

Federal Tax Incentives as Industrial Policy

This evidence casts doubt on the desirability of tax incentives as industrial policy. It is questionable whether such programs as the Economic Recovery Tax Act of 1981 are the best means to stimulate business activity in general, and it appears that the use of such incentives unwittingly creates winners and losers among U.S. businesses.

The general effects of business tax incentives are undesirable for at least three reasons. As shown in the preceding section, the largest of these programs in terms of tax expenditures, the investment tax credit and accelerated depreciation allowance, bias economic decision making. Specifically, they encourage firms to substitute capital for labor (thus exacerbating unemployment), equipment for structures, and short-lived for longer-lived assets. In addition, these programs reward many firms for doing what they would have done anyway. The growing businesses that qualify for the largest relative amount of credits and deductions would mostly have been able to expand, albeit less rapidly, without having had their profitability increased. Third, the increasing use of business tax incentives has further shifted the burden of the tax system from corporate to individual taxpayers at a time when government programs for individuals are being cut.

The unequal effect of tax incentives on different types of businesses is also undesirable since the firms that benefit most are not necessarily the ones that should be rewarded. As just discussed, we may not want to reward large and diversified firms or growing businesses that are already healthy. We also may not want to reward marginal firms since we would thus postpone their day of reckoning. Evidence suggests that if the tax laws had not been liberalized in recent years, industrial outcomes would have been quite different in the United States. The steel industry is a case in point. Several times during the past decade, firms in that industry were able to report positive after-tax profits only because they received tax credits. If those credits were not available, the firms would have had to shut down, diversify into other product lines even more than they have, or undertake a vigorous program of retooling to become competitive with the foreign steelmakers that have captured much of the U.S. market. In one sense, the "protectionist" nature of tax policy is good since employment in distressed sectors has been preserved. But in the long run this protectionism is inefficient. If marginal firms had closed down, overall productivity would have been higher in the United States. If marginal firms had been forced to restructure themselves, they might have undertaken *more* investment than they actually did.

The inescapable conclusion is that the United States lacks a coherent and explicit industrial policy. There is no five-year plan as in the Soviet Union and other command economies. There is no indicative strategy as in Great Britain and Canada. And there is no formal cooperation between the state and corporate sector as in France and Japan (Bergson, 1964; Cohen 1969; and Pinder, Hosoni, and Diebold, 1979:19–22). There is, instead, an uncoordinated assortment of federal, state, and local tax, regulatory, and expenditure programs, including the incentives described above. This ad hoc approach to industrial development has some obvious difficulties. Because there is little coordination within and among levels of government and little consistency among different programs, government intervention is less effective than it might be. Moreover, because industrial policy is not clearly focused, other national goals, such as balanced regional development, are more difficult to achieve. This is particularly true since general policies, especially tax incentives, have distinct urban consequences.

The need for a clearly defined industrial policy has been widely recognized, especially in conservative quarters. Felix Rohatyn of Lazard Frères has recommended a new Reconstruction Finance Corporation for this purpose (Burke and Brokaw, 1981). Schwartz and Choate (1980) have proposed a "sectoral approach to economic policy." The Trilateral Commission has urged the United States to adopt an industrial policy "coordinated with the other branches of structural policy" (Pinder, Hosoni, and Diebold, 1979). And *Business Week* (1981) has argued that "macroeconomic policies [are] not likely to solve the problem of sectoral fragmentation. . . . Instead government policies will have to be carefully targeted to meet special needs."

FEDERAL TAX POLICY AND URBAN OUTCOMES

The first part of this section enumerates the inadvertent urban consequences of the nontargeted tax incentives discussed in the previous section. The second part discusses recent proposals to use additional tax incentives to help particularly distressed urban areas. The last part evaluates the use of tax incentives as an instrument of urban policy.

Table 8.3. Investment Tax Credits Received by Los Angeles and Philadelphia Manufacturing Industries, 1963–1976*

	Los Angeles		Philadelphia	
Industry	Total (×1000)	Per production hour	Total (×1000)	Per production hour
Food and kindred products	$36,644	$ 18	$33,386	$ 16
Textile mill products	5,446	21	7,149	14
Apparel and other textile mill products	8,024	3	5,387	2
Lumber and wood products	4,131	10	1,361	9
Furniture and fixtures	6,861	6	2,469	6
Paper and allied products	15,274	21	20,625	18
Printing and publishing	19,955	16	14,572	10
Chemicals and allied products	29,635	36	40,513	34
Petroleum and coal products	40,498	89	37,534	54
Rubber and plastics products, etc.	23,576	19	14,132	25
Stone, clay, and glass products	15,865	16	13,303	22
Primary metal industries	17,792	13	37,043	23
Fabricated metal products	37,988	13	21,038	9
Machinery, except electrical	48,228	18	33,090	15
Electrical equipment and supplies	46,909	14	22,287	10
Transportation equipment	67,206	9	18,208	12
Instruments and related products	12,713	15	6,777	12
Miscellaneous manufacturing	7,242	5	4,416	7
Total manufacturing		$342		$298

* These data were constructed by multiplying the value of each year's investment in equipment by the national average effective investment tax credit rate for that year, k_t, or

$$R_{jk} = \sum_{t=63}^{76} R_{tjk} = \sum_{t=63}^{76} (k_t \, I^e_{tjk})$$

Urban Effects of General Tax Incentives

Because industries are affected differently by tax incentives, we can expect metropolitan areas with different compositions of industry to be affected differently as well. But even when metropolitan areas have the same mix of industries, they can benefit to different degrees from federal business tax programs since there are location-related differences among plants belonging to the same industry which allow them to qualify for different amounts of credits and deductions, and since the "multipliers" of metropolitan areas differ. In addition, tax incentives accelerate changes in industry composition that would have occurred eventually in any case. These are discussed in turn below.

Location-based Differences within Industries

There are significant differences related to location among plants belonging to the same industry. A steel plant in Houston, for example, may be as different from a steel plant in Buffalo as it is from a textile mill. First, since Houston is a newer metropolitan area than Buffalo, the steel plant located there is likely also to be newer. Because the plant is newer it will be more productive, not only because it has had less time to deteriorate but also because it incorporates more recent advances in steelmaking technology. Second, since wages are generally lower in Houston than in Buffalo, production in all types of plants will most likely be done with a higher ratio of workers per machine since low wages encourage the use of labor. Third, since Houston is a growing market, the steel plants located there will themselves grow more rapidly than steel plants in Buffalo that face stagnant local demand.

Because of these intraindustry, intermetropolitan area differences in the age of plants, the mix of capital and labor used in production, and the growth rate of markets, the receipt of business tax incentives differs across metropolitan areas that have the same mix of industries. This is illustrated in table 8.3, which shows tax credits received by manufacturing industries located in the Los Angeles and Philadelphia metropolitan areas. If there were no intraindustry, intermetropolitan area differences, there would be no variation in the amount of tax

---

where R_{jk} is the entry in the table, or tax credits received by "firm" jk, and I^e is the value of equipment investment undertaken. The subscripts "j" and "k" are indices for industry and location, respectively.

Data for k_t are from Data Resources, Inc. (U.S. Central Data Bank). k_t is less than the statutory rate for year t since some assets in I^e_{tjk} have service lives of less than seven years. Intermetropolitan area differences in the distribution of assets by service lives are assumed to be negligible.

credits received by similar industries in the two metropolitan areas once differences in the scale of production were accounted for. Yet we see that the intraindustry variation is substantial in most cases. The average textile mill in Los Angeles, for example, received $21 in investment credits for each hour of work performed by a production employee over the 1963–1976 period, while the typical textile mill in Philadelphia received only $14 for each hour of work performed. This reflects the fact that the textile mills of Los Angeles were generally newer than those of Philadelphia, and the market for its textile products grew faster during that time. Similarly, petroleum and coal refineries in Los Angeles received over 60 percent more tax credits per hour of production work than refineries in Philadelphia received. In some cases Philadelphia's plants earned more tax credits than their Los Angeles counterparts. Steel mills, for example, received $23 per production hour worked in Philadelphia compared to $13 in Los Angeles. This is not surprising since steel production was substantially more capital-intensive in Philadelphia. Hence, more equipment needed to be bought per production employee and, consequently, more tax credits were generated.

Table 8.3 provides another interesting insight. For all manufacturing industries, Los Angeles received around 15 percent more tax credits per production hour worked than Philadelphia ($342 vs. $298) between 1963 and 1976. This is significant since Los Angeles was economically more vibrant during that time.[6] Thus, business tax incentives tend to reinforce regional growth rate disparities by rewarding plants in growing areas (such as Los Angeles) relatively more than plants in stagnant or declining areas (such as Philadelphia). These plants can then use the additional after-tax revenue to finance more growth.

Metropolitan Area Multipliers

The amount of credits and deductions initially received by an area's businesses is not the full measure of the urban impact of tax incentives. When businesses increase wages, raise dividends, expand investment, or cut prices as a result of having received those credits and deductions, more money ends up in the hands of workers, shareholders, and consumers. If this money is spent locally or put into savings that are ultimately invested in local businesses, the local benefits of tax incentives are multiplied.

The degree to which tax benefits multiply within an area depends on (1) how many workers, consumers, and shareholders of businesses that have received tax credits and deductions the area contains, (2) what taxpayers who have received additional income as a consequence of incentives do with it, and (3) how large and competitive local markets are.

To understand the importance of the first of these, consider a hypothetical country that has one manufacturing plant and two metropolitan areas, area A and area B. Assume that the plant is located in area A. Since a plant's work force usually lives nearby, a tax-policy–induced increase in wages will initially benefit people in area A alone. A policy-induced decrease in the price of output, however, could benefit residents of both areas. If the good were mostly consumed locally (for example, newspapers and dairy products), the initial benefits of price cuts would be concentrated among residents of area A. But if the good were exported to area B, the benefits of price cuts would also be exported. Consumers in both metropolitan areas would end up with more disposable income as a result. Similarly, if shareholders lived only in area A, policy-induced increases in dividends or in the value of shares would be limited to that area, but in the more likely case that shareholders lived in both metropolitan areas, the increased property wealth would be spread widely.

The full urban effect of business tax incentives depends on more than the initial receipt of additional income by an area's residents. It depends as well on how that income is used. That part which is spent on consumption goods could be spent within the local area or in another metropolitan area. And that part which is saved could be used for local investment or exported to another area to finance investment there. In the simple example used above, area A could benefit less than area B even if all workers and shareholders lived in area A if the extra wages paid and additional dividends distributed were spent to buy imports or if the incremental savings were loaned to new enterprises in area B. If each area in our hypothetical country contained several manufacturing plants, the full urban impact of policy-induced reductions in prices or increases in demand would depend also on the interplant linkages within and between areas. To illustrate: suppose the hypothetical country contained two factories, an auto plant and a steel mill. Then, if tax policy changes induced an increase in the demand for cars, the steel plant would also be affected since steel is used in auto production. Additional employment and wages would be generated in both industries, then, not just in the auto plant. The distribution of benefits between areas A and B would depend on the locations of the plants. If they were in the same urban area, there would clearly be a greater stimulus effect than if the auto plant were in area A and the steel plant in area B (or vice versa). The example can be elaborated further by adding the location of car dealers and maintenance, parts, and other services. If these were all concentrated in one of the two areas, the benefits of tax incentives would also be concentrated.

The receipt of additional income by area residents and its ultimate disposition—and, hence, the metropolitan area multiplier—depend, finally, on the size and organization of the local market and firm. The size of the market is important since it determines the number of consumers and shareholders an area contains. If everyone in areas A and B owned an equal share of the plant and consumed an equal amount of the manufactured good, more initial nonwage benefits would flow to the larger of the two areas. Size also determines the degree to which additional income is exported as consumption spending or savings. The larger the local area, the less "leakage" there is likely to be and, hence, the larger the multiplier would be. The organization of the market determines the likelihood of policy-induced cost reductions being passed on to consumers and of policy-induced productivity increases being reflected in wages. If there were only one employer (as in the preceding example), tax benefits would be less likely to be shared with workers in the form of higher wages than if there were intense competition for labor. Even with several employers, benefits might not be passed on to workers unless those workers were well organized. Similarly, if there were no competition in the output market or if consumers were not well organized, policy-induced decreases in costs would not likely be passed on as lower goods prices. The size and organization of the firm itself are important in this context since they determine the likely spatial distribution of shareholders. Small, closely held corporations are typically owned by a few individuals who live near their businesses, while large, public corporations are usually owned by a dispersed population of shareholders.

Plant Mobility

Some metropolitan areas are more attractive production sites than others, for example, because they have cheaper or better disciplined labor forces, more readily available supplies of energy, or lower local taxes. Businesses that are not tied to particular locations because of market or resource dependence will tend to move to these metropolitan areas. Since tax incentives add to recipient firms' after-tax cash flow, they increase the ability of the businesses to make this move. In a 1976 study, George Peterson noted that the investment tax credit and accelerated depreciation allowance encourage firms to write off capital installed in declining cities more quickly than they otherwise would have, and then reward the firms for starting anew. Once faced with the decision of where to place their capital, said Peterson, firms choose locations in growing areas. Roger Vaughan (1977) made the same observation. He concluded that "tax credits, applied without regional targeting, generally represent a subsidy to growth areas . . . at the expense of those areas that are growing more slowly."

Urban Effects: A Summary

In sum, business composition, urban size, and local market conditions seem to be the most important determinants of the effects of general tax incentives on metropolitan areas. Business composition is important since there are significant interindustry and intraindustry differences in the characteristics that condition firms' eligibility for and use of tax incentives. Business composition also affects the size of the local consumption multiplier. The size of the urban area is important since large metropolitan areas have more linkages and less "leakage" and, hence, bigger multipliers. Market conditions are important since they determine the attractiveness of an area for future investment and affect the rate of growth. Other factors also affect the degree to which tax incentives influence local economies. These include the structure of business ownership and the degree of industrial concentration.

Targeted Tax Proposals and Urban Outcomes

Another set of tax incentives proposed by presidents Carter and Reagan and various members of Congress would also have urban consequences. But unlike the existing general tax programs—whose urban effects are largely inadvertent—these proposals are specifically intended to affect particular distressed areas. It is questionable, however, whether the benefits of any of the targeted plans would be sufficient in light of the projected costs.

President Carter introduced a "differential" investment tax credit as part of his 1978 national urban policy.[7] By this plan firms would have received an additional 5 percent tax credit (on top of the general 10 percent tax credit) for investment outlays made for equipment placed in designated areas. The estimated annual tax expenditure associated with this credit was $1.5 billion (Goldsmith and Derian, 1979).

Carter's differential tax credit would have had many of the same effects as the general investment tax credit discussed in the second section. For example, the differential credit would have favored capital more than labor, equipment more than buildings, and longer-lasting more than shorter-lived assets, and would have rewarded certain kinds of businesses more than others either for behaving as they would have in any case or for being able to change their behavior to receive more credits. These more favored firms would generally have been large, growing, and capital-intensive. Thus, if the differential credit succeeded in changing the location patterns of firms, they could well have created enclaves within distressed urban areas that were dominated by businesses with those characteristics.

In one sense this is desirable since jobs would have been moved to where they were needed most. Large, capital-intensive businesses are not the best employment providers, however. Multiplant firms with separate headquarters have no particular stake in the long-term development of the areas in which they locate production facilities. Research by Harrison and Bluestone (1981), Rees (1977), Squires (1983), and others indicates that capital mobility is higher for these types of firms than for smaller, locally owned businesses. Capital-intensive firms, moreover, provide relatively few jobs per dollar of output. The jobs these firms would have offered to area residents would likely have been in the secondary labor market, again boding poorly for the area's future development since those types of jobs generally impart few skills, pay poorly, and have no future.

Two further criticisms of the 1978 plan are that (1) it may not have been lucrative enough to alter location behavior and (2) even if it were sufficiently lucrative, it would simply have "shuffl[ed] a dwindling or more or less fixed supply of jobs from one place to another" (Pred, 1977). The first of these criticisms is based on the accepted wisdom among economists that small, interjurisdictional tax rate and incentive differentials do not play a major role in the location decision of firms contemplating long moves (Oakland, 1978; Schmenner, 1978). The Carter proposal, therefore, would mostly have benefited firms that planned to locate in designated areas anyway. The second of these criticisms is perhaps the most damning of all. The United States suffers from widespread unemployment. The national jobless rate has exceeded 9 percent twice since 1975 and has been above 7 percent for more than half of the past eight years. "Beggar thy neighbor" unemployment policies, such as the differential tax credit, are hard to justify then since the areas firms vacate are likely themselves to have high unemployment.

The enterprise zone bills recently proposed by members of Congress and the president avoid some of these criticisms.[8] Each of the bills would increase employment tax credits as well as investment tax credits for firms operating in the zones. Thus, unlike the Carter proposal which would have only rewarded firms for undertaking investment, the enterprise zone bills would not bias firms toward the use of capital. The value of tax incentives included in the various enterprise zone bills is also larger than the value of Carter's national urban policy incentives, so businesses would be more likely to move into the zones in response to the incentives. In fact, Lawrence Revzan (1982) has estimated that the president's proposal would add upwards of two percentage points to the profits of a typical firm locating in a zone.

The use of tax incentives in enterprise zones is subject to criticism nonetheless. Jobs would still be shuffled from one place to another without increasing total employment. In addition, by using so many tax incentives simultaneously, the enterprise zone packages would erase virtually all of the tax liability of zone businesses. Consequently, the associated tax expenditure would be high. By January 1986, for instance, the Reagan proposal would cost the Treasury as much as $1 billion in forgone revenue (in 1982 dollars) (U.S. Department of Treasury, 1982). Even those proposals that apply more equally to the purchase of capital or the hiring of labor would favor some types of businesses more than others. For example, larger businesses with substantial taxable income would benefit more than small businesses, especially in the president's version, since the proposed tax credits are not refundable. The Reagan proposal would also unwittingly favor businesses belonging to the service, wholesale and retail trade, and finance, insurance, and real estate sectors since these businesses have technical, market, and organizational characteristics that would enable them to take particular advantage of the incentives offered (Hopeman, 1982).

The basic problem with the enterprise zone measures, as with President Carter's 1978 initiative, is that recipient businesses stand to benefit far more than the residents of the targeted areas. Since the proposals do not address the underlying problems that make the designated areas "distressed" in the first place, the incentive that must be provided to induce businesses to suffer the disamenities of zone location must be large. In the enterprise zone bill sponsored by representatives Kemp and Garcia, for instance, sixty cents of each dollar of benefit—including federal tax expenditures and new privately generated wages—would go to businesses, and forty cents would go to newly hired low-income workers.[9] The split would be even more uneven

under the Reagan plan since there would be considerably more investment and employment tax credits available for businesses and fewer tax
credits for employees. Furthermore, if the deteriorated infrastructure
and high crime within enterprise zones were not corrected, businesses
would surely move from the zone at the termination of the program,
leaving area workers unemployed once again. The particular plan
advanced by President Reagan would have further problems for zone
residents. Businesses in the designated areas would not have to hire
zone residents or other low-income individuals to benefit from most of
the tax breaks. If this happened, zone residents might actually be
made worse off. The new industrial activity and the residential development it attracted could increase local property values, driving up
taxes for existing property owners and making new property purchases
even more unlikely for low-income residents. Renters in the zone could
especially suffer since local governments applying for zone status would
be expected "to prohibit rent control [on] new dwelling units built
within the zone and on all existing units as they became vacant" (U.S.
Department of Treasury, 1982).

Federal Tax Incentives as Urban Policy

Just as there is no coherent and explicit industrial policy in the United
States, there is no clearly articulated urban policy. Principles regard-
ing urban outcomes have been included in such legislation as the
Public Works and Economic Development Act of 1965, the Comprehensive Employment and Training Act of 1973 (Title II), the Housing
and Community Development Act of 1974, the Trade Adjustment
Assistance Act of 1974, the Full Employment and Balanced Growth
Act of 1978, and most recently, the enterprise zone bills discussed
above. But either these bills have lacked sufficient budget authority to
make a difference (for example, the 1978 act), have been ill-conceived
(as have many of the enterprise zone bills), or have been offset by
other policies, most notably untargeted federal tax incentives.

This chapter sheds light on the last two of these problems. The
leading enterprise zone proposals are ill-conceived as urban policy
since (1) they would not create net new jobs, (2) they do not address
the real causes of urban decline, and (3) they are designed to help
businesses rather than distressed populations. The 1965, 1973, and
1974 acts noted above and other legislation with targeted components have provided some relief for distressed areas (Glickman, 1980;
Vaughan, 1977). But most of these acts have been cut back or elimi-

nated by the Reagan administration. In addition, as shown in the third section, general tax incentives have had a countervailing effect. In short, they have helped economically healthy metropolitan areas more than economically distressed places.

ALTERNATIVES FOR INDUSTRIAL
AND URBAN POLICY

Federal tax incentives have been criticized in the preceding sections as both industrial and urban policy. General and targeted incentives alike have been labeled ineffective, inefficient, and inequitable. They have been characterized as ineffective because they cannot always achieve their stated goals. As corporate tax rates approach zero, general tax incentives become less effective as a way to modify the behavior of businesses. And because they shuffle existing jobs from place to place, targeted incentives are not likely to achieve their primary objective of new job creation. Federal business incentives have been called inefficient as industrial and urban policy because they encourage suboptimal resource use. Specifically, existing incentives distort economic decision making by applying unequally to capital and labor and to different types of assets. And proposed targeted incentives would apply unequally to different urban areas. In addition, tax incentives lead to an inefficient use of public resources. The amount of tax revenue forgone as a result of using investment incentives, for example, may well exceed the value of induced investment, and the cost per new job created using general or targeted incentives may be significantly higher than if alternative policies were used. Finally, tax incentives have been labeled inequitable because they are generally more beneficial to the individuals, businesses, and metropolitan areas that need help the least. They tend to favor higher-income over lower-income individuals, and large and growing over small or declining businesses and urban areas.

Some of these problems can be reduced by modifying the tax laws. Some important changes would be to eliminate the capital bias of general business tax incentives, to replace the 10-5-3 depreciation provision with a more rational set of guidelines, and to use tax incentives in a more discriminating way. The first of these modifications can be achieved, in part, by integrating the employment tax credit program now on the books with the investment tax credit program. The employment tax credit subsidizes firms for part of the wage bill of "hard-to-employ" workers. In addition, the investment tax credit rate could be made uniform for all types of assets. The second suggested change has also been proposed by Auerbach and Jorgenson (1980) and Vaughan (1981), who argue that "first year cost recovery" is less distorting and more equitable than 10-5-3 depreciation. Under first-year cost recovery, businesses get to deduct in the year of acquisition the present value of depreciation of assets purchased. This is better than the 10-5-3 rule because it does not arbitrarily assign a depreciation period (ten, five, or three years) to assets. If a machine is scheduled actually to last eight years (rather than five), the business would claim depreciation based on that eight-year life. The third modification—to use tax incentives in a more discriminating way—can be achieved by limiting them to firms that meet certain performance requirements. Instead of adding incentive on top of incentive as presidents Carter and Reagan proposed to do, it would be more effective to remove unneeded incentives, for example, for growing firms that would have undertaken investment and earned profits anyway. This third suggested change would include closing tax loopholes such as the lease-back provision of the 1981 Tax Act, which was discussed in the second section.

This "fine tuning" of tax policy would reduce the deleterious effects of federal tax incentives, but it would not eliminate them. In the final analysis, policy makers must recognize that business tax incentives are inherently limited as industrial and urban policy. Because individual and corporate taxpayers are not uniform, they will inevitably be treated differently by uniform tax laws; and because metropolitan areas differ, they too will be affected in different ways by tax policy. Perhaps most importantly, it is doubtful whether the tax system can be used to achieve both desired industrial and desired urban outcomes at the same time. As Glickman (1981) argues, "There is a built-in contradiction between national economic growth and 'reindustrialization' on the one hand and our attempts to aid distressed areas on the other." A similar theme is struck by Goldsmith and Derian (1977), Cameron (1979), and others.

Because of the limitations of tax incentives as industrial and urban policy, further steps need to be taken. Business incentives should not be seen as a substitute for people-oriented policies. Social programs, especially those targeted to distressed areas, need to be restored. To the extent that these programs increase the employability of individuals and make certain places more suitable for business location (for example, by improving housing and reducing crime), they would not conflict with programs directed at businesses. Other remedies for industrial and urban decline need also to be explored. These might include fundamental changes in the tax structure and in federal policy toward business organization and ownership. Finally, the "wickedness" of industrial and urban problems (to use Webber and Rittel's [1974] metaphor) and the confounding effects of industrial and urban programs make better planning, evaluation, and policy coordination essential. In short, the United States must formulate explicit industrial and urban policies. This, at least, would make tradeoffs easier to understand and the debate about programs better informed.

NOTES

1. The transportation equipment industry also includes aircraft, boat, and other types of transportation goods plants. The Department of Commerce breaks the transportation equipment industry into two finer levels of aggregation. "Motor vehicles and supplies," for example, is at the next level of disaggregation, and "batteries" is at the finest level of disaggregation.
2. This is not to say that personal tax rates have not been reduced or corporate tax rates have not been increased on occasion. For instance, in the early 1950s, corporations paid an excess profits tax, and in the early 1970s, they were subject to a 5-to-10-percent surtax. Individual tax rates were cut in 1964 and 1981 by rather large amounts.
3. The biggest reason for this is "bracket-creep," or the necessity for individuals to pay more taxes because inflation has raised their nominal incomes into higher-taxed brackets. The 1981 Tax Act included tax indexing after 1984 to address this problem.
4. For instance, the distributions of real estate investment trusts were made tax exempt in 1961, and extraction firms were allowed to claim special resource depletion allowances until 1975.
5. Consider, for example, the article in the March 15, 1982, *Wall Street Journal*, p. 16, entitled "GE's Huge Tax Leasing Benefits Expected to Heighten Controversy Over 1981 Law." The article explains that GE was able to reduce tax payments by $280 million because of the leaseback provision.
6. In a ranking of 147 metropolitan areas according to their degree of economic distress, Garn (1981) put Philadelphia in thirteenth place and Los Angeles in fiftieth.
7. The 1978 national urban policy is discussed at length in the *Journal of Regional Science* 19 (February 1979). The policy itself is described in U.S. President, 1978.
8. These bills include HR3824, introduced by Representatives Kemp and Garcia; HR2950, sponsored by Representative Rangel; HR2965, introduced by Representative Nowak; S1240, sponsored by Senators Heinz and Riegle; and S2298, the administration's bill.
9. Author's calculation ignoring indirect benefits, but assuming that 75 percent of employees live within the zone.

REFERENCES

Ando, A.; Brown, E. Cary; Solow, R.; and Karaken, J. "Lags in Fiscal and Monetary Policy." In Commission on Money and Credit, *Stabilization Policies*. Englewood Cliffs, N.J.: Prentice-Hall, 1963.

Auerbach, A., and Jorgenson, D. "Inflation-Proof Depreciation of Assets." *Harvard Business Review* (September/October 1980):113–18.

————, and Summers, L. Testimony before U.S. Congress, House of Representatives, Committee on Ways and Means, March 22–28, 1979. In *A Review of Selected Tax Expenditures: Investment Tax Credits*. Washington, D.C.: U.S. Government Printing Office, 1979.

Bergson, A. *The Economics of Soviet Planning*. New Haven: Yale University Press, 1964.

Bischoff, C. "The Effect of Alternative Lag Distributions." In *Tax Incentives and Capital Spending*, edited by D. Fromm, Washington, D.C.: Brookings, 1971.

Bradford, D. "Tax Neutrality and the Investment Tax Credit." NBER Working Paper No. 269 (August 1978).

Burke, W. S., and Brokaw, S. "A New Reconstruction Finance Corporation? A Critique of 'Mr. Fixit's' Proposal." *Journal of Contemporary Studies* (Summer 1981):91–99.

Business Week, June 1, 1981:100.

Cameron, G. C. "The National Industrial Strategy and Regional Policy." In *Regional Policy: Past Experiences and New Directions*, edited by D. Maclennan and J. B. Parr. Oxford: Robinson, 1979.

Coen, R. "The Effect of Cash Flow on the Speed of Adjustment." In *Tax Incentives and Capital Spending*, edited by G. Fromm. Washington, D.C.: Brookings, 1971.

Cohen, S. S. *Modern Capitalist Planning: The French Model*. London: Weidenfeld and Nicolson, 1969.

Eisner, R. "Tax Incentives for Investment." *National Tax Journal* 27 (September 1973).

————, and Nadiri, M. I. "Investment Behavior and Neoclassical Theory." *Review of Economics and Statistics* 50 (August 1968):369–83.

Feld, A. "Tax Policy and Competition." Report to the Bureau of Competition and Office of Policy Planning and Evaluation, Federal Trade Commission, 1979.

Ford, G. F. "The President's Address to the Nation Announcing His Decision to Sign HR2166." *Weekly Compilation of Presidential Documents*. Washington, D.C.: Office of the Federal Register, National Archives and Records Section, GSA, April 7, 1975, p. 319.

Fowler, H. Testimony before U.S. Congress, Senate Finance Committee. In *Suspension of Investment Credit and Accelerated Depreciation*. Washington, D.C.: U.S. Government Printing Office, 1966, p. 14.

Garn, H. *Urban Economic Development Strategies: Improving Economic and Fiscal Performance*. Washington, D.C.: Economic Development Administration and the Urban Institute, 1981.

Glickman, N. "Emerging Urban Policies in a Slow-Growth Economy: Conservative Initiatives and Progressive Responses." Institute of Urban and Regional Development Working Paper No. 353. University of California, Berkeley, June 1981.

————, ed. *The Urban Impacts of Federal Policies*. Baltimore: Johns Hopkins University Press, 1980.

Goldsmith, W. W., and Derian, M. J. "Is There an Urban Policy?" *Journal of Regional Science* (February 1979):93–109.

Hall, R., and Jorgenson, D. "Tax Policy and Investment Behavior." *American Economic Review* 57 (1967):391–415.

———. "Application of the Theory of Optimal Capital Accumulation." In *Tax Incentives and Capital Spending*, edited by G. Fromm. Washington, D.C.: Brookings, 1971.

Harberger, A. "Comments." In *Tax Incentives and Capital Spending*, edited by G. Fromm. Washington, D.C.: Brookings, 1971.

Harrison, B., and Bluestone, B. *Capital and Community*. Washington, D.C.: Progressive Alliance, 1981.

Hopeman, Anna. "The Effects of Enterprise Zones on Industry Location Decisions." Unpublished paper, Duke University, April 1982.

Jorgenson, D., and Stephenson, J. A. "The Time Structure of Investment Behavior in United States Manufacturing, 1947–1960." *Review of Economics and Statistics* 49 (February 1967):16–27.

Journal of Regional Science, "Toward a National Urban Policy—Critical Reviews." Vol. 19 (February 1979):67–131.

Kennedy, J. F. "State of the Union Message to Congress." *Public Papers of the Presidents of the United States, January 20–December 31*. Washington, D.C.: U.S. Government Printing Office, 1961.

Luger, Michael I. "Tax Incentives and Tax Inequities." *Journal of Contemporary Studies* 5 (Spring 1982):33–49.

Mayer, T. "Plant and Equipment Lead Times." *Journal of Business* 33 (April 1960):127–32.

Musgrave, R., and Musgrave, P. *Public Finance in Theory and Practice*. New York: McGraw-Hill, 1980.

Nixon, R. "The Challenge of Peace." *Weekly Compilation of Presidential Documents*. Washington, D.C.: Office of the Federal Register, National Archives and Records Section GSA, September 6, 1971, pp. 1168–74.

Nixon, R. *Newsweek*, October 18, p. 18.

Oakland, W. "Local Taxes and Intra-Urban Industrial Location: A Survey." In *Metropolitan Financing and Growth Management Policies: Principles and Policies*, edited by G. Break. Madison: University of Wisconsin Press, 1978.

Peterson, G. "Federal Tax Policy and Urban Development." Washington, D.C.: Urban Institute Working Paper, 1976.

Pinder, J.; Hosoni, T.; and Diebold, W. *Industrial Policy and the International Economy*. New York: Trilateral Commission, 1979.

Pred, A. *City Systems in Advanced Economies*. New York: Wiley, 1977.

Rees, J. "Manufacturing Change, Internal Control, and Government Spending in a Growth Region of the U.S." Paper presented at the 24th North American Meeting of the Regional Science Association, November 1977.

Schmenner, R. W. *The Manufacturing Location Decision: Evidence from Cincinnati and New England*. Cambridge, Mass.: Harvard-MIT Joint Center for Urban Studies, 1978.

Schwartz, G., and Choate, P. *Revitalizing the U.S. Economy: A Brief for National Sectoral Policies*. Washington, D.C.: Academy for Contemporary Problems, 1980.

Squires, G. "Capital Mobility Versus Upward Mobility: The Racially Discriminatory Consequences of Plant Closings and Corporate Relocations." Chapter 6 in this volume.

State and Local Government Law Program. "Tax Incentives for Economic

Revitalization: New Directions for the 1980s?" State University of New York at Buffalo, School of Law, November 1981.

Sunley, R., Jr. "Toward a More Neutral Investment Tax Credit." *National Tax Journal* 26 (June 1973).

Ture, N. *Accelerated Depreciation in the United States, 1954–1960*. New York: Columbia University Press for NBER, 1967.

U.S. Code Congressional and Administrative News 6 (August 1981):1.

U.S. Congress, House of Representatives, Committee on Ways and Means. *President's Proposal on Suspension of Investment Credit and Application of Accelerated Depreciation*. Hearings, 89th Congress, 2d Session. September. Washington, D.C.: U.S. Government Printing Office, 1966.

————. *The Administration's General Economic Program*. Hearings, 94th Congress, 2d Session. January 22. Washington, D.C.: U.S. Government Printing Office, 1975, p. 5.

————. *Tax Aspects of the President's Economic Program*. Hearings, 97th Congress, 1st Session. February. Washington, D.C.: U.S. Government Printing Office, 1981, pp. 6–11.

U.S. Department of the Treasury. "The Administration Plan for Enterprise Zones." Unpublished paper. January 15, 1982.

U.S. President. *The President's 1978 National Urban Policy Report*. A Biennial Report to the Congress prepared by the U.S. Department of Housing and Urban Development. Washington, D.C.: U.S. Government Printing Office, 1978.

Vaughan, R. *The Urban Impacts of Federal Policies:* Volume 2, *Economic Development*. Santa Monica, Calif.: Rand, 1977.

————. "The Job Development Administration: A National Employment, Education, and Training Policy." Unpublished paper. Albany, N.Y., September 1981.

Wall Street Journal, March 15, 1982, p. 16.

Webber, M. M., and Rittel, H. "Dilemmas in a General Theory of Planning." *DMG-DRS Journal: Design Research and Methods* (January–March 1974):31–39.

9

Regional Economic Policy and the New Corporatism

DAVID WILMOTH

The debates around reindustrialization and associated social contracts pose a dilemma for progressive regional economic policy in the United States.[1] Given the regressive implicit regional policies of the Reagan administration, the various investment planning proposals for reindustrialization appear to offer opportunities at least for debate about appropriate directions for regional policy, and possibly for contributions from the labor movement and progressive planners. Yet it is clear that most of the reindustrialization proposals under current discussion are corporatist in form, with big business and big government forming tripartite, "top-down" planning committees in nominal collusion with big labor at a time when the labor movement has rarely been weaker. Leo Panitch (1981) defines corporatism as "a political structure within advanced capitalism which integrates organized socio-economic producer groups through a system of representation and cooperative mutual interaction at the leadership level and mobilization and social control at the mass level."

At one extreme, corporatism is an integral part of facism. Less extreme forms have been embodied in some parts of the New Deal and in European social democracy. Under corporatist systems political power tends to be organized by economic sector and integrated at the top by authoritarian leadership. Democratic political representation by area tends to be overshadowed by sector-based representation, and in the economy market freedom tends to be replaced by industrial planning. Because current regional problems are caused by unprecented changes in the industrial structure of the economy, modern corporatist proposals are taking a new form. The main question asked by this chapter is: Do recent reindustrialization proposals offer good opportunities, or are they politically too dangerous?

One approach to answering this question is to examine the context of specific reindustrialization proposals over the last five years and the evolution of regional policy. An understanding of recent domestic economic policy, especially the nature of economic crisis and differing perceptions of the same economic and social conditions, is vital to understanding the origins of such policy proposals. The roots of recent proposals lie in the failure of earlier approaches. Regional economic policy has gone through several stages, for convenience here called early Carter, late Carter, and early Reagan.

On the grounds of countercyclical stimulus to the economy, the early Carter administration boosted assistance to state and local governments even after signs of general economic recovery were apparent. Part of this at least was an attempt to redirect public sector resources to areas "in distress." Lagging private investment in particular worried the administration. Espousing the theme of "public-private partnership," the Carter administration's explicit urban and regional policies concentrated on stimulating private investment in these distressed areas,[2] even against the contradictory and more powerful across-the-board subsidies to private investment elsewhere. Targeted economic development proposals dominated urban and regional policy debate and the administration's budget proposal.

What hopes the Carter administration may have had for remedial regional redistribution were dashed against the hard realization that the economic crisis of the late 1970s was not a simple cyclical matter, but one threatening the industrial structure of the whole economy. Calls from business, labor, and congressional quarters for state-led "reindustrialization" took some time to penetrate the Carter administration. First, the administration repudiated the social policies and programs of the 1960s,[3] to shift the emphasis of regional policy onto business development policy with a nod toward small business. Later the Carter administration found itself forced by circumstance to jettison even these regional economic interventions. It turned to an "economic revitalization" package of proposals that was corporatist in form and less remedial in terms of regional redistribution. In effect, industry policy eclipsed regional policy, and an earlier "jobs-to-people" emphasis turned to a "people-to-jobs" strategy.

This helped clear the way for the Reagan pursuit of "supply-side" and monetarist domestic economic policies that are now widening social and regional disparities. But even as the chances of corporatist planning take a back seat for a while, proposals for investment planning from capital, labor, and even within the Reagan administration itself are gaining currency. Furthermore, in the face of dangerous regional disparities, explicit regional policy is gaining a place in these new proposals. If the Reagan strategy succeeds, some state coordination of a new wave of investment may be needed; certainly there will be a greater need for setting infrastructure priorities. It is more likely that the strategy will not succeed, and in the ensuing crisis, corporatist proposals will be ready to take over. Either way, it is argued below, there may be a future for these proposals later in this administration or during the next one. Whether such a new political arena would offer new opportunities for progressive regional policy, or new dangers of top-down corporatist planning, still remains an open question. What follows gives some recent historical context to this question and offers criteria for answering it.

EARLY CARTER

The Carter administration came to power with the international oil crisis and the legacy of the 1973–1975 recession dominating domestic policy. Though Northeastern and North Central regions were hardest hit by these problems, Carter's first big policy initiative, the energy policy, was criticized as antiurban and anti-Frostbelt because its subsidies for Western-based synthetic fuels development would hasten Sunbelt growth and Northeastern decline (Markusen and Fastrup, 1978; Western Urban and Regional Policy Collective, 1978).

In addition to his energy policy, Carter engaged in the more routine economic pump-priming. The administration extended employment, public works, and fiscal assistance to state and local governments. With the inevitable delays in authorization and spending, the economic stimulus package took effect long after economic recovery was under way, but the assistance nevertheless helped many city governments and constituted an implicit urban and regional policy (Stanfield 1980b:1468). However, state and local government reliance on countercyclical spending was obviously risky, given that regional distribution effects were secondary to general economic effects, and that recovery could remove this indirect rationale. Furthermore, the explicit retargeting of assistance programs, especially community development block grants (CDBG), sharpened regional rivalries in and out of Congress (Markusen and Fastrup, 1978; Stanfield, 1977b). The compromise dual formula settled upon for the latter program, by which localities were funded according to the old formula or a new one that favored cities with old housing stock, whichever was greater, did not satisfy the new Sunbelt lobbies, which felt they had lost the fight. Because of the basis of his constituency, Carter had to walk a tightrope on regional allocation questions. In his words, "I don't see it as an economic war between the North and the South. . . . I think the problems are nationwide, and the focusing of attention on employment opportunities would be much more on a community-by-community basis than it would North versus South" (Stanfield, 1977a:140). Public sector constituents for regional policy were reasonably satisfied.

Business was a more demanding constituency. The distinctive emphasis of the new administration lay not in its public sector programs but in its support, through ostensibly urban and regional programs, for private investment. Private investment has been more and more heavily subsidized since at least the Kennedy investment tax credits and other stimuli (Luger, 1981), but by 1977 Carter's advisers thought lagging investment was still the weakest link in economic recovery. This view strongly influenced urban and regional policy. Urban Development Action Grants (UDAGs) offer a good example of perhaps the most successful program in legislative and political terms. (The National Development Bank, UDAG's intended longer-term counterpart, was less successful. That is examined later.) The UDAG program provided grants to private development projects that would otherwise not be feasible in cities with high unemployment rates and other indicators of distress. Certain private development projects (characteristically hotels, convention centers, and shopping centers) in targeted cities were awarded direct federal grants in order to "leverage" additional private investment. UDAGs fitted the political requirements of the time: leveraging appeared to make scarce federal dollars go a long way; targeting on areas "in distress" appeared to focus them effectively; and offering grants ultimately to corporations rather than to local governments appeared to ensure that jobs so created were private, and hence permanent, by contrast with jobs created within, or fully by, the state. In practice, none of these held very strongly. It was impossible to ascertain in advance whether a UDAG really would tip the scales toward feasibility. Congressional "log rolling"—and the administration's anticipation of Congress—ensured that benefits were widely spread geographically. It was at least debatable whether service jobs in new downtown hotels and convention centers were more stable than public service jobs. But for the above reasons, and for the flexibility it gave the administration in awarding the grants, UDAGs became popular with property developers and inner-urban investors.

But countercyclical dollars and UDAGs were no substitute for an urban and regional policy. In April 1977 Carter set up an interagency Urban and Regional Policy Group (URPG) to prepare a policy statement (Wolman and Merget, 1980). If the city government officials and property developers were reasonably satisfied with the early programs of the Carter administration, minority organizations and community groups were more and more critical of the administration's apparent neglect of social programs and lack of support for community-based organizations (for example, Humphrey, 1977; Jordan, 1977). Such criticism goaded Carter into ensuring closer White House supervision of urban and regional policy formation. This, combined with tight budget deadlines and a White House study of the possibility of reorganizing community and economic development programs, both put pressure on URPG and worsened interagency conflicts. Proposals to stimulate private economic development were central to the URPG's work because they addressed the central economic questions of the day, namely economic recovery, shortage of private investment, and unemployment, and because they appeared to reverse the increasingly discredited approach of relying on the creation of public sector jobs instead of jobs in private industry. In this interagency process, the Economic Development Agency's (EDA) nonurban background, Treasury's overview of the economy, and White House anticipation of congressional opposition all widened the earlier Department of Housing and Urban Development (HUD) focus on cities and regions in distress toward communities across the country and "pockets" of poverty within otherwise ineligible wealthy areas. When a bland compromise set of principles was put to Carter, he replied:

1. include all cities;
2. analyze existing programs first;
3. encompass federal, state, and local governments and private and neighborhood groups and volunteers. (U.S. President, 1978.)

These three points sum up, in a pithy way, the urban and regional policy that emerged. The first is of most interest here. The regional politics of Congress, the broad mission of participating agencies, and the politics of presidential constituencies all caused URPG to propose spread-out targeting. So avidly did it second-guess Congress that at least one program was criticized widely there for targeting too broadly (Donsky, 1978:1963).[4] Even so, the administration tried to make political capital out of the idea of targeting itself. It still appeared to limit spending to needy areas, even if that included most of the population for some programs. The net effect of geographically spreading program funding, of relying on marginal changes to existing programs, and of providing something for all interest groups was that Carter's 1978 urban and regional policy proposals were scattered, weak in relation to recognized urban problems, and not especially novel.

When they finally were released, long after publicly announced deadlines, the April 1978 proposals were focused on urban economic development, especially the stimulation of private investment through subsidies to developers (Hager, 1978). A differential investment tax credit was proposed as an incentive to business investment in inner urban areas, even though the enormous tax subsidies to business in general had the opposite net effect of encouraging capital movement out of "distressed" areas toward growing regions (see chapter 8 and Western Urban and Regional Collective, 1978). This happened because investment incentives encourage industrialists to build new plants, which are usually located away from inner-city areas in suburban locations or nearby developing regions. Antirecession assistance was to be continued through revenue sharing programs and labor-intensive public works. Tax credit incentives to employers to hire the unemployed and an urban volunteer corps were also proposed as means of creating employment. A state strategies program was proposed to encourage states, on a competitive basis, to prepare urban and regional plans. Within the federal government, an Interagency Coordinating Council was to be set up, and new constraints to be placed on federal procurement and facility location to pursue urban and regional objectives. All new and major federal initiatives affecting urban and regional development would be subject to urban and community impact analyses, to be prepared by the proposing agencies. There were many other proposals.

The most innovative and controversial proposal was for a national development bank, a version of the "urbank" idea that had been around federal circles since the Johnson administration. It proposed a new institution governed by three hitherto contending cabinet secretaries (Treasury, HUD, and EDA) that would finance businesses to remain, expand, or locate in economically depressed urban and rural areas through a combination of grants, loan guarantees, tax exemptions, and direct loans. The proposal was presented by the press as the "centerpiece" of the Carter strategy (to the extent that the miscellaneous collections of proposals had any center at all), and in many respects the most innovative. It was also the largest single spending item, both in budgetary terms and in terms of federal credit obligations. It proposed a new financial institution with considerable powers of discretion (if not, at the outset, resources fit for the task). Consideration of the development bank more than any other proposal created an arena for designing a fundamental shift in the focus of U.S. urban and regional policy: a move away from social policy to business development policy, from local countercyclical and redistributive spending to corporate reindustrialization. This change in regional policy was marked not by a change in administration, but by a mid-term, mid-business-cycle change in strategy arising from a late realization of how serious the larger economic crisis had become. Within severe constraints, the bank was attractive to the administration for several reasons. It assisted private capital investment relatively directly, little mediated by local governments or community groups. Much of its assistance was off-budget, mostly loan guarantee authorities and loan loss coverage. It spoke the language of development finance, not remedial programs to the poor or disadvantaged, though it retained a somewhat misleading impression of being focused on unemployment in areas of distress.

The bill to create the urbank failed to be reported out of congressional committee. The proposal was made very late in the 95th Congress and was weakly backed by White House lobbying. For the next congressional session, the administration retreated in several respects. It proposed to build on an existing agency and programs rather than creating a new one—thus scuttling the main feature of the "bank." Carter proposed to allocate even less money to the program than before, and to broaden the geographical targeting criteria even further in anticipation of congressional widening. (After Congress dealt with it, 90 percent of the U.S. population lived in eligible areas.) EDA, on whose public works reauthorization bill the development finance provisions were "piggybacked," appeared to have won the interagency battle, but it was a pyrrhic victory indeed. After passage by the House and Senate, the bill lay dormant in conference. As part of an emergency antiinflation package early in 1980, Carter tried to defer the bill, but as the 1980 elections approached, the Carter White House changed position and desperately lobbied for conference resolution of the stalled public works bill. But committee jurisdictions, personal intransigence, irritation at the White House style of lobbying, and preelection party politics kept the conferees deadlocked until the elections. Carter's national development bank was dead.

Private economic development was clearly the focus of Carter's urban and regional policy proposals; the largest portion of funding was oriented to the business community, as tax breaks, loans, loan guarantees, and outright grants. Transfer payments to individuals and grants to city governments were seen only as short-term expedients. A variety of constituencies approved of this situation. Organized labor was happy enough with the proposals, though some had qualms about the subminimum wages allowed in job creation programs (U.S. HUD, 1977a, 1977b). As a large constituency that voted for Carter, the poor and the unemployed in distressed areas would receive nothing directly, in part because services "to people" were defined out of the meaning of urban and regional policy. They would be served by the trickle down of affluence from restored local economies and the assumed increase in employment that would result from CETA, job credits, and business expansion incentives, as well as direct welfare payments not regarded as "urban and regional" (Donsky, 1979:24).

For the first time, the administration claimed, the federal government had formulated an explicit national urban policy. However, in addition to the weak political support in the first place, political and economic conditions changed, thus further preventing full implementation. First, economic recovery was more sluggish than expected, with the weakest part of capital accumulation being insufficient private investment in productive activities. Capitalists claimed incentives for themselves and cutbacks for everyone else, not by lobbying hard, but through a successful ideological offensive to make their problems synonymous with the economy's problems, hence society's problems. The effect was to shift the focus away from social policy toward business development policy, especially toward subsidies to private investment in a situation where capital markets were increasingly crowded with potential borrowers. Second, a related mood of fiscal conservatism and a movement for deregulation gained in Congress, with domestic social programs and business regulations coming under especially close scrutiny. Bad relations between an "outsider" White House and Congress did not help matters. The effect of this fiscal conservatism was to curb the rate of growth of payments to local sectors of the state, where responsibility for most urban services and regional development was vested, and to have the explicit urban and regional policy arena separate out "people"-related problems from "place"-related ones. In these and other ways, urban policy turned its back on much of social policy. Third, among smaller capitalists, sharper competition for relatively fewer public and private resources, coupled with the demystification explicit in the rewriting of supposedly objective spatial allocation formulae of federal programs, both ended earlier opportunities for enacting any measures targeted toward areas "in distress." The anticipated experience of regional rivalry, especially in the House, brought the administration to curb its earlier "pro-city" tilt toward the declining urban areas of the Northeast and North Central regions, to despatialize urban policy by alluding to "communities," and to ensure, in the president's very words, that all cities were included.

In short, the early Carter administration searched unsuccessfully for a way out of the underlying economic crisis first by countercyclical means that were targeted regionally, and secondly by means of weaker-targeted investment incentives for private economic development. Neither involved removal of important investment decisions from normal politics or corporate choice; even the unsuccessful national development bank was to have been governed by cabinet secretaries at least indirectly accountable. The "new partnership" between government and business was only a rhetorical reflection of the Carter administration's probusiness priorities.

LATE CARTER

The unprecedented inflation of 1979 and onset of a much-forecast recession during 1979 and 1980 caused the administration to look twice at its usual stock of countercyclical state and local pump-priming programs and to decide not to promote them. This had the effect of a policy of fighting inflation with unemployment and recession even during an election year. A rising deficit, voter dissatisfaction with traditional bromides, and, above all, a growing awareness that something more basic was wrong with the structure of industry all influenced this abandonment of conventional countercyclical programs. This time, there was less scope for growth in social policy except where legally mandated and therefore "uncontrollable" programs were involved. Worsening unemployment in large cities gave further justification for an urban and regional policy focused on economic development, but worsening inflation and another general recession were translated into increased congressional opposition to federal spending. Indeed, Carter attempted to balance the last budget over which he had any implementation control. This possibility was later ruined by some "uncontrolable" anticyclical spending triggered by a deteriorating economy (Vaughan, 1979). Inflation still dominated domestic policy, resisting all efforts to quell it, short of full recession. In the words of *Business Week*,

> Wishful thinking has been the hallmark of the Carter administration economic policy from the beginning. For most of [1979], President Carter's economic advisers kept seeing the recession—their last weapon against inflation—just around the corner. Treasury Secretary G. William Miller even declared the slump "half over" last fall [1979], well before it had begun. (Wildstrom, 1980.)

The crisis was deeper than the administration feared, and its stock of acceptable domestic economic and regional policies was depleted.

By the last year of the Carter administration, policy attention moved away from the spatial structure of the economy—battles among new regional lobby groups notwithstanding—to the more basic problems of its sectoral and industrial structure. With this move regional policy took a position even more subordinate to national economic policy, even though there were significant, usually implicit, regional dimensions to the new industrial policy.

Earlier discussion around regional policy, for example at the 1978 White House Conference on Balanced National Growth and Economic Development (U.S. White House Conference, 1978), did show a conflict between those who considered the economic crisis then to be serious and endemic to the industrial structure, and those who argued for nothing more than mildly ameliorative urban and regional policy. But by late 1979, as the economic outlook worsened into recession and the associated political prospects for Carter's reelection looked dimmer,[5] those arguing that there was something more serious than a cyclical downturn gained the upper hand. In August 1980 Carter said, "This is no time for an economic stimulus program," and he repudiated the emphasis of urban and regional policy that had prevailed early in his administration. An administration official admitted that "[t]his time, instead of trying to stimulate consumer purchasing, we're going to encourage investment in industry, productivity and energy conservation" (Stanfield, 1980a:1468). The countercyclical programs of 1978 and 1977 had actually been very useful to cities and regional development bodies, and the new "tightfisted approach to this recession has confused and enraged some members of the liberal-labor community" (ibid.).

Despite more and more subsidies and greater prospects for infla-

tion outlook, investment was still not picking up. Even though the concepts of "insufficient" capital (in neoclassical theory capital is always
available, at a price), and of capital markets "crowded out" by too
many borrowers may be problematic, the rate of growth of net fixed
business capital stock during the 1970s was 25 percent lower than
during the 1950s and 1960s (U.S. Comptroller General, 1980:i), and
the capital shortage in 1980 much more pressing than in the mid-1970s
(Carson-Parker, 1980:72). Some capital-intensive industries where
productivity was going slowly, such as autos, rubber, and steel, were
closer to collapse. The economies of the regions in which they were
concentrated were consequently in a precarious situation (Rohatyn,
1981b:19). Economists spoke of a distinctly one-sided recession, with
other industries—energy, electronics, and chemicals for example—growing rapidly. Despite implicit federal encouragement of capital investment by means of investment incentives that grew faster than the rest
of the budget and the economy, the 1974–1975 recession was not
enough to do the job of industrial restructuring needed for the next
period of economic growth. Another recession was necessary, but it
ran the risk of a full "economic calamity," to use the later words of
President Reagan. To avoid a deeper crisis, some finance and corporate capitalists wanted the state to give more promotion and direction
to investment.

Business Week led the way by popularizing new "reindustrialization" proposals, followed enthusiastically, if somewhat vaguely, by the
rest of the media (Business Week, 1981c; Fortune, March 9, 1981;
Hershman, 1980; Newsweek, September 8, 1980; Pierce and Steinbach,
1980; Time, February 23, 1981; and U.S. News & World Report,
September 22, 1980). Others called it recapitalization (Miller, 1979).
The Carter administration called its set of investment incentives economic revitalization, in typical style metaphorically associating business activity with life itself.

Most of the reindustrialization proposals under discussion had
common elements: a "social contract" under which labor would peace-
fully accept lower wages and new technology, government would cut
nonmilitary spending and deregulate, and business with new profit incentives would once again make productive investments. To the extent
that this could encourage further capital flight out of older industries
and regions, one might have expected opposition from people in areas
that would lose jobs.[6] But by 1980 the rhetoric of austerity and the
ideological closure of Keynesian options muted opposition, while reindustrialization proposals sought a new "social contract." As this

vague term became popular, it attracted strange bedfellows. Almost everybody was for reindustrialization, but there were at least three different groups under the reindustrialization blanket.

The first were radical conservatives, who associated a reactionary utopia of small-scale free enterprise capitalism with the dismantling of the welfare state (such as it was) and the promotion of private investment through across-the-board profit incentives. Their supply-side strategy dominated the policy of the Reagan campaign and much of the Reagan administration's economic strategy, if not the later cabinet composition: severe cuts in nonmilitary spending, deregulation, and regressive (that is, prorich) tax cuts. The National Association of Manufacturers and the U.S. Chamber of Commerce came up with reindustrialization programs compatible with this strategy (*Business Week*, 1980:34). The strategy was not explicitly targeted on particular industries or regions, though implicitly it favored big oil and the Sunbelt. While trying to assist U.S. industrial development by the above means, this group usually dissociated itself from the avowed "reindustrialists."

This second self-defined group for reindustrialization was made up of corporate liberals who argued for a much more explicit industrial policy of support for particular industries and associated regions. Careful nurturing of the growth industries—for example, computers, robotics, and genetics—and adjustment assistance or euthanasia for declining industries and regions were at the heart of this strategy. It tended toward national investment planning, though most of the group would not call it that (Tabb, 1980). Felix Rohatyn was the best known of the group (Rohatyn, 1979, 1980, 1981a, 1981b), as befitted a finance capitalist who designed New York's Municipal Finance Corporation and Emergency Financial Control Board, the city's de facto receivers. Without strong federal intervention in industrial and regional policy, Rohatyn saw the whole United States declining just as New York had. Many of the demands of this group amounted to calls for a corporatist state, with tripartite big-business, big-labor, big-government committees deciding upon future patterns of investment for industries and regions. Their proposals carried through as alternatives during the Reagan administration, so they are further considered in the next section.

In a sense, the above groups were the two poles of the main debate on reindustrialization since left proposals were not relevant.[7] There was also a center group arguing for government assistance tar-

geted on research and development and on new investment in manufacturing and infrastructure, rather than on consumption and services
to the working class. This third group was pragmatically conservative
and wanted to target goverment assistance to capital formation, not
just to profits, as did the first group, or to specific industries and
regions, as did the second group. This is what Carter's economic revitalization strategy tried to do, alongside ad hoc congressional assistance to distressed entities such as New York City and Chrysler corporation.

Carter's economic program for the eighties statement continued
the rhetorical theme of a "new partnership" between government and
private business evident in earlier national urban policy statements.[8]
Under this program an Economic Revitalization Board would be made
up of representatives of business, labor, and an unspecified "public"
sector. In such a partnership, Irving Shapiro, chair of the du Pont
Corporation, and Lane Kirkland, president of the AFL-CIO, accepted
joint chairmanship. Their first tasks were to propose arrangements for
an Industrial Development Authority and to propose separate arrangements for remedying the effects of industrial dislocation, for improving
worker skills and job training, and for meeting health and safety regulations. The purpose of the authority would be to "help mobilize public
and private resources, including pension funds, to restore private
industrial development and create jobs in areas affected by economic
dislocation" (U.S. White House, 1980a).

Though it was up to the Economic Revitalization Board to make
appropriate recommendations, it is clear that the tripartite public
sector–business–labor structure would be perpetuated (Shapiro, 1980:
1810). Urban and regional problems were to be addressed, but they
were of secondary importance. In Shapiro's words, "The basic mission
is to restore the health of the American economy. Part of that includes
decaying cities, but from my perspective it's the economic issues that
are the driving force" (ibid.). Kirkland wanted to take a more inter-
ventionist position, but in the direction of tax incentives to particular
firms rather than toward an urban and regional policy (Business Week,
1980d). The regional policy people who had worked together in URPG
managed to have some regional emphasis included (Kaplan, 1980),
but even within the Department of Commerce, EDA had little to say
on what was increasingly seen as a matter for sectoral policy, not regional policy (Hausner, 1980).

In its emphasis on industries in distress, Carter's economic revital-

ization proposal, general as it was, moved toward a corporatist solution to economic crisis, one compatible with the center "pragmatic"
camp of reindustrialism described earlier and reminiscent of the
Reconstruction Finance Corporation (RFC).[9] Urban and regional
problems, though addressed, were clearly secondary. Open confusion
around emergency legislation for saving Chrysler, excessive politicization of regional resource allocation, and the failure of economic development programs to deal with the structure of the economy all argued
for a new approach to state investment priority setting at least one step
removed from electoral politics and involving government, business,
and labor leaders. This was an attempt to find a corporatist solution to
the economic crisis. However, Carter, Shapiro, and Kirkland agreed
that the proposals would not take effect until after the 1980 elections.

The progressive downgrading of areal assistance to people, governments, and locally based industries went a step further with President Carter's Commission on an Agenda for the Eighties. While not
endorsing its specific recommendations, Carter did not publicly dis-
avow them either. It was published in the last days of the administration at a crucial time electorally, though this apparently was not the
political design of the White House. At least some administration officials' thinking had moved. Accordingly, this report may well have
influenced the Reagan administration.[10]

On the basis of an analysis which found that "contrary to conventional wisdom, cities are not permanent" and can be left to depopulate,
that "technological, economic, social and demographic trends" are
"near immutable," and that the New Deal "commitment to continuing
federal involvement in the functioning of local economies was never
intended," the report proposed, "It may be in the best interests of the
nation to commit itself to the promotion of locationally neutral economic and social policies rather than spatially sensitive urban policies
that either explicitly or inadvertently seek to preserve cities in their
historical roles" (U.S. President's Commission, 1980:165). In this context the growth pains of the Sunbelt were held to be "no less traumatic" than the shrinking pains of declining regions. The main emphasis would have to be on reindustrialization, sending people to where
the new jobs would be, not encouraging new jobs where unemployed
people already lived. This flatly reversed the "jobs-to-people" strategy
of the early Carter administration. No U.S. Government document has
ever argued so strongly for the neglect of declining regions.

On industrial policy, the commission took a no less laissez faire
attitude:

The aim of government policies should be to facilitate the access of all industries to adequate capital, ideas, and labor, rather than to direct resources toward some sectors or industries and away from others. Not only are efforts by government to designate "winners" and "losers" likely to be fraught with difficulty . . . but *the very imagery is that of divisiveness and politicization rather than consensus and cohesion.* Instead, the emphasis should be on maintaining diversified industrial strength, competitiveness, and technological dynamism, with policies that encourage resources to flow to their most productive uses. At the same time, it is essential to provide *temporary* assistance to workers and communities hurt by the transitions resulting from technological progress and changing patterns of international trade [emphases added]. (Ibid.:65.)

The new corporatists wanted the "divisiveness and polarization" of redistributive regional policy replaced by a "consensus and cohesion" over reindustrialization policy focused on production and fueled by profit incentives. But this report was published and not used, and the 1980 elections denied Carter the chance to put his other "revitalization" policies into practice.

EARLY REAGAN

Clearly, the early Reagan administration is not pursuing corporatist policies. It does not need to make any concession toward labor, and indeed is doing its best to attack and ignore the various parts of the labor movement. Yet corporatist ideas are gaining currency not only in opposition to the administration's domestic economic policies, but within the new administration itself. In the context of the Reagan administration's implicit regional economic policies, these proposals are discussed here. Their chances of implementation and ultimate success are discussed in the next section.

The ostensibly neutral regional policy implied by the Reagan administration's version of supply-side economics in practice disguises a strong implicit regional policy. The bias toward certain industries such as oil and certain sectors of state activity such as military development have strong regional implications, for example for the South and West, where energy boom towns and defense projects will be disproportionately located. The accelerated disinvestment from older industries in North Central and Northeast regions enabled by domestic economic policies is causing regional dislocation on a massive scale. Cuts in programs and elimination of such agencies as EDA will have negative regional effects that mirror their current regional spending patterns. New, explicitly spatial policies such as "enterprise zones" (Le Gates and Wilmoth, 1981) may have some effects in designated areas. The consolidation of programs and devolution of responsibilities to the state level will undoubtedly have differential regional effects as some states reduce service standards or eliminate some services altogether. Though the aggregate regional consequences of all these policies are not yet calculable, from the point of view of equitable regional distribution they are far from benign. The economic vulnerability of whole industries and the regions in which they are concentrated has given rise to a new round of corporatist proposals to reconstitute the RFC.

Of the new RFC proposals made, those of William Moorhead, the AFL-CIO, the Felix Rohatyn were among the most influential. They also represent three different urban policy constituencies. Long a promoter of development banking arrangements, Rep. William S. Moorhead (D-Pa), chair of the House banking committee, proposed a new RFC in his last term of office (Moorhead, 1980). Referring to the cumbersome legislative solutions found for resolving the crises of New York City and Chrysler Corporation, Moorhead proposed an RFC that would (1) offer corporations and cities equity, not just more loans and therefore more debt, (2) issue its own obligations in the market, and (3) be able to borrow from the U.S. Treasury. The RFC would not only bail out entities in distress—with "tough and mean" provisions—but would also help reindustrialization by offering corporations not in distress financial assistance to modernize. The proposal itself was not reported out of his committee, but it reflected the views of liberal Democrats toward reindustrialization by one of their best-placed people. Rep. James Blanchard's more recent proposal for an RFC in a bill called "the United States Revitalization Act" was along the same lines (Newsweek, 1981:29).

As if encouraged by Kirkland's role as joint chair of Carter's Economic Revitalization Board, the AFL-CIO soon thereafter, in February 1981, called for a new RFC (Kirkland, 1981). This proposal, like the others, called for appointees from business, labor, and government to be on the board. The RFC would offer a broad range of tax and nontax subsidies. However, the AFL-CIO proposal put more emphasis than the others on the basic manufacturing sector and on investments in areas that were economically distressed. Other eligibility factors would include industries with "bottleneck" capacity problems, high-risk but high-growth possibilities, competition with foreign-government–

supported firms, and, not least, risks of bankruptcy or failure that would have repercussions on production elsewhere (ibid.:2). The RFC would be financed in part by pension fund set-asides (ibid.:7).[11] The proposal did not mention a municipal window.

The New York City fiscal crisis spawned Rohatyn's proposal (Alcaly and Mermelstein, 1977:300–01). Arguing that national and indeed international financial stability was at stake in New York City's near collapse[12] (and that $30 billion, about 20 percent of the capital of the U.S. banking system, could have been declared insolvent), Rohatyn feared that the United States as a whole would also suffer a similar crisis unless drastic economic and political changes were adopted. The good relations apparently forged in the heat of crisis in New York City among government, finance, and labor leaders led him to believe that a similar entente could be struck at the national level. Administering the bitter medicine of economic restructuring could not be done through democratic means alone; the changes would have to be decided upon "away from the political hurly-burly," while he nevertheless appeared accountable via public appointments (Rohatyn, 1979:8). A tripartite RFC was the central part of his solution for solving the national economic crisis: "We in New York City found ourselves at war and created the equivalent of a coalition government to manage an austerity program. That coalition of government, business, and labor works. A similar coalition must be created at the national level if we are to show the rest of the world that our democratic system really works" (ibid.:19).

By this means, investment would be allocated and attracted to industries and enterprises in danger, and the RFC would "play a major part in a regional policy" (Rohatyn, 1981b:19). The RFC would also be able to buy equity in firms and would have a city window for direct municipal finance. The federal government would capitalize it at $5 billion and authorize it to issue $25 billion in government-guaranteed bonds that would be used to "leverage" more private money, especially OPEC petrodollars (ibid.). "Only an RFC that is publicly accountable but is run outside politics, like MAC in New York State, could provide such capital as well as negotiate the often stringent concessions that would have to come with it" (ibid.:18). Labor would be "asked to make their contribution in the form of wage concessions and changes in work rules that would increase productivity" (ibid.). In the same way that New York City politics lost democratic control of city budgets to appointed committees dominated by financiers, so would industrial policy and regional policy be shielded from politics and subordinated to an RFC or a Temporary National Economic Committee

(Tabb, 1980:54). This overt corporatist structure of Rohatyn's solution had considerable appeal to finance capitalists, city officials, and Democrats looking for a new approach. At first dismissed as the ideas of a "gadfly" and as unnecessarily alarmist, Rohatyn's proposals came to the cover page of magazines like Newsweek (1981:26–35) and gained wide currency through the media.

The social and regional development purposes of a new RFC and other development banking arrangements appealed to liberals disenchanted with the conservative ideology then dominant. Even some radicals were attracted by the prospect of central investment planning for the above-mentioned allocation priorities.

AN EVALUATION

What political conclusions can be drawn from the recent history of regional policy and the rise of reindustrialization proposals with corporatist aspects? How corporatist really are the proposals? What are their chances of coming to the center of regional policy consideration? Should they be opposed or supported? What are their implications for progressive regional investment planning?

By contrast with other advanced capitalist countries, the United States has had little recent experience with corporatist structures, certainly not in the field of investment planning.[13] Carter's revitalization proposals and calls for a new RFC by the AFL-CIO, finance capitalist Rohatyn, and Business Week all involve tripartite government-business-labor committees. To the extent that the proposals involve producer group integration into economic policy making, they are corporatist. Though none of the proposals are close to implementation, it is prudent to speculate about the possibilities.

Will such proposals come to the fore? At present they are more the property of corporate liberals within and around the Democratic party. Though their influence is undoubtedly growing as the economy fails to recover and as the media disseminate their ideas, they do not as yet have broad support among all fractions of capital. Indeed, there is a strong ideological aversion among labor as well as capital to government intervention in the pattern of investment. Faltering old industries and capital-short new industries prefer ad hoc assistance for the few (preferably them) rather than systematic attention to the investment needs of many. The supply-side strategy of service and budget cuts, tax concessions, military spending, and deregulation is still dominant. Economic policy is corporatist now only in the sense that reactionary policy could be seen as leading to the possibility of "friendly fascism" (Gross, 1979). Corporatism, however, as defined here excludes the simple repressive integration of labor into the fascist state. The real corporatists, those who would have tripartite business-labor-government committees setting industry and possibly regional priorities for investment, have little influence in the Reagan administration. Rohatyn, Kaufman, Minsky, and other finance capital jeremiads, who argue that debt expansion and underinvestment have put the whole economic structure in danger of collapse without a new RFC, are hardly in favor at the White House (Carson-Parker, 1980). Their remedies for government intervention imply too much industrial and regional direction. Radical as Reagan's intervention may be, it has not advocated explicit industrial and regional priorities and business-labor-government tripartite committees.[14]

However, the tripartite reindustrialization proposals may well see another day. As the supply-side strategy of spending cuts, tax cuts, deregulation, and remilitarization deepens the economic crisis, then industry calls for emergency assistance, allocating scarce capital, and clamping down on class struggle by state incorporation (as well as by more direct repression) may be hard for the administration to resist. Certainly the Rohatyn proposals are growing in influence within the Democratic party as a counter-Reaganomics, as Kirkland and others became converts (Bedell, 1982:6). Even if the supply-side strategy works, there could be such severe economic disproportionalities, not to mention regional political movements, that the administration might see a new RFC or development bank as expedient. The regional problems addressed by such arrangements are not going to go away even if, as laissez faire advocates quote President Kennedy, "a rising tide lifts all boats" (U.S. White House Conference, 1978, I:53). Perhaps wishfully, *Business Week* (1980d:35) reported that "with George Schultz working for him, Reagan is likely to turn to the tripartite approach too." Charles Walker, a right wing lobbyist and very prominent member of Reagan's election campaign, has joined the chorus. The purpose of his RFC would be to "deter rather than encourage congressional bailouts such as those for Lockheed, New York City and Chrysler" (ibid., 1981a:13).

Should these reindustrialization proposals be opposed by progressives or not? The main considerations have to do with the extent of democracy permitted or denied and the strength of labor relative to capital and the state.

The proposals are explicitly designed to deal with the difficulties of investment priorities at a time of economic crisis, when normal politics would seem incapable of sufficient resolution. Appointed bosses are at last one more step removed from popular, congressional, or even executive politics. Despite the attractive possibilities of national investment planning, it is likely that current versions under discussion would be vehicles for undemocratic domination of state resource allocation by finance and corporate capital. Furthermore, this summit planning is very centralized, far removed from the potential of community control over investment decisions. The decisions of such bodies are not popularly accountable, accessible, or visible. The technocratic appearance of rationality is characteristic of corporatist decision making (Gross, 1980). In these ways, the proposals attempt to depoliticize parts of economic policy. But it could cut the other way too. By intervening where the state may not have done so before, they re-politicize other economic decisions. The possible future failure of investment planning to save particular industries or the U.S. competitive position could further politicize such arrangements. In short: though less democratic than other public sector arrangements, and though centralized and top-down, reindustrialization proposals could extend the realm of state politics into what is now private decision making.

The role of labor has a similar ambiguity. Labor is virtually excluded from economic policy decisions now, so a corporatist arrangement that included labor even as a junior partner would appear to offer some advantage. But the advantages of consultation may be chimerical. Given the ideological consensus on austerity policies and the current offensive by the U.S. state against the whole working class, tripartite agreements may well be more likely to enforce repressive social contracts that legitimate further losses in wages, working conditions, and political power. Winpisinger expresses this clearly:

> The Chrysler deal was not labor-management cooperation or tripartite decision-making. For the [United Auto Workers Union] and the workers, it was a "non-choice" at best and job blackmail at worst. It was Government intervention, on the side of the employer, to an extreme degree. Therefore, to those who have the Chrysler case in mind as they call for greater cooperation between labor and management, we in the machinists' union say "thumbs down"—to be unduly polite. (Winpisinger, 1981:Ey 23).

The answer to whether tripartite planning arrangements benefit labor or not depends more on the terms and conditions of labor participation, not on anything intrinsic to corporatist arrangements. From the present point in the Reagan administration, it would appear that policy-making arrangements that incorporate a labor point of view are worth fighting for, *if* that participation involves more than just the labor leadership and if the conditions of such participation include more than an internally repressive accommodation within the labor movement. In the absence of a broad socialist movement, to refrain from such participation would be to invite even more disastrous defeats.

NOTES

I am grateful for detailed comments from Jim Shoch, Evan Jones and Ann Markusen, and for helpful discussion at the Conference on Urban Political Economy.

1. *Regional economic policy* here means federal policies that implicitly or explicitly affect the spatial distribution of economic activities.
2. The phrase *distressed area* is of course highly ideological; places as such cannot be "distressed." People who live and work there may well be distressed, but to say that the aim of the program would alleviate their conditions would be inaccurate. Place-based programs such as many of those recommended by the urban policy statement were aimed at the physical development of such areas—that is, fixed capital—as if that would necessarily improve the conditions of life of those using the area. Services to people directly were excluded from national urban policy consideration in the definition of the task, over the opposition of the Department of Health, Education and Welfare. This "person vs. place" argument pervaded the urban policy discussions of the Carter administration.
3. And to an extent the whole post–New Deal period.
4. This program was fiscal assistance.
5. The 1980 recession was also the most forecast economic downturn in history.
6. Indeed, the Chrysler bailout, and some years before, the New York City loans, were both instances of federal amelioration of the effects of structural change.
7. However, a UAW-based proposal for "rational reindustrialization" for Detroit is gaining attention.
8. The URPG and Carter cabinet tried to avoid stamping their administration with grandiose "New Deal," "New Frontier," or "New Society" labels, in part because of the low level of legitimacy to which the federal level of the state had sunk, in part as an effort to convey modesty (a more attractive cousin of austerity), and in part to avoid the risk of grandiose programs of legislation failing—spectacularly—in Congress.
9. The RFC was one of the most important agencies of President Roosevelt's New Deal. It was a means of bailing out industries then in distress by offering them finance on favorable terms.
10. However, David Stockman, Reagan's budget director, did ridicule it. One of the political purposes of the commission was to help plan for Carter's second term (Glickman, 1981).

11. Cf. Rohatyn's proposed OPEC sources of finance.
12. Former Undersecretary of State George Ball warned that without federal support to New York City's crisis, communism would achieve a great victory (Auletta 1980:91).
13. Panitch (1981:29) points out, "However great the incidence of class collaboration in America, its practice is little elaborated in the institutional field of the central administrative apparatus of the state, where trade unions are largely excluded from participation in policy making."
14. One could make a strong case that "big oil" (Cockburn and Ridgeway, 1982) and Sunbelt capitalists (Markusen and Wilmoth 1981) are the implicit winners.

REFERENCES

AFL-CIO Executive Council. "The National Economy." *In These Times,* March 4–10, 1981:18.
Alcaly, Roger, and Mermelstein, David, eds. *The Fiscal Crisis of American Cities.* New York: Vintage, 1977.
Auletta, Ken. *The Streets Were Paved with Gold.* New York: Vintage, 1980.
Bearse, Peter. "Influencing Capital Flows for Urban Economic Development: Institutions or Institution Building?" *Journal of Regional Science* 19 (1979):79–92.
Bedell, Bean. "Royhatyn Plots Economic Strategy." *Guardian,* March 24, 1982:6.
Business Week. "How Sudden Oil Wealth Is Splitting the States." May 12, 1980a:91.
———. The Reindustrialization of America. Special issue. June 30, 1980b.
———. "Carter's Options for Industry." August 18, 1980c:104–06.
———. "A Revitalization Board Comes to Life Slowly." October 6, 1980d: 34–35.
———. "The RFC: A Born-Again Lender Under Reagan?" April 13, 1981a:13.
———. "Dislocations That May Deepen." June 1, 1981b:62–64.
Carson-Parker. "The Capital Cloud Over Smokestack America." *Fortune,* February 23, 1981:70–80.
Cockburn, Alexander, and Ridgeway, James. "Oil Slicks. The Boys Behind Reagan." *Village Voice,* January 28–February 3, 1981:1, 17–19.
Donsky, Martin. "Business Aid, Regionalism Spark Urban Grant Dispute." *Congressional Quarterly Weekly Report* 36 19, May 13, 1978, pp. 1171–74.
———. "Carter's Urban Policy Floundering on Hill." *Congressional Quarterly Weekly Report* 36 30, July 1978, pp. 1960–63.
———. "Urban Aid: 'A Time of Austerity.'" *Congressional Quarterly Weekly Report* 36 48, December 2, 1978, pp. 3379–83.
———. "Carter, Congress Weigh Federal Role in Urban Economic Development." *Congressional Quarterly Weekly Report,* January 6, 1979: 24–29.
Gross, Bertram. *Friendly Fascism: The New Face of Power in America.* New York: Evans, 1980.
Hager, Barry M. "Carter Aides Proud of Urban Policy Process." *Congressional Quarterly Weekly Report* 36 14, April 1, 1978, pp. 783–86.

Hausner, Victor. Personal interview, 1980.
Hershman, Arlene, with Levenson, Marc. "The 'Reindustrialization' of America." *Dun's Review* (July 1980):34–43.
Higgins, James. "Road to Fascism." *The Nation,* January 3–10, 1981:4.
Humphrey, Hubert. Quoted in *Los Angeles Times,* July 28, 1977, p. 29.
Jordan, Vernon. Quoted in *New York Times,* March 28, 1977.
Kirkland, Lane. Testimony before the Ways and Means Committee, House of Representatives, on the administration's tax proposal and the AFL-CIO's alternative. March 24, 1981.
LeGates, Richard, and Wilmoth, David. "More Sweatshops Are Not the Answer." *In These Times,* March 11–17, 1981:6.
Luger, Michael. "Some Micro-Consequences of Macro Policies: The Case of Business Tax Incentives." *Proceedings of the National Tax Association— Tax Institute of America* (forthcoming).
Markusen, Ann, and Wilmoth, David. "The Political Economy of National Urban Policy in the USA: 1976–81." *Canadian Journal of Regional Science* (forthcoming).
————, and Fastrup, Jerry. "The Regional War for Federal Aid." *The Public Interest* 53 (Fall 1978):87–99.
Miller, S. M. "The Recapitalization of America." *Social Policy* (November–December 1979): 5–13.
Moorhead, William S. "Reconstruction Finance Corporation." In *Congressional Record,* 126 156:E 4836–7, Oct. 15, 1980.
NADO News. "Comparison of House and Senate Public Works and Economic Development Bills." November 30, 1979:2–3.
Nathan, Richard, et al. *Lessons from European Experience for a U.S. National Development Bank.* Washington, D.C.: Council for International Urban Liaison, January 1979.
Newsweek. "Mr. Fixit for the Cities." May 4, 1981:26–35.
Panitch, Leo. "Trade Unions and the State." *New Left Review* 125 (January–February 1981):21–43.
Peirce, Neal R., and Steinbach, Carol. "Reindustrialization—A Foreign Word to Hard-Pressed American Workers." *National Journal,* October 25, 1980:1784–89.
Rohatyn, Felix. "Public-Private Partnerships to Stave off Disaster." *Harvard Business Review* (November–December 1979):6–9.
————. "The Coming Emergency and What Can Be Done About It." *New York Review of Books,* December 1980:20–26.
————. "The Older America: Can It Survive?" *New York Review of Books,* January 22, 1981a:13–16.
————. "Reconstructing America." *New York Review of Books,* March 5, 1981b:16–20.
Shapiro, Irving. Interview in *National Journal,* October 25, 1980:1810.
Stanfield, Rochelle L. "Is the Man from Georgia Ready to Help the States and Cities?" *National Journal,* January 22, 1977a:137–41.
————. "Civil War Over Cities' Aid—The Battle No One Expected." *National Journal,* August 6, 1977b:1226–27.
————. "Don't Call It Economic Stimulus, Call It Long-Term Economic Renewal." *National Journal,* September 6, 1980a:1468–87.
————. "Carter's Urban Development Bank—Dead but Not Buried." *National Journal,* Oct. 11, 1980b:1700–01.
Tabb, William K. "The Good News Is That There Is No Good News." *Social Policy* 11 (November–December 1980):52–57.

U.S. Comptroller-General. *An Analytical Framework for Federal Policies and Programs Influencing Capital Formation in the United States.* Washington, D.C.: General Accounting Office, September 23, 1980.

U.S. Department of Housing and Urban Development. Minutes of meeting on the urban and regional policy with the AFL-CIO representatives. September 2, 1977a.

———. Notes on labor's response to the urban policy for the secretary's meeting with editors of trade union magazines. Undated memo, 1977b.

U.S. President. Memorandum to Patricia Harris and Stuart Eisenstat. Jan. 25, 1978.

———. Commission on an Agenda for the Eighties. *A National Agenda for the Eighties.* Washington, D.C.: Government Printing Office, 1980.

U.S. White House. Executive Order 11297. Mar. 21, 1978a.

———. *New Partnership to Conserve America's Communities.* Washington, D.C.: White House, Mar. 27, 1978b.

———. *Economic Growth for the 1980s.* Washington, D.C.: White House, August 28, 1980a.

———. "Economic Program for the 80s." Fact sheet. Washington, D.C.: White House, August 28, 1980b.

———. Conference on Balanced National Growth and Economic Development. *Final Report.* 6 vols. Washington, D.C.: Government Printing Office, July 1978.

Vaughan, Roger J. *Inflation and Unemployment: Surviving the 1980s.* Washington, D.C.: Council of State Planning Agencies, 1979.

Watkins, Alfred J. "Felix Rohatyn's Biggest Deal." *Working Papers* (September–October):44–52.

Western Urban and Regional Collective. "A Critique of Carter's Urban Policy." Berkeley, Calif., 1978. Mimeo.

Wildstrom, Stephen H. "A Self-Correcting Recession Isn't Likely." *Business Week,* June 16, 1980:61.

Winpisinger, William W. "Who It Takes to Tango." *New York Times,* Nov. 15, 1981: EY 23.

Wolman, Harold L., and Merget, Astrid E. "The Presidency and Policy Formulation: President Carter and the Urban Policy." *Presidential Studies Quarterly* 10 (Summer 1980):402–15.

10

Reindustrialization:
A Debate Among Capitalists

GOETZ WOLFF

In the past few years, business leaders have shown increasing concern about the state of the U.S. economy. They see stagflation, insufficient productivity, decreasing profit levels, lagging technology, too little investment in productive capital, and lack of competitiveness in world markets. And they don't like any of it.

At the same time, business leaders are careful to distinguish between these serious problems and other problems which they accept philosophically. Plant closings, in their view, are merely manifestations of a period of change and disruption for older, declining industries. The Snowbelt is losing to the Sunbelt; the United States is losing to Japan and to industrializing Third World nations; steel, rubber, textiles, and autos are losing to computers, aerospace, and machinery.

Integral to this process of change are the impetus of capitalists to increase their profits so as to enlarge the reproduction of capital (that is, increase capital accumulation) and a concomitant class struggle in which workers tend to resist increased exploitation. To increase accumulation, a variety of strategies are pursued, including the disciplining of labor in order to keep wages low (and to reduce wages if they have risen) and the replacement of demanding and unruly labor with machines. In addition, capital seeks out cheaper, more docile labor. Thus, the growth in manufacturing jobs has taken place in regions and countries where wages tend to be lower and where unions are less evident and/or less militant.

This article was written in 1981.

But capital doesn't only strike out geographically in search of higher profits. There also exists competition for investment among sectors of the economy (and within sectors). As was noted above, in the area of manufacturing, there are sectors that have been growing ("sunrise") while others have been declining ("sunset"). In addition, the goods-producing sector as a whole has been giving way to the services sector (Ginzberg and Vogta, 1981:48).[1]

For many economic analysts, this is but a natural process resulting from the births and deaths in the corporate species. They conveniently overlook the human costs that are involved in these changes. For them, a readjustment and restructuring will work itself out as corporations and individuals seek out the more profitable sectors and regions in which to invest. As this happens, the less profitable regions will adjust their business climate so that they will become more attractive to investment in the future. Most economists expect this process will result in a convergence of regional incomes.

Nevertheless, even the businessmen and their economists are concerned with the way in which these structural changes are going to come about. From their point of view, will the changes come soon enough, or will America be left in the lurch while other countries surge ahead? How disruptive will this working out of "natural" market forces be? What corporations will suffer the greatest losses? Will the United States risk losing some basic industries that are critical to military production? Their primary concern is how their own economic positions might be adversely affected by the economic changes brought on by the dynamics of capitalism.

This is where the idea of *reindustrialization* comes in. It's a single name given to a number of different policy proposals for dealing with the economic maladies manifested by the United States. Credit for coining the name is claimed by Amitai Etzioni, a sociologist and former senior adviser to President Carter. Because the economic problems are so complex, there isn't any agreement yet among business leaders as to which route is the best way out of the economic crisis. But if we are going to understand what business has in mind for the nation, we have to be able to distinguish among the various plans which are being proposed.

We can identify at least three major strands in this reindustrialization debate among business leaders and their spokesmen. One might be called the *unfettered-capitalism* version of reindustrialization because it is advanced by those who still have a great deal of faith in the free market. They believe that most of the economic problems of the

United States have their roots in excessive government-business interdependence. A second strand, called the *Business Week* version because of the now-famous issue which delineated the problems facing the U.S. economy and provided a strategy for rebuilding it, is advocated by those who believe that for better or worse, the fates of government and business are linked. A third version of reindustrialization, *pragmatic state capitalism,* agrees with the second, but goes one step further and suggests that it is in the long-term interests of capitalism for government to take a guiding role in reindustrialization. It also holds that the most pressing needs of labor, minorities, women, and poor should be taken into serious account in the restructuring process.

Although the three reindustrialization plans aren't as sharply distinct as I'm portraying them, it is necessary to recognize that with each version, different tactics and strategies are being proposed, and consequently working people will be affected differently. This means too that different responses may be called for, depending on the version of reindustrialization which is being promoted.

UNFETTERED CAPITALISM

Reindustrialization by unfettered capitalism relies upon a perspective of free enterprise which sees government as an impediment to the success of capitalism. Of course, this is the perspective that dominates the rhetoric—and to a surprising extent the actual policies—of the Reagan administration.[2] The solutions that make up this reindustrialization approach can be capsulized into a strategy of less government and more capitalism.

Specifically, this strategy wants to strip away or reduce virtually all social buffers (unemployment insurance, food stamps, COLA, the minimum wage) which have made life more tolerable and secure for workers and their families in the past half-century. These free enterprise economists and politicians complain that the labor force has extracted a "cushy" existence which discourages productivity and keeps market forces from allowing wages to fluctuate with the demand for labor. Another proposal is the creation of enterprise zones, recommended by the Heritage Foundation and presented to Congress as the Kemp-Garcia Urban Jobs and Enterprise Zone Act,[3] which has some disconcerting similarities to the export platforms (free trade zones, or FTZs) that are most common in Asian nations which border on the Pacific Basin. Closely related is the proposal to drop the minimum wage for young people—a first step toward a more widespread modification of the minimum wage, and thus the wage structure in general. Another tactic focuses on unions, for they are to "be considered an obstacle to the optimum performance of our economic system" (Rees, 1977). The thrust of these proposals and tactics is to make American labor cheaper, and thus more competitive with Third World workers.

Direct benefits for industry are also advocated in this approach to reindustrialization. Here the assumption is that as government "gets out of business," business will be able to choose the most efficient strategies to compete in the world economy—unrestricted by so-called costly health, safety, and environmental regulations. (The costs will not go away—they will be borne not by business but by the workers in the form of injury and illness.) It is believed that the most profitable directions for investment will somehow be the ones that meet the needs of the nation. Thus, the way forward is to cut taxes drastically through accelerated depreciation for capital purchases such as equipment and buildings, through decreased corporate tax rates, and through decreased personal income taxes in the upper brackets.

Unfettered capitalism does not ignore the poor, the minorities, and "the truly needy"—in its rhetoric. One repeatedly encounters references to concern for the less well-off, and how workers and job seekers will gain with the soon-to-come booming, restructured, revitalized economy. But as the Reagan program takes shape, it becomes increasingly clear that this rhetoric was never anything more than a perfunctory window dressing.

BUSINESS WEEK

The second version of reindustrialization, the *Business Week* approach, includes some related proposals coming from other sources. For example, the *Time-Life* empire has jumped into the fray with a special project on American renewal in which *Fortune* advocates a slightly more cautious, and somewhat more broad-brushed, set of proposals. However, to avoid complicating this brief review, I will focus most of my attention on *Business Week*.

It should be noted that *Business Week* doesn't oppose the labor sacrifices that are explicit strategies in the unfettered capitalism version. Thus, it endorses Amitai Etzioni's statement that reindustrialization will require "10 years of belt tightening." Likewise, *Business Week* is supportive of cuts in personal income taxes as well as liberalized depreciation allowances, increased investment tax credits, and cuts in the corporate income tax. However, the somewhat more "liberal" *Business Week* perspective acknowledges that the government, if dominated by the appropriate business interests, can serve as an important coordinating agent in overcoming the anarchy of the capitalist system. A key aspect of the approach, therefore, is that *selective* budgetary and tax policies will strengthen industry by rewarding investment in the production of capital goods, by encouraging research and development, and by promoting exports. It is not simply a matter of putting money in the hands of investors, as in the unfettered capitalism approach to reindustrialization.

Business Week wants to forge a "new social contract," a tripartite consensus between business, labor, and government in order to achieve the needed climate for restructuring American industry. In particular, the worker-versus-owner adversarial relationship (class struggle) is to be replaced by a partnership which *Business Week* calls a "collaborative relationship" in shops and factories. By such an arrangement, policies would emerge that represent the needs and contributions of all the economic elements. And among the first to "contribute" to the "needs" of business will be labor. "As part of the new social contract, unions will come under pressure to limit wage gains in the first phase of reindustrialization" (p. 88). *Business Week* attempts to balance this bargain by affirming the need for "high employment and decent wages"— the point being, nevertheless, that business is the implicit decision maker about what is needed and how the needs are to be fulfilled.

The *Business Week* position still fears government as potentially unmanageable, because the electorate is made up of more workers than capitalists. Thus, it says, "It will be legitimate for government to work with the private sector in developing a road map for healthy industrial development, showing which industries should be encouraged to grow and which have only a limited future." But "it will not be legitimate for government to legislate a new industrial structure. Nor will it be legitimate for government to take over sick industries to preserve obsolete jobs." This principle has been taken to heart by Governor Jerry Brown, who wants to "go with the flow" of industrial growth. In California he has proposed a state reindustrialization program which would aid research in microelectronics, encourage new firms in high-technology sunrise industries, and create an "industrial reinvestment fund" (*Business Week*, 1981:40). Whether these new industries will provide accessible and well-paying jobs to those being displaced by reindustrialization is open to question.

Both *Business Week* and *Fortune* take note of minorities, women, and the needy—and they are quick to emphasize that reindustrialization must be fair. But not very well hidden in this rhetoric are statements such as, "Each social group will be measured by how it contributes to economic revitalization," and "The drawing of the social contract must take precedence over the aspirations of the poor, the minorities, and the environmentalists" (*Business Week*, 1980:86). "In the 1970s, however, the egalitarian thrust went too far. . . . Now, without overreacting and subordinating equality too much, we need to restore the balance in our values, as we have so many times before" (Bowen:115).

Finally, it should be noted that *Business Week* is not blind to possible failings within the leadership of capital. It is critical of business management itself for a short-sighted, quick-profit approach which hasn't had the nerve to grab hold of the long-range opportunities confronting the American economy.

Before we turn in the third version of reindustrialization, it should be pointed out that while *Business Week* did the "outreach" work with its special issue, the outlines of the problem and the strategies for dealing with it were already formulated by the Trilateral Commission in 1979 (Trilateral Commission, 1979). There is no need to leap to assumptions of conspiratorial machinations to acknowledge the role of multinational corporations and financial interests in formulating the agenda for discourse on industrial policy. However, it is significant to note that such a powerful configuration of economic/political interests was concerned with this issue. Thus we may speculate that the *Business Week* version will be most likely to be adopted as policy in the long run.

PRAGMATIC STATE CAPITALISM

To the left of *Business Week* is an approach to reindustrialization which places even greater reliance on government involvement and includes an explicit strategy for dealing with the problems of the disadvantaged regions and sectors of the United States. Felix Rohatyn, an investment banker and chairman of New York City's Municipal Assistance Corporation, best typifies the pragmatic state capitalism approach to reindustrialization (Rohatyn, 1980a; 1981a, 1981b, 1981c). Although this approach causes distress at the *Wall Street Journal* and heart failure among some of the advocates of unfettered capitalism, it must be remembered that the goals are basically the same: maintaining the health of the capitalist system. Rohatyn sees an even greater need for government involvement and direction of the capitalist economy than *Business Week*—but always for the long-term benefit of the capitalist economy.

While *Business Week* hesitantly considers the creation of a Reconstruction Finance Corporation as an option, Rohatyn embraces and advocates the idea without apology: in addition to intervening in the economy "to shore up America's troubled older industries by providing equity capital . . . it would have the right to insist on management changes." Because an America "half rich, half poor; half suburb, half slum . . . is a recipe for social strife," the RFC could "also play a major role in shaping regional policy," aiding regions and cities that are hit particularly hard by economic changes. Such an intervention by the government is not meant to be a permanent one, however. "The RFC should never become a permanent stockholder in any corporation." Rather, it would gradually remove itself as the economy becomes regenerated. Rohatyn is undaunted by those capitalists who suggest that this strategy involves excessive interference in the free market system: "Free markets are clearly desirable, but we do not in fact live in a free-market economy and never will; we live in a mixed economy in which prices and capital are, and will be, subject to governmental influence."

The basic thrust of Rohatyn's proposal is that the United States has to maintain its basic industries, for both national security and the economy as a whole depend on these industries. "Is it rational, in the name of the mythical free market, to let our basic industries go down one after the other, in favor of an equally mythical 'service society' in which everyone will serve everyone else and no one will be making anything?" Furthermore, rather than waste precious capital by having to build new plants and the related infrastructures in one part of the nation while the other sections die "natural deaths," the reindustrialization project he envisions "will provide work enough for everyone as far as the eye can see."

Before this approach to reindustrialization is accepted as the best one, we have to remind ourselves how Rohatyn arrives at his solution: it involves business interests dominating government policy making, and it involves "belt tightening," which means that the workers will pay for most of the changes he advocates, even though he claims that everyone will pay a price. It is the workers who bear the greater burden with frozen wages or givebacks, with higher energy costs, with reduced social services, with cutbacks in unemployment benefits. Thus the price of pragmatic state capitalist reindustrialization involves giving up the "padded society," as Rohatyn characterizes it. The problem is that this "padding" is a lot thinner for the workers than it is for the corporate interests who will be deciding where the padding gets reduced.

CONCLUSION

What does all this mean for the United States? It seems pretty obvious that the unfettered capitalism approach wants little more than to convert the United States into a Milton Friedman–approved Hong Kong free market economy. It will rely upon unemployed workers (the "reserve army"), forcing labor to become cheaper and more productive, thus encouraging new plant openings and expansions in the United States. And too, as the declining industries die off, it is assumed that a new set of suitable replacement sunrise industries will be ready to take their place. Whether the laid-off workers will have the skills to fit into the sunrise industries and the "freedom" to move to the location of the new plants seems more certain in supply-side economic texts than in the real world.

The *Business Week* approach would keep government in the picture as an agent of general direction ("indicative planning"), and there would be some concern with having labor included in the planning for shifts that take place. The question, though, is which elements of labor will be speaking for the workers. Although *Business Week* wants to avoid major disruptions in declining industries, at the same time it doesn't want to maintain "sick industries to preserve obsolete jobs." And while on the one hand *Business Week* talks of labor nestling in *with business* as a way to improve communication and achieve a "collaborative relationship," it doesn't oppose corporate attempts to dismantle unions and prevent workers from organizing independently of management.

Pragmatic state capitalism holds out hope for those sectors and regions where industries have been in decline because this approach is aware that you don't simply throw away investment in capital and skilled human beings. In addition, the Rohatyn approach is more concerned with the "less fortunate" in our economy, although the concern is pragmatic, based on fear of adverse consequences arising from "social strife"—that is, disruption and disorder. In that sense, the Rohatyn approach is far more sensitive to the nature of the struggle between the classes. But as has already been noted, the cost of the strategy will ultimately be borne by the workers, who will have to accept pay cuts, givebacks, and declining social services. And in the long run, the strategy of pragmatic state capitalism may create an even closer bond between business and government, resulting in what Bertram Gross has called "friendly fascism" (Gross, 1980).[4]

None of the various reindustrialization advocates consider the fact that state and local government accounted for about one-fifth of the additional jobs in the United States in the past twenty years. The government has played a special role in absorbing employable citizens in a changing economy. But now, obviously, that role will be much smaller. Not only will there be a decline in services by the government, but fewer jobs will be made available in precisely the major growing sector in which wages were higher and increasing at a rapid rate. The service and trade sectors, also growing during the past twenty years, tend to pay less than the manufacturing jobs that are being eased out. Thus, many of the "job opportunities" in the nonmanufacturing sectors are (and will be) lower-paying, less unionized, and more likely to be dead-end (see also Rothschild, 1981).

If, as *Fortune* asserts, reindustrialization has become "an 'empty-bottle' word," into which various wines have been poured, it should be recognized that whatever the vintage, all have come from the same capitalist vineyard. What needs to be added to this debate on reindustrialization is a perspective which speaks for the workers and progressives, not only for corporate interests.

NOTES

1. According to my own calculations from the *Handbook of Labor Statistics* (1979), the proportion dropped to 29.7.
2. A book that is taking on the status of a tome for the administration's approach is George Gilder, *Wealth and Poverty* (New York: Basic Books, 1981). Budget Director David Stockman ordered it for distribution to his colleagues.
3. For a discussion of the Kemp-Garcia bill by its authors, see U.S. Congress, 1980, pp. 205–24.
4. See also Lens, who looks at reindustrialization in general and notes its resemblance to Mussolini's corporate state (1980:44).

REFERENCES

Bowen, William. "How to Regain Our Competitive Edge." *Fortune*, March 9, 1981:84.

Business Week. "The Reindustrialization of America." Special issue, June 30, 1980.

————. "California's Own Reindustrialization Program." January 26, 1981.

Butler, Stuart M. *Enterprise Zones: Pioneering in the Inner City.* Washington, D.C.: Heritage Foundation, 1980.

Etzioni, Amitai. "Reindustrialization: View from the Source." *New York Times,* June 29, 1980.

Ginzberg, Eli, and Vojta, George J. "The Service Sector of the U.S. Economy." *Scientific American* 244 (March 1981).

Gross, Bertram. *Friendly Fascism: The New Face of Power in America.* New York: Evans, 1980.

Lens, Sidney. " 'Reindustrialization': Panacea or Threat?" *The Progressive* (November 1980).

Rees, Albert. *The Economics of Trade Unions.* Chicago: University of Chicago Press, 1977.

Rohatyn, Felix. "The Coming Emergency and What Can Be Done About It." *New York Review of Books,* December 4, 1980, pp. 20–26.

————. "Putting the U.S. Economy Back on Its Toes." *Los Angeles Times,* February 15, 1981, part V, p. 1.

————. "Reconstructing America." *New York Review of Books,* March 5, 1981, pp. 16–20.

————. "A Matter of Psychology." *New York Review of Books,* April 16, 1981, pp. 14–16.

Rothschild, Emma. "Reagan and the Real America." *New York Review of Books,* February 5, 1981.

Trilateral Commission. *Industrial Policy and the International Economy,* Triangle Paper 19. New York: The Trilateral Commission, 1979.

U.S. Congress, House of Representatives, Subcommittee on the City. *Urban Revitalization and Industrial Policy.* Hearings, 96th Congress, 2nd Session. September 16, 17. (Washington: U.S. Government Printing Office, 1980), pp. 205–24.

Part Four

LOCAL POLICY

11

Motor City Changeover

DAN LURIA and JACK RUSSELL

Detroit's economy is being killed by industrial disinvestment. Detroit's major manufacturers have not returned to the city the wealth we have created. On the contrary, the profits produced by Detroit labor have built new factories elsewhere, or been distributed to stockholders, or funded often ill-advised corporate adventures. In 1947, the city held over 280,000 manufacturing jobs in some 3,300 firms. Today, Detroit hosts less than 100,000 such jobs in fewer than 1,700 firms. This industrial disinvestment has eroded our tax base and distorted our expenditure priorities. It is *the* fundamental cause of the municipal fiscal crisis we now confront and with which we will continue to struggle for years.

We believe that the 1980s will determine Detroit's fate: either industrial Detroit will be rebuilt and recover an important position in the national economy, or disinvestment will destroy the life chances of our youth, our capacity for local self-government, and much of the useful wealth created by three generations of Detroiters. By the 1990s, Detroit will either be a diversified manufacturing center of a new kind, or it will be a discarded city of vacant factories and abandoned homes from which the remaining affluent shield themselves in residential enclaves and a well-fortified downtown.

If Detroit is to survive as a city in which working people can prosper, we must redefine and reorder our development priorities. We believe that a rational economic development strategy for Detroit must be a least-cost program to retain and create tens of thousands of

high-wage, cyclically insensitive industrial jobs. This essay is a first
sketch of such a program. Before we present our arguments, however,
we should enter three caveats.

*First, we are not opposed to the relocation of investment capital
within cities of a metropolis, regions of a nation, or even the nations of
the world.* We oppose only its unplanned, socially wasteful, and privately controlled movement. Once the relatively high wages enjoyed
by Detroit auto workers had filled up the city's available space with
single family homes, it was inevitable and desirable that those forms
of auto production requiring extensive space would subsequently be
built in suburban and rural greenfields. But it was neither inevitable
nor desirable that metropolitan Detroit be politically balkanized into
hostile municipalities differentiated by class and race; that metropolitan tax base sharing would thus become impossible; that a powerful
auto/oil/construction/consumer durables lobby would decree the federal highway and mortgage policies that replicated the suburban phenomenon; that Detroit would be gutted by freeway trenches rather
than served by mass transit; nor that the city's commerce would be
mauled by the placement of major shopping centers just beyond its
borders. The spatial catastrophe of metropolitan Detroit is a sufficient
argument for greater social control of investment.

We will not advocate the socially irrational imprisonment of private capital within Detroit or southeastern Michigan. We *will* argue
for radically increased government authority in the economy; for new
structures that allow bargained planning between private capital, labor, and government; and for an overall economic development plan
that will eventually allow the city and its agencies to appropriate and
reinvest locally some of the wealth the planned, semi-public economy
creates.

Second, we are not opposed to Detroit's Renaissance. We *do* believe it should be demystified. The much-celebrated rebirth is in essence an attempt to protect the value of existing investments and future profit opportunities in the downtown hub. The banks, retailers,
utilities, and other businesses downtown have been threatened by the
disinvestment of Detroit, especially since 1967. The Renaissance was
their self-interested redevelopment strategy long before it became the
keystone policy of the Administration of Mayor Coleman Young. By
logic and law, many of the downtown businesses are less mobile than
industry. They must stay and protect their futures. We hope they build
and succeed.

We do challenge, however, the terms they offer for development, the logic of their strategy, and the absurd conceit that somehow their success will be the salvation of a city ravaged by industrial disinvestment. Even if our skepticism is unfounded, and downtown Detroit *is* recommercialized on the foundation of a substantial new market-rate residential community, it is not at all obvious what that offers most Detroiters. To what extent, we ask, would the huge economic damage wrought by industrial disinvestment be repaired by a flourishing service economy in the hub?

During the past 30 years, Detroit has lost 27 percent of its population but nearly 70 percent of its jobs in manufacturing. In 1981, over 400,000 Detroiters—one in every three—received some form of public assistance. No rebirth of downtown, even if it succeeds against heavy odds, will provide the resources to heal our community. A different conception of economic development must address the needs of the majority.

Third, we acknowledge the important efforts at community development in Detroit, but argue that these efforts at best only partially balm the wounds of disinvestment; they do not constitute a cure for the disease. Detroit needs all the housing dollars and programs we can get, but we should understand that the neighborhoods created by a high-wage, high-employment industrial economy between 1910 and the 1950s will not be renewed, especially at today's costs, in an economy based on transfer payments from the federal government and on low-wage service employment. The best housing program for Detroit would be one that reopens our plants and employs our homeowners.

Similarly, most neighborhood commerce cannot survive drained by the suburban malls and dependent on the Detroit poor. If Detroit can reindustrialize and employ our people, then neighborhood merchants will have a chance. If industrial disinvestment continues unchecked, we will have boutiques for the downtowners and party stores for the people.

The small manufacturers and job shops, long an important element in most Detroit neighborhoods, are also endangered by disinvestment. As the big plants close, orders dry up; family owners are forced to consider relocation or closing.

Efforts to regenerate our housing stock, stabilize some neighborhood commerce, and assist our small manufacturers are essential. During the Reagan years, we will have fewer resources for this work. But even if we had twice the funds, this work would only slow our decline rather than rebuild our economy.

What *will* rebuild it? This essay argues the outlines of an answer.

Let us begin with a paradox: the very severity of Detroit's industrial disinvestment may create an opportunity. In a sudden, severe, and traumatic decline in automobile industry activity in the city of Detroit, tens of thousands of workers have been permanently dismissed. Several major plants have closed; more will follow. Smaller plants that built components for obsolete technologies or products have been abandoned. Orders from smaller parts suppliers have ceased. Tool and die shops are without work. In less than 30 months, multiple shocks have broken many of the crucial links that had held together Detroit's ailing but still viable automotive industry.

Are these links permanently broken, or can they be reforged? In some quarters, optimism about *Michigan's* future in the automotive economy runs high. Transport economies and attempts to emulate Japanese-style inventory management may recentralize in our state some of the previously lost major elements of the industry. Southeastern Michigan still has important comparative advantages in labor skills, transport infrastructure, abundant water, and the substantial remaining share of auto production. But *Detroit* cannot hope to win back much of what *we* have lost; our built environment is a huge barrier to major new industrial construction. The staggering public costs borne to prepare the new Cadillac Plant site indicate the price extracted for merely retaining 6,000 of the 14,000 Cadillac jobs we had less than a decade ago. Detroit will do well to retain just the auto jobs we still had in 1981.

Much of our auto industry, then, is gone or going. But in the wake of its passing there remain crucial resources which, we argue, constitute the opportunity to rationally reindustrialize the city. Capital leaves, but labor skills remain. Plants are closed, but not razed. Railways and freeways still tie the factories together and connect them to the nation. The links between the hundreds of small- and medium-sized vendors and the major facilities are damaged, but not broken beyond repair. The engine of production that was built over the span of a half-century has not yet been scrapped, nor should it be. Detroit can still bend metal.

We believe that Detroit can and must take a bold step forward during the 1980s. To survive as a city where working people can prosper, Detroit must forge a new role for local government in planning the redevelopment of industry in a frostbelt city. There are industrial products that the American economy and the world must have. If we are bold, we can build them, and as we do so rebuild our city.

THINKING RATIONALLY ABOUT REINDUSTRIALIZATION

A rational economic development agenda must be centered on replacing the declining private activities of the city—auto assembly, parts, and machining—with new activities that take maximum advantage of the existing industrial linkages. There are many activities that produce desirable goods and services for a national as well as a local market that fail to exploit these linkages. For example, a bakery may produce bread for the Midwest market, but it doesn't salvage the tool and die shops whose auto industry orders are drying up. Similarly, there are activities that require inputs from existing intermediate goods suppliers, such as buses and rail and subway cars, but for which existing public policy anticipates no predictable unmet local, regional, national, or international demand.

What process, then, can be followed to identify workable production activities? A rational response to this question begins with the identification of a set of key criteria across which potential economic development ventures may be compared. These include:

1. *Scale of job creation.* Would the ventures provide substantial employment to residents of Detroit?
2. *Conservation of capital.* Would the firms producing the proposed outputs be able to reuse a significant portion of Detroit's existing stock of industrial facilities and idle or underused machinery and equipment? Could they take advantage of the city's in-place industrial infrastructure (see also #5 and #9, below)?
3. *Local economic impact.* Would the new activities, at full scale, play a role in the local economy similar to that of auto in the past? Would they constitute a set of major "exports" from Detroit to the national and even international market, bringing resources in from faster-growing regions and from abroad?
4. *Characteristics of markets.* Are the demands for the proposed product lines sufficiently strong and enduring to justify large capital investments? Are the markets located properly?
5. *Use of Detroit's comparative advantage.* Would the contemplated ventures take full advantage of the city's existing skilled metalworking labor, industrial infrastructure, and of the key linkages among cognate metals industry activities spawned by the region's legacy of auto dependence?

6. *Market countercyclicality.* Is demand for the ventures' outputs stable or highly cyclical? If it is cyclical, does its cycle counteract or reinforce the shocks to the local economy that come from dependence on auto?

7. *Labor cost barriers.* Do the private sector firms producing similar or identical products pay wages as high as those to which Detroit workers are accustomed as a result of auto's past high profitability? And are they as high as those they could expect in light of the decline of U.S. auto companies' market power?

8. *Transport cost barriers.* Is the cost of moving the proposed products from Detroit to market destinations prohibitively high? Or are there classes of products whose size, price, and existing production sites allow Detroit manufacture more readily than others?

9. *Advantages of publicness.* Do some products make more sense than others as candidates for public or public/private production? Are there products whose cost of production could be especially reduced by city policies?

10. *Profitability for entry.* Are the private firms now producing similar outputs characterized by above-average, and less cyclical than average, profitability? Does selection of the product lines we propose move Detroit into a national sector growing fast enough to allow new entrants?

Translating these criteria into an answerable question about new production in Detroit, we can ask: *What projects can re-employ a large number of skilled and semi-skilled workers, at or near their accustomed wage, taking maximum advantage of the area's concentration of metalworking capital stock and labor force training and of the city's northern deep waterway location, producing products for a growing, undersupplied, long-lived national and international market for which the business cycle is either absent or opposite to the auto/ auto parts demand cycle?*

Others have asked the "diversify into what?" question. In a study for the Detroit Metropolitan Industrial Development Corporation by John Mattila and Wilbur Thompson, the answers were meat packing, industrial inorganic chemicals, farm machinery, and electronic instruments. Unfortunately, Mattila and Thompson used our criteria 5, 6, and especially 7 only, being innocent of 1, 2, 3, 4, 8, 9, and 10. Moreover, having identified the new product lines, they ended their analysis without offering any ideas on how to move into their production.

Chamber of Commerce commentator George Moffett tried to fill the gap, saying that "if it can be proved that there are large-scale [presumably local or regional] demands . . . [that] cannot be filled by local producers, we would have . . . an indisputable selling point for involving . . . prospects in meeting those demands." To the contrary, we will show that criteria 1, 2, 3, and 4 require proof that unmet demands be national in scope. Even if in some cases they are, many rational private firms would still hesitate to initiate production in Detroit on anything close to the required scale. The city of Detroit and its people, however, have an interest in initiating what many rational private investors will not do on their own. We believe that in the 1980s and beyond only local government, its agencies, and its close associates in worker-controlled organizations can create the new productive sector which can arrest the destruction of Detroit's industrial base. To be sure, there is an important, essential, and profitable role for private capital in such a sector, but only to the extent that it conforms to the rational mandates of the public development plan.

Let us return to our ten criteria and the question we generated from them. It is our view that the industries into which Detroit can move must be high-wage, metals-based, and national market-oriented ones. The new activities should take advantage of Detroit's superb rail and Great Lakes transport advantages, and should be characterized by a pattern of demand that counters the roller-coaster ups and downs of the automotive sector. These criteria favor production of physically large, heavy products not all of which are purchased by individual consumers whose incomes are subject to the cyclical swings that are quickly mirrored in auto and other consumer durables sales figures.

Finally, because the start-up costs for the production of capital goods are substantial, the period between investment decisions and payoffs may be relatively long. Thus our precious venture capital must be targeted only on those producer goods for which a rapidly growing and long-lasting market can be conclusively demonstrated.

OUR PRODUCTION LINE: ENERGY HARDWARE

Has this set of criteria, and the exclusions it dictates, exhausted the stock of viable projects? Hardly. There are at least four that meet all of the criteria: (1) deep natural gas and heavy oil production and up-grading equipment; (2) residential and industrial steam/electric co-generation units; (3) large coal- and diesel fuel-fired industrial process engines; and (4) minemouth coal gasifiers.

A rational economic development plan for Detroit would invest in the conversion of abandoned or underutilized industrial capacity to production of deep gas and heavy oil equipment—steam injectors, com-pressors, pumps, and the like—and make a serious effort to capture significant shares in the developing regional, national, and even inter-national markets for minemouth gasifiers, cogenerators, and industrial engines.[1]

Deep Gas and Heavy Oil Equipment

As easy-to-tap reservoirs of natural gas and crude oil are exhausted, more and more energy industry resources are being invested in pros-pecting for deep deposits of natural gas and "completing" known fields of heavier crude oils. The stock of structures and machinery that re-quire gas and oil products will not be junked despite waning supplies of cheap, easy-to-extract hydrocarbon fuels. Thus a massive market in the hardware associated with drilling deeper, faster, and in more loca-tions is assured. In addition to the traditional equipment required—pipe, rigs, bits, derricks, masts, wellheads, etc.—the depth, viscosity (thickness), impurity, and pressure conditions of oil and gas below about 8,000 feet promise a growing market in pumps, steam injection engines, steam compressors, and oxygenators. Simply put, to take full advantage of reserves of "sour" oil and gas, horsepower must be avail-able to force the fuels out and upgrade them to pipeline (gas) and refinery (oil) quality.

Orthodox industrial location thinking would not immediately link the need for oil and gas field equipment with the underused capacity of Detroit; but in the new energy world of the 1980s and 1990s we may well have a major comparative advantage for the production of the pumps, engines, compressors, tubular goods, and other componentry now demanded in the field.

Cogenerators and Industrial Process Engines

A legacy of cheap, accessible, domestic hydrocarbon fuels has not only produced an economy that runs on oil and gas; it has also stimulated a pattern of use that, at today's prices, is unaffordably wasteful of them.

The best case in point is the structural divorce between the use of heat and the use of electricity. When oil or gas products are burned, the energy embodied in them is released in the form of heat. In both structures (homes, office buildings, and factories) and processes (steelmaking, smelting, etc.), however, individuals and corporations purchase fuels for heat and electricity for light, for appliances, and to power non-oil/gas machinery. The heat lost in burning oil and gas—from 30 percent in most residential burners to over 55 percent in some industrial processes—is simply wasted: it does no work. Meanwhile, electric utilities purchase oil, gas, coal, and uranium, and burn (or, in the nuclear case, bombard) them to make the steam that drives electrical turbines. On average, they lose over 60 percent of the available heat content in the fossil fuels they burn.

An increasingly attractive alternative, and one assured a growing market, is to *co*generate heat and electricity from the same fuel input. Engines or burners that do this are called cogenerators. Markets exist, and are expanding rapidly, for cogenerators that heat houses and halve electricity bills all the way to massive cogenerators that provide virtually all of the heat and power needs of multi-plant industrial complexes. The smallest units look, weigh, and are built much like relatively low-compression small car engines; those that would suit a small factory, like truck engines; and the largest types, like industrial process engines. Two Detroit-suited product lines thus emerge; small, medium, and large cogenerators; and, as a spinoff as well as a lease on the life of existing investments, industrial process machine-driving engines.

Minemouth Gasifiers

Finally, the U.S. is unquestionably on the verge of a major new industry geared to reconcile the existence of a 400-year supply of coal with a capital stock that was built to run on what appears now to be a 40- to 70-year supply of oil and gas. For all the talk of making Colorado's shale deposits into a 500-year supply of diesel fuel or of producing massive volumes of heating oil from West Virginia and Kentucky bituminous coal, the only proven technologies that resolve the mismatch between the form in which U.S. hydrocarbons exist in nature and the forms in which they are consumed involve the conversion of coal into gaseous fuels embodying between one-seventh and two-fifths of the heat content of natural gas. A full discussion of the "energy path" that diverts natural gas to replace heating oil, replaces it with coal-derived gaseous fuels, and upgrades oil refineries to make less heating oil and boiler fuel appears later in this paper. For now, the important fact is that, in the face of uncertain policy, the investment community is voting in the marketplace for the machinery that turns coal into "synthesis gas" at the coal-mining site.

There are at least three attractions for Detroit in the production of such gasifiers. First, unlike the equipment used to liquefy shale or coal, gasifiers need not be huge to be commercial scale. There are today at least three companies straining to meet the demand for gasifiers that cost just $830,000 and that convert as little as 25 tons of coal per day into "syngas"; 92 percent of U.S. coal mines, it should be noted, have daily output exceeding 50 tons. Second, unlike coal liquefaction equipment, which must be custom-built and optimized to process a particular type of coal, syngasifiers can transform coals of widely differing heat, water, and sulfur content into clean gaseous fuels. This greatly increases the range and siting of their application. Third, where commercial scale liquefaction equipment must be built near, and partially assembled on, the process site, minemouth gasifiers are small enough to be transportable fully built, allowing their producers to capture most of the value-added they embody. In fact, Detroit may well be the one place in the U.S. that could host *all* of the jobs required to produce gasifiers, from steelmaking from scrap all the way to final product assembly.

There is an important overlap between the equipment, labor, and technical skills, and structures used for Detroit's current product lines (cars, trucks, buses, and the machinery neded to transform the metals from which their components are made) and the factors of production necessary to make the equipment used in deep natural gas, heavy oil, and coal gas production, and to fabricate cogenerators and engines.

But do our four proposed product lines meet all ten of the criteria with which we began? First, our work date convinces us that they satisfy criterion #2 by conserving the value of the existing capital stock. All are manufactured of iron, steel, and aluminum; many are made using machine tools of the type used in the auto industry (certainly, the tool conversion problem is far smaller than that posed by the auto-to-warplane transition of the 1940s). Some—notably the smaller cogenerators and pumps—can be made using idle capacity in engine plants, whether now open or closed down. Others—valves, gasifier chambers, and the castings used in their production—are typically not assembly-line outputs; hence, many existing multi-story plants are suitable for their manufacture. In fact, the use of multi-story plants may not be as inefficient relative to single-story, land-intensive ones as most planners assume. Important new innovations in high-rise storage and counterweight inter-floor stock movement, coupled with rising land and site preparation costs, are making refurbishing of existing multi-story structures an increasingly attractive alternative to single-story, greenfield construction.

The transition from auto to energy hardware manufacture requires planning. Some of Detroit's advantages will be lost if the area's remaining large car and light truck assembly, engine, and casting plants are allowed to put their equipment up for auction in the internal machinery market. A serious effort at rational diversification would include the immediate inventorying of the capital stock of the city and the region. We contend that past efforts by government to attract new enterprises would have fared better had Detroit and Michigan assumed an activist role in the capital goods market; after all, a cheaper lathe can make the same contribution to the "business climate" as a cheaper worker compensation program.

Second, the product line descriptions above should suggest why we are satisfied that all four product areas meet criteria #3–6. They can replace auto's "export" role; they supply strong, growing, and long-lived industrial markets; they take advantage of Detroit's human and physical capital base; and they are relatively immune to major demand variation. The energy hardware market is fully national, universally agreed to be a major growth center, and—to the extent it exhibits any cyclicality—reacts favorably to precisely the energy price and supply hocks that devastate auto production levels.

But what about criterion #1, the contribution they could make to large-scale Detroit employment? And what about our four product lines' relevance to criterion #7, the labor costs of firms producing them?

To study employment impacts of different product line investments, we have used Bureau of Labor Statistics (BLS) employment requirements tables published in May 1980 and based on input-output relationships that existed in 1977. These tables show the number of full-time jobs, direct and indirect, created or maintained by each $1 billion (in 1972 dollars) of sales. We have examined the jobs per billion dollars in sales in a number of industries that produce outputs similar or identical to the four we are proposing for Detroit's new sector.

To illuminate the method, imagine an industrial park, a set of buildings and rail spurs surrounding a once-abandoned truck assembly plant. Imagine further that this industrial park, this complex, produces

Table 11.1. Employment Impact per $ Billion of Sales in Construction, Mining, and Oilfield Equipment

Industry in which jobs created or maintained	Number of such jobs	Number of such jobs Detroit could capture
Construction, mining, and oilfield equipment (e.g., gasifier) itself	21,429	21,429
Engines, turbines, and generators	634	634
Metalworking machines	924	924
Industrial machinery	2,145	2,145
Machine shop products	619	619
Motor vehicles and equipment	331	331
Ferrous stampings	215	215
Steel furnaces and foundries	4,424	4,424
Scientific instruments	216	5–108
Material handling equipment	488	30–488
Screw machine products	325	20–163
Railroad equipment	183	3–45
Tire and rubber	220	220
Metal and coal mining	376	0
Aluminum production	248	0
Assorted other industries, from zinc mining to rivet making to intercity trucking	18,355	1,240–9,200
Total	51,522	31,839–40,545

minemouth coal gasifiers; in fact, the finished gasifiers exit from the old truck plant. Many of the inputs that go into the gasifiers are made within the complex; others are trucked in from other Detroit shops; and still others have to be brought in from outside the city. Using the BLS input-output tables for the industry group that produces "construction, mining, and oilfield equipment," table 11.1 presents the number of jobs that each billion dollars in gasifier sales could be expected to generate. It also shows, under the "Jobs Detroit could capture" heading, the maximum number of jobs producing inputs to gasifiers that could be created or retained in Detroit if the city were to aggressively exploit potential linkages, both on and off the complex site. To the extent that the planners of a new sector failed to assemble land and pursue procurement targeting as effectively as they might, the gasifier plant would be less well linkaged to the local metalworking economy; the number of non-gasifier jobs would thus be lower.

Table 11.1 should be read to mean that the development of a

gasifier-producing capacity that generates one billion dollars in annual sales could provide local employment for between 32 and 40 thousand workers, depending on the extent to which Detroit's metalworking industry could be mobilized as part of the effort. Repeating the process embodied in table 11.1 for cogenerators, pumps, and industrial process engines ("Engines, turbines, and generators") and for steam injectors, compressors, and oxygenators (various "Standard Industrial Classifications," or "SICs"), we conclude that a new energy hardware sector generating about $6 billion in annual sales (in 1980 dollars) could employ 100,000 Detroiters. The capital base that produces that level of sales obviously presupposes a large-scale infusion of capital.

But will Detroit's infamous high wage barrier disqualify it from taking advantage of this major opportunity for reindustrialization? Can the product lines we propose replace the disappearing auto sector jobs at similar wage and benefit levels? The answers appear to be "no" and "yes," respectively. Using another BLS source for data on hourly wage rates, and updating 1980 Bureau of National Affairs surveys on fringe benefits (table 11.2), we can determine hourly labor costs for the SICs now important to Detroit's economy as well as for the SICs covering the product lines we have proposed for the future.

It appears that Detroit's blue collar, primary labor market work force is accustomed to highly paid, if insecure and seldom year-round, employment. Certainly, most of our proposed product lines fall in SICs—344, 351, and 354–56—that do not offer average remuneration at

Table 11.2. Hourly Labor Costs, January 1982

SIC no.	Industry title	Base hourly rate, including COLA	Hourly cost of fringes	Total hourly compensation
371	Motor vehicles and equipment	$11.43	$7.87	$19.30
	GM, Ford Masters	11.67	7.98	19.65
	Chrysler Master (U.S.)	9.48	7.78	16.56
351	Engines and turbines	11.19	6.83	18.02
354	Metalworking machinery	9.39	6.26	15.65
356	General industrial machinery	8.80	5.94	14.74
355	Special industrial machinery	8.51	5.75	14.26
336	Nonferrous foundries	8.42	5.01	13.43
344	Fabricated metal prod.	8.18	4.87	13.05
	U.S. manufacturing average	8.16	4.31	12.47

the GM Master Agreement level. It is not obvious, however, that GM's hourly compensation figure is the relevant standard of comparison. First, Chrysler is the largest auto employer in Detroit; its January 1982 hourly compensation averaged only $0.54 per hour more than the average of SICs 351, 354, and 356. Moreover, without cost-of-living protection, by mid-1982 Chrysler workers made less than the 351/354/356 average. Second, there is severe downward pressure facing auto industry wages in this period. The U.S. policy of protecting low-wage, low-productivity industries while not protecting high-wage, high-productivity ones such as auto has undermined the oligopoly power of the Big Three; when oligopoly power wanes, super-profits dry up, and when that happens labor rates tend to fall relative to those prevailing in other industries. It seems obvious to us that, in the long run, Detroit's working class is better off taking part in a transition into industries producing for growth markets than crossing its fingers that both wages and employment levels in auto hold up.

In the short-term, however, no new public or public/private production sector can guarantee to provide employment at Big Two labor rates. What *can* be fought for, and eventually won, is secure employment at adequate wages. A city government not tied to a redevelopment strategy wholly dependent on luring private capital, along with organized workers who can realistically assess the future of an unprotected, unplanned, and disinvested auto sector, could choose to bargain a wage/security trade-off, provided that policy and planning were able to keep fringe benefits and the "social wage" relatively high. Workers value job security highly; thus, when one conceives of security as a "fringe benefit," it becomes possible to think of workers in a new publicly managed energy hardware sector receiving a *social* wage superior to that of today's autoworkers, but at a direct hourly wage rate as low as $8 an hour. We will return later to the role of other public sector activities in reducing the wage cost of a given living standard; for now, we stress that job and income security, along with the potential benefits of the new and less alienated production relations that might be possible in such a sector, constitute major parts of our living standard.

Moving on, to determine whether Detroit's distance from nonlocal equipment demands represents a market-constraining force (criterion #8), one must find out how much of our proposed product lines' delivered cost would be accounted for by transportation. Examination of rail and truck freight rate charts makes clear that transport costs are dependent on a constellation of nine factors:

—weight of products being shipped
—number shipped per order
—dimensions of products shipped
—extent to which one-way movements are matched by return trips
—degree of product containerization
—speed with which delivery must be made
—whether destination is on or off main rail lines or highways
—whether products require special handling
—level of carrier insurance coverage required

To see how these nine factors impinge on the product line choice calculus, we compare Matilla and Thompson's top choice, packaged meats, with a 35-ton engine representative of many of the outputs suggested in our agenda. Converting our findings into shares of delivered cost (table 11.3), we conclude that production of low-volume, high unit price goods is the best way to obviate any comparative locational disadvantage that Detroit may suffer.

The critical variable, of course, is not the absolute dollar cost of shipping the two sample outputs being compared, but rather shipping cost as a share of value-added. Assuming conservatively (see table 11.3) that Detroit could capture 60 percent of the value-added in the cogenerator, and assuming very liberally that city producers could capture 50 percent of the value-added in packaged meats, we can compare the ratio of shipping cost to local value-added for the two product lines (table 11.4).

Packaged meats, we infer from the above, could at most compose part of a Detroit industry that sought to capture slightly more of the

Table 11.3. Transport Costs by Size and Destination

Product	Dimensions	Weight (lb)	Mode/Destination	Cost
Industrial cogenerating engine	40'x14'x10'	70,000	1—Rail/Los Angeles	$3,400
			2—Rail-barge/Gulf Coast	2,800
			3—Barge/Chicago	1,100
Packaged meats	Full truck: 48'x9'x13'	30,000	1—Truck/Los Angeles	4,700
			2—Truck/Gulf Coast	1,900
			3—Truck/Chicago	800

Table 11.4. The Effect of Shipping Cost on Price

	Price at delivery ×	Local value-added =	"Local price"	Shipping cost as % of local price
Industrial cogenerating engine	$1,800,000	0.60	$1,080,000	1– 0.32% 2– 0.26 3– 0.16
Packaged meats	64,000	0.50	32,000	1–14.69 2– 5.94 3– 2.50

value-added in the meat products sold in southeastern Michigan. As a national "export" product line, it is distinctly inferior to large capital goods. The best way to minimize the disadvantages of Detroit's distance from major markets is to strive to supply those markets with high unit cost products. Our proposed product lines qualify.

ON THE PUBLIC ACCOUNT

Having dealt with the extent to which our agenda's six proposed product areas satisfy our first eight criteria, we recognize an additional responsibility to readers who may be justifiably skeptical about our agenda because it seems to fly in the face of past events. Why, one might well ask, hasn't Detroit's economy already begun the transition from auto dependence to industrial diversification? If the linkages indeed exist, if the existing capital stock is to some significant extent reuseable, and if labor costs are not an insuperable barrier, why hasn't private investment in energy hardware already occurred?

The answer, to which we have already alluded several times, is that the full potential of the linkages is unrealized because real planning exists now only at the firm level. The private sector employs a restrictively narrow accounting method that foregoes the full value of the efficiencies provided by a sound industrial infrastructure, while overvaluing the quick achievement of returns that allow high dividend payouts. In the next several pages, we contrast this narrow, socially irrational method of allocating resources with the method David Smith has labeled "public balance sheet accounting" or "social cost-benefit analysis."

To assess whether and in which activities a public sector or joint public/private sector set of enterprises might succeed where purely private ones would not even venture (criterion #9), we present a matrix constructed from work done by Barry Bluestone and Bennett Harrison in their *Capital and Communities*. It shows that there are at least two "cases" in which a public or public/private mode might produce where in a private mode production would not occur. The reader will quickly see that the energy hardware products described above fit into case #4; this genre of analysis also suggests that more product lines are feasible, those that fall into cases #2 and #3 (table 11.5).

In case 1, the firm in question is unprofitable, so much so that it would be cheaper to close it and pay unemployment insurance and even welfare to its work force than to keep operating it, particularly since it's not importantly hooked up to the rest of the local economy. Both "full cost enumerators" and "private accounters" would, and should, shut such a plant.

In case 2, the firm is losing money, but not so much that a rational social cost-conscious accountant would shut it, whether or not it was significant to the economy. Full cost enumerators would keep the plant open; private accounters would shut it.

In case 3, the firm isn't profitable, and the losses may be so great that it would appear cheaper to shut it down and pay workers off; but it's central enough to the local economy that the economy-wide social costs of closing it might exceed the total costs of operating it. Full cost enumerators, if the planning mechanism valued its linkages, would keep such a plant open, while private accounters would unambiguously close it.

Table 11.5. Social Accounting Matrix

Case	Profitable?	Socially cheaper open than closed?	Productively linkaged?
1	No	No	No
2	No	Yes	Either
3	No	Either	Yes
4	Yes	Yes	Either
5	Yes	No	No

In case 4, the firm is profitable and may be well-linkaged. Full cost enumerators would let it close only if there existed full employment and better uses for the resources invested in it. Private accountors, however, might well choose to close it, if its profitability were below some target rate of return believed to be available elsewhere.

Finally, in case 5, the firm is profitable, but for the community in which it operates its costs exceed its benefits. For example, it may be a heavy polluter. Full cost enumerators would want such a plant closed. Its private owners, however, would keep it open unless they could make more profit investing elsewhere.

Are there social benefits of job-creating investment that are overlooked in private sector accounting but explicitly enumerated in our approach? Might a city deem an enterprise requiring an ongoing subsidy "socially profitable" and hence worthy of support?

First, by creating or retaining jobs, a social cost-benefit approach results in capturing the gains of not having to provide as much unemployment insurance, general relief, and crime control; to settle as many insurance claims; to incur such exorbitant health costs; and to levy such high tax rates. Many jobs are sacrificed today because the costs enumerated above are borne by the public sector, rather than by the private investors whose decisions are responsible for them.

Imagine a Detroit enterprise that employs 250 workers earning $15,000 each per year, of whom two-thirds own homes and half live in Detroit. The enterprise, let us say, is losing $500,000 per year. Assuming that closing the facility makes private accounting sense to its owners, let us ask whether closing the facility is also rational for the total society. On the negative side, operating the plant costs society $500,000, the private loss. On the positive side, keeping the enterprise open garners the society about $172,000 in property taxes, $57,000 in worker-paid city income taxes, $138,000 in state income taxes, and $487,000 in federal income taxes. It also saves $920,000 in unemployment insurance (a one-time cost), welfare, and food stamp transfer payments. Adding these social benefits, one gets about $1,770,000 in year one and $850,000 each year thereafter. Netting out the annual $500,000 loss, over a decade society is better off to the tune of $4.4 million by keeping the plant open.

Second, this sort of calculation understates society's saving: by keeping the plant open, the city may be preserving other jobs in enterprises supplying the plant. While the degree of "linkagedness" of a firm to the rest of the local economy is difficult to quantify, it is important to understand that it can be increased by rational planning.

In fact, planning an ever-more-interconnected sector is the essence of the reindustrialization task in Detroit. In return for a subsidy, for example, the city can require that a firm increase its ties with other local firms. By making the firm do so, the city (1) earns a return on its subsidy, (2) captures tax revenues and their future stability, and (3) foregoes the costs associated with continued disinvestment. The savings can then be used to seed new enterprises in the sector, to invest in cost-cutting infrastructure projects, or even to reduce local tax rates.

Third, to the extent that keeping the plant open constitutes part of a broader plan to integrate salvaged labor and capital resources into a new, planned public or public/private sector, the city's new sector planning authority can reduce its subsidy liability by offering workers in the enterprises the income–job security trade-off described earlier. Success in doing so can be a powerful tool in convincing private capital that, if it is willing to play by the rules—secure employment, accountability to a citywide enterprise linkage plan, etc.—it too can enjoy the benefits of what a private accountant would consider lower labor costs.

These aspects of publicness are difficult to cost out. When and if Detroit goes shopping for investors in its emerging new sector, its pitch will have to include quantitative estimates of what publicness promises the venturesome lender or partner. It would not do merely to argue that interfirm sectoral planning is more efficient; investors will want to know *how much* more efficient.

Again, a precise estimate of the cost advantage accruing to public/ worker production is not feasible; but a lower limit—a minimum— figure *can* be derived. Basically and oversimply, it is composed of that part of our private sector counterparts' after-tax profits that leak out of the investment stream as dividends. Of the firms producing the product lines we have identified, we calculate that approximately 39 percent of those companies' net income is lost to these uses. Thus, 39 percent of a 7.4 percent after-tax return on sales, or 2.9 percent, constitutes the minimum quantifiable advantage of public/worker enterprise for our product lines.

We maintain, of course, that the true "public edge" is far greater than that. In addition to nonquantifiable factors such as planning to maximize linkagedness, there may be ways to exploit two other programs to swell the advantages of public/worker production. First, to the extent that the smaller scale of our start-up enterprises allows them access to industrial revenue bond financing, they might realize a capital cost edge of as much as 5–6 percent over other, larger producers, depending on prevailing interest rates. Preferential use of tax abate-

ment policy—an altogether appropriate use of this oft-misused tool—
might assist in lowering the interest rate the bonds would have to pay
to attract buyers.

TOWARD THE RATIONAL REINDUSTRIALIZATION OF DETROIT

We have called for the redeployment of Detroit's idled industrial resources in the production of an initial group of products particularly
suited to our city's existing capacities. Believing that the challenges of
industrial disinvestment must be met with a bold political departure,
we look to local government to take the lead in initiating a continually
bargained economic development plan in which workers and government join private enterprise as co-planners in the realm of production.

Such bargained planning is not business as usual in America. We
therefore face a tangle of problems which encumber such a departure.
Before we can claim that our economic development agenda is a pragmatic possibility, we must address several current legal, financial, and
spatial obstacles.

Legal

At present, Michigan law narrowly constrains the public role in economic development. The Michigan Constitution clearly limits the types
of money-generating enterprises in which a city may be engaged. The
Constitution prevents the state or any of its subdivisions from owning
stock in a privately operated enterprise, or from establishing a state
or municipally owned bank. It also limits the role of public credit.

State law regulates permissible investment of public employee retirement funds. Only 1 percent or less of a given fund's assets may be
in the common or preferred stock of a given corporation, and that
stock must have paid a dividend in five of the past seven years. No
fund may own more than 5 percent of a given corporation's stock. In
Michigan, start-up enterprises seeking capital through equity offerings
to public employee pension funds clearly face severe limitations. The
strict limits imposed by the Michigan Constitution are also reiterated
in state development finance legislation.

Financial

To fully implement the rational reindustrialization of Detroit will
require, over time, billions of dollars of both private and public invest-

ment. But the Reagan supply-siders are currently eviscerating the existing federal programs that could provide some of the public capital.

Even if these federal programs were to remain in place, mobilizing capital for the start-up enterprises of Rational Reindustrialization would be challenging. Private providers of debt or equity capital will look carefully at new firms with unusual ownership and management structures, especially when they have neither a track record nor the investment tax advantages of established, profitable corporations.

Existing Michigan economic development programs such as industrial revenue bonds, tax abatement, or modest and targeted loan guarantees could cheapen the price of capital or reduce the cost of enterprise, but by themselves could only facilitate, rather than assure, access to development capital.

Spatial

Most of the Detroit plants that have been or will be idled by disinvestment are multi-story buildings constructed between 1910 and the 1940s. Although many of the product groups discussed earlier as the core of Rational Reindustrialization can be produced efficiently in such facilities, this is not so in all cases at all scales. Some potential private investors in a reindustrializing Detroit may require new facilities; this poses the costly and politically painful task of land assemblage in an intensely built environment. The continuing agony of providing the 465 cleared acres said to be necessary for the new GMAD plant in the Central Industrial Park is well known: a $200 million public expenditure (*excluding* the cost of financing debt), the complete destruction of a community, and abject capitulation by government to the dictates of a potential private investor. The city of Detroit controls but one 60-acre site with industrial potential, and has identified only a handful of privately held sites in even the 15–40 acre range. Industrial land assemblage in Detroit will require a new relationship with private investors, superior replacement housing for relocated residents, a continuing public presence in the developments facilitated, and access to public development capital at the federal level on a scale unlikely under Reagan.

It is not possible to take up all the problems and tasks we can anticipate. We possess neither the space, the necessary special knowledge, nor the bravado. We will, however, engage some of the major obstacles defined above by imagining the specific forms they might assume in three distinct phases in the long march of rationally reindustrializing Detroit. For the sake of orderly exposition, we will discuss an early Pilot Project Phase; an intermediate "Mixed Enterprise Zone" Phase; and a more distant Mature Plan Phase.

Pilot Project Phase

The event that creates the possibility of implementing this initial phase has become a bitter commonplace in contemporary Detroit: a major industrial facility is closing and hundreds, perhaps thousands, of workers face permanent unemployment. We assume a year or more of lead-time between announcement and closing; the presence of a major union; a plant work force with strong leadership; and some interest in averting disaster on the part of the surrounding community, the vendors to the facility, and local and state government. The objective in this phase is to reopen the facility as an enterprise in which the workers and community hold equity and thus can participate in bar-gained planning of the new company's development. The product line of the new venture would be based on the criteria, and probably selected from among the examples, we have described. Hence, as the firm eventually prospers, the legitimacy of the Rational Reindustrializa-tion agenda will be reinforced: local government, other endangered workers and manufacturers, and potential investors will be embold-ened to attempt similar ventures.

Feasibility

The first step must be a campaign to mandate and properly conduct a feasibility study for reopening the closing plant. The initiative of the threatened workers and the affected union will be crucial. They will have to gather the support and generate the momentum to enlist local and state government, vendors, community organizations, and perhaps even the existing corporation.

The key participants in the study would be the workers and the union; local and state governments and their economic development agencies; representatives of community organizations whose member-ships include many plant workers; and, at some point, one or more Detroit-based financial institutions interested in investing in the pro-posed venture. The participants would retain necessary consultants for special studies on the proposed product line's current and future mar-ket; on current production technology, costs, and anticipated improve-ments; on financing options; on the forms of corporate governance and management structure suited to the purposes of the participants; and on how best to accommodate existing or pending state law and regulations. The feasibility study should be conducted so as to maximize the educational impact of the inquiry and public support for the proposed undertaking. The feasibility study process would be consummated in a final report that could also function as the initial business plan of the new enterprise.

Governance

The new enterprise should be structured to maximize access to potential capital while insuring a strong worker and community voice. We propose a model with five components.[2] An *operating company* with a management including elected union representatives would organize production, marketing, planning, and the other traditional aspects of enterprise as a for-profit business. An Employee Stock Ownership Plan (ESOP) with a committee, under union control, would provide the vehicle for worker equity, facilitate access to certain sources of capital, and confer significant tax advantages. A nonprofit, tax-exempt *community corporation* would provide a locally accountable entity that could accept contributions from local and national charitable organizations to provide capital for and assume equity in the new enterprise. The community corporation might also prove useful as a pass-through mechanism for donated buildings and equipment. *Individual investors* would be offered stock, though care must be taken not to unnecessarily dilute worker and community equity and influence in corporate governance. Finally, the *Detroit EDC* would function as a conduit for government grants, as a lessor of equipment and/or plant if industrial revenue bonds are used, as a continuing source of technical assistance, and as an indirect voice of local government in corporate affairs.

How would such a complex structure be governed, and how would bargained planning occur at the level of the firm? The common stockholders would be sovereign, electing a board of directors that would make policy for management. To maximize the policy impact of worker equity and to strengthen the hand of the union, both the allocated and unallocated shares in the ESOP would be voted by the workers (or by their elected representatives in the ESOP Committee, which might overlap with the union leadership or be a special union office). The stock held by the ESOP, the community corporation, and by individual local residents would be voting common stock. If it would not compromise the general appeal of firm offerings, the by-laws of the operating company might require that both the ESOP- and community corporation–held shares elect a certain minimum number of directors. Additional capital would be sought through nonvoting preferred stock available to all.

The procurement of high quality—but controlled—management personnel would be essential. To attract private investors and government support, to navigate the dangers of the launch, and to build the operating company's standing in the marketplace will require experienced and aggressive managers. But these managers must also understand the unusual character of the company. They must be prepared to accept policy direction from a board in which the voice of the workers and the community is strong, even dominant. They must conduct relations with a union strengthened by the equity position of its members. And they must willingly participate in both the formal and informal processes of bargained planning, often yielding to the voice of the shop floor on the organization of production, heeding the union or the ESOP Committee's recommendations on local procurement targeted to union shops, and accepting the dictates of the city on hiring. Such unusual individuals may well find work in such new enterprises highly attractive: a work force inspired to exceptional productivity by its equity position and policy role; a plant equipped with state-of-the-art technology; the special support of local government; and high visibility in a nationally known innovation are all benefits to be expected. To recruit the best available talent, however, substantial material incentives may also be necessary. Direct salaries above the norm in the industry, cash bonuses for top-flight performance, and advantageous options on nonvoting preferred stock should be considered.

The union would function both as the traditional collective representative of the workers in daily and contractual relations with the operating company and, through the ESOP, as a voice in corporate governance. The precise relations between the ESOP and the union would be defined in practice, and would be influenced by such considerations as the interaction between the union local and the international or bargaining tactics at contract time.

This sort of enterprise structure clearly contains elements of political contest as well as common interest. It would, in the embryonic form of an individual pilot project, embody the dynamic class tensions that would play themselves out in a fully implemented, mature Rational Reindustrialization plan.

Financing

The financing of the enterprise should be designed to realize substantial capital for start-up, to maximize equity in relation to debt, to reap

the maximum tax advantages available to its unusual structure, and—
for political as well as business and tax reasons—to allow a rapid rise
to profitability. Money will be necessary at the launch for the acquisition of building and equipment, for initial operating capital, and to
fund the ESOP trust.

In the best possible case, the plant that will house the new enterprise would be donated by the former corporate owner to the tax-
exempt community corporation, which would then bestow it upon the
operating company. The former owner would realize tax advantages,
and might be particularly amenable to this course of action if also
engaged in bargaining with the City Council over permission to receive
tax abatement and/or industrial revenue bonds for new investments
elsewhere in Michigan.

Securing financing for the Employee Stock Ownership Plan (ESOP)
is essential. The typical elements of an ESOP are the company, the
ESOP trust and trustee, the initial lender, and the employees and their
ESOP committee. The operating company would establish the plan
and the trust and designate the trustee. A lender would make a loan
to the trust, which would use the proceeds to purchase common stock
in the operating company. The company would at the same time agree
to pay the trust the equivalent of the trust's principal and interest
payments to the initial lender. The shares would be held by the lender
as security for its loan to the trust; as the plan begins to operate and
payments are made on the loan, progressively more stock would be
released to the ESOP trustee and then distributed to the accounts of
the employees on the terms of the plan.

The benefits to the operating company are substantial. If an initial
lender can be found, the new enterprise can enjoy an immediate, interested market for its common stock. The most likely lender will be a
local commercial bank interested in the full banking business of the
operating company and that of its workers and supporters. Although
the company is required to make payments to the trust in the manner
of a loan, the entire payment (both that dedicated to interest *and* the
principal on the trust's obligation to the lender) is tax-deductible. (In
realizing the benefits of the ESOP, it will be important to prevent its
substitution for an adequate and independent pension plan for the
employees of the operating company. The union must guard against
an "economy" such as this.)

Beyond the sale of voting common stock to the ESOP, the company would seek initial capital by offering the same securities to the
community corporation and to local private investors. Given political

support for the venture and the ideological appeal of its main product
(e.g., fuel-saving hardware), certain foundations might give grants to
the community corporation for the purpose of purchasing equity in the
operating company.

To seek other equity capital, particularly from church and other
institutional investment trusts, the operating company could also issue
nonvoting preferred stock without diluting worker and community
power in company governance. Since at first the enterprise would presumably seek market entry with aggressive pricing of its product, initial purchasers of stock should have modest expectations about near-
term dividends.

It will be important, however, to show profitability as soon as
possible. We think that can occur: given the substantial investment in
new equipment, the special tax status of the ESOP financing, and the
predictable net operating losses in the early years of the enterprise,
the company will have huge tax benefits to carry forward to future,
profitable years. If potential investors can be convinced of the company's prospect of stable profitability in the future, then the anticipated cash flow from the deductions carried forward can be sold in
advance, at start-up, for precious early capital. Investors might well
go for such a "tax loss sale": after all, the new company is *not* a worker
takeover of a troubled firm in a declining industry, but a publicly
assisted mixed venture entering a booming industry.

In light of these possible solutions to the start-up obstacles, it is
perfectly reasonable to expect that one or more of Detroit's major factories could be saved from closing. A former auto engine plant, for
example, might be reopened to produce a small cogenerator similar to
Fiat's TOTEM, which is based on a four-cylinder auto engine and can
deliver substantial savings in heat and electricity costs for individual
residences, small apartment buildings, and stores. Such a product
would have both a local and a national market. Beyond the expected
tax abatements, the city could assist by requiring procurement of the
cogenerators for publicly assisted new construction, assuring that some
orders would already be in hand at launch. Further, the city and
its EDC could discuss with potential local vendors to the new enterprise the possible relationship between their cooperation with the company and their prospects for future incentives from the city. Even at
the pilot project stage, the advantages of publicly directed linkages
would begin to emerge.

Mixed Enterprise Zone Phase

We foresee a time when the aggregation of pilot projects, together with certain legislative and political developments, will make possible a larger, more coordinated application of our agenda. As auto disinvestment continues and the limits of the downtown Renaissance become clearer to the electorate, local government may be compelled to use its available economic development tools in unprecedented ways in a bold quest for jobs, tax base, and restored legitimacy. At that point, Rational Reindustrialization can be attempted in a single large industrial tract of Detroit. Local government would nurture the potential linkages among a substantial number of both traditional private and pilot project firms in the tract.

As auto-dependent suppliers look for replacement orders, as some plant closings lead to successful pilot project reopenings, as the earlier new ventures become profitable and expand, and as private corporations become interested in major investments in the zone, local government can shape both the terms and the character of growth in the zone by its aggressive use of economic development tools.

Tax Increment Financing

A Tax Increment Finance Authority (TIFA) can designate one or more development areas in which tax revenues from net increases in property valuation go not to the city's general fund but to an account controlled by the Authority, which can use the funds to finance revenue bonds based on the cash flow of the tax increment. These resources are applied to the economic development of the increment district. Broadly constructed, state law may even allow a TIFA to assume an equity position in zone enterprises.

Enterprise Zones

In the current legislative proposal, enterprise zones may be designated by local government with the approval of the Secretary of HUD in consultation with Commerce, Labor, and Treasury. The criteria are quite loose: any continuous urban zone characterized by vacant land and buildings, an unemployment rate 1.5 times the national average, most residents' incomes below the city median, and 4,000-plus residents despite pervasive depopulation would qualify several times over. All the significant industrial tracts of Detroit would thus be candidates for designation.

Because of contemplated limits on the number of zones to be

designated nationally during the early years of the program, intense competition among cities is likely. Beyond political trade-offs, cities that can demonstrate greatest need, broadest local support, and most potential for job creation will be the winners. If Detroit wants to win, it should ask: how can a local government supportive of Rational Reindustrialization combine a tax increment development area with an enterprise zone to create stable industrial employment on a large scale?

If such a Detroit zone were drawn to include several vacant and available industrial facilities, the federal tax incentives could be used to attract new, private investors. If, for example, Schlumberger, Nucorp, or another major energy hardware producer eager to ride the 1980–2000 drilling surge grows understandably frustrated with its unfilled orders from uncoordinated and overextended vendors, and if it were cautious of the costs of major new construction, the in-place industrial linkages of southeastern Michigan might prove very attractive, especially in a Detroit mixed enterprise zone in which innovative public policy had begun to efficiently rationalize the relations among many separate producers. Under such circumstances, the federal incentives offered in the zone might induce both the major private investment *and* the entering corporation's participation in the general planning process of the zone.

Pension Fund Capital

To implement Rational Reindustrialization in a major industrial zone of Detroit will require more development capital than will be available from worker/community equity, government grants, and conventional lenders. For the mixed enterprise zone to flourish, access to pension fund capital will eventually be necessary.

Pension funds in the United States control huge resources. They hold over $550 billion in assets, equivalent to 27 percent of GNP. Their $100 billion investment in corporate bonds represents nearly 15 percent of all long-term private corporate debt in the country. A building political contest of great import is developing around two simple questions: Whose dollars are in the funds? How should they be invested? In an August 1980 statement, the AFL-CIO Executive Council strongly encouraged affiliates to bargain for joint administration of benefit funds. The highest priority for redirected investment identified by the Council was "a new independent institution, partially supported by pension funds and aimed at promotion of employment as part of a broad program for the reindustrialization of America"—in essence, a public development bank in which workers would have a policy voice.

Major obstacles confront the aggressive pursuit of such a goal. Most start-up and smaller enterprises are excluded from investment simply because they are unproven or too small to merit the necessary research. Finally, all pension fund investment policies are influenced by the "prudent man" doctrine which, as conventionally interpreted, requires trustees to invest conservatively, based on the narrowest measures of return to plan beneficiaries. Ironically, such caution has often produced poor performance.

For workers to gain some influence over their deferred earnings held in pension trusts, a sustained campaign will be required. Unions must bargain for joint administration. Public funds must be freed from socially irrational regulations. A doctrine of "social prudence" must be asserted, one that charges trustees with an affirmative responsibility to consider social criteria in investment policy. Vigorous use of the public balance sheet approach must be used to demonstrate the full economic value of targeting investments—especially from the public employee funds—to the communities of plan participants. Many regional and national risk pooling and capital targeting instruments must be developed, so that workers have the tools to safely direct the power of their pensions.

Unions must win creation of and joint control over a state or area investment bank that guarantees a minimum rate of return to pension fund investments and targets a portion of its resources to zone enterprises. For example, as the pilot project building small cogenerators matures to profitability, new equity capital from the regional fund could help finance its expansion into much larger industrial cogenerator production.

Eminent Domain

Only public authority will be able to accomplish the major spatial rationalizations that may be required within the zone. A mixed enterprise zone embracing and overlaying a federally mandated enterprise zone and a city-designated tax increment finance district should include as much existing open space as possible, to reduce the need for industrial land assemblage in the future. While Detroit has very little such space well served by the necessary transport and utility infrastructure, we have noted the potential cost advantages of major reinvestment in existing facilities as compared with entirely new "greenfield" developments. While greenfield expansion often appears to minimize production costs, its huge—and often publicly assumed—capital costs as compared with the "brownfield" or retrofit alternative calls that appearance into question.[3] We are convinced that when all costs are fully and properly enumerated, the bottom line will be urban reinvestment.

Detroit's multi-story factories need not be industrial dinosaurs marked for extinction. We have noted that many of the product lines we recommend for Detroit are large, relatively low-volume-per-week goods suited for fabrication in rehabilitated multi-story factories. We would also point out that many of the smaller, start-up enterprises that will bloom in our agenda can share multi-story facilities converted, through government initiative, into "industrial condominiums."

Nevertheless, the need for land assemblage will inevitably arise as reindustrialization proceeds. Rational Reindustrialization projects a new conception of the land assemblage process, in which public/worker/community authority dominates. The municipal exercise of eminent domain will not commit such blight-by-announcement but be the outcome of open, protracted discussion within the planning mechanism. If housing must be taken, relocated residents will move into an already constructed replacement community reflecting their preferences, a community financed by federal and state governments and the bonding power of the Tax Increment Finance Authority or the Economic Development Corporation. Some homes might even be physically relocated; in any case, neither residents nor businesses will lose the relationships that are their sustenance.

Bargained Zone Planning

Who should govern the mixed enterprise zone? Through what structure should decisions to wield the development tools we have described be made? We envision an incorporated, democratically constituted Planning Authority that brings together (1) representatives of workers (both unions and boards of worker-owned firms); (2) private enterprise (big and small manufacturers, banks and other lenders, utilities); (3) communities (e.g., a zone-wide council of neighborhood organizations); and (4) government (EDC/TIFA, the city). Each of these four blocs would have a set number of members elected or appointed to the Authority board by the entities it represents.

Having recognized common interests in the process of establishing the zone and the Authority, the representatives would still necessarily bring contending interests to the governance of the zone. Open debate at the board table and in public would test the strength of the blocs represented; ultimately, each entity has the power to withhold its participation in the economy of the zone. These social contests, sometimes mild and sometimes sharp, would be resolved by adoption of a zone contract or bargained planning agreement binding on all participants.

As the political experiment of the mixed enterprise zone matures, the bargained planning agreement would embrace a wider and wider range of economic activity: wage and hiring policy; coordinated production of intra-zone orders; development and maintenance of infrastructure; distribution of government resources; coordinated targeting of capital; efficient materials movement; and even formal merger of some zone enterprises. The Planning Authority would, in effect, levy a tax or "user fee" on zone enterprises, at first simply to finance its oversight role but later to enable it to make ongoing targeted investments within the zone.

The commitment to a mixed enterprise zone would obviously constitute a major shift in the priorities of local government. Downtown commercial interests would be told to rely more on market forces and be asked to forego their claim on public development resources. The citizenry would be asked to consider surrendering part of its tax resources to targeted use in the zone. The federal government would have to be won over to the logic of a city using public balance sheet accounting and be persuaded to cooperate. Such a federally tolerated, well-developed mixed enterprise zone would be the highest stage of Rational Reindustrialization attainable in Detroit without a major restructuring of American politics. To go further, large resources are essential.

Mature Plan Phase

How large? We can assign rough round numbers to suggest the resources necessary to fully reindustrialize Detroit as a model of frost-belt recovery: to create 100,000 new industrial jobs, close to $4 billion in new investment would be required over time. We will not discuss here how the public component of this investment might be raised. For now, suffice it to say that, for Rational Reindustrialization to progress to full form, Reagan and the free market troglodytes who shape his economic policies must go, to be replaced by a federal administration whose solution to the crisis of the 1980s is incipiently state-capitalist. While it does matter whether this evolution is dominated by antidemocratic pragmatists such as Felix Rohatyn or by genuine liberals seeking a state-capitalist regeneration of a more redistributively just society, in either case corporatist institutions would be created. A crucial test of strength for progressives would be our ability to marshal the forces necessary to condition these institutions. If a Rohatynesque national development bank were founded, would city movements, trade unions, and other mass organizations of the working class and poor have sufficient strength in the streets and in Congress—and sufficient clarity on what is desirable—to shape part of the bank's mandate? Could we insure that some of its resources would be targeted to the Rational Reindustrialization of the frostbelt?

The fullest implementation of our agenda may very well depend on the convergence of the left and progressive forces in America into a national social-democratic movement with clear objectives and political power. This national bloc could influence federal energy, development finance, transportation, housing, and urban policy in ways that would favor a full capital-conserving, job-creating industrial program for Detroit.

At the local political level, mature Rational Reindustrialization requires the advent of a city administration that shares our agenda's fullest objectives. Its leaders would represent a mobilized people in negotiations with private capital, with Washington, and with other industrial communities of southeastern Michigan. As the scope of bargained planning came to encompass a widening range of city life, a popular movement would emerge, one that could elect and protect a creative leadership and which would provide the training ground for thousands of resourceful citizens guiding the planning contest in the factories and neighborhoods of Detroit.

NATIONAL POLICY AND RATIONAL REINDUSTRIALIZATION

The agenda described in this paper would be all the more feasible if certain national policies begin to be implemented in the 1980s. First, a national response to the current automotive sector crisis could slow the loss of key inter-firm linkages in the Detroit economy. Second, a national energy policy centered on fuel substitution and coal conversion, rather than on the production of diesel fuel from Western shale, would place Detroit in a better position to capture a significant share of the U.S. energy hardware sector. Third, because start-up costs for our "Mature Plan" phase are large, an approach to national, regional, and urban revitalization based on an integrated federal capital targeting mechanism, such as a Reconstruction Finance Corporation with access to Energy Security Trust Fund monies, would make financing Detroit's future far easier.

We will examine each of these national areas in turn.

Policy for the Auto Transition

An agenda to rationally reindustrialize Detroit's economy would be well served by a national policy aimed at slowing the decline of the U.S. automotive sector. The downsizing of the city's main industry is occurring at a dangerous pace; if the linkages that bind together the industrial economy are ruptured by too many sudden jolts—bankruptcies, lost orders, skilled work force migration—the cost of rebuilding the area's economy will be far greater. A managed approach to the auto crisis is important in buying time in which to marshal resources for rational conversion of Detroit's industrial base.

Specifically, in order to slow the decline of the U.S. industry, steps must be taken to retain North American employment and to narrow the gap between the price of the labor-power embodied in U.S. and Japanese nameplate vehicles sold here. The key step is enactment of "local content requirements" that would mandate that all vehicles sold in high volumes in the U.S. contain at least 75 percent North American value-added by some future date. Such requirements would simultaneously induce Japanese investment in the U.S. and Canada; reduce the downward pressure on U.S. manufacturing wages (and hence on frostbelt tax bases); speed the integration of Japanese auto unions into the worldwide auto productivity/labor rate norm; and slow the outsourcing of work by the Big Three to offshore shops. For those who argue that local content mandates would raise car and truck prices, we respond that the U.S. government can and should demand auto price restraint as a quid pro quo for reducing the threat to the Big Three's market share from low-wage foreign producers.

Policy for the Energy Transition

Rational Reindustrialization in Detroit is not strictly dependent on which policies are adopted to deal with U.S. overdependence on scarce petroleum-based fuels. The least-cost energy future for the nation, which we describe below, is also the one most conducive to Detroit's role as an energy hardware producer. Only one policy emphasis in the energy field—massive subsidization of the synthesis of diesel fuel feedstocks from Western oil shale—could sabotage the planning process we have described. Any other policy direction, including a nonpolicy of letting "the market" determine fuel mix, will favor the substitution of gas for oil and the emergence of coal as the prime synthetic gas feedstock.

Detroit's future will continue to depend on the health of the auto industry for at least the next 30–50 years. That fact dictates our strong interest in the U.S. having adequate supplies of high-heat content liquid fuels for the transportation sector. That interest, in turn, leads us to advocate a 1980–2020 energy policy that frees up high-quality liquid fuels from sectors that can easily be switched to gas. Basically, the so-called energy crisis is rooted in the absence of such fuel-switching: scarce petroleum-based fuels for which there are no affordable substitutes available to the transportation sector are being wasted on stationary uses that *can* be cheaply and quickly switched.

What should be done? First, large industrial and electric utility boilers should be, and are being, switched over to coal. Second, the possibility of interfuel substitution should be maximized by policies encouraging large-scale production of low- and medium-BTU gas from coal. Such coal-based syngas once enjoyed a significant industrial market, and is being produced today—at half the cost of new natural gas—without subsidy and despite the lack of an explicit national policy favoring it; conscious policy, however, could accelerate the return of this proven industrial gas supply technology.

As more and more coal-based gas becomes available to industries that have not been able to switch from oil or natural gas to coal, they will switch to coal gas, freeing up oil for transportation fuels and natural gas for home heating. To make this thoroughly rational redistribution of fuels among sectors feasible, a third step is already underway: the upgrading of U.S. refineries to crack almost all crude oil into light fuels suitable for transportation.

These three steps would mean that by the end of this century, about 70, rather than today's 50, percent of U.S. oil use would be in the transportation sector. Assuming an on-road vehicle fleet of 160 million units averaging 28 miles per gallon, and adding about 800,000 barrels a day (B/D) for aircraft, by 2000 the U.S. transportation sector can get by on about 7.5 million barrels a day (MBD) of petroleum products. Based on the consensus forecast that U.S. crude oil production in 2000 through 2020 will be about 7.0 MBD, at 70 percent transport fuels per barrel, the sector's domestic shortfall is only 2.6 MBD of product, less than half what the U.S. now imports.

Unless too many of the resources needed to finance fuel switching and refinery upgrade flow instead into unnecessarily expensive, long lead-time shale and direct coal liquefaction projects, the coal gas-based energy transition can and will occur. Liquid fuels will be directed where their use is most efficient, and gasoline will be supplemented more and more by synthetic liquid fuel made from coal gas.

This is the rational 1980–2020 energy and transportation fuels strategy, and the stable, secure industrial jobs lie in the production of the hardware for energy production, storage, upgrading, and (coal) gasification. Moreover, because of the affordability of the low- and medium-BTU gas from coal that underpins this energy path, policies that contribute to its development should have great appeal to non-energy capitalists who, like consumers, must treat energy as a cost. We argue that this common interest creates the basis for an alliance of the public sector, the citizenry, and elements of the nonenergy business community to preserve, and win a share of, the Energy Security Trust Fund financed by the tax on the windfall profits of oil companies due to price decontrol.

Policy for Capital Targeting

At some point in the 1980s, the nation will confront the failure of Reagan's laissez-faire, supply-side stewardship of economic policy. Despite continued stagnation and Reagan's abuse of the working class and poor, welfare-warfare liberalism will not recover: its demise was the predictable result of its ideological bankruptcy and programatic disarray. With the legitimacy of government as a source of security and an engine of growth in question, a period of danger and opportunity will arrive in American politics. With laissez-faire discredited no less than redistributive liberalism, the debate will center on the objectives, forms, and costs of qualitatively new state interventions in the economy.

Contending champions of the restructuring of the accumulation process will advance industrial policies that speak to debates over regional competition, energy sources and costs, urban recovery, and the renewal of basic infrastructure. Despite their differences on these matters, all serious participants in the contest will assume the necessity of major state spending. Vulgar critiques of "big government" will wilt before the hard fact of social decay. One example: a recent estimate of the cost of merely maintaining and renewing the existing U.S. highway, mass transit, railroad, water and sewer, and harbor systems during the next two decades presents a staggering $1,225 billion bill. Some of these costs will be assumed locally, but the figure suggests the scale of federal intervention that will be required just to maintain the possibility of an industrial economy, let alone to achieve steady growth.

In this context, what is the approximate magnitude of the capital needed to establish the Mature Plan version of Rational Reindustrialization in Detroit? What does the capital stock required to equip 100,000 well-paid workers cost? This is not an easy question. We *can* determine an upper bound on the funds required by examining capital-output ratios in the firms producing goods similar to those we propose for a new sector in Detroit. This method tells us that approximately $60,000 in annual sales are associated with each job, and that a capital investment of about $0.75 is required to yield each $1.00 in annual sales. By this reasoning, the $6 billion in annual sales required to employ 100,000 workers would entail capital requirements of some $4.5 billion.

But this is only an upper limit, because it assumes that the new Detroit energy hardware sector would be put together the way its capital-wasting private sector counterparts were: in new plants, with relatively untrained labor pools, and forced to procure intermediate inputs from profit-maximizing market suppliers. There is, admittedly, no scientific way to quantify the savings that might accrue to Detroit's attempts to maximize the use of existing and potential linkages and work forces, but rough estimates are possible. First, based on U.S. Department of Transportation analyses of the cost advantage that Japanese automakers reap due to industrial *complexes*—as opposed to isolated plants—it would not be unreasonable to reduce our capital needs figure by 10 percent, to $4.05 billion. Second, assuming conservatively that one-third of new sector operations could be housed in existing, older facilities, the Office of Technology Assessment's spring 1980 study that found a 30 percent savings to "rounding out" existing steel plants versus building new ones suggests an additional reduction, to $3.65 billion (i.e., $4.05 billion reduced by one-third of 30%).

This large sum seems modest when compared with the hundreds of billions of public and private dollars that will be required to restructure the national economy. However, we are still left with the basic question: where will the money come from to rationally reindustrialize Detroit? Part of the necessary $3.65-billion investment will be made by traditional private enterprise seeking the long-term benefits of the Detroit approach. Part will be raised by worker-owned enterprise from local and regional investors and lenders, especially those with access to pension fund resources. Part will be provided from the revenues of local and state government. Part *must* come from a federal capital targeting mechanism.

The federal government has, of course, always targeted capital in one way or another, and the history of more formalized national development banking reaches back at least to Hoover's Reconstruction Finance Corporation. As corporatism advances, the confusion and parochial infighting that surrounded Carter's National Development Bank proposal will abate; it will be time to seriously debate capital targeting. The severity of the situation presented by Reagan's denouement, and the broad political base required to legitimate the bold swing to major new state intervention, will compel a resolution of differences.

But the national development bank that emerges from the push and pull of regional and class interests refracted in the federal government will almost certainly be an institution shaped primarily by corporatist forces. However, those forces will need allies against the ideological right, and to get them will have to make important—if reluctant—concessions to a progressive bloc in Congress.

For what should that bloc fight?

Corporatists such as Felix Rohatyn will conceive of the bank as an investor in infrastructure renewal, a stabilizer of municipal finances, and a source of equity capital for essential but troubled industries in need of a corporate safety net. For them, the bank would be an institution "beyond politics" and thus more able to extract intensely political concessions from cities and unions while disciplining less corporatist lenders and companies.

The progressive bloc would concur with the general proposition of investment in infrastructure and agree that the bank should have a municipal window. When cities come to borrow at that window, however, the terms of the loan will be a matter of intense debate. On the crucial issue of the bank's industrial investment policy, the progressive bloc and the forces it represents must advocate a "buy-in" complement to the corporatist "bail-out" strategy: there should be a requirement that failing firms falling into the corporate safety net bounce out with the added vigor of worker equity, financed perhaps by the development bank's guarantee of a loan to an ESOP trust. On the basis of such equity, a recovering auto parts supplier in Detroit might diversify and be brought into cooperation with the Mature Plan for reindustrialization of Detroit.

The decisive issue for our Detroit agenda would be the bank's capacity and willingness to take a minority equity position in the fully or partially worker-owned enterprises that were born in the mixed enterprise zone phase of Rational Reindustrialization and that would now be seeking new capital for expansion. Progressives should fight to require that a certain percentage of the bank's loans, loan guarantees, and especially equity purchases are targeted to the kind of enterprises that underlie our agenda in Detroit. In light of the industrial dimensions of the energy path previously described, its obvious contribution to a secure and affordable energy future, and its broad appeal to all energy consumers in all social classes, we can even envision the new development bank drawing from the Energy Security Trust Fund and investing in the expanding worker/public firms in Detroit.

Finally, such an RFC-like bank that targets a portion of its capital to the kind of urban economic development program we advocate for Detroit should be made to gradually separate these investment demands from block-grant–funded community development. The necessary work of community renewal would then not be slowed by the funding needs of large-scale development, while the capital requirements of Rational Reindustrialization would not be constantly subjected to debate among parochial neighborhood interests.

OUR AGENDA CAN WORK

The foregoing is not merely wishful thinking unrelated to an assessment of what is possible. The large-scale energy hardware we have sketched uniquely satisfies three central requirements:

1. Properly managed, such a sector can unfetter the city's industrial engine and provide a socially controlled source of investible surplus, while maintaining secure, well-paid employment.
2. Only such a sector, grounded in the existing plants and—where possible—equipment of the city and region, can maintain living standards during the transition process. That is, only such a plan preserves capital from the incomplete accounting of private capitalists.
3. Only public management can effect the conversion from auto industry dependence to planned energy hardware development. This is because only an integrated program of land assemblage, affordable replacement housing, intra-sectoral input procure-

ment, and rational tax policy can overcome the parochial conflicts among developers, communities, creditors, and service
deliverers that large-scale redevelopment inevitably entails.

Some may object that a revitalization plan that gives such heavy
emphasis to public investment is utopian in the United States of the
early 1980s. We would agree, of course, that for the foreseeable future
most productive activity in Detroit will be organized by private capital. It is not inevitable, however, that the *leading* growth sectors will
be in purely private hands. In fact, there are several reasons why it
probably will *not* be the private sector that provides the dynamic
push to the regional economy, if such a push occurs at all.

For the very reasons that explain our tentative choice of public
projects, the activities around which any recovery will be centered
will require massive scale. It is extremely unlikely that private capital
would take the risk of betting large chunks on what will obviously
look to less venturesome minds on Wall Street like the longest of long
shots. Unlikely, yes; absurd, no: the more farsighted *may* understand
the power of a well-linkaged set of new enterprises; the capitalist class
is not a monolith. There are Walter Wristons, but there are also Ar-
mand Hammers; there are Citibank traditionalists, but there are also
the foreign loan departments of the central banks of social-democratic
nations involved in North American energy joint ventures. Nor need
government always remain a passive junior partner in a narrow, busi-
ness-dominated agenda. In fact, as the fiscal crisis inevitably deepens,
the public sector will realize that a strong role in production is its only
insurance against unending private disinvestment.

The market alone will never save the economies of cities such as
Detroit. Even though disinvestment has eroded the cost of land, it cannot drive down the cost of either labor-power or capital fast enough
or far enough to recreate the conditions for expanded reinvestment.
Most important, even if private investors were inclined to take the
gamble, they would lack the tradition, skill, experience, and resources
to do the one thing that could radically lower their overall costs: the
coordination of core and supplier firms and their work forces in the
new industries. If Westinghouse, for example, were to establish a coal
gasifier operation in Detroit, it would tend to order components from
its current, non-Detroit suppliers. Given the excess demand position
of the industry, it might have to wait months for delivery. A public
enterprise sector, however, could decide that, simultaneously with the

conversion of idle auto capacity, excess production capacity in the auto parts/tool and die sector should be given over to making gasifier components that would otherwise be scarce.

Even if there are ways to foster the development of a small public or mixed public/private production sector, some may call it folly to think of a new sector that could employ 100,000 workers. We disagree, though obviously we do not imagine immediate implementation of the Mature Plan version of Rational Reindustrialization. It is our view, however, that the hurdles to be overcome in bringing this agenda into being are, in some important ways, independent of the scale of the proposed activity. Many of the legal, financial, regulatory, political, and ideological obstacles that attach to a fairly grandiose conception of a new sector apply with equal force to a small version. Moreover, unless our agenda speaks to the core need of the disinvested local economy for a large number of stable, well-paid, metalworking jobs, it will at best operate at the margins of reform.

Detroit is too far gone to be salvaged by even the best decentralized, neighborhood-based projects often advocated by adherents of the small-scale entrepreneurial model of revitalization. Many of those projects have a role to play in Detroit, as we noted earlier in distinguishing national capital targeting from community development funding. But they cannot form the core of a rational plan for rebuilding an industrial economy.

The best available writing on what we call the "localist/communitarian" alternative, Martin Carnoy and Derek Shearer's *Economic Democracy*, argues that a needs-oriented sector based on small businesses can be built on a big enough scale, i.e., small, but repetitively, to "make . . . fights against [service and employment] cutbacks unnecessary by substantially reducing . . . economic distress." We have tried to test that hypothesis for Detroit by seeing how much a low-profit, needs-oriented sector could reduce living costs in the city. In the most charitable case imaginable, some 35 percent of local consumption could be locally produced in such a small business sector. Even if that sector could sell output at 15 percent below its current prices—which we doubt—living costs would be reduced only 5 percent.

Such a reduction in what we earlier termed "the cost of reproduction of labor-power" could, of course, help maintain the "social wage" associated with a given direct wage. But producing basic necessities for local consumption cannot rebuild the economy, and so cannot justify any substantial claim on the resources that could become available for basic reindustrialization. Moreover, while an agenda such as ours, that aims directly at the creation of a new emphasis for the manufacturing base, *can* sustain the small business sector so critical to the decentralized vision, the small business sector *cannot* restore industrial vitality.

We share with Carnoy, Shearer, and other progressive redevelopment activists a commitment to the notion that only a new political culture can sustain the movement necessary to build a new urban economy. In the Detroit case, we believe that Rational Reindustrialization is a workable agenda which, if implemented, could initiate the process of a steadily growing planned, semi-public sector, the management of which would create the possibility of a mass political culture of involvement, competence, and productivity. Such a culture could lift the transition toward real public/worker governance out of the realm of theory and into the real world of industrial and community planning.

We foresee a future Detroit in which the hours of work per job could be progressively reduced in favor of increased employment through worker and community power in economic planning. We foresee a Detroit in which workers, collectively, can become managers, and in which the tension between increased current benefits and increased investment for growth can be openly debated and resolved. In the place of a Detroit whose factories are vacant monuments to the limits of purely private economic power, we want a Detroit whose factories are open and alive with constructive debate over conflicts between the full development of new work relations and the needs of a democratically determined general development plan.

This future Detroit is possible.

NOTES

1. If one assumes a different set of national energy, transportation, and tax policies, a number of other product lines meet the ten criteria. For example, if a set of tax and regulatory changes transferred all or most nuclear power and/or synthetic fuel subsidies to manufacturers and consumers of solar equipment, Detroit could capture a significant share of what would be a burgeoning Midwest market for flat-plate solar collectors for space and water heating and cooling in new structures. Similarly, a shift in policy toward more rational urban commuter and national freight transportation systems would swell demand for product lines—buses, light and heavy rail cars, and rail electrification equipment—for which major componentry could be manufactured in Detroit for the national market.

   It would not be sound local-level economic development planning, however, to base a reindustrialization agenda on outputs for which existing national policy, however mistakenly, promises no predictable mass market. On the other hand, while this paper is confined to product lines realistic under current national policy, a more speculative and generic application of our perspective would study which cities could expect to capture significant shares of the bus, rail car, and rail electrification markets, should they evolve in the future. Detroit would appear to have the means to stake a major claim in a future rail electrification hardware industry; Cleveland, Cincinnati, Dayton, and Philadelphia appear to enjoy advantages that might earn them a large part of the rail car market; and Youngstown, Pittsburgh, Seattle, and Memphis seem suited to strong entries in the bus manufacturing business. Finally, there are markets that, while currently speculative, can be anticipated. For example, it is a good bet that there will soon be a major international market for $200–300 receiver "dishes" that will process transmissions from direct broadcast satellites (DBS). Any city with a substantial stamping/metalworking sector should prepare for entries into that market as it develops.

2. During the late 1970s, a team of consultants coordinated by the National Center for Economic Alternatives did extensive work on behalf of the Ecumenical Coalition of the Mahoning Valley in their campaign to reopen the Campbell Works of the Youngstown Sheet and Tube Company as a community-controlled corporation. The NCEA team did important work on the structure of worker and community ownership. We have benefited especially from the insights of Brad Dewan and Karl Frieden. See their *Recommendations of Worker/Community Ownership Structure for Reopened Campbell Works* (Washington, D.C.: National Center for Economic Alternatives, 1978).

12

Economic Crisis and Political Response in the Motor City

RICHARD CHILD HILL

The nation's sixth largest city, Detroit has a central city population of 1.3 million encompassed by 3 million additional residents living in over seventy suburban communities. But the significance of the Motor City transcends its demographic dimensions. Locus for the growth of the auto industry, terrain where the postwar relationship between Big Capital and Big Labor was first institutionalized, national staging point for black political struggle, exemplar of the syndrome of problems labeled the "urban crisis," and touted model of a "new urban renaissance," Detroit symbolizes and substantiates the central economic and political issues facing U.S. industrial capitalism. It is known as "the birthplace of good times and bad," and the forces shaping Detroit shaped the nation.

Detroit's past growth trajectory was set by the rhythm of auto production. Today economic crisis and global reorganization in the auto industry place the Motor City at the heart of the debate over alternative reindustrialization and urban revitalization strategies for the United States. The Motor City is at a crossroads. What happens in Detroit will once again serve as a beacon for the nation.

A CITY IN CRISIS

Situating Detroit

Imagine picking up a pen and applying it to a map of the United States. Beginning with Buffalo, run a line through Pittsburgh, Wheeling,

Cincinnati, Louisville, St. Louis, and to Kansas City; then angle north-
ward to Des Moines, Minneapolis, and finally east to Milwaukee, Flint,
Detroit, and Cleveland. You have sketched the contours of the Midwest manufacturing belt. Beneath this soil lie limestone, coal, and iron
ore for the production of steel—the structural fabric of an industrial society. The Midwest is interwoven by rivers and lakes providing for the
transshipment of factory products to international markets. Over 40
percent of the labor force in the manufacturing belt has traditionally
worked in the basic industries: steel, machine tools, rubber, electrical
machinery, and auto (Jacobs, 1970).

Within the manufacturing belt is an "automotive realm." The geographical apexes of the automotive realm form a triangle stretching
from Oshawa, Ontario, to Cincinnati, Ohio, to Milwaukee, Wisconsin.
Until recently, 90 percent of the automotive employment in North
America rested within this triangle, and the automobile industry set
the pace for urban industrial growth in the manufacturing belt. It
turned out millions of products at relatively low cost; constituted the
largest consumer of steel, rubber, and oil products; provided the key
stimulus to production in highway construction, housing, and the repair and plastics industries; and was responsible for one-quarter of the
value of all retail sales, the vitality of one in six businesses, and a parallel percentage of jobs (Cray, 1980:7).

The heart of the automotive realm beats in metropolitan Detroit.
Spurred by the development of the automobile and mass production
techniques, Detroit's population grew from 250,000 in 1900 to 1.8 million in 1950. The Motor City had by now become the hub of a massive
urban-industrial system. Transportation and communication arteries
daily carry the products manufactured in the rubber plants of Akron
and Kitchener, in the metal foundries of Chicago and Cleveland, in
the machine tool shops of Cincinnati and Windsor, in the steel factories of Gary and Buffalo, in the electronics and hydraulic research
labs of Columbus and Dayton—all to the Motor City for final processing, assembly, and distribution throughout the nation and the world
(Sinclair: 36). In 1940 nearly half of Detroit's metropolitan labor force
worked in manufacturing, with one-third employed in motor vehicle
production. By 1970 the metropolitan area figures had dropped to 37
and 18 percent respectively. Yet 42 percent of Detroit's central city industrial workers continue to work for the auto producers, and an additional 37 percent are employed by auto-related manufacturers (City of
Detroit, 1978, table III-13).

The Web of Uneven Development

Detroit once billed itself as the "largest factory town in the world." But some two decades ago, the economic tide began to turn against the Motor City. Detroit became enmeshed in a web of uneven development spun first by the flow of industrial and commercial capital to the suburbs and then to the Sunbelt and, more recently, by the reorganization and decentralization of the auto industry on a global scale.

Local Dimensions: City Versus Suburb

The spatial growth of the auto industry shaped the physical and social contours of the Detroit region. Auto companies expanded their operations through a leapfrog locational logic. A new plant was constructed next to a major railroad line, in open terrain at the perimeter of the burgeoning metropolis but within reasonable proximity to the urban labor force. Once built, the factory attracted complementary metal and machinery industries, and then residential subdivisions. Further expansion repeated the process farther out (Sinclair, 1972:36).

Prior to World War II, the auto industry developed in or within close proximity to the central city of Detroit.[1] During and after World War II, factory construction and spatial growth moved to the suburban and exurban fringe of the region.[2] As in the past, complementary metal and machinery industries clustered around the new factories, and residential growth and services followed industrial expansion. Suburban expansion was facilitated by federal financing for a massive highway network and further spurred by Federal Housing Administration practices which ensured loans for new suburban homes while often redlining older areas in Detroit (Serrin, 1971).

Industrial corridors following the major railroad lines and residential corridors siding the major highway arteries split the Detroit region into sectors. Working-class suburbs emerged in the industrial corridors. Wealthier suburbs, housing the administrative and professional groups associated with the auto industry, developed along the radial freeway arteries (Sinclair, 1972:38).

As manufacturing plants located in suburban industrial corridors, as commercial establishments flocked to suburban shopping malls, as warehouse facilities gravitated from loft structures at points of central city railway convergence to single story structures located on suburban interstate freeway points, and as the magnet of suburban office complexes attracted professionalized service activities, two Detroits came into being. Suburban Detroit developed into a thriving economy stimulated by high levels of capital investment and a population earning a per capita income above the state average. The central city of Detroit, on the other hand, had increasingly become a segregated bastion of unemployment, underemployment, and poverty amid one of the wealthiest metropolitan regions in the world (Taylor and Willits, 1971:18).

The social costs of postwar economic growth in Detroit fell heavily upon the inner city black population. The boom years of World War II lured Southern migrants to jobs opening in Northern industrial centers. Then, during the 1950s, the mechanization of Southern agriculture pushed millions of agrarian workers off the land. Primarily black, poor, unskilled, and unfamiliar with the urban scene, this wave of migrants poured into the aging urban core of Detroit and other Northern industrial metropolises in search of work. What they encountered was confinement to lower-paying jobs, and prohibitions against entering most suburbs and many central city neighborhoods through policies of racial exclusion and by the high cost of housing (Fusfeld, 1973: ch. 1).

Between 1930 and 1970, Detroit's black population more than quadrupled while the city's white population decreased by 56 percent. In 1940, 91 percent of the central city population was white. By 1978 Detroit was 59 percent black. By then 87 percent of the region's black population lived in Detroit. Detroit was now a black majority city encircled by a white suburban ring (Schnore et al., 1976:89–90; City of Detroit, 1978:23).

Black Detroiters found residential space by spreading outward from the lower east side and the near northwest side to a concentric area ranging five or six miles from the central business district (Sinclair, 1972:48). White residents often identified "neighborhood succession" with "ghetto expansion," and the turmoil unleashed by this "succession" process undermined neighborhood efforts to conserve inner city communities. Blight spread rapidly through Detroit's central core. Today Detroit is composed of a predominantly black central area surrounded by a belt of mixed neighborhoods, with predominantly white communities to the northwest, northeast, and southwest of the city.

The City Planning Commission classifies Detroit subcommunities into three zones according to land use, age of physical structures, and degree of residential blight. They are: the inner city, within Grand Boulevard; the middle city, a three-mile-wide belt encircling Grand Boulevard; and the outer city, in the northwest, north, and northeast (City of Detroit, 1978:20). These "cities within the city" are the physical expression of a deeply rooted social inequality and correspond to patterns of racial segregation. Those social groups bearing the costs of uneven development tend to be segregated in the inner city and transition zones. The working poor and the unemployed live in neighborhoods bordering industrial corridors with obsolete and abandoned manufacturing facilities. Here population decline and unsuccessful competition with suburban shopping malls resulted in blighted retail strips, housing deterioration, and the decline of entire neighborhoods. Rates of infant mortality and diseases like tuberculosis show a similar concentration in the inner subcommunities and a decline toward the outer rim, as does the incidence of most types of crime (Sinclair, 1972:48).

Regional Dimensions: Snowbelt Versus Sunbelt

The regional distribution of the nation's economic activities also changed rapidly over the past two decades. Capital investment, employment, personal income, and population growth favored the South and West ("Sunbelt") over the Northeast and Midwest ("Snowbelt"). And the pace of uneven regional development escalated as a Sunbelt economic axis formed around oil, petrochemicals, defense industries, "space-age" technology, agriculture, and leisure to assault the economic supremacy of the manufacturing belt and the automotive realm.

Between 1970 and 1980, Sunbelt nonagricultural employment increased at four times the rate of the Snowbelt. During that decade the Snowbelt lost 870,000 manufacturing jobs, and the Sunbelt gained 1.7 million. And the Northern industrial regions experienced a net outflow of population to the Southwestern states. Between 1970 and 1976, for example, 650,000 workers moved from the North to the South. Projections suggest that population growth in the Sunbelt will outpace the Snowbelt by a factor of four to one during the next two decades (Mazza and Hogan, 1981:5).

This shift in economic activity from Frostbelt to Sunbelt has variously been attributed to: (1) characteristics of the Northern labor force including union membership, higher wages, and strike potential; (2) labor-related legislation in the North including closed shop agreements and higher worker compensation and unemployment and disability benefits; (3) regional differentials in state and local taxes; (4) federal government spending favoring the Sunbelt; (5) regional differences in energy costs; and (6) stricter enforcement of pollution regulations in the Snowbelt (Mazza and Hogan, 1981:24).

It is difficult to specify the sources of uneven regional development with precision because the relative importance of each factor varies by industry and firm.[3] Nonetheless, by the early 1970s, it had become clear that older industrial cities in the North, whose economies were dependent upon mature and declining industries, were critically affected by regional shifts in investment and employment growth. With outdated production facilities, a highly unionized labor force, and a public infrastructure in poor condition, Detroit was finding it increasingly difficult to retain business activity and to attract new capital investment.

Global Dimensions: The Reorganization of the Auto Industry

In 1980 the U.S. auto industry experienced its worst economic downturn since the 1930s. The auto giants lost a combined $3.5 billion, 250,000 auto workers were given indefinite layoffs, and 450,000 more lost their jobs in industries supplying the Big Three (Shaiken, 1980: 345). The deep slump in the auto industry issued from a combination of factors: economic recession, rising energy prices, a saturated U.S. market for fuel-guzzling cars, and intensified foreign competition—all translating into a falling profit rate. Given the geographical organization of U.S. auto production, the severe hardship wrought by the auto crisis centered in Detroit and the industrial cities of the automotive realm and manufacturing belt.

The crisis in the auto industry is immediate, close-at-hand, and painfully visible. Less apparent, but of far greater long-run significance, are far-reaching structural changes occurring in the industry. Today the ferocious competition among transnational corporations focuses upon a common objective: the development of the world car. The world car, "suitable for American highways, European city streets, and African trails," is a small, energy-efficient vehicle with standardized, interchangeable components, designed to be manufactured and marketed throughout the world. The development of the world car is a vast cost-cutting strategy meant to lower the expenses of design and engineering, realize economies of scale, and enhance manufacturing flexibility by allowing the car giants to multiply their production locations for major components. The success of the world car is meant to counter foreign competition at home and abroad and thus renew the vitality of the U.S. automobile and supplier industries (Hainer and Koslofsky, 1979).

Investment requirements to build the world car and enter expanding markets are very high and are forcing capital-short firms to merge with more powerful competitors—a repeat of the historical trajectory of the U.S. auto firms but now on a global scale (*Le Monde*, 1980). Intensified international competition heralds the introduction of new labor-saving technology: auto components are increasingly produced by computer-controlled machine tools and assembled into the final car by robots (Shaiken, 1980:345). And with the development of the world car, explicitly designed to be assembled with components produced from around the world, global sourcing has become a distinctive feature of the auto industry's new international division of labor.[4]

These structural changes in the auto industry suggest the employment crisis afflicting the industrial heartland of the United States will be less than fully ameliorated by the return of vitality to the U.S. auto industry. The downsizing of automobiles will permanently reduce employment in the supplier industries. Intense competition today will likely lead to overproduction tomorrow as corporations attempt to maximize efficiency from economy of scale. Advanced industrial nations will continue to confront the possible failure of enormous, home-based auto corporations. More automation suggests production will now outstrip employment growth at a more rapid rate. And global sourcing portends reduced employment in the United States and threatens to undermine the collective bargaining and strike power of unions in the auto industry.[5]

A Structural Crisis

From the close of World War II to the late 1960s, Detroit's economy bounced back with each upswing of the business cycle. But then recession-level unemployment failed to respond to economic expansion. Tough and resilient from weathering cyclical ups and downs, the Motor City now confronted a challenge of a different sort. Detroit was beset by a persistent, structurally rooted, economic crisis. A few indicators tell the tale.

1. Detroit's population peaked in 1953 at 1.85 million inhabitants. During the next quarter century, the central city lost 487,000 people (Holli, 1976:269).
2. Between 1968 and 1977, Detroit employment dropped by 208,-200 jobs—one-third of total employment in the city (City of Detroit, 1978:27). Since the late 1940s, 50 percent of the Motor City's industrial firms and 70 percent of its manufacturing jobs disappeared (Luria and Russell, 1981:5).
3. Unemployment became permanent. The population of Detroit

declined 13 percent since 1970, but the employed labor force
declined 20 percent. Outmigrants tend to be employed persons.
Left behind are the elderly, disabled, and discouraged workers
(City of Detroit, 1978:23). Unemployment in the central city
of Detroit, investigations have concluded, "is more the result
of inadequate demand for employees of any kind than a lack of
skills or training among the unemployed" (New Detroit, 1974:
iv–v).

4. Detroit's bleak employment picture coincides with a rapid rise
   in welfare case loads. Between 1969 and 1974, the number of
   Aid to Families with Dependent Children (AFDC) and General Assistance (GA) recipients living in the city increased
   from roughly 80,000 to approximately 256,000 persons—a total
   increase of 167,000 or 187 percent (State of Michigan Task
   Force, n.d.). By 1978 one in three residents of Detroit—400,000
   in all—received some form of public assistance (City of Detroit, 1978: table III-9).

5. Disinvestment, job loss, and the concentration of the region's
   poor and unemployed in the central city threatened Detroit
   with fiscal collapse. Increased service needs and stagnant land
   values eroded the property tax—Detroit's primary source of local revenue. The city responded with increased income and
   utility taxes, and citizens of Detroit came to pay nearly four
   times the tax rate of the average city in Michigan (City of Detroit, 1977:140). Even so, tax revenues fell far short of increased expenditure demands. So, despite the need for increased
   services, the number of city employees and social service outlays were steadily cut back (ibid., 1976).

In June 1981, fully 60 percent of the city's 1.2 million residents
were receiving some form of government assistance. Local income tax
revenues had fallen by $30 million in 1980–1981. The city ended its
fiscal year $120 million in the red and projected an additional $150 million deficit for fiscal 1982. To fend off bankruptcy, Detroit implemented an austerity plan. Wage concessions totaling $77 million were
extracted from the city's 20,000 workers. Increases in the payroll tax
levied on Detroit residents and suburban commuters brought in $94
million. And the city went to the bond market and borrowed an additional $100 million to help pay off the debt (Business Week, 1981:
55–56; Peirce, 1981).

With continued disinvestment, Detroit has found it ever more difficult to create the physical infrastructure and produce the public services which attract private investment. With further tax increases and declining city services, the danger facing Detroit, as one fiscal analyst has observed, is "at the stage of fiscal crisis, disinvestment becomes a cause of disinvestment" (Russell, 1981).

WHAT IS TO BE DONE?

Detroit's fate has been wed to an economic base controlled by a small number of multinational corporations. Corporate stability and growth are premised upon the capacity to respond to changing national and international costs and conditions. The profit logic that once brought investment and growth to Detroit now brings disinvestment, decline, and decay. Industrial and commercial capital flow to suburbs and Sunbelt. The auto industry is reorganizing and decentralizing on a global scale. The Motor City's factories—Detroit's "raison d'etre"—are being abandoned. And there is no reason to believe that an "invisible hand" will transform today's disinvestment into the conditions conducive to the scale and kind of new investment necessary to rebuild Detroit tomorrow. No, the issue is plainly political: what is to be done to save Detroit?

The Dependent City

If a city government is to play more than a marginal role in determining its own economic fate, it must have a genuine development capacity. That is, a city government must have the capacity to (1) *organize* development—to plan, coordinate, and implement development projects; (2) sufficient *financial* resources to realize development projects; (3) control and assemble *land* to meet the specifications of development projects; (4) *retrain* its labor force to meet the skill requirements demanded by development projects; and (5) *evaluate* the consequences of development projects as they bear upon the public interest and in light of changing conditions in the local, national, and international economy. And the city must have an overall economic development *strategy* which interconnects these development capacities within a concretely reasoned and economically defensible image of the city's future.

Legal rules defining the relationship between government and the private economy, and the city's constitutionally prescribed location within the nation's system of government, have severely circumscribed the economic development capacity of city governments in the United States.

The accumulation of capital takes place in private enterprises. Governments are barred from producing and appropriating surpluses to reinvest in their own expanding enterprises. However, governments have the authority, the mandate, and indeed the need to create and sustain conditions of private profitability. So, as night follows day, the capacity of a city government to foster development depends upon its ability to attract and maintain private investment. In the absence of private accumulation and reinvestment, the city's own power to govern wanes.[6]

In the U.S. federal system, the level of government expenditures, the distribution of government expenditures by function, and the methods and capacities for obtaining revenue vary among federal, state, and local governments and between relatively autonomous units within levels of government. The federal government takes in the largest share of tax dollars, monopolizes the more progressive tax sources, and spends the largest part of its budget on military and social welfare outlays. State and local governments share the welfare bill and have policing functions, but a large share of their budgets is devoted to infrastructure and services which directly condition economic development. Local governments, for example, assume major responsibilities for schools, fire protection, sanitation, transportation, and the like. State and local governments gain the major share of their revenues from the most regressive taxes: sales taxes, flat rate income taxes, and property taxes (Netzer, 1970:170).

During the past two decades, the heaviest demands for new government spending have been made on state and local governments, particularly the latter (Fleming, 1973:33–39). With circumscribed tax-raising capabilities to match their increasingly heavy expenditure demands, the fiscal solvency of older, industrial cities like Detroit became increasingly dependent upon federal and state government transfers. Moreover, within the U.S. federalist system, cities have only those rights of self-government constitutionally granted to them by state governments. This subordinate relationship between the city and state governments places added constraints upon municipal development capacity since state constitutions limit the scope of local authority to raise taxes, buy, control, and sell property, and negotiate with private investors (Friedman, 1974:5; Reeves, 1970).

Governing responsibility is not only divided among federal, state, and local governments but also between relatively autonomous units within levels—for example, between states and between local units of government. Metropolitan regions are dotted with hundreds of municipalities, school districts, and other types of single and multipurpose units of local government. Uneven development, in the context of a metropolis fragmented into local jurisdictions with their own taxing powers and expenditure priorities, produces uneven fiscal development and disadvantages the central city in relation to its suburban neighbors (Hill, 1974). In the absence of a strong regional government, externalities impose further fiscal damage on central cities whose public investments in health, education, and cultural facilities "spill over" their boundaries to the benefit of the suburbs while region-wide problems such as unemployment and poverty "spill into" the central city (Brown, 1970; Neenan, 1971).

Little wonder that the politics of cities have been described as a "politics of dependency" (Katznelson, 1976). Economic investment and location decisions are made in corporate boardrooms, not in city hall. Individual households choose residential locations within a regional context which is at best only partially influenced by central city policy decisions. Programmatic state and federal decisions bearing upon urban economic development issues are often made by political figures without urban constituencies. The city, therefore, takes on the role of managing the consequences of decisions made elsewhere. Local policies become marginal relative to the market and broader political forces shaping the urban terrain.

But within these "rules of the game," the economic development role played by city governments has significantly expanded during the past decade. A brief synopsis of key events in Detroit helps explain why.

In the late 1960s, the inner cities of many Northern metropolises erupted in flames. A structure of racial discrimination, economic oppression, and political exclusion had burdened black inner city residents with the costs of uneven development and central city decay. Detroit was no exception. The July 1967 "great rebellion" in Detroit—an outpouring of street violence which left forty-two people dead and thousands injured—marked one of the most intense outbreaks of civil rebellion in the history of urban America (Conot, 1974; Widick, 1972).

The outburst of mass violence shocked the civic and business elite into a determination to do something about the deterioration of the inner city. Detroit's mayor and the state government invited representatives from business, labor, government, and the city's neighborhoods to a meeting. The meeting established the New Detroit Committee, the forerunner of the National Urban Coalition. This coalition organized to pressure for federal and state urban programs and to channel private resources to reconstructing the central city (Graves, 1975).

By the early 1970s, it was crystal clear that the flow of capital to suburban, Sunbelt, and foreign locations was the fundamental impediment to the physical and economic revitalization of the central city. With the scent of smoke still lingering, and backed by the support of the Motor City's major corporate heads, Detroit's urban coalition renewed its pressure for federal and state programs—now directed toward augmenting the city's development capacities and creating public "incentives" to compensate Detroit for its disadvantages in competing for private investment with the "growth centers" of the suburbs and Sunbelt (New Detroit, 1974).

The political effort mounted in Detroit, and multiplied by similar efforts in numerous Northern urban centers, produced results. State governments in the Frostbelt created a variety of grant, loan, and tax incentive programs to encourage private investment: programs often were targeted to distressed urban areas (Vaughn, 1979). New state legislation also enabled central city governments, like Detroit, to expand their local development capacity.[7] In addition, federal programs including urban development action grants, community development block grants, the HUD Section 108 loan program, and grants and loans by the Economic Development Administration were created or amended to facilitate economic development in distressed cities (U.S. House of Representatives, 1980).

Urban economic development in the 1970s thus came to be characterized by a local public/private "merger." This consisted of the creation of local development organizations which intertwine public and private interests; the growth of a "dual investment process" as the involvement of public funds in what previously would have been considered private development increased dramatically; and a redefinition of the public interest to encompass private development projects which retain or expand jobs and investment.

The Detroit Strategy

Working closely with the city's major corporations, and operating within the framework of available state and federal enabling legislation and programs, Detroit's public officials have designed a strategy for economic development in Detroit. An overall economic development program provides a comprehensive blueprint and rationale for the city's economic revitalization efforts. And Detroit's development efforts are organized through a structure which knits together private development organizations and public development agencies.

Detroit's capacity to organize development centers upon a cluster of economic development corporations (EDCs)—organizations now constitutionally authorized to wield expanded development powers and designed to coordinate public and private development efforts through a system of overlapping memberships modeled upon the interlocking corporate directorate system in the business world. The activities of these EDCs are in turn overseen by an Overall Economic Development Program Committee composed of representatives from the EDCs, chaired by the mayor, and staffed by the city's Planning and Community and Economic Development departments (City of Detroit, 1978; appendix H).

In the past city government has been able to acquire land through urban renewal funds and to provide public improvements through its routine capital expenditures. Today state enabling legislation has authorized EDCs to utilize public funds to acquire, hold, develop, and dispose of land. Transfers from private to public ownership can now be accomplished with greater ease.[8]

Economic development corporations are also authorized to wield expanded financial powers. They can issue industrial revenue, tax increment, and job development authority bonds and establish industrial revenue districts. They can receive and administer grants and loans from higher levels of government. And they can offer further public incentives for private development like land banking and tax abatement schemes. This structure has afforded city development officials added capacity to "leverage" scarce funds provided by federal and state programs and the city's capital improvement budget to attract private investment and to initiate private development projects in Detroit.

The most comprehensive statement of Detroit's current development strategy is the "overall economic development program."[9] This development plan is organized around four general objectives: (1) to retain and modernize Detroit's indigenous commercial and industrial activities; (2) to attract and develop new commercial and industrial activities which have the potential to expand employment, sales, and tax revenue; (3) to improve Detroit's overall capacity for economic development; and (4) to increase the role of minority entrepreneurs in the economic development process. These objectives are applied to seven key geographical sectors which play individually unique yet interrelated economic functions in Detroit's space economy: (1) the riverfront; (2) the central business district (CBD); (3) the central functions area; (4) industrial corridors; (5) the port of Detroit; (6) housing and neighborhoods; and (7) transit corridors.

Detroit's general development objectives are a riverfront teeming with tourist and convention crowds; a strong CBD serving as the financial pillar to the region's economy; a central functions area thriving on headquarters activities, culture, and research and development–related jobs; and a surrounding expanse of neighborhoods whose population stability and economic well-being are assured by the retention and attraction of modern industries to renovated industrial corridors and port facilities. All are to be interconnected by an efficient and rapid public transit system. This is the best of all possible worlds: the full flowering of the Detroit Renaissance.

But in this world of scarce resources, access to development funds is shaped by the size and use provisions of state and federal programs and by the profit calculus of private investors. "Leveraging"—the matching of scarce public incentives to restricted private interests—is the name of the game. Development priorities must follow.

The necessity to establish investment priorities raises a series of questions. (1) Should retention of existing industry or attraction of new industry be given priority? (2) In what directions should diversification of the economy be pursued? (3) Should new investment concentrate on commercial or industrial activities? (4) Should new investment be targeted to a few large, big-business oriented projects or toward a larger number of projects on a smaller scale? Clearly these are not mutually exclusive alternatives. Rather, the basic issue is what underlying logic and corresponding mix of investment is most likely to maximize the city's development across all geo-economic sectors?[10]

In Detroit, as in all large U.S. central cities today, the logic shaping investment priorities and the practical application of development plans is the corporate center strategy.[11] That is, overall investment priorities are geared to transform this aging industrial city into the modern corporate image: a financial and administrative and professional services center for auto and related industries; a research and development site for new growth industries (such as robotics, new auto materials and components technology, and leisure-related activities); an emphasis upon recommercialization rather than reindustrialization; and an orientation toward luxury consumption that is appealing to young corporate managers, professionals, convention-goers, and the tourist trade. In areal terms, the Detroit strategy affords priority to the creation of a "golden arch" radiating from the riverfront through the central business district to the central functions area; the creation of upper-income, gentrified neighborhoods within this arch; and the construction of a transportation system closely knitting the activities in this arch into a unified whole.

Urban Crisis or Urban Renaissance?

Will this corporate center strategy revitalize Detroit? It seems doubtful. The Renaissance of the urban core in Detroit is fragile. The central place activities performed by the riverfront, CBD, and central functions areas are tied to the economic well-being of the region as a whole. And the economic vitality of the region remains tied to manufacturing. Continued industrial disinvestment threatens to undermine the whole Renaissance effort.

In a blue-collar, union town, a development strategy which emphasizes headquarters functions, recommercialization, leisure activities, and high-technology industries seems unlikely to produce the number of jobs at the level of remuneration required to reconstruct Detroit. New technology-based industry starts small, produces few jobs in the short term, and flirts with failure. Recommercialization and the transition toward a leisure economy are targeted toward the better-paid professional, technical, and managerial groups. But for Detroit's less-advantaged workers, the Renaissance means trading a former possibility for blue-collar jobs at decent wages for the future probability of scarce, low-paying, dead-end service work—all at a high public cost per job.[12]

In short, the corporate center strategy—the Detroit Renaissance—will not in itself end the traumas induced by industrial disinvestment. At best the Detroit Renaissance will reverse the historical correlation between privileged residence and distance from the inner city by creating a gold arch surrounded by deteriorating and impoverished workers' neighborhoods. At worst it will itself collapse under the weight of continued industrial disinvestment and fiscal decline.[13]

Detroit must stem the tide of industrial disinvestment and draw upon its manufacturing past to reconstruct an industrial future. It must do so on a scale that will replace the number and kinds of jobs that have left town. If the city is to survive and thrive, there must be

a well-conceptualized and coordinated *national* commitment to reindustrialization, targeted to revitalize cities like Detroit, and backed by
a massive investment of financial resources. The problem is clear. But
the means for achieving a solution founder against firmly entrenched
obstacles.

U.S. federal urban policy lacks coordinated planning and agreement on what ought to be done. There is little coordination between
urban programs and general economic policies. Federal, state, and
local urban programs are fragmented; program requirements are often
in flux; and financing is unpredictable. And the commitment of federal
revenues for urban redevelopment falls woefully short of what is required.

The reign of the market, the fragmentation of government institutions and programs, and the lack of federal planning, coordination,
and control mean that urban economic development strategies are
formulated within the context of bitter local, regional, and national
competition as governments attempt to outdo one another in marshal-
ing public incentives to court private favor.

Public incentive programs, rather than working to attract private
investment where it would otherwise not go, actually appear to be
wasteful of scarce public revenues. So many governments have proliferated so many incentives that these enticements may have lost their
selective power to attract (Vaughn, 1979; Peirce and Steinbach, 1980).
More to the point, there is little evidence that public incentives
strongly influence corporate location decisions. Public tax incentives
are usually less important corporate lures than wage, land, transportation, and energy costs and the presence of a network of suppliers. And
these are factors often beyond the control of local governments (Jones,
Bachelor, and Wang 1981; Mazza and Hogan, 1981).

The terms currently defining the "public/private partnership" development strategy also raise serious issues of accountability. Private
influence over the development process was traditionally based upon
technical expertise and the ability to relocate capital. Now economic
development corporations have become an instrument through which
the private sector more or less *directly* allocates public resources and
wields public powers. As the definition of the public purpose with
respect to eminent domain and other government powers is enlarged
to encompass unemployment reduction through retention, expansion,
and attraction of private economic activity, it becomes less possible
to recognize a potential conflict of interest or, indeed, to even distinguish between public and private interests.

Alternative Strategies To Save Detroit

The Reagan administration is likely to continue to promote the public/ private partnership, some targeting to distressed areas, and the leveraging of private investment through public incentives. All of these principles are embodied in the hotly debated Kemp-Garcia urban enterprize zone proposal incorporated in the 1980 Republican platform. Kemp-Garcia designates areas of high unemployment and poverty in cities as enterprise job zones. State and local governments reduce property taxes, and the federal government reduces social security, capital gains, and business taxes for enterprises which locate in and draw a majority of their employees from these targeted areas.

But the Reagan administration is also scaling down HUD programs, plans to scuttle the Economic Development Administration, and is incorporating various urban programs into broader but more weakly funded block grants to localities. This means a drop in federal revenue available for economic development projects, even less federal policy review and coordination over urban development programs, and heightened city competition for scarce resources.

Current federal policies will aggravate uneven regional development. Supply-side tax cuts suggest increased movement of manufacturing firms from North to South. Increased defense spending disproportionately benefits the Sunbelt at the expense of the Snowbelt. Federal welfare cuts will hurt the North more than the South. And the decontrol of oil and gas prices signals a massive transfer of capital to energy-producing Sunbelt regions and higher energy costs to consumers in the Snowbelt. The implications seem clear: further job and capital flight, unemployment, and fiscal deterioration in Northern industrial cities.

The policies of the Reagan administration notwithstanding, today's rising debate over U.S. industrial policy foreshadows the future necessity for large-scale government intervention in response to regional competition and uneven development, the dwindling sources and rising costs of energy, renewal of basic industrial and urban infrastructure, and city revitalization. The stakes are high and bold policy alternatives have been forthcoming. Two recent proposals reflect the range of alternative positions emerging from the current debate.

Felix Rohatyn, senior partner in the New York investment firm of Lazard Frères and Company, has forwarded an alternative industrial policy committed to reconstructing urban infrastructure and reorganizing basic industries (for example, auto, steel, glass, and rubber).

The twin objectives are to improve the competitive position of U.S. firms in world markets and "even out" the burdens and benefits of economic development across U.S. cities and regions.[14]

Rohatyn criticizes the laissez faire market posture of the current administration. In contrast, he argues the reality and the merits of state intervention and the "mixed economy." Rohatyn is unsympathetic to proposals urging the government to "pick the winners" by facilitating investment in high-technology growth industries. He maintains that government lacks the expertise to do so, that winners already win without government assistance beyond tax subsidies for research and development, and that the focus of industrial policy should be upon basic industries. Rohatyn opposes government "bailouts" to large, non-competitive organizations backed by only enough capital to allow them to "limp along." He believes that "losers must be turned into winners" through infusion of enough capital to allow them to reattain a competitive market position. And Rohatyn gives little credence to public sector employment strategies. Rather, he argues the merits of government support for reorganization and employment expansion in the private sector of the economy.

The catalyst in the Rohatyn strategy is the proposed creation of a national development bank designed to mobilize and coordinate the large sums of equity capital required to reorganize basic industries and reconstruct urban infrastructure.[15] This development bank is also viewed as a key instrument for the creation and enforcement of a "new social contract" between business and labor in the United States. Through a bargained tradeoff, equity capital to firms and job security to workers are to be exchanged for union wage concessions, work rule changes to increase productivity, matching financial commitments by banks and union pension funds, and tax support and reduction in service costs by state and local governments.

The Rohatyn plan integrates economic, regional, and urban policy, provides high-level policy coordination through the instrument of the national development bank, confronts competitive disadvantages now outside the city's control, and potentially raises and targets the enormous sums of capital which will be required for reindustrialization and the revitalization of our most deeply distressed cities. It remains unclear, however, to what extent increasing the competitive position of basic industries in world markets will redound to the benefit of industrial cities like Detroit. If, as in the auto industry, modernization means the increasing use of capital-intensive technology and

global sourcing strategies, reindustrialization may well remain di-
vorced from employment expansion and urban revitalization. Moreover, this national development bank, which is viewed by Rohatyn as
"publicly accountable but outside politics," seems destined to be
neither.

The outlines of a contrasting redevelopment strategy have
emerged from work done by the National Center for Economic Alternatives and like-minded groups grappling with the issues of capital
flight, uneven regional development, and worker and community dislocation in the United States. Like the Rohatyn plan, this strategy
argues the merits of focusing upon basic industries, increasing government authority in the economy, developing new structures to pool
investment capital, and linking industrial policy to efforts at urban
revitalization (Alperovitz and Faux, 1980). But the two strategies
part company over the methods for achieving these objectives.

This redevelopment strategy focuses less upon the reorganization
of basic industries than upon the planned conversion of idle and
underutilized infrastructure, plant, and equipment to the production
of alternative goods for which there is a clear social need and a potential economic demand. The calculus governing what is to be produced
encompasses social benefits beyond private profits. These indirect benefits derived from employment retention include lower unemployment
insurance and costs for welfare, health, and crime control—costs which
are borne today by the public sector rather than by the private investor. Here the role of government in the economy includes not only
the current range of public incentive tools and the proposed national
development bank but also extends to the creation of joint public/
private or full public enterprises capable of producing a reinvestible
surplus. And the meaning of development planning is extended to
include workplace governance, employee ownership plans, and combined business, worker, neighborhood, and city representation at the
enterprise and redevelopment area planning levels.

In chapter 11, Dan Luria and Jack Russell propose a public sector
conversion strategy, embodying these tenets, for the "rational reindustrialization" of Detroit. They suggest replacing declining auto
assembly, parts, and machining industries in Detroit with new activities that take maximum advantage of linkages between idle labor
skills, infrastructure, plant, equipment, and industry. The replacement industry, they argue, must be "high wage, metal based, and
national market oriented." And they identify a range of products which

meet these criteria: (1) deep natural gas and heavy oil production and upgrading equipment; (2) residential and industrial steam/electric cogeneration units; (3) large coal- and diesel-fuel–fired industrial process engines; and (4) minemouth coal gasifiers. The authors thus propose that investment in Detroit be targeted to the conversion of abandoned or underutilized industrial capacity to the production of these energy hardware products.

Luria and Russell also develop a three-phase scenario meant to illustrate the institutional possibilities and requirements for implementing their conversion plan. First, the *pilot project* phase represents a possible response to a major plant closing. Here they outline the possibilities for converting the plant to a community-controlled corporation. They suggest the establishment of an operating company, an employee stock ownership plan, and a community corporation attracting individual investors as well as use of the Detroit economic development corporation as a conduit for government grants. Conversion financing tools would include urban development action grants, industrial revenue bonds, a secure lender (such as the EDA or a local commercial bank), and plant purchase through stock sales. Second, the *mixed enterprise zone* phase involves a broader, coordinated application of their development plan to a large industrial tract. Here the authors propose combining tax increment district financing with enterprise zone designation, outline pension funds as a possible source of capital, discuss new procedures for the use of eminent domain authority through a combined public/worker dialogue, and suggest the creation of a bargained zone planning authority made up of workers' representatives, business, neighborhoods, and the city. Finally, the *mature plan* phase sets a 100,000 industrial job target, would require $4 billion in new investment over time, and anticipates support from a national development bank.

This public sector conversion strategy recognizes that modernization of basic industries is in itself unlikely to revitalize distressed industrial cities like Detroit. This strategy also addresses the issue of public accountability by seeking to establish new institutional arrangements for joint public/private participation in the development process. However, it runs up against stiff obstacles posed by the rules governing urban economic development in the United States. Michigan law sharply restricts the range of revenue-generating enterprises a city can create.[16] There are a number of legislative hurdles to be surmounted before public and private employee pension funds can be drawn upon for investment capital. And land assembly in a densely built environment remains a dilemma.[17]

CONCLUSION

Bluntly put, Detroit's plight is that of a city which is no longer competitive within the institutional rules of the game. Private corporations accumulate and reinvest capital; Detroit does not. Capital is mobile; Detroit is not. In the absence of national and regional development planning and coordination, Detroit's own strategy has been shaped through bitter rivalry with other governments for corporate smokestacks and skyscrapers. Mobilizing public incentives to leverage private resources, city officials now call themselves "entrepreneurs in the public interest." But in the nature of the case this version of the public interest boils down to the needs of private investors.

In any era the United States could ill afford to throw away the labor force, managerial and technical expertise, and network of companies, services, and capital investments concentrated in Detroit and scattered across the auto realm and manufacturing belt. To do so in an age of impending scarcities is economically wasteful, politically irresponsible, and morally indefensible. Recognizing this, the rules of the game come into question: First, what should be the role of government authority in relation to economic development? Second, what should be the nature of our intergovernmental system as it relates to development planning on a national, regional, and local level? Last, what are the limits as well as the strengths of private profit as the equation governing urban development?

The issues are not planning versus the market, centralism versus localism, or private versus public accounting. Today the government underwrites the market; local autonomy counts for little without central planning and resources attached; and any accounting scheme which ignores the social and personal costs of economic dislocation makes a mockery of the public interest. Rather, the issue concerns the terms upon which new institutional relationships between government and economy and among levels of government are to be forged. At root the question that confronts advocates of private sector reindustrialization plans and public sector conversion strategies alike is political: can broad popular support be mobilized for the institutional changes implied? The future of the Motor City and the industrial heartland of the United States will hang upon the way that question is answered during the decade ahead.

NOTES

This is a revised version of a paper originally prepared for presentation at an international conference, "Economic Crisis and Political Response in the Auto City: Detroit and Turin," organized by the Harvard University Center for European Studies (Detroit, Michigan, December 10–13, 1981).

1. More specifically, it grew within the confines of an urban core composed of the central city of Detroit, the inner suburbs of Highland Park and Hamtramck, Dearborn to the southwest, and Windsor across the Detroit River (as the locale for the Canadian subsidiaries of the Ford and Chrysler corporations). A few auto facilities were also located outside the core in Flint, Pontiac, and Lansing—locations for once independent companies now absorbed as internal divisions within the General Motors Corporation (Sinclair, 1972:36 ff.).

2. Past location considerations—major railroads, undeveloped land, and proximity to a sufficient labor supply—were now supplemented by a national defense policy urging the dispersal of war production to satellite cities as a protection against nuclear attack. Between 1947 and 1955, the Big Three constructed some twenty new plants in the suburbs of the Detroit region (Jacobs, 1981).

3. Lewis Mandell's research (1975) suggests that wage costs and labor-related legislation are the most important sources of disinvestment in the Detroit region.

4. Global sourcing is both a large-scale cost-cutting strategy and a corporate response to the national political requirements of those less-developed countries which have imposed local content laws (requiring a certain percentage of locally produced components) on their domestically assembled cars. As components produced in a range of individual countries are going into an increasing number of autos built by American auto companies and their foreign competitors, imports of components by domestic companies are rising dramatically. The U.S. imports of auto parts amounted to $6.8 billion in 1979 alone (McDowell, 1980; Woutat, 1980).

5. When facilities for the production of standardized parts are duplicated, slowdowns or strikes at one national site can be countered by increased production at another while final assembly production in a third nation continues unhampered. Moreover, it is estimated that wages at Ford installations in the Philippines and Brazil, for example, are approximately 10 percent the U.S. payrate while in Mexico wages run about 40- to 50-percent of the U.S. rate of pay (Woutat, 1980).

6. As Goldsheid (1964:205) noted, "When poor men conquer power over the poor State this is but a meeting of the dispossessed."

7. State funding in grants and loans is usually a relatively small share of the public costs of local development projects. More significant has been the role of state governments in granting new powers to local governments to facilitate development efforts (Jones, Bachelor, and Wang, 1981).

8. EDCs are authorized to buy land through options, planned purchases, and "opportunity" purchases. Public Act 87, passed by the Michigan legislature in 1980 and popularly known as the "quick take law," also establishes procedures by which a municipality can obtain title to a property acquired through its eminent domain powers before reaching a settlement with property owners for just compensation. This considerably reduces the time required to assemble land for development projects while raising serious issues of due process of law.

9. This document (City of Detroit, 1980) synthesizes and renders up-to-date previous Detroit economic revitalization plans including the Detroit master plan, the moving Detroit forward plans of 1975 and 1977, the 1978 comprehensive economic development strategy, and material from the city's capital agenda, public works program, and community development block grant program.

10. The criteria currently used by the city for evaluating development project priorities are: (1) number of jobs created or retained and cost per job; (2) the long-range impact of an investment with respect to diversification, spinoff, and growth potential; (3) probability of attracting private sector interest; and (4) total "leverage" generated in public and private monies (City of Detroit, 1980:4).

11. Robert Fitch labels this approach to urban development the "national center strategy" and traces its origin to plans developed and implemented in New York City during the second decade of this century. This urban development strategy corresponds to changes in the spatial organization of national and multinational corporations: the increasing centralization and concentration of conception, coordination, and control activities ("headquarters" functions) and the regional, national, and international decentralization of production activities. Therefore, it seems best characterized as a corporate center strategy for urban development.

12. City and state planning officials well recognize this problem and have commissioned a number of studies of potential growth industries for southeastern Michigan. Mattila and Thompson (1980) review this literature and offer a thoughtful analysis of potential growth industries. Using a variety of criteria including cyclical stability, wage rates, assets per worker, value added per BTU, male/female labor force composition, world market demand, and size and employment growth potential, they point to the following industries with growth potential for the Detroit region: meat packing, chemical industries, farm machinery, electric machinery, wholesaling of electrical goods, mail order houses, and a range of services (for example, advertising, computers, management, engineering, commercial photography, and film production and distribution).

13. For example, the Renaissance Center—a $600 million riverfront hotel-office complex masterminded by Henry Ford II—is meant to symbolize the rebirth of Detroit, signal to the investment community that Ford and his financial partners are committed to the city's future, and provide a linchpin for redevelopment of central Detroit in the modern corporate image. Yet it has recently become apparent that the Renaissance Center is in severe financial difficulty. Having lost $103 million since opening in 1977, the Renaissance partnership has been in default on its $197 million first mortgage for the last fourteen months and is now attempting to sell some of its assets (Luke and McNaughton, 1981).

14. The ensuing discussion of Rohatyn's proposal is derived from a speech

he delivered to the Detroit Economic Club, reprinted in the *Detroit Free Press* (Rohatyn, 1981).

15. This national development bank is modeled upon the Reconstruction Finance Corporation (RFC) and the Municipal Assistance Corporation (MAC) in New York City. The RFC, created by Herbert Hoover in 1928, saved a number of banks, cities, and businesses during the Great Depression and helped underwrite synthetic rubber production and the construction of defense plants during World War II. The MAC, under the leadership of Rohatyn, recently helped "rescue" New York City from a severe financial crisis.

16. For example, a city in Michigan cannot own stock in a private enterprise and a city- or state-owned bank is unconstitutional.

17. Wilbur Thompson has recently proposed a "clearing and clustering" land assembly strategy. It would provide land for manufacturing complexes by relocating residents into reconstituted neighborhoods with an eye also to savings in city service production and delivery (U.S. House of Representatives, 1980).

REFERENCES

Alperovitz, Gar, and Faux, Jeff. "Beyond Bailouts: Notes for Next Time." *Working Papers for a New Society* (November–December 1980).

Brown, Peter. "On Exploitation." *National Tax Journal,* (March 1971).

Business Week. "Behind the Fiscal Bind That Plagues Detroit." June 29, 1981.

City of Detroit. *Report of the Mayor's Task Force on City Finances.* Detroit: City of Detroit, February 1976.

———. *Moving Detroit Forward: A Plan for Urban Economic Revitalization.* Detroit: City of Detroit, 1977.

———. *The Overall Economic Development Program.* Detroit: City of Detroit, 1978.

———. *Annual Overall Economic Development Report and Program Projection.* Detroit: City of Detroit, 1980.

Conot, Robert. *American Odyssey.* New York: Morrow, 1974.

Cray, Ed. *Chrome Colossus: General Motors and Its Times.* New York: McGraw-Hill, 1980.

Fitch, Robert. "Planning New York." In *The Fiscal Crisis of American Cities,* edited by Robert E. Alcaly and David Mermelstein. New York: Vintage, 1977.

Fleming, Thomas L. "Manpower Impact of State, Local Government Purchases." *Monthly Labor Review* (June 1973).

Friedman, Lewis. "City Budgets." *Municipal Performance Report* (August 1974).

Fusfeld, Dan. *The Basic Economics of the Urban Racial Crisis.* New York: Holt, Rinehart and Winston, 1973.

Goldsheid, Rudolf. "A Sociological Approach to Problems of Public Finance." In *Classics in the Theory of Public Finance,* edited by Richard A. Musgrave and Alan T. Peacock. New York: St. Martin's, 1964.

Graves, Helen M. "New Detroit Committee/New Detroit, Incorporated: A Case Study of an Urban Coalition, 1967–1972." Ph.D. diss., Wayne State University, 1975.

Hainer, Marg, and Koslofsky, Joanne. "The World Car: Shifting into Over-
    Drive." *NACLA Report on the Americas* (July–August 1979).
Hill, Richard Child. "Separate and Unequal: Governmental Inequality in the
    Metropolis." *American Political Science Review* (December 1974).
Holli, Melvin, G., ed. *Detroit*. New York: New Viewpoints, 1976.
Jacobs, Jim. "Our Thing is DRUM!" *Leviathan* (June 1970).
———. "Suburbs and Disinvestment." Unpublished paper, 1981.
Jones, Bryan D.; Bachelor, Lynn W.; and Wang, Richard. "Rebuilding the
    Urban Tax Base: Local Policy Discretion and the Corporate Surplus."
    Paper presented at the Midwest Political Science Association meetings,
    Cincinnati, 1981.
Katznelson, Ira. "The Crisis of the Capitalist State: Urban Politics and Social
    Control." In *Theoretical Perspectives on Urban Politics*, edited by
    D. Hawley. Englewood Cliffs, N.J.: Prentice-Hall, 1976.
Le Monde. "A Detroit, L'Omelette Se Prepare en Cassant des Oeufs."
    March 4, 1980.
Luke, Bob, and McNaughton, David. "RenCen Loses $33.5 Million; Behind
    on Debt." *Detroit News*, October 25, 1981.
Luria, Dan, and Russell, Jack. *Rational Reindustrialization: An Economic
    Development Agenda for Detroit*. Detroit: Widgetripper Press, 1981.
Mandell, Lewis. *Industrial Location Decisions: Detroit Compared with
    Atlanta and Chicago*. New York: Praeger, 1975.
Mattila, John M., and Thompson, Wilbur R. *Detroit Area Economic Oppor-
    tunities Project*. Detroit: Detroit Chamber of Commerce, 1980.
Mazza, Jacqueline, and Hogan, Bill. *The State of the Region: Economic
    Trends in the Northeast and Midwest*. Washington, D.C.: Northeast-
    Midwest Institute, 1981.
McDowell, Edwin. "Made in USA—With Foreign Parts." *New York Times*,
    November 9, 1980.
Neenan, William B. "Suburban-Central City Exploitation Thesis." *National
    Tax Journal* (June 1970).
Netzer, Dick. *Economics and Urban Problems*. New York: Basic Books, 1970.
New Detroit, Inc. *Action Program Against Unemployment*. Detroit: New
    Detroit, May 1974.
Peirce, Neal. "Detroit Recovery Plan a Model." *Lansing State Journal*, July
    18, 1981.
———, and Steinbach, Charles. "Reindustrialization: A Foreign Word to
    Hard-Pressed American Workers." *National Journal*, October 25, 1980.
Reeves, H. Clyde. "Have State Policies Produced the Current Urban Prob-
    lems?" *Public Administration Review* (March–April 1970).
Rohatyn, Felix. "Back from Bankruptcy: New York's Lessons for Detroit."
    Detroit Free Press, June 4, 1981.
Russell, Jack. "Disinvestment and the Fiscal/Social Stress of Detroit." Un-
    published paper, February 1981.
Schnore, Leo F.; Andre, Carolyn D.; and Sharp, Harry. "Black Suburbaniza-
    tion, 1930–1970." In *The Changing Face of the Suburbs*, edited by
    Carry Schwartz. Chicago: University of Chicago Press, 1976.
Serrin, William. "Detroit Grows Lean While Suburbia Fattens." *Detroit Free
    Press*, November 1, 1971.
———. "Cash Flows Out of the City." *Detroit Free Press*, November 3,
    1971.
Shaiken, Harley. "Detroit Downsizes U.S. Jobs," *The Nation*, October 11,
    1980.

Sinclair, Robert. *The Face of Detroit: A Spatial Synthesis*. Detroit: Wayne State University, Department of Geography, 1972.

State of Michigan Task Force. "City of Detroit vs. Rest of 3-County SMSA: ADC and GA Recipients as Percent of Total City Population, 1969–1974." Lansing, Mich., n.d.

Taylor, Milton, and Willits, Richard. *Detroit: Agenda for Fiscal Survival*. East Lansing, Mich.: Institute for Community Development, 1971.

U.S. House of Representatives, Committee on Banking, Finance and Urban Affairs, Subcommittee on the City. *Hearings on Urban Revitalization and Economic Policy*. Washington, D.C.: U.S. Government Printing Office, 1980.

Vaughn, R. J. *State Taxation and Economic Development*. Washington, D.C.: Council of State Planning Agencies, 1979.

Widick, B. J. *Detroit: City of Race and Class Violence* (Chicago: Quadrangle, 1972.

Woutat, Donald. "Auto Money Moves South of the Border." *Detroit Free Press*, March 2, 1980.

13

Bringing the Third World Home: Enterprise Zones for America?

WILLIAM W. GOLDSMITH

The centerpiece of the Reagan urban program is a development scheme called enterprise zones. The plan would offer extra tax and regulatory concessions to induce business to invest in depressed areas. The problem is that Reagan has already given away so much of business' tax base that he has little left to offer. The enterprise zone idea leads logically to concessions by the only group left with much to concede—workers. Trade unionists are already facing widespread demands for givebacks. In their pure form, enterprise zones attract industry by insisting on wage concessions, as well as waivers of health, safety, and environmental regulation. Reagan's version begins by waiving minimum wage for youths.

It is a mark of the exhaustion of liberal postwar policies in urban renewal, housing, and job development that this approach is being taken very seriously, and not just by conservatives. A key congressional enthusiast is the Democrat from the South Bronx, Representative Robert Garcia. Across America, mayors, city councils, and state administrations hungry for jobs are debating the shape of enterprise zones.

What makes this idea thinkable is radical change in the structure of the world economy. During the past twenty years, corporate capital has become increasingly diffused. Modern communications have permitted central financial and accounting controls over far-flung

Reprinted from *Working Papers for a New Society* (March/April 1982).

manufacturing networks. Today, complex industrial goods can be fabricated in relatively primitive settings, by a workforce paid far below levels prevailing in industrial societies.

In this new global economy, private capital enjoys vastly increased leverage to extract wage concessions as its price for staying put. The result is nothing less than a serious erosion of economic and political rights. Enterprise zones do far more than retain and attract jobs. They become a wedge to cut deeply into the social safety net of the modern welfare state and to reduce the political power of workers in advanced industrial countries.

This idea did not spring full-blown from the brow of some conservative policy intellectual. The Third World already has a good deal of experience with these special production enclaves, often known as "platform economies" or "free production zones." Conditions in these tax-free, duty-free, sub-minimum wage areas suggest the sort of economic development that enterprise zones portend for the United States. And even the relatively successful cases, like Singapore and Puerto Rico, are nothing we should wish to emulate, economically or politically.

As Berkeley planner Manuel Castells has suggested, national governments in the Third World increasingly serve as political intermediaries, caught between the demands of their displaced, urbanized populations and requirements set by global corporations. The enterprise zone idea reflects the growing pressure on governments of advanced countries to play essentially the same role.

In effect, enterprise zones would keep American jobs from being exported—by bringing the Third World home to the United States.

Before turning to enterprise zones in greater detail, one should stop to recall just how radically the new global economy has changed the relations between industrial capital and the Third World. Historically, early industrial expansion sought trade in commodities. Raw materials were imported from underdeveloped countries; manufactured goods were produced in the mother country for sale at home and overseas. This process built industry in Europe, and later in America and Japan, at the expense of local Third World industry. For example, English cities exploded with textile production, while the traditional Indian textile manufacturing industry collapsed.

Later, manufacturing operations were established in overseas territories, but mainly to serve local markets. As European and North American industry established outposts in the Third World, however, they remained something essentially grafted onto local social systems. This external sector was seldom fully integrated into the local economy.

In this long process of the expansion of industrial capital, the great bulk of benefits went to the already industrialized countries. Development elsewhere was stunted, skewed, even reversed. Andre Gunder Frank has termed this process "the development of under-development."

But traditionally, the poor countries were not really part of a worldwide production system, except as suppliers of raw materials. In the past two decades, that has all changed. Today, worldwide cor-porations can supervise minutely specialized manufacturing opera-tions from distant headquarters, so that in the industrial sector of the global economy relations between workers and owners increasingly ignore national boundaries.

In the new international economy, global corporations manufac-ture at multiple sites for export to world markets. They also import Third World labor to the metropolitan countries. Hence, we purchase underwear and transistor radios made in Kuala Lumpur, Volkswagens made in Germany by Turks, and beans harvested by Mexicans in the United States. In this context, it becomes harder and harder for the domestic workforces of the industrialized countries to defend their privileged position as islands of high wages, relatively decent work conditions, and social benefits.

This internationalization of industrial production is all remark-ably recent. As late as 1960, there was virtually no Third World pro-duction of manufactured goods for export. By the late 1970s, however, there were many hundreds of thousands of workers in multinational corporate plants producing for export from scores of sites in more than sixty countries of Asia, Africa, and Latin America. Today there are more, probably millions of such workers. Aside from the availability of raw materials or energy sources, such production is based on three main considerations: an available labor force that will do good work for low wages, an international transport and communication system, and a system for dividing tasks, allowing subdivision into easily or-ganized, supervised, and controlled units of production.

Although foreign plants may be located all over some Third World countries, many "world market factories" are located in such free production zones. These zones are legal islands, where foreign corporations and their officers are usually treated to the special con-siderations that are recommended by the United Nations Industrial Development Organization: exemption from duty on machinery and raw materials, from income tax, and from other normally applicable taxes; freedom from restrictions on foreign exchange; preferential rates on financing, local transportation, and facility rental; provision of utilities, roads, office buildings, and factories; and provision of multiple business and personal services. Usually health and safety regulations are minimal, labor has few rights, and there is little environmental protection.

American domestic corporations are also assisted by special provisions of the U.S. Tariff Code, which allow duty-free reimportation to the United States of products assembled abroad. Under articles 806 and 807, components may be shipped abroad for processing, then reimported with a sizeable duty exemption as long as there will be further processing in the United States. Duty is not assessed on the original components, but only on fabrication costs overseas. In 1978, after six years of growth at 20 percent per year, imports under this preference amounted to $7.2 billion. Of this, one-third was from underdeveloped countries, where such exports grew at a rate of 26 percent per year.

These tariff provisions accelerate the movement toward runaway shops. Among the world's poor countries, Mexico is a striking example of the ability of low wage areas to attract runaway industry. Mostly along the border with the United States, more than 100,000 workers, almost exclusively young women, work in scores of factories that re-export goods to the United States.

In Ciudad Juarez, many work in the large Bermudez Industrial Park, where they process or assemble components for such corporations as GE, Westinghouse, Bendix, American Hospital Supply, RCA, and Sylvania. At the other extreme, in Tijuana, young women sew clothing in fly-by-night sweat shops. In 1978 firms shipped over $700 million in taxable value under 806–807 from Mexico alone. The actual value of the goods was approximately twice as much. From Taiwan came $400 million and from Singapore, Malaysia, and Hong Kong, about $200 million each.

The idea of enterprise zones in advanced industrial countries was first promoted in Great Britain by Professor Peter Hall of Reading University as a means to cut wages so that British workers could somehow compete with their brethren in the colonies. The so-called "free ports . . . to be based on fairly shameless free enterprise," as Professor Hall expressed it, would abate taxes on profits, capital gains, sales, and personal income, allow imports and sales free of duty, eliminate all but the most basic regulations, and cut social services and labor protection to the bone. Strong trade unions would be officially discouraged. As Professor Hall put it, "Wages would find their own level. . . . Small, selected areas of inner cities would be simply thrown open to all kinds of initiative, with minimum control. In other words, we would aim to recreate the Hong Kong of the 1950s and 1960s inside inner Liverpool or inner Glasgow." Such legislation, watered down to meet political realities, has become the cornerstone of the urban program in Mrs. Thatcher's Conservative government.

British enterprise zones are now defined as depressed areas in big cities in which local taxes on industrial and commercial property are to be abolished (municipalities to be reimbursed by the national government), capital gains and corporate income taxes are to be reduced, local zoning waived, and government paper work simplified to aid business and encourage international trade. These provisions are to apply for a decade and are to be renewable. To date, eleven such zones have been formally recognized by the British government, but no new enterprises are operating yet.

In the United States the idea was promoted first by the ultraconservative Heritage Foundation, in Washington, which put out an American version of the British proposal in 1980. Now embodied in at least five federal bills, in proposed legislation in more than twenty states, and under active discussion in city halls everywhere, enterprise zones promise to become the main element in U.S. urban policy. An Illinois bill, for example, although successfully vetoed by Governor Thompson in September 1981, was nearly repassed over his veto. Organized labor and civic groups played a large role in the defeat. The bill provides useful illustrations of the possibilities for local legislation. The original Illinois proposal called for suspending all zoning and buiding codes, eliminating minimum wages, initially abolishing property taxes, prohibiting any state aid not provided in the enterprise act itself, weakening unions (through right-to-work laws), and weakening or eliminating all environmental regulations and health and safety laws.

Besides Reagan's new plan, one key federal bill is the proposal by Congressmen Jack Kemp and Robert Garcia, the 1981 "Urban Jobs and Enterprise Zone Act." The Kemp-Garcia bill would eliminate taxes on capital gains, halve taxes on corporate income, liberalize treatment of business losses, and give the firm a tax credit equal to 5 percent of the wages paid each employee in the zone—and another 5 percent when employees are low income people.

An earlier draft also eliminated social security taxes and drastically cut regulations. Because of opposition from Garcia, the minimum wage reductions and drastic regulation waivers were dropped from the bill. Ironically, technical analysis shows that the remaining provisions are unlikely to attract investment or provide jobs. The current White House version of an enterprise zone emphasizes tax cuts mainly, but President Reagan has also been an enthusiastic advocate of sub-minimum youth wages and freer entry for foreign guest workers.

Except for the special cases of Taiwan, South Korea, and Singapore, not a single poor, capitalist country since World War II has developed in a way that both increased incomes and improved income distribution. As it turns out, even the successful cases, which were continuously stimulated by our Asian military preparations and by wars in Korea and Vietnam, are problematic.

Before moving to evidence about the majority—the places that *didn't* develop—let's consider two of these peculiar "successes," Singapore and Puerto Rico. They are particularly interesting, even though exceptional, because they survive almost entirely as "factories" producing for the global marketplace. They really are precursors of today's enterprise zones.

The international development community considers the city-state of Singapore a model of successful development. It is an almost laboratory-controlled case illustrating the effect of investment by global corporations in branch plants that manufacture products for re-export to world markets. It also suggests how this process influences domestic political life.

As in much of the Third World, political life in Singapore is controlled by a corporatist state, whose eagerness to help depress wages and control labor strife in order to attract multinational investment has undermined the domestic business class and stunted political opposition. The economic relationship between domestic workers and their foreign employers virtually dominates the political context in Singapore. The constant threat that these employers will move their operations elsewhere determines to a great extent how, when, and why local business and the government act.

In the 1960s, the ruling People's Action Party embarked upon a program to attract foreign industrial investment. They began by cutting corporate taxes for investors from 40 percent to 4 percent. This did attract new investment, but because it was highly capital intensive, unemployment continued to grow, worsened by the loss of domestic markets when Singapore became independent from Malaysia in 1965 and British military bases were closed after 1966.

Then, in 1968, tough new labor legislation effectively eliminated collective bargaining by reducing benefits to laid-off workers, cutting bonuses and pay for overtime work, reducing maternity leaves, holiday leaves, and fringe benefits, and authorizing full management control over promotion, transfer, and dismissal. This left for negotiation only wages, on which disputes go to the Ministry of Labor and a special labor court. Since the government also acted drastically to weaken unions, decisions have consistently favored management. Strikes and lockouts have been virtually eliminated. In 1955 strikes cost industry nearly a million lost person-days, and in 1963 nearly 400,000 lost person-days; since 1970 the losses have dropped to no more than a few thousand per year, an average of only five or ten workers out on strike each day in a country of 2 million.

In this "favorable investment climate," as it is called in the business press, manufacturing invesment in labor-intensive industries shot up. From 1963 to 1974 industrial employment increased 560 percent, by 170,000 workers, the biggest increases being in textiles and electronics, the bulk of the new employees being young, unskilled women. Immigrant workers (one-eighth of the labor force by 1973) and children, whose legal work age was reduced to twelve, were needed to fill labor shortages.

Although Singapore is something of a success story compared to the even worse conditions of much of the Third World, wages remain shockingly depressed. Prevailing wage for all production work in 1974, for example, was $16.72 for a forty-four-hour week—under $900 a year. Worker dissatisfaction is now expressed in high absenteeism, high quit rates, and of course pressure to raise wages, all of which makes Singapore somewhat less desirable for foreign investors.

Puerto Rico's foreign investment history, although it began fifteen or twenty years earlier, is remarkably similar. After some experimentation with planning and nationalization, the Puerto Rican leadership decided in the late 1940s to open the island to foreign corporations for branch plant manufacturing.

Under "Operation Bootstrap," special provisions of U.S. law abolished corporate income taxes in Puerto Rico, provided subsidized feasibility studies and infrastructure investment, and guaranteed to investors the protections of domestic U.S. law and American courts. Initially, this program did succeed in attracting outside investment to produce growth rates that were extraordinarily high, averaging about 35 percent per year in textiles, metal, and machinery, and well over 8 percent in every other sector but agriculture and food. Per capita GNP grew 354 percent in real terms from 1947–1973. This was a heyday for government-assisted free enterprise, with subsidies for feasibility studies, roads, utilities and factory buildings, free labor training, and active recruitment, all close to home and under the full protection of U.S. laws.

The Singapore development may still progress in a fashion, but the Puerto Rican experiment is in real trouble. Even with 40 percent of its popoulation having left for the U.S. mainland, conditions on the island are difficult. First, export growth has virtually ceased. From 1968 to 1974, while Asian producers increased their apparel exports to the U.S. market by 370 percent, Puerto Rican exports stagnated, leading to net factory lay-offs for 23,000 workers. Second, unemployment, always a problem in Puerto Rico, has hovered between 30 percent and 40 percent since 1974. Third, family poverty is severe, and without food stamps, which go to seven of every ten families, there would be widespread hunger and disruption.

Why did Puerto Rico decline? In a sense, the entire development strategy was contradictory. To the extent that it succeeded, thereby raising wages, it reduced the attraction for investors, and failed. There was no mechanism for internal generation of development, no central planning, no government investment, no real development policy aside from *laissez-faire*. Inherent in a mode of development that emphasizes low-skill, high-tech production, and depends on corporations' ability to operate anywhere in the world, is the danger that they can simply relocate whenever wages threaten to rise. In this sort of global economy, in which selling prices are rigid and only low labor-cost operations can survive, it is all too easy for new plants to open, for orders to be shifted from one source of supply to another. Such a dependent development program causes local employment to be whipsawed between local wage increases and foreign low wage competition.

For years, the government in San Juan has been troubled by this dilemma. To attract branch plants, it has kept wages down, but as its own statistics show, this is a losing game. While the average hourly wage in Puerto Rican textile factories was just $2 in 1974, in its competitors—the Philippines, Sri Lanka, Haiti, Malaysia, India, Pakistan, Singapore, and the Dominican Republic—hourly wages in textiles were grouped between 14 and 33 cents. At the same time, pressured by the workforce, which is itself heavily influenced by mainland U.S. wages and prices, the government has allowed wages to rise (although they have not risen above 50 percent of U.S. mainland wages). Once again we see a government stuck between the unyielding demands of global industry and the unfulfilled aspirations of its people.

When Third World countries gear themselves to become low-wage outposts of global industry, stagnation seems to be the logical outcome. Hospitality to branch plants of multinational corporations fails to generate a balanced local economy. Wages stay low, because other Third World countries always are available to pay even lower wages.

Puerto Rico and Singapore, as even partial successes, are very much the exception. Singapore is small. It can expel its foreign labor. It has no impoverished rural hinterland. It may survive on receipts of international banking, commerce, and commodity trade, because it is at an extraordinary international crossroads. And it may capitalize on its educated labor force through centralized planning to introduce more technically advanced manufacturing, with higher wages.

In the rest of the world, things are worse. Just as global competition has snatched textile employment away from Puerto Rico, first to Asia and then back to Haiti, the Dominican Republic, and Central America, so it will displace employment elsewhere too. In general the vast majority of the sixty-odd countries that hope to develop with platform economies cannot succeed, because there are not enough jobs to go around. For to the degree any country threatens or manages to raise its wages, the global corporations will threaten to or actually move elsewhere, where wages are still lower.

Consequently, aside from the exceptional cases, things are dismal indeed. In most countries with free production zones, labor is astonishingly cheap. Hourly wages for unskilled manufacturing workers in branch plants in 1975 were about 15 cents or less in India, the Philippines, Thailand, Mauritius, and Haiti; they were 25 cents or less in Indonesia, Malaysia, Taiwan, Lesotho, Liberia, Swaziland, Colombia, and Honduras. Add it up: 25 cents an hour is $10 a week, hardly more than $500 a year for the best of these cases.

Given levels of productivity that are comparable to plants in the United States, it is difficult for any industrialist to resist foreign location, and fewer and fewer with the capability have resisted each year. Even in nearby Mexico unskilled labor is paid as low as $1 an hour. Giant corporations are closing U.S. plants more rapidly than small firms because the former are more easily able to modify their operations in industrial countries and then organize and finance operations abroad.

This brings us back to the United States, where the problems of plant closing and capital flight lie behind the urban unemployment that stimulates calls for enterprise zones. Let's try now to make sense of the situation.

The prospects for American workers in the new global economy bring to mind a rather disreputable Marxian phrase that was all but laughed out of the vocabulary of mainstream economics during the postwar era—the reserve army of the unemployed. During a brief thirty-year moment of the "American Century," U.S. workers could enjoy the benefits of America's remarkable dominance of the world economy. Granted, even America has always had its secondary labor market where racial minorities, women, and foreign migrants worked at low-paying, unskilled jobs. But there remained a substantial primary labor market as well, where many American workers (the vast majority of them white and male) were protected—whether by trade barriers, technological limits to a truly global factory system, American dominance of manufacturing for export, or, most important of all, the hard-won gains of the American labor movement. Just as all these factors helped to expand the boundaries of the primary labor market, the new international economy and its offspring, urban enterprise zones, are potent weapons for shrinking them. The under-employed people of the Third World constitute an authentic reserve army that can undermine the wages and benefits of workers all over the world.

It is of course very unlikely that wages of American workers can be cut so low, even in enterprise zones, that they could compete effectively with the platform economies of the Third World. If nothing else, the high cost of living in the United States precludes industrial wages of $14 a week.

But even the attempt to impose this competition on American workers will radically reduce their standard of living and their political power, and will transform the role of the state. During the period of American domination of world trade, American workers were able to seize a measure of political power and the state was more or less neutral in labor relations. Measures like the Wagner Act helped labor to organize, while unemployment insurance, minimum wage, and occupational health and safety laws improved labor's economic capacity to bargain.

But the new global economy radically changes the bargaining

power of domestic labor, and the enterprise zone proposal is a device to shift explicitly government's role from neutral party to overt ally of corporate industry. Even without government playing this role, workers have already felt the growing pressure for wage concessions. In November 1981, the Ford Motor Company threatened to close a plant employing 1,300 workers in Sheffield, Alabama, unless the workers agreed to a 50 percent cut in wages and fringe benefits, to bring costs at the plant in line with global competition. In December, the United Auto Workers released its locals to negotiate separately, to reduce wages where they feel it necessary to provide assistance to otherwise unprofitable plants. Perhaps the most astonishing evidence of such a long run plan is Ford's for duplicating production plants in Western Europe. Their plants are designed normally to operate at half-capacity precisely so that managers can confront labor with a stronger hand.

In this climate, financiers and corporate planners are increasingly candid about what they expect from governments. Does a country have the temerity to raise minimum wages or impose regulations? Walter Wriston, Chairman of Citicorp, has a ready reply: "As a last resort, all the multinational company can do in its relation with a sovereign state is to make an appeal to reason. If this fails, capital, both human and material, will leave for countries where it is more welcome." Wriston, it turns out, was not lecturing some obscure Third World country. His words were directed to the British (in 1976).

In pure form, enterprise zones call upon government to create planned depressions, rather than letting the market generate chaotic spontaneous ones. They are quite consistent with other proposals of the Reagan administration, such as more liberal entry for "guest workers," tolerance of high unemployment rates, and reduction of a broad range of social supports, all of which depress wages. In effect, enterprise zones would officially bless the *de facto* dual labor market, since workers in such zones would have fewer protections and rights than other workers.

The danger, however, is that enterprise zones would not stay contained. Once industry became accustomed to lower wages, lower taxes, and limits on workers' rights in enterprise zones, these provisions would tend to spill over elsewhere. Why should GM tolerate a high wage, unionized work force in Detroit when a government-approved domestic Third World is available, say, in St. Louis?

As medicine to rejuvenate American cities, the enterprise zone proposal is entirely self-defeating. Rather than creating new oppor-

tunities for depressed areas, it would mainly depress standards elsewhere in America. It would accelerate the erosion of America's status
as a relative island of affluence. The worst affront, however, is to political democracy. For enterprise zones enshrine not just a dual labor
market, but a dual citizenry. And in time, the result would be a single
pool of low wage workers, with diminished rights as citizens.

Part Five

WHAT IS TO BE DONE

14

After Advocacy:
The Transformation of
Community in England

ROBERT KRAUSHAAR

Since the end of World War II, there have been important structural changes occurring in most advanced industrial countries. The trends in postwar capitalist development include the concentration and internationalization of capital, structural change and rationalization of production, and concomitantly, an extensive increase in state intervention in the economy and related areas of society. The negative effects of these changes—regional imbalances, structural unemployment, fiscal crises—are features common to most of the Western countries.

With one of the weaker economies among Western industrialized countries, and with the oldest infrastructure, England has suffered perhaps the most adverse effects. In addition, major aspects of this restructuring (such as plant closings, urban fiscal problems, and the economic decline of older industrial regions) have surfaced in England before other industrial countries, including the United States. For these reasons, the interrelationships of all these problems to the underlying structural changes occurring are clearer and offer a good perspective on the American conceptualizations.

At this moment new types of organizations are trying to address these issues in the United States. Many are community-based, focusing on the local and regional impacts of global problems. What links these efforts together is a concern not simply with incremental day-to-day issues, but with the distribution of power, both political and economic, in America (see Boyte, 1980; Carnoy and Shearer, 1980).

This essay concerns an earlier transformation that occurred in England and its implications for grass-roots action in the United States. It is divided into three sections. The first presents a general overview of the context within which the English efforts took place. Specifically, it examines the limitations inherent in traditional community action as a form of radical practice and outlines the radical perspectives that eventually evolved within the English context. The second section is a case study of one local project—its theoretical framework for action and its actual strategies. The third section is a brief overview of contemporary American community initiatives and their interrelationships with the English experience.

THE COMMUNITY DEVELOPMENT PROJECT

The Community Development Project was established in Great Britain in 1969. Its purpose was to be: "a neighborhood-based experiment aimed at finding new ways of meeting the needs of people living in areas of high social deprivation, by bringing together the work of all the social services under the leadership of a special project team and also by tapping resources of self-help and mutual help which may exist among the people in the neighborhoods" (Home Office, 1969).

As pointed out by Marris and Rein (1972:13), it was similar to the American Community Action Programs in that its stated strategies were "coordinated planning, community participation, experiment and research." *Coordination* was to come about "through consultation and action among the separate departments of Central and Local Government and voluntary organizations, and the people of the local communities" (Home Office, 1972). *Participation* was seen as a "full and positive opportunity [for the community] to express its needs and views and aspirations effectively and . . . those seeking to cooperate with them should be receptive and sympathetic towards the ideas and even criticisms that can result" (ibid.). The projects were to be run as *experiments* which would "constitute a wise and worthwhile addition to traditional ways of tackling the problems of social welfare" (Home Office, 1971).

For a variety of reasons, not the least being that the program contained the same inherent flaws that hampered the American programs (such as the mistaken assumption that the government bureaucracies would automatically cooperate with one another), this attempt at social engineering quickly broke down at the national level. After barely a year, the local projects were in effect cast adrift. The Home Office contented itself with the day-to-day administration of the program and denied any responsibility for its overall direction.

The local projects, at this point, did not necessarily have any concrete alternative explanations for the decline of the communities they were working within. Nor did they have any cohesive strategies of action to undertake. The entire project became an exploration of alternative explanations and strategies, seeking effective methods of coping with their everyday reality. No one ideological perspective or operational strategy was ever agreed upon by all of the local projects. As one participant remarked, "Diversity becomes the keynote in CDP. Projects are strung out on a continuum, from 'rat-catchers' to social theorists" (Smith, 1974:382).

Some of the local projects used more traditional models of community development such as "Locality Development" or "Social Planning" (Rothman, 1974). But at least half of the local projects became so alienated in what they regarded as an untenable position, caught between the demands of the state and the needs of the community, that they felt the necessity to explore alternative, and for the most part radical, approaches (Kraushaar and Loney, 1980).

The alienated CDP workers found few guideposts to follow in their quest for both theoretical and practical alternatives. Traditional community work had evolved as a method "to help people to adapt their way of life to the changes they accept or have imposed upon them" (Batten, 1957:5). The CDP workers, who considered the problems the result of government policy and economic conditions, could not accept a model based upon a 'blaming the victim' philosophy (Ryan, 1971). Alternative models of change were needed.

One alternative contemporary model was community action, defined in 1970 as a way "to verbalize discontent, articulate grievances, to form a pressure group with which to confront authority in a militant struggle for righting wrongs, gaining power, acquiring new resources and better service or amenities" (Hodge, 1970:70). This form of radical community organizing was more prevalent in the United States than in England, with Saul Alinsky (1946; 1971) its most noted practitioner.

From the perspective of the alienated CDP workers, however, this model was inadequate. Conflict could not be seen as a short-term tactic to achieve specific results. It must, of necessity, be defined in terms of the historical and continuing struggles between particular organizations or classes. Community action, in short, was theoretically deficient in relation to the evolving CDP perspective.

First, it was overtly pluralistic in nature, assuming that the existence of diverse pressure groups would provide an adequate representation of people's real interests. By doing so it helped to perpetuate a myth "which prompts individuals to view society as one based on diffused power, where every person may have a significant impact on the decision-making process" (Mazziotti, 1974:43).

Second, it led to an inherent dependence on issues defined by the state itself and influenced the types of local organizations. As Cockburn (1977:159) concluded: "It takes a shape that is expected, anticipated and even proposed by the state. In a sense (to use an ecological metaphor) the state is the environment that offers a vacant 'niche,' a milieu that will reward and foster a certain kind of behavior, and the fledgling institutions of struggle step in to fill it." When community struggles are local in nature and somewhat isolated from other working-class organizations and activities, this symbiotic relationship with government institutions is difficult to avoid.

Third, it led to an isolation, both functional and geographical, of the problems at hand. Community action tended to divide problems into separate components and not take into account the fact that the problems were actually "aspects of one central problem whose roots are not at all local but are to be found in the total social system which creates inequality and constantly reinforces it" (Coates and Silburn, 1972:10). It stresses the "community" as an entity in itself, something that could be isolated and treated without regard to other "communities" or the overall society. The limitations of this concept were even more obvious in the context of economic decline experienced by the CDP project areas, when any services or amenities fought for and won were usually acquired at the expense of another similar, but less organized, community.

Finally, and most important, the nature of the political situation changed and with it the relevant issues, strategies, and organizational forms. The problem could no longer be seen as the consequence of local maldistribution of resources to be corrected via organizational efforts and consequent political strength on the part of those adversely affected. Instead, a broader conceptual and more political approach was needed to confront the disinvestment of capital and retrenchment of public services occurring in Britain.

In response, the CDP workers evolved a new form of community work to better fit their theoretical perspective and their everyday activities. This strategy can best be defined as pragmatic radicalism (Kraushaar, 1979). It was *radical* in that its aims and strategies were geared toward resisting what were seen as the inevitable hardships imposed in the working class by a capitalist economic and political system. One important distinction from past efforts at the community level was an insistence on an underlying structural analysis within which to base actions. As one writer commented, "A fair criticism of radical community action is that, until recently, the theoretical framework within which that action took place was naive, evangelistic and highly personalized" (Stevens, 1978:93).

It was *pragmatic* within that overall framework because of the contradictory nature of practice. For example, it was not usually possible to choose an issue to organize around, even though broad categories of issues could be defined. Yet each issue that did arise needed to be put in the proper perspective so that the "most appropriate and feasible points of intervention" could be identified. In addition, certain levels or types of activities were indicated which were difficult to attain. In these cases there was a need to develop intermediate or even marginal strategies, the advantage of the overall framework being their recognition as such. As one CDP report put it, there was the necessity of "seeing the links between what appears to be the obvious mundane day-to-day activities and the strategic objectives" (National CDP, 1974).

Pragmatic radicalism started with a basic assumption that the uneven nature of capitalist development had pernicious effects on both individuals and communities. Structural changes occurring within England only served to exacerbate these effects. This was central to the CDPs because it meant that the fortunes of each community were intimately related to the state of local industry, which in turn is dependent on processes at work in the wider society. As the economic base of each area changed over time, so the basis of the local community was transformed. Therefore, an essential aspect was that the overall process could only be understood in terms of the interrelationship between industry and community. To look at the community in isolation from its industrial base was to artificially divide elements of the same process (see National CDP, 1977a).

In effect this required a transformation of the concept of community. Previous definitions only confuse both local dependencies on wider issues and the necessity of linking production and consumption. The Community Development Project was one of the first community organizations in England to go beyond traditional concepts of advocacy and attempt to evolve an effective strategy that would allow community groups, unions, and to a certain extent, local governments, to work together on common concerns.

THE TRADE UNIONS

Central to the evolving economic focus of the CDPs were the trade unions. Their organization and strength was a key component in the achievement of significant gains in controlling the flow of capital and jobs. Yet historically, especially after World War II, the British trade union movement had been almost totally economistic—focusing on wage demands and productivity deals to the exclusion of all else. This phenomenon, which Lenin called "trade-union consciousness," was not uniquely British. Almost without exception, the union movement in the advanced industrial societies has been predominantly concerned with "the immediate and limited demands associated with wages, hours and contracts" (Miliband, 1977:133).

As with most other existing institutions, the trade unions have evolved within the present structure of society and, as such, can only function within its logic. Trade unions perpetuate by their very existence the notion of labor as a commodity to be bought and sold. They seek contractual relationships with businesses, advancing incremental demands within a shared consensus of industrial relations. In addition, as they grow and age, they become more bureaucratic and conservative. New objective conditions, even innovative ideas, frequently threaten the status quo and thus are resisted.

In the British context, the official union leadership was closely linked with the National Labour party leadership. Several commentators would argue that the union structure had been coopted, functioning more as a "junior partner of capitalist enterprise" than as a working-class organization (Miliband, 1973; Coates, 1975; Westergaard and Resler, 1975). Therefore, any actions which would endanger that relationship were to be resisted.

As a result of all these constraints, the formal union structure found it extremely difficult to deal with unusual situations and always preferred economistic responses. The issue of plant closures, for example, was defined in terms of possible redundancy payments. The decline of the British economy, however, presented unique problems. The velocity of change, its spatial impact, and the changes taking place at the point of production were issues beyond the scope of the traditional union mandate, a mandate centered around input and influence at the national political level.

The national government, given its own constraints, could only react to, rather than direct, the changes. It simply was not able to deal effectively with plant closures and large redundancies. It was in the process of rationalizing its own operations, closing coal pits and steel mills and reducing government employment and services. Consequently, the brunt of the decline of industrial Britain fell on the individual worker, who rapidly became disillusioned with the national union leadership. Whatever resistance there was came from shop floor organizations such shop stewards and combine committees.

The CDP workers saw this occurring within the same context as the decline of the working-class communities. Most of the projects were located in areas of industrial decline, of which a few were communities almost entirely dependent on large declining industries. Therefore, work at the industrial level, in particular in support of factory-level union organizations, was a logical extension of the CDP's economic definitions of community decline.

NEWCASTLE COMMUNITY DEVELOPMENT PROJECT

The Newcastle CDP is a good example of the degree to which the work of the CDPs evolved over time. As one of the last local projects to be operationalized, the sophistication of its efforts by the time it closed in 1978 show the end result of an extensive attempt by the radical CDPs to transform previous conceptions of community.

Benwell, the Newcastle project area, was built primarily for workers employed by one of the largest engineering companies in Britain. By the 1890s the area represented the most advanced section of British industry, with heavy engineering and shipbuilding at the forefront of technological advances. At its peak, during World War I, one Vickers armaments factory alone employed over twenty thousand workers.

The 1920s saw the beginning of industrial stagnation with several dramatic plant closures. The decline has continued, except for a brief reprieve during World War II, up until the present day. Benwell is still dependent upon these declining industries, however, with Vickers still employing 50 percent of the local workforce and occupying a large area of the waterfront. The employment levels at Vickers have dropped to under five thousand workers, and any profits are invested elsewhere, leaving only marginal adjustments made locally to the aging infrastructure.

Benwell was chosen as a CDP project area because of this legacy. Most new employers provide only low-paying, often exploitative jobs. The housing stock, much of it built for factory workers in the late nineteenth century, had deteriorated because of age and a lack of investment. The local government had adopted a policy of locating new industry in suburban new towns and redeveloping the inner areas for new housing. This had accelerated the decline of the entire industrial West End of Newcastle, which included Benwell.

In originating industrial work, the Newcastle CDP was helped in the high percentage of overlap between the home and work population of Benwell and the existence of a few powerful unions which represented a majority of the Vickers workers. With a long history of shop floor independence, these local unions were actively fighting the decline of local industry, albeit from a weak bargaining position and a concentration on the issue of redundancy.

As it evolved, the strategy of the CDPs with regard to work within local unions was to get them to recognize:

1. The complex ways in which their lives are determined not just by pay and conditions at the workplace but by the wider economic and political structure, and particularly by the operations of the central and local state;
2. A common interest with sections of the working-class outside the workplace—the retired, the unemployed, the redundant and the claimant;
3. The possibility of influencing what happens in the city outside the workplace, more actively and effectively than through existing forms of representation on the City Council. (Benington, 1974:2.)

Finally, the CDP attempted to help local shop-level committees reorganize in order to effectively address new adverse conditions, including redundancies and closures.

Concerning this last point, the Newcastle CDP's most extensive connections were with the workers at Vickers. For several years it acted as the secretariat for the working group of shop steward conveyors for all six Vickers plants in the area. It was active in research, report writing, and the dissemination of information during strikes. When one plant was threatened with closure, the CDP set up a campaign committee, acted as secretariat and researchers, and coordinated the efforts of all six plants. "We also developed that work on the national level. The Vickers shop stewards set up a national combine committee and we have been involved in helping them on several matters, including publicity and printing flyers. I even helped them organize a week-long course at a college on the issue from a national perspective" (private interview).

Similar, albeit less extensive work, was done with other local shop stewards' committees. One example was an attempt to take over a recently closed factory (Tress Shop Stewards, 1978). All of this was considered officially part of Newcastle CDP's local work. Most of the shop stewards' meetings, for example, took place in the CDP offices.

The Newcastle CDP also worked through shop stewards' committees to involve the unions in local issues which directly affected union members. When the site of a closed Vickers plant was to be redeveloped, the original plan was for light industry and warehousing. The Vickers shop stewards, concerned that only a few poorly paid unskilled jobs would result, mounted a campaign to get the city planning committee to require an industrial development scheme. The CDP workers provided the organization and background research, including an estimation, based on comparable experience elsewhere, that an adequate industrial plan could create about four hundred skilled union jobs, as opposed to the originally expected fifty to one hundred low-paid ones.

The Newcastle CDP also felt it important to work with the local trades council. These local union organizations were in existence before the Labour party and the National Trades Union Congress and were central actors in working-class attempts to organize both politically and economically. Few of the remaining trades councils engaged in any vital activities, their power having been eroded by the Labour party and the TUC activities at the national level ("Trades Councils," 1974). Because it was the only organization which involved all the local unions in regional concerns, the Newcastle CDP saw itself as an important link between workplace and community issues.

While the Newcastle Trades Council was active before the intervention of the CDP workers, the scale and scope of that activity changed significantly. By providing support services to the trades council, the CDP helped it to publish a newspaper, organize resistance to public expenditure cuts, and to play a leading role concerning local plant closures. Even more significant from the CDP perspective, the trades council promoted activities that included the retired and the unemployed and began to work on issues that concerned unions and communities. Public expenditure cutbacks affected both those who provided and those who received the services. In addition, since several of the CDP workers were official delegates to the trades council from their respective unions and one CDP worker was for several years the secretary to the council, this allowed the CDP to extend the scope and legitimacy of its own work.

Perhaps the most difficult goal was to overcome "trade-union consciousness" and generate an understanding of events beyond the workplace. One major strategy in this regard was the emphasis all the CDPs placed on "upward research." This entailed the collection of discrete information about specific companies and their activities[1] (Canning Town CDP, 1977). If not only the activities of the major local companies but also their impact were detailed, a better understanding of the reasons for local economic decline would evolve. This information was also crucial in challenging the threats of redundancies, closures, and transfers (for the U.S. equivalent, see Bluestone and Harrison, 1982).

For this reason, the Newcastle CDP established the North East Trade Union Studies Information Unit, which continues even though the CDP has officially ended. The unit provides a resource center with three full-time workers and a workers' library which collects all the information that is of general interest to workers in the area. The staff also collects information on changes in the industrial structure of the region, employment trends, redundancies, and wage movements in an effort to monitor employment and industrial situations.

In addition, the unit undertakes research or consults for various local unions, runs periodic conferences on key issues, and organizes short courses and workshops. Its reports have included one on workers' occupations in the Northeast and another on direct labor as the answer to the chaos in the building industry (North East Trade Union Studies Information Unit, 1977).

The Newcastle CDP, through its own research capacity, also compiled information and conducted studies on particular sectors of work which directly affected Benwell. Much of this helped the smaller unions, which had little research capacity of their own. Other parts, such as work on the building industry, were given to tenant associations and the relevant trade unions to promote cooperation on common concerns. The CDP's final effort at upward research was a series of reports which concentrated on such topics as the history of capitalist development in the region, warehousing and distribution in West Newcastle and its implications for workers, commercial development in Benwell, and youth unemployment (see Benwell Community Project, 1978a; 1978b; 1978c; 1978d; 1979a; 1979b; 1980; 1981).

THE AMERICAN CONTEXT

The Community Development Project originated as a typical action-research poverty program. A multitude of such programs have been implemented in several industrialized countries (see National CDP, 1977; Miller and Kraushaar, 1979). What was unique about the CDP was its rejection of previous models of intervention and subsequent evolution of pragmatic radicalism in an effort to work effectively within a changing economic environment. No other community program, in either the United States or England, approached the sophistication of the CDP during the same period.

Since that time, however, other community projects have focused on these same concerns. Both theorists and activists in the United States, for example, have rallied to the banner of "economic democracy" (see Carnoy and Shearer, 1980; Hayden, 1980). The main concern has become the transfer of economic decision making from the few to the many. "For us, the two essential elements of any strategy of fundamental reform in the United States today are: (1) the shift of investment control from corporate domination to the public; and (2) the reconstruction of economic decision-making through democratic, worker- and worker/consumer-controlled production" (Carnoy and Shearer, 1980:4).

In the process, a new consciousness has evolved. Flacks (1974: 229–30) describes it as a "post-industrial consciousness . . . rooted in a definite class." This evolution was partly a result of a general disillusionment with the strategies of organizing throughout the 1960s, but primarily due to economic conditions. Economic austerity generated by the concentration of wealth and power in the multinational corporations is in contrast to the surplus conditions of the 1950s and 1960s. Because the economic context has changed, the organizational strategies of the 1960s are no longer adequate. Emerging instead is a struggle aimed at challenging the structure of power and decision making and the domination of "corporate, militarist or conservative interests" (ibid.:230–31).

Another major focus has been in coalition building. At the community and local levels, greater efforts to unite with regional and national organizing efforts have begun to surface. This expansion also has meant that voluntary structures and institutions of everyday life, such as religious groups, schools, and clubs, are becoming directly involved. This is significant, for these community groupings have previously been the bulwark of the conservatives. Alliances have been formed between the poor, minorities, and the working class over certain issues.

One example of this change is the Ohio Public Interest Campaign (OPIC). It is a statewide coalition of union, church, minority, and community organizations formed in 1975 to "attack the roots of the problems, the structure and behavior of the giant corporations, national and global" (Boyte, 1980:103). At the moment OPIC is lobbying for a state law which would require large corporations to give advance notice of closures, grant redundancy pay for the retraining and resettlement of workers, and reimburse the affected communities for the resultant dislocation.

Another organization is Massachusetts Fair Share, which has been able to forge an alliance between blacks and working-class whites on issues that transcend race. It is a statewide organization, and each local chapter sends representatives to a monthly assembly that plans overall strategy and policy. Its strength has been an ability to focus on local issues such as street repairs and housing rehabilitation while lobbying successfully for state actions to help alleviate these local problems. For example, through protest and organizing efforts, it was able to pressure insurance companies to pay $9 million in back taxes to the city of Boston. At the same time, it lobbied the legislature in order to have insurance reform laws enacted. Other victories have included a state law establishing differential property tax rates for residential and commercial property and local campaigns against banks that discriminate in their lending practices (ibid.: 97–102).

While these initiatives are new in several ways, they are also solidly based within the native brand of radicalism—populism—which has a legacy of resisting big business as well as big government. A major goal of these new community organizations is to shift the present U.S. focus on the evils of too much government over to the pernicious efforts of corporations. They have also turned inward in an attempt to reinforce ties of culture, trust, and community. "Community stands at the heart of the current activists' vision of the future no less than of their plans for the present. They look to community to nurture the ethos and institutions that will serve as alternatives to those of corporate capitalism" (Lustig, 1981:103). While an older generation of radicals sought to dismantle local, voluntary, and traditional structures, the new model of practice sees in these very institutions and customs the "capacity and the inspiration for insurgency" (Boyte, 1980:179).

CONCLUSIONS

The emerging efforts at a new kind of community action in the United States, along with the continuing initiatives in England, are crucial in the present zero-sum context, where structural changes and capital shifts can easily lead to conflicts over shrinking economic resources. With little tradition of coordination or even communication, however, the economic conditions and a focus on the relevant issues are frequently insufficient. The CDP strategy was to act as a catalyst in this regard. As one CDP worker explained: "We might be considered a communications linkpoint between various elements of the wider community that might not necessarily work together. Our individual work is not anything that the tenant groups or unions wouldn't do themselves at times, but since we have credibility with both—and the relevant information—it makes it easier to get them to work together" (private interview).

Ultimately, the Community Development Project wanted alternative workers' organizations which would be uniquely qualified to tackle the problems of uneven economic development. Some of the new trade union initiatives, such as combine committees, revitalized trade councils, and local resource and intelligence units, were initial steps in that direction. In a practical context, however, the best the CDPs could do was to juggle the old and the new.

Nevertheless, the Community Development Project can be seen as a first step in the transformation of community action to fit a changing political and economic context in both the United States and England. The necessity of that transformation is no longer the issue; rather, it is the search for ways to achieve it that will be a major concern in the 1980s.

NOTE

1. "Downward research," by contrast, entailed the gathering of mass statistics about the people and workers in CDP areas and was seen as an instrument of social control by the radical CDPs.

REFERENCES

Alinsky, Saul. *Reveille for Radicals.* Chicago: University of Chicago Press, 1946.

————. *Rules for Radicals: A Pragmatic Primer for Realistic Radicals.* New York: Vintage, 1971.

Batten, T. R. *Communities and Their Development.* London: Oxford University Press, 1957.

Benington, John. "Strategy in CDP." Paper presented to CDP Conference, York, England, September 24, 1974.

Benwell Community Project. *Storing Up Trouble: Warehousing and Distribution in Newcastle.* Final Report No. 1. Newcastle: Benwell Community Development Project, 1978a.

————. *Permanent Unemployment.* Final Report No. 2. Newcastle: Benwell CDP, 1978b.

————. *Private Housing and the Working Class.* Final Report No. 3. Newcastle: Benwell CDP, 1978c.

————. *The Making of a Ruling Class: Two Centuries of Capital Development on Tyneside.* Final Report No. 6. Newcastle: Benwell CDP, 1979a.

————. *From Blacksmiths to White Elephants: Benwell's Changing Shops.* Final Report No. 7. Newcastle: Benwell CDP, 1979b.

————. *Adamsez: The Story of a Factory Closure.* Final Report No. 8. Newcastle: Benwell CDP, 1980.

————. *West Newcastle in Growth and Decline.* Final Report No. 11. Newcastle: Benwell CDP, 1981.

Bluestone, Barry, and Harrison, Bennett. *The Deindustrialization of America.* New York: Basic Books, 1982.

Boyte, Harry. *The Backyard Revolution.* Philadelphia: Temple University Press, 1980.

Canning Town CDP. *Canning Town to North Woolwich: The Aims of Industry.* London. Revised ed. Canning Town CDP, 1977.

Carnoy, Martin, and Shearer, Derek. *Economic Democracy: The Challenge of the 1980's.* White Plains, N.Y.: Sharpe, 1980.

Coates, David. *The Labour Party and the Struggle for Socialism.* London: Cambridge University Press, 1975.

Coates, Ken, and Silburn, Richard. "The Scope and Limits of Community Action." *Community Action* (February 1972).

Cockburn, Cynthia. *The Local State: Management of Cities and People.* London: Pluto, 1977.

Coventry Workshop. *Progress Report 1976–1977.* Coventry, England, January 1978.

Flacks, Richard. "The New Working Class and Strategies for Social Change." In *Strategies of Community Organization,* edited by Fred M. Cox, et al. Chicago: Peacock, 1974.

Great Britain, Home Office. "A Major Experiment in Improving the Social Services for Those Most in Need." Press Release, July 16, 1969.

————. *CDP: Objectives and Strategies.* Unpublished paper, 1971.

————. *CDP: A General Outline.* CYN/72 13/10/3. Unpublished paper, 1972.

Hayden, Tom. *The American Future: New Visions Beyond Old Frontiers.* Boston: South End Press, 1980.

Hodge, Peter. "The Future of Community Development." In *The Future of* the Social Services, edited by William A. Robson and Bernard Crick. Harmondsworth: Penguin, 1970.

Joint Docklands Action Group Resource Center. Docklands—The Fight for the Future. Unpublished paper draft, September 1977.

Krauschaar, Robert. "Pragmatic Radicalism." International Journal of Urban and Regional Research (1979): 61–80.

——, and Loney, Martin. "Requiem for Planned Innovation: The Case of the Community Development Projects." In The Year Book of Social Policy in Britain, 1978, edited by Muriel Brown and Sally Baldwin. London: Routledge & Kegan Paul, 1980.

Lustig, Jeff. "Community and Social Class," Democracy (1981): 96–111.

Marris, Peter. "Images of Progress 2: America." New Society 39 (1977): 9–10.

——, and Rein, Martin. Dilemmas of Social Reform: Poverty and Community Action in the United States. Second edition. Harmondsworth: Penguin, 1972.

Mazziotti, Donald F. "The Underlying Assumptions of Advocacy Planning: Pluralism and Reform." Journal of the American Planning Association (January 1974).

Miliband, Ralph. The State in Capitalist Society: The Analysis of the Western System of Power. London: Quartet, 1973.

——. Marxism and Politics. London: Oxford University Press, 1977.

Miller, Tom, and Kraushaar, Robert. "The Emergence of Participatory Policies for Community Development: Anglo-American Experiences and Their Influence on Sweden." Acta Sociologica, 22 (1979): 111–33.

National CDP. "Report of Action Strategy Committee to the Industry and Employment Collective." Unpublished paper, 1974.

——. The Costs of Industrial Change. London: Home Office, 1977.

North East Trade Union Studies Information Unit. A Guide to the Unit. Newcastle: Benwell CDP, 1977.

North Tyneside CDP. North Shields: Living with Industrial Change. Final Report, volume 2. London: Home Office, 1978.

O'Malley, Jan. The Politics of Community Action: A Decade of Struggle in Nottinghill. London: Spokesman, 1977.

Rothman, Jack. "Three Models of Community Organization Practice." In Strategies of Community Organization, edited by Fred M. Cox et al. Chicago: Peacock, 1974.

Ryan, William. Blaming the Victim. New York: Vintage, 1971.

Smith, George, "Community Development: Rat-Catchers or Theorists?" New Society (1974): 380–82.

Stevens, Bob. "A Fourth Model of Community Work?" Community Development Journal (1978).

"Trades Councils: Can They Link the Struggles at Work and at Home?" Community Action 16 (1974): 12–16.

Tress Shop Stewards. The Closure of Tress: A Fairey Story. Newcastle: Shop Stewards of Tress Engineering, 1978.

Westergaard, John, and Resler, Henrietta. Class in a Capitalist Society: A Study of Contemporary Britain. Harmondsworth: Penguin, 1976.

15

The Incidence and Regulation of Plant Closings

BENNETT HARRISON and BARRY BLUESTONE

As the American economy enters the 1980s, a great deal of public attention has been drawn to the phenomenon of plant shutdowns. Even before the advent of the most recent recession, newspapers were reporting major closings and cutbacks in a wide range of industries, including (but by no means restricted to) automobiles, steel, and rubber.[1] The conventional explanations for these alleged business failures range from straightforward competitive disadvantages, both domestically and internationally, to excessive government regulation, for example, with respect to health and safety or environmental protection.

Many U.S. business closings are unquestionably the result of an inability to successfully compete with other enterprises. Yet, building upon the research of a number of other investigators, we have found this explanation to be at best insufficient and often incorrect.[2] The inference that a closing always represents a business failure may be completely misleading in a world of large, multiplant, multilocational corporations, operating under modern management methods. The implications for measuring and regulating capital mobility in such a world are profound.

As one might imagine, the large and apparently growing number of corporate shutdowns and relocations in the United States has generated the beginning of organized resistance. This is due especially to

Reprinted from F. S. Redburn and Terry F. Buss, eds., *Public Policies for Distressed Communities* (Lexington, Mass.: Lexington Books, 1982).

American trade unionists who have learned how other western countries use public authority to regulate private capital mobility, or at least to shelter workers from precipitous closings and cutbacks. This resistance is reflected in the legislative drives in nineteen states and in the U.S. Congress for so-called plant closing laws.

Our objective in this chapter is to analyze the new legislation, together with other complementary approaches to the orderly regulation of private capital disinvestment, especially as it occurs in the form of large-scale plant or store shutdowns. First, however, it will be helpful to put the magnitude of the problem in perspective. We therefore begin by reviewing recent data on the incidence and employment impact of shutdowns during the 1970s, in particular industries, by region, and by form of ownership.

A TYPOLOGY FOR COMPREHENDING HOW CAPITAL MOVES

A shutdown is but one, albeit the most extreme, form of the reallocation or movement of capital. It is of course possible for capital to literally move—that is, to be physically shifted by its owners—by closing down operations at one location, selling off the old plant, loading the equipment onto a van, a widebelly jet, or a railroad car, and transporting it to a new site, where a new building is constructed and operations are resumed.[3] This kind of dramatic move gets newspaper and TV headlines, but it is not very common.

Using data from the Dun and Bradstreet Co., a private business credit rating service, David Birch of MIT concluded that, between 1969 and 1976, only about 2 percent of all private sector annual employment change in the United States was the result of such overt physical relocation. During the 1969–1970 recession, the rate was even lower: perhaps 1.5 percent per year, a statistic which has been widely quoted both by academic researchers[4] and by spokespersons for big business, seeking to prove that the growing attempts to restrict capital flight and to make business more accountable to the public "are a solution to a nonexistent problem."[5]

Such explicit physical relocations are undoubtedly infrequent. But admitting this in no way trivializes the problem, for outright plant relocation per se represents only the tip of an iceberg in studying the process of capital shift. There are a number of ways that owners may and do move their capital from one place to another.

1. *Redirect profits.* The multibranch corporation may not, in the short-run, physically remove any of the older plant's capital stock, but will instead reallocate profits earned from that plant's operations to its new facilities, for example, for new product development. Such milking of a profitable plant is especially common among conglomerates, whose managers describe some of their acquisitions as *cash cows.* This most subtle and virtually invisible form of disinvestment is disinvestment nevertheless. The loss of control over its own retained earnings greatly increases the chances that an establishment will run into trouble in the future.[6]

2. *Redirect profits and depreciation (overall cash flow).* Both large and small companies may run down their older facilities (for example, by not replacing worn-out machinery), and use the savings in the form of depreciation allowances to reinvest in other branches of their own firms, in other businesses, or perhaps in financial instruments.

3. *Remove physical capital.* Multiplant, multistore, and multioffice corporations may gradually shift some machinery, inventories, materials, and so on from their older to their new facilities located in some other city, state, or country. The old facility remains in operation, at least for the time being. If actual physical capital has been removed, their operations are now subject to a lower level of productive capacity. On the other hand, especially where the labor process is characterized by benchwork assembly, and materials (for example, clothing pieces or electronic components such as silicon chips) are sent to new plants for assembly, the old facility may actually be said to be undergoing a planned reduction in its rate of capacity utilization. The same thing occurs when management cuts back operations domestically and subcontracts various production activities (for example, assembly, or manufacture of particular components formerly made in-house) to other companies.

4. *Shutdown or bankruptcy.* Companies may go the last step, and completely close the older facility. Land and/or buildings may be put on the market, and the machinery sold for scrap to other branches or to other firms. If the owner formally declares bankruptcy, chapter XI of the bankruptcy laws provides a procedure which enables even small businessmen to retain a surplus from their creditors which may then be reinvested in new

economic activity or used as a kind of pension. The latter practice is common among small entrepreneurs who want to retire
but have no heirs to whom to leave their business or can find
no one else who wants to run it.

5. *Actual physical relocation of the facility to a new site.*

In all five cases (which should properly be understood as aspects
of a continuum describing capital shift), some form of capital is real-
located from one plant, office, store, warehouse, or hospital to another.
Sometimes the transfer takes place among the branches of a single
firm and sometimes it occurs across firms, possibly mediated by a
bank, insurance company, or local public development authority. In
other cases, the transfer takes the form of finance capital (profits or
savings reinvested elsewhere). In only relatively few cases does it consist of actually transferring a large volume of capital goods themselves—machinery, equipment, materials, or parts of buildings—within
or among firms, over space.

Regardless of the particular form of capital involved, in nearly all
cases, the old and new facilities coexist for at least some period of
time. This is illustrated in the upper panel of figure 15.1. Often, the
older facilities are eventually closed down completely, particularly
after the newer ones become fully operational. But the timing can vary
enormously. Some corporations like General Electric have operated
parallel plants for thirty years or more, while conglomerates like Genesco, Sheller-Glove, and Lykes have milked a number of their acquired subsidiaries dry in a decade or less. Alternatively, the old plant
may never be shut down entirely.

In special cases, the old closure and the new opening occur more
or less simultaneously, or at least in rapid sequence, as shown in the
lower panel of figure 15.1. This kind of instant migration of a plant is
clearly only a special case of the more general type of capital shift.
Not surprisingly, because money, time, and effort are necessary to shift
capital goods across space, relatively few shifts are of this rather extreme kind.[7] It is these shifts which account for the 1.5 to 2.0 percent
employment change noted by Birch and others.

Moreover, since operating a multibranch firm is invariably more
costly and difficult than running a single branch enterprise, small businesses with fewer capital resources are least likely to exhibit the parallel plant pattern. Indeed, they are most likely to make simultaneous or
rapidly sequential moves when they do actually relocate their own

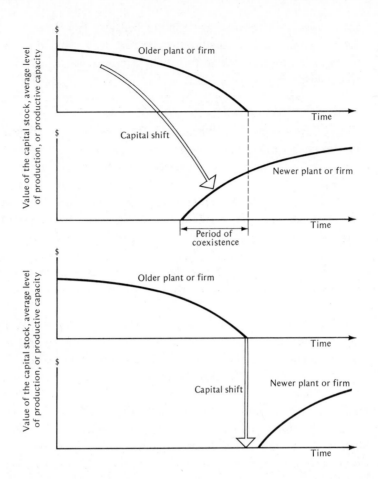

FIGURE 15.1. Possible Types of Capital Shift Between Business Establishments or Plants, over Time.

facilities. All of the researchers who have studied the Dun and Bradstreet data agree that the great majority of what can be called simultaneous movers are, in fact, single plant firms, with an average (according to Jusenius, Ledebur, and Birch) of less than twenty employees.[8] This class of runaways has attracted considerable attention and created serious problems for workers in the textile, apparel, shoe, and electronics industries. But as we will see in the next section, when the other forms of capital investment and reinvestment are accounted for, large employers become an increasingly visible part of the process.

THE INCIDENCE AND IMPACT OF ESTABLISHMENT SHUTDOWNS IN THE 1970S

Few people have the necessary time, access, or money to pierce the veil of privacy which firms have put around their investment transactions.[9] In this context, the federal government's unwillingness to require companies to disclose the details of their investment activity makes direct measurement of the different kinds of capital movements identified earlier virtually impossible.[10]

Still, even without a systematic, comprehensive picture of cutbacks, rundowns, and the subsidy of new plants at the expense of older ones, the study of plant closings alone is justified because by releasing at least some resources that may be reinvested elsewhere, *every shutdown represents a potential capital shift.*

Because of the lack of other sources, it has been necessary for us to resort to a reanalysis of the same private Dun and Bradstreet data discussed earlier. The 1969–1976 Dun's Identifiers file covers some 5.6 million business establishments, about 88 percent of which are single-unit, independently owned and operated, with the rest being the branches, subsidiaries, and headquarters of corporations. Dun and Bradstreet compiles these data as a by-product of its credit rating and market research activities, and sells them to business groups and researchers. They are expensive, hard to use, and sometimes contain inaccurate information (including, but by no means limited to the undercounting of migrations). Nevertheless, they are by far the best—certainly the most comprehensive—data available on the subject.[11]

We, like others, have relied on the help of David Birch, who has by now made great headway in mining this valuable source. He has also prepared an extract of the Dun and Bradstreet data for us for New England, in connection with our own ongoing research on regional economic development. This extract provides greater detail than Birch himself has made available in his own publications. What follows draws upon both Birch's published work and our own analysis of this Dun and Bradstreet extract.[12]

Table 15.1 displays the aggregate employment effects of establishment startups, shutdowns, and relocations through the mid-1970s for each of the nine census regions. By our estimate, about 22 million jobs were eliminated or relocated in the United States, which comes to an average of 3.2 million jobs per year. Establishments in the northeast destroyed about 118 jobs through closures for every 100 new jobs created through openings, while establishments in the south elimi-

Table 15.1. Jobs Created and Destroyed in U.S. Private Business Establishments, 1969–1976

Region	Number of jobs in 1969 (in thousands)	Jobs created		Jobs destroyed	
		Openings and immigrations	Expansions	Closures and outmigrations	Contractions
U.S. as a whole	57936.1	25281.3	19056.1	22302.3	13183.2
Snowbelt	32701.2	11321.5	9470.4	11351.7	7212.1
Northeast	15824.6	4940.4	4347.5	5881.5	3589.0
New England	3905.3	1251.2	1131.0	1437.2	952.1
Mid-Atlantic	11919.3	3689.2	3216.5	4444.3	2636.9
Midwest	16876.6	6381.1	5123.0	5470.2	3623.2
East North Central	12563.6	4670.6	3581.8	3962.6	2651.7
West North Central	4313.0	1710.6	1541.2	1507.6	971.5
Sunbelt	25234.9	13959.8	9585.7	10950.5	5971.0
South	16044.5	8934.2	5964.6	6824.3	3803.3
South Atlantic	8204.1	4651.2	2913.0	3547.9	2014.2
East South Central	3065.2	1518.2	1089.9	1211.0	631.9
West South Central	4775.2	2764.8	1961.7	2065.4	1157.2
West	9190.4	5025.6	3621.1	4126.2	2167.8
Mountain	1941.9	1226.1	953.6	977.9	481.0
Pacific	7248.5	3799.6	2667.6	3148.3	1686.8

nated an average of only 76 jobs through business closings for every 100 created. The rate of shutdown appears lower than expected in the midwest, but remember that these data do not cover the years after 1976. The great wave of auto, steel, and tire closures occurred during the closing years of the decade.

Not surprisingly, there is particular interest in the shutdown behavior of larger establishments. We should expect that the rate of turnover of capital, as exemplified in this research by startups and closings, is greatest for small business. This hypothesis is confirmed by the figures in table 15.2. In all but one row of the table, for trade and services as well as for manufacturing, given that the establishment started prior to the end of 1969, the odds of shutting down before the end of 1976 show a very strong tendency to fall, the larger the establishment. The only exception is the wholesale and retail trade sector in the northeast, which suffered a number of major closings (for example, in the department store and food wholesaling industries) during this period. In general, though, the largest establishments were the most likely to have survived the two recessions of this highly unstable period. What is of course most astonishing is the overall rate of the aspect of capital turnover which we are measuring. Even among those establishments in the sample that had more than one hundred employees in the base year (1969), as we look across the four regions in table 15.2, between a sixth and a third of them were out of business by 1976.[13]

Let us now concentrate just on the largest manufacturing plants, those with, in 1969, 100 or more employees. Birch's published tables (not shown here) provide us with the sample sizes of each employment size class. With these, we can use the probabilities of closing from table 15.2 to compute the number of closings of established (pre-1969) plants and stores in the sample in each industry and region. Table 15.3 displays the results. We are not surprised to see that by far the largest number of closings of large established manufacturing plants in the sample occurred in the northeast. Moreover, with only 24 percent of the nation's population in 1970, the northeast suffered 39 percent of the shutdowns of large manufacturing plants.

What *is* surprising is the larger number of closings (of this scale) in the south than in the north central region. Even more dramatically, the rate at which large established manufacturing facilities have closed—that is, the probability of a shutdown by 1976, given being in operation in 1969—was actually higher in the south than in any other part of the country. One answer to this puzzle is that there has been

Table 15.2. Probabilities of Going Out of Business During 1969–1976 for
Businesses Existing in 1969, by Size of Establishment and Region in 1969,
and by Major Industrial Sector

Region in 1969 and industrial sector	Number of 1969 establishments in the sample (000)	Size of establishment in 1969, by reported number of employees				
		1–20	21–50	51–100	101–500	501+
		Probabilities of closing by 1976				
Northeast						
Manufacturing	76	.53	.40	.37	.33	.21
Trade[a]	295	.60	.35	.34	.36	.57
Services	51	.61	.42	.43	.39	.29
Total[b]	514	.59	.37	.36	.33	.26
North Central						
Manufacturing	63	.48	.30	.27	.27	.15
Trade[a]	296	.57	.33	.30	.28	.27
Services	56	.60	.39	.38	.41	.30
Total[b]	519	.56	.32	.28	.27	.17
South						
Manufacturing	49	.53	.36	.36	.34	.28
Trade[a]	335	.59	.33	.30	.23	.23
Services	63	.61	.41	.40	.39	.34
Total[b]	565	.58	.35	.33	.32	.27
West						
Manufacturing	41	.53	.39	.36	.31	.16[c]
Trade[a]	182	.60	.38	.34	.29	.33
Services	35	.62	.41	.40	.42	.36
Total[b]	318	.59	.38	.35	.32	.23

Source: Birch, *The Job Generation Process*, Appendix D.

a Includes wholesale and retail trade.
b Measures all private sector employment recorded by Dun and Bradstreet: manufacturing, trade, and services, plus other industries not recorded here (farming, mining, transportation, utilities, and finance).
c Includes only eighty-six establishments.

a secular acceleration in the propensity of especially multiregional conglomerates to decentralize their operations globally. The south became fully integrated into the modern international capitalist system later than did the north. By the time it did, in the years following World War II, corporate branching, milking, profit target setting, and relocation practices were in far greater use everywhere. The south—precisely because of its latecomer status—was experiencing the effects

Table 15.3. Closings Occurring by December 31, 1976, of Manufacturing Plants in Existence on December 31, 1969, with More Than 100 Employees at That Time, by Region

Region			Manufacturing plants with more than 100 employees in the 1969 sample		
Name	Number of states	Percentage of U.S. population	Number of plants in the sample in 1969	Number in the sample closed by 1976	Probability of closing by 1976, given existence in 1969	Interregional percentage distribution of closings
Northeast	9	24.1	4,576	1,437	.31	38.6
North Central	12	27.8	3,617	904	.25	24.2
South	16	31.0	3,101	1,042	.34	28.0
West	13	17.1	1,155	344	.30	9.2
Total	50	100.0	12,449	3,727	.30	100.0

Source: See table 15.2 (Population statistics are from *1970 Census of Population*).

disproportionately. Thus, for example, it took seventy-five years for the northeast to lose the bulk of its old mill-based industry to the sunbelt (and more recently to foreign countries). Yet already, within a much shorter time span, the sunbelt has undergone extensive restructuring and overseas migration of, for example, textiles, apparel, and electronics assembly. Clearly, we need more research on this intriguing finding.

So far, these results pool the corner grocer, the multinational corporation's branch plant, and the successful family business which has been acquired by a diversified conglomerate. For several reasons, the data should be broken down according to *who owns the business*. Small, independently owned (often family-run) businesses can be expected to have high failure rates. They are generally more vulnerable to the business cycle, have more restricted access to debt finance (and/or must pay more for it), and have no parent or home office to bail them out of trouble. Corporate branch plants presumably have all of these advantages—along with access to the corporation's own internally retained earnings—as, in theory, do the subsidiaries of conglomerates. To the extent that the mode of operation of the modern conglomerate is organized around the acquisition of profitable subsidiaries, conglomerate closings are more likely to be the result of a planned strategy to increase company-wide profits. The closing of an independently owned business is more likely to constitute a truly involuntary failure.

Our estimates of startups and closings by type of ownership are unfortunately limited at the moment to Massachusetts and New England. Similar counts could indeed be constructed for other states and regions, but Birch has not done so, and our own extract from the Dun and Bradstreet file is limited to New England. Table 15.4 presents establishment openings and closings flows for Massachusetts and for New England, and the associated employment impacts, distributed by form of ownership. Thus, the small family drug store (as well as the not-so-small high technology partnership) are listed as *independents*. The headquarters and branch plants of, for example, General Electric, General Motors, General Dynamics, and Data General are listed under the heading *corporations*. Finally, there is a separate listing for such *conglomerates* as Gulf and Western, Genesco, United Technologies, and all of their many large (and small) subsidiaries.[14]

Between 1969 and 1976, plant closings in Massachusetts cost the state about 739,000 jobs. For New England as a whole, closings (and outmigrations) eliminated 1.4 million jobs. Most important, corpora-

Table 15.4. Startups (or Reorganizations) and Closures of Private Establishments in Massachusetts and New England, by Type of Ownership: 1969–1976

	Ownership form[a], Massachusetts			Ownership form[a], New England		
	Independent	Corporate	Conglomerate[b]	Independent	Corporate	Conglomerate[b]
Establishments						
Closings	83.4%	13.4%	3.1%	84.5%	12.9%	2.6%
Openings	68.4%	29.7%	1.9%	73.1%	25.0%	1.8%
Ratio of closings to openings	1.6	0.6	2.2	1.5	0.7	1.8
Jobs						
Job destruction	48.8%	38.4%	12.8%	49.6%	38.6%	11.8%
Job creation	29.7%	65.4%	4.9%	34.9%	59.1%	6.0%
Ratio of jobs destroyed to jobs created	1.9	0.7	3.0	1.7	0.8	2.3

Source: Extract from the Dun's Identifiers File, prepared for us by David L. Birch.

Note: Closings includes outmigrations; *openings* includes inmigrations.

[a] *Ownership form* refers to the relationship of the establishment (factory, office, division, store, hotel, etc.) to its parent firm, if any. *Independent* establishments operate at only one location, and have no parent. A *corporate* headquarters or branch facility is an establishment which is part of a multifacility enterprise, and which carries the identification (that is, DUNS) number of the parent corporation. A *conglomerate* headquarters or subsidiary is an establishment which is part of a family of often quite heterogeneous businesses, all owned by a single parent but each carrying its own DUNS number. These definitions represent our interpretations of file descriptions distributed by Birch. For further discussion, see Birch, *The Job Generation Process*, and Bluestone and Harrison, *The Deindustrialization of America*, ch. 2.

[b] The *conglomerate* openings in the table represent either literally new establishments or—probably more commonly, although we have no way to tell—preexisting businesses which have been acquired and then reorganized sufficiently radically to prompt Dun and Bradstreet to assign a new DUNS number to them. (Acquired companies which retain their original identities and DUNS number are not counted as new openings, and do not appear in this table.) Analogously, conglomerate divestitures may sometimes appear here as apparent closings, even though they have been bought up and continued to be operated by some other corporation.

379

tions and conglomerates together were responsible for only about 15 percent of the shutdowns, which is consistent with the earlier national finding (table 15.2) that smaller establishments have a higher probability of closing. Yet this relatively small group of corporate and conglomerate establishments was responsible for half of all the jobs lost directly through shutdown. Moreover, we are certain from our fieldwork on subcontracting and procurement networks in the region that a great many of those closings of independently owned businesses were the indirect result of losses of orders and other spillovers generated by the corporate shutdowns.

In particular industries the differences between opening and closing behavior by type of ownership become even more sharply defined. Table 15.5 shows openings and closings (and, because of how we measure them, relocations and reorganizations) for the entire period 1969–1976, for ten important New England industries, both mature and growing. The rate at which conglomerates have closed New England business establishments relative to their rate of openings or acquisitions exceeds that of either independent or corporate owners in eight of the ten industries in table 15.5. For example, take two industries that are very important to (and quite typical of the old and new economic bases of) the region: metalworking machinery and department stores. For every new job created by an independently owned business between 1969 and 1976, 1.6 jobs were destroyed in metalworking and 1 in department stores. But in establishments controlled by conglomerates, for every job created, 4.6 jobs were destroyed in metalworking, while 4 were eliminated in department stores.

While conglomerates controlled a small percentage of all businesses prior to 1976 (although they were responsible for a much larger proportion of all jobs), conglomerate *behavior*—the acquisition of existing facilities in diverse product and service lines bearing little or no relation to the acquirer's original industry—seems to have increased during the closing years of the decade. Thus, for example, U.S. Steel now reinvests a sizeable share of the surplus appropriated from its steel operation into chemicals, nucleonics, and real estate. General Electric (also labeled a corporation rather than a conglomerate in the tables) makes everything from toaster ovens to jet engines. And Mobil Oil now owns the Montgomery Ward department store chain.

In other words, the findings on the disproportionate high rate of shutdowns exercised by conglomerates between 1969 and 1976 may be a harbinger of things to come as more and more conventional corporations behave like conglomerates—buying and selling, opening and

closing operations in order to meet profit targets. In 1979 alone, acquisitions totaling $40 billion were made by U.S. corporations, more
than the total spent on research and development by all private firms
nationwide.[15]

EXISTING POLICY RESPONSES

State governments across the country, and the last several U.S. Con-
gresses, have not been completely oblivious to the problems created
by shutdowns, relocations, and conglomerate reorganizations. While
resisting pressures from public interest groups to directly regulate the
pace of private capital disinvestment, governments at all levels have
become heavily involved in what we choose to call a welfare strategy
for dealing with public demands for help.

The prevailing policy approach consists of tax and other subsidies
or incentives to private companies. In a virtual stampede, literally
thousands of jurisdictions across the country are adopting tax abatement schemes and other business subsidies in the belief that these are
necessary requirements to lure employers to their communities or to
retain those companies they already have. The rush has created what
Business Week, in its May 17, 1976, issue, called "The Second War Between the States." There is now extraordinarily wide agreement in the
research community that these subsidies have no demonstrable impact
on business location behavior, and what is more, entail high opportunity costs in the form of foregone public revenue.[16] If so, then the policy amounts to regressive income distribution: windfall profits for the
corporations, and a deadweight loss to the public.[17]

The other policy is the redistribution of income through federal
grants, in order to at least partially compensate workers who lose their
jobs as the result of shutdowns. In fact, this welfare approach constitutes the standard government response used since the 1930s to cope
with the exigencies of economic development. Limited compensation
has been available to the unemployed in the form of state-provided
unemployment insurance, job retraining programs, and public assistance. While these programs were never designed to specifically help
the victims of plant closings, they have of course been utilized by
those who have found themselves in this perilous position. Particularly for non-union workers, these three programs often serve as the
first, second, and ultimate lines of defense against poverty. Yet while
they are used, none of these programs are particularly well-suited to

Table 15.5. Startups (or Reorganizations) and Closings of Private Business Establishments in Ten Industries in New England, by Type of Ownership: 1969–1976

Industry and form of ownership (standard industry classification codes in parentheses)[a]	Startups or reorganizations		Closings		Rate of change		
					Ratios of closings to openings		Net % change in employment associated with startups and closings
	Establishments	Jobs	Establishments	Jobs	Establishments	Jobs	
Women's apparel (233)					1.9	2.0	−10.1
Independent	56%	42%	67%	53%	2.2	2.5	−10.5
Corporate	41	52	28	39	1.3	1.5	−7.8
Conglomerate[b]	3	6	5	8	3.4	2.9	−20.0
Paper mills (262)					1.0	1.3	−2.1
Independent	40	8	39	7	1.0	1.3	−1.8
Corporate	56	89	51	91	0.9	1.3	−2.4
Conglomerate[b]	4	3	10	2	2.0	0.5	+2.0
Commercial printing (275)					1.2	1.2	−1.9
Independent	79	35	89	53	1.4	1.8	−4.2
Corporate	16	33	7	32	0.6	1.1	−2.3
Conglomerate[b]	5	32	4	15	1.0	0.6	+9.9
Shoes (304)					2.6	4.2	−18.4
Independent	40	17	49	33	3.1	8.1	−24.7
Corporate	54	76	37	51	1.8	2.9	−13.4
Conglomerate[b]	6	7	14	16	6.0	9.5	−28.4

Metalworking machinery (354)					1.6	1.6	−4.4
Independent	74	15	81	24	1.8	2.6	−4.4
Corporate	23	78	15	58	1.0	1.2	−2.3
Conglomerate[b]	3	7	4	18	2.2	4.6	−10.5
Computers (357)					0.9	0.8	+3.3
Independent	43	8	56	10	1.2	1.1	−0.5
Corporate	51	91	36	89	0.6	0.8	+3.9
Conglomerate[b]	6	1	8	1	1.1	1.2	−1.4
Aircraft engines (372)					2.0	3.6	−3.3
Independent	57	7	57	10	2.1	5.3	−4.6
Corporate	37	91	28	55	1.6	2.2	−1.6
Conglomerate[b]	6	2	15	35	4.5	76.2	−22.8
Department stores (531)					0.7	0.5	+11.3
Independent	9	4	14	8	1.1	1.0	0.0
Corporate	82	93	60	69	0.5	0.4	+17.4
Conglomerate[b]	9	3	26	23	2.1	4.0	−27.0
Grocery stores/Supermarkets (541)					2.3	1.0	+0.3
Independent	75	38	93	64	2.8	1.7	−6.4
Corporate	24	61	6	27	0.6	0.4	+18.4
Conglomerate[b]	1	1	1	9	3.0	12.5	−24.6
Hotels/Motels (701)					1.2	0.8	+3.4
Independent	72	39	87	70	1.5	1.5	−5.8
Corporate	26	59	10	20	0.4	0.3	+4.6
Conglomerate[b]	2	2	3	10	1.7	3.9	−21.5

Source: **Extract from the Dun's Identifiers File.** [a] **See table 15.4.** [b] **See table 15.4.**

the task of compensating those adversely affected by plant shutdowns per se. This is because income losses resulting from shutdowns tend to be far more substantial and long-lasting than the personal losses associated with any other cause of unemployment.

Unemployment insurance (UI), for example, replaces only a fraction of weekly earnings, and under normal circumstances is only available for a maximum of twenty-six weeks. The average weekly benefit under UI was a mere $78.60 in 1977, a year in which nearly 2.8 million workers exhausted their benefits before finding new jobs (during the depth of the recession in 1975, almost 4.2 million workers exhausted their benefits).[18] Since a significant minority of plant closing victims are without jobs for more than six months,[19] UI—as presently constituted—provides only temporary, and usually inadequate, relief.

Trade Readjustment Assistance (TRA) augments unemployment compensation for those workers who can prove that liberalized trade relations greatly contributed to the elimination of their jobs. TRA first became law in 1962, as a quid pro quo with organized labor, designed to overcome the protectionist demands of the AFL-CIO.[20] Its provisions and coverage were substantially expanded in 1974, and again in 1977. Nevertheless, "the current adjusted assistance program has been criticized as 'burial insurance' because it provides little more than unemployment-type benefits without enabling the worker to obtain future employment."[21] Except for the cash grants, few workers have demanded the retraining or relocation subsidies. Perhaps this is because comparable jobs, for what are often middle-aged or older workers with very specific skills, are hard to find, so that retraining or migration assistance may be of little practical value. Moreover, many workers who have established themselves in their communities are reluctant to sell their homes, remove their children from the local school system, and move away in search of work.

COLLECTIVE BARGAINING APPROACHES
TO PROTECTING WORKERS

Of course, for workers who belong to unions, the first defense against precipitous dislocations resulting from plant or store closings is without doubt the negotiated contract between labor and management. In recent years, some unions have made significant breakthroughs in negotiating protection for workers' jobs, wages, or at least severance benefits.

For example, new contracts between the United Food and Commercial Workers and several meat-packing firms prohibit the latter from closing a plant and then reopening it on a non-union basis within five years of the shutdown.[22] A clause in a contract between the Amalgamated Clothing and Textile Workers Union and the Clothing Manufacturing Association of the United States, negotiating on behalf of a certain garment firm, prohibits the employer, during the life of the contract, from removing plants from the city (or cities) in which they are located. In still another case, the Graphic Arts Union recently succeeded in getting the printing industries of metropolitan New York to agree to a provision in its members' contracts according to which: "In the event that an employer shall move its factory, this agreement shall remain applicable to the plant at its new location."[23]

But these stories do not mean that the labor movement has solved the problem. Quite apart from the fact that three-quarters of the American labor force has no trade union protection at all, most of those whose jobs are covered by collective bargaining agreements receive very weak protection from dislocation related to shutdowns or large cutbacks. Table 15.6 displays figures for 1977–1978 on the proportion of American and Canadian contracts which provide for advanced notification to employees of impending shutdowns. In the United States, in 1978, while three-quarters of the 400 contracts surveyed by the Bureau of National Affairs (BNA) made some provision for prenotification to workers (although only 29 percent called for advanced notice to *unions*), 81 percent provided for only one week's notice or less. The Canadian record is much the same.

Moreover, the record for large manufacturing companies is much

Table 15.6. Presence in Collective Bargaining Agreements of Provisions for Advanced Notification of Layoff Due to Plant Shutdown or Cutback

	Canada (1977)		United States (1978)	
All contracts surveyed	341	100.0%	400	100.0%
No provision for prenotification	121	36.0	100	25.0
Some provision	220	64.0	300	75.0
One week or less	180	82.0	244	81.0

Source: Bob Baugh, Department of Research, International Woodworkers of America, "Shutdown: Mill Closures and Woodworkers," IWA, Portland, Oregon, December 3, 1979, p. 8, based on data from Labour Canada and from the U.S. Bureau of National Affairs.

Table 15.7. Presence in Collective Bargaining Agreements of Provisions for Income Maintenance in the Event of Layoff Due to Plant Shutdown or Cutback

	Canada (1977)		United States (1978)	
All contracts surveyed	341	100.0%	400	100.0%
No provision	144	42.0	204	51.0
Some provision	197	58.0	196	49.0
Severance	161	47.0	148	37.0
Supplemental Unemployment Benefits (SUB)	81	19.0	64	16.0
Other	—	—	36	9.0

Source: Baugh, "Shutdown: Mill Closures and Woodworkers," p. 11.

Note: Percents may sum to more than 100 because some workers are eligible for more than one benefit.

worse than the BNA averages suggest. According to the U.S. Department of Labor, of 826 contracts active on July 1, 1976, covering 3.4 million workers in manufacturing plants with 1,000 or more employees, only 111 contracts (covering 353,000 workers) provided for any sort of advanced notification. That amounts to only 13 percent of the contracts, covering only 10 percent of the workers.[24]

Table 15.7 shows the incidence of income maintenance provisions in union contracts in 1977–1978 in Canada and the United States. Half of all American workers covered in some respect by a contract receive no income protection of any kind. Only a sixth of all workers were even eligible in 1978 for Supplemental Unemployment Benefits—long-term company-paid unemployment insurance—negotiated as part of their contracts.

LABOR LAW REFORM

The American labor movement has long been unanimous in its opinion that workers need far greater protection than is now available. A key element in enhancing that protection would be removing the fetters that the Taft-Hartley Act placed upon the ability of unions both to organize in businesses and locations where workers are presently unorganized, and to protect themselves from a variety of unfair labor

practices by management. The repeal of Section 14(b) in particular—
the granting to states of the power to prohibit the union shop without
which union locals' financial survival is made far more precarious—has
become something of a crusade in recent years. Our own research
supports the view that business is aware of and responsive to the attractiveness of such anti-union jurisdictions as sites for branches of relocated facilities.[25]

A second major area of labor law reform that seems especially
pertinent to the subject of capital flight is the clarification of the
extremely ambiguous state of affairs that currently prevails with respect to the problem of *successorship*. In 1964, the U.S. Supreme
Court ruled that unions had the right to bring grievances before the
National Labor Relations Board when an employer disappeared by
merger and the new employer refused to recognize the union. For example, this occurred when Perdue, a determinedly non-union employer, acquired three plants from Swift and Company in Delaware
and Maryland, all of which had been unionized under Swift.[26] As we
saw earlier, this sort of disappearance seems to have become increasingly common in the past twenty years, and another merger wave, led
this time by the computer and semiconductor industries, appears to be
in the offing. But in 1972, in the *Burns* decision, the Burger Court effectively reversed the previous Warren Court ruling, arguing that a
successor's honoring the contract

> does not ensue as a matter of law from the mere fact that an employer
> is doing the same work in the same place with the same employees as
> his predecessor . . . a potential employer may be willing to take over
> a moribund business only if he can make changes in corporate structure,
> composition of the labor force, work, location, task assignment, and na-
> ture of supervision. Saddling such an employer with the terms and con-
> ditions of employment contained in the old contract may make these
> changes impossible and may discourage and inhibit the transfer of
> capital.[27]

Given our own finding that the typical acquisition is anything but mor-
ibund, this decision represents a major setback for organized labor.
Senator Harrison Williams (Democrat-New Jersey) has submitted legislation to amend the Taft-Hartley Act to make it an unfair labor
practice for an employer who assumes ownership or operation of an
ongoing business to refuse to assume all of the terms and conditions of
a predecessor contract. Thus far, the legislation has had little success.

PLANT CLOSING LEGISLATION

In the past several years, national labor law reform has been thwarted
in the U.S. Congress. But even if the various changes being sought by
labor were to be achieved, for example, with respect to successorship,
common situs picketing, or the repeal of 14(b), there would still be
at least three major problems to overcome. First, the case-by-case collective bargaining approach is insufficient for reaching every worker
directly at risk, as labor unions are simply not financially strong enough
today to organize all employers. Second, protection needs to be extended beyond those workers who are immediately affected by company restructuring strategies, to cover everyone whose income security
is threatened. And finally, collective bargaining is obviously incapable
of providing for the rebuilding of the local economic base in the wake
of major shutdowns. Thus, many have called for legislation that addresses the whole range of problems created by plant and store closings
and cutbacks.

The European Experience

In June 1978, a delegation made up of officials from three American
unions (the auto workers, steel workers, and the machinists) and several government agencies visited Sweden, West Germany, and England to study how those governments—and the unions in those countries—were dealing with what is, after all, an international problem.
They found that

> Without exception . . . all three (countries) had programs for coping
> with the adverse effects of economic dislocation upon workers and com-
> munities. . . . In all three countries, corporations are legally obligated
> to give advance notice [to] workers, unions, and the national employ-
> ment service before closing a plant or dismissing workers for economic
> reasons. Before initiating layoffs, moreover, a company must first nego-
> tiate the matter with its employees' union or the plant's works joint
> labor-management council. . . . The planned reduction is handled en-
> tirely by attrition and no dismissals are necessary. The time gained gives
> affected workers and potential new employees the chance to arrange
> for alternative employment. . . . Advance notice triggers into action
> labor market boards at the national, regional, local (and in some cases,
> workplace) levels.
>
> Some might argue that Western Europe's statutory programs to
> protect workers and communities against economic dislocation are
> costly and burdensome to corporations. [Yet] many of the same corpora-

tions which can be counted on to oppose such programs in the United States have been investing heavily over the last thirty years, and for the most part have operated profitably, in the three countries we visited and in others which have long experience with legislation to cope with the effects of economic dislocation.[28]

The Swedes have the most highly developed programs for relocating workers, for example, by bringing employment service computer terminals right inside the old plant as soon as notice of the eventual closing is given, and by statutorily requiring all employers to list vacancies in these computerized files (in strong contrast to the American employment security system, where filing is de facto voluntary and has been shown again and again to be very selective). Moreover, the Swedes have a wide variety of programs for replacing the eroded local job (and tax) base, through direct public enterprise and grants and loans for new private sector startups. In West Germany, a firm contemplating a shutdown is required to give its reasons to the local works council, and to open its books so that the council will have free access to all corporate data relevant to evaluating the reasons for the decision and its likely impact on the region in which the plant is located. Although not yet strictly enforced, the Codetermination Act of 1976 calls for one year advance notice by West German businesses of intended closings.

It is also worth noting that each of these three countries has pushed the welfare approach considerably beyond what is available in the United States. Severance pay, mandatory transfer rights, guaranteed social security credits, health benefits, and adequate income maintenance benefits are provided by the company (or as a last resort, by the government) until the individual is reemployed. Retraining, mobility assistance, and guaranteed employer-paid relocation expenses are also mandated in most cases. Through such measures, the governments in these countries have tried as much as possible to fully compensate workers who lose their jobs through no fault of their own.[29]

Legislative Attempts in the United States

In 1974, then Senator Walter Mondale (Democrat-Minnesota) and Congressman William Ford (Democrat-Michigan) introduced the National Employment Priorities Act (NEPA) into the U.S. Congress. The act would have created a National Employment Relocation Administration to investigate complaints, rule on whether the plant shutdown or relocation was justified, and, if not, recommend the withholding of various tax benefits. The proposed program has been criticized for being administratively impractical, as well as for lacking criteria for determining justified capital disinvestment. The program constituted an open invitation for every firm to blackmail the government into giving it the various financial subsidies provided for in the bill whenever extra cash was needed. The language of Title VI made any firm, even if it was just *thinking* of closing or transferring operations, eligible for loans, grants, interest subsidies, and technical assistance. In any case, the bill was never reported out of committee.

At this point, the effort to organize plant closing legislation shifted to the states. In late 1975, the Ohio Public Interest Campaign (OPIC) was formed to educate citizens and organize resistance to the wave of plant closings and corporate demands for tax abatements and credits that was sweeping the midwest. OPIC is a coalition of labor unions, senior citizens, civil rights and consumer organizations, and church groups, based in Cleveland, with offices all across the state. In July 1977, a new plant closing bill, the Community Readjustment Act, drafted by OPIC, was introduced into the Ohio Senate by Senator Michael Schwarzwalder (Democrat-Columbus). In spite of a major organizing effort in 1977–1978, the bill died in committee. Through continued effort, and in the wake of a new rash of steel mill closings, the revived 1979 version (Ohio Senate Bill No. 188) began to win more widespread support, including approval by the Senate Finance subcommittee (but not by the entire body) in 1980.

The OPIC-Schwarzwalder bill contains six key provisions, which have come to define the basic agenda for the many similar bills which have followed in many other states:[30]

> prior notification of major cutbacks and total shutdowns, varying from six months to two years;
>
> discharge or severance payments for all workers, whether or not they are unionized;
>
> continuation of health insurance coverage for some period following the layoff, paid for by the company;
>
> increased rights of transfer to other plants or stores in the company's system (if any);
>
> lump sum payment to the local municipality, to help finance economic redevelopment;
>
> preparation by joint company-union-government committees of economic impact statements, to facilitate the redevelopment effort.

Two other states—Maine and Wisconsin—already have modest plant closing laws on the books (Maine reformers are attempting to strengthen theirs). In every case, the provisions apply only to shutdowns of (or substantial cutbacks in) the establishments of firms with some minimum number of employees (generally 100, but the details vary from state to state).

Much impressed with what they had learned on their June 1978 tour of western Europe, upon their return to the United States the UAW members of the study group issued a seven-point program for dealing with problems related to plant closings in this country. During the next year, through conferences with the staffs of OPIC and those of other unions, the UAW plan grew into a twenty-seven-point program which was published in a joint communique of the three unions that had made the European tour.[31] This statement represents the most comprehensive set of recommendations ever set forth.

The rapid growth of activity at the local level, and the deteriorating economic situation in the country as a whole, made a new initiative in Washington appear more likely in 1979. After long consultations with the UAW Research Department, on August 31, 1979, Michigan Congressman Ford reintroduced his (considerably altered) bill into the U.S. House of Representatives. Co-sponsored by Senator Donald Riegle (Democrat-Michigan) and fifty-eight others, the new National Employment Priorities Act of 1979 (H.R. 5040) has begun to attract attention through hearings around the country, and (more recently) as a result of growing and vocal opposition in the business press. The main provisions of the Ford-Riegle bill cover: prenotification (so workers and communities have time to plan readjustment), severance pay, successorship, transfer rights, the protection of benefits for a period of time following the shutdown or layoff, grants and loans to failing businesses under certain specified circumstances, economic redevelopment assistance to local governments, and grants and loans to workers to help them buy out closing businesses in order to operate them as cooperatives. A companion, but not identical bill, introduced into the Senate by Harrison Williams, is called the Employee Protection and Community Stabilization Act of 1979. And an earlier bill by Congressman Peter Kostmayer (Democrat-Pennsylvania) and Philip Lundine (Democrat-New York), designed to provide federal loans and loan guarantees for worker buy-outs, became a Carter administration–supported amendment to the National Public Works and Economic Development Act of 1979. This legislation sought to renew (with greatly increased funding and authority) the nation's economic programs. Senator Steward (Democrat-Alaska) further promoted this directive toward worker ownership with an amendment to the Small Business Administration Reauthorization Act (S. 918), requiring SBA to extend its entire range of technical and financial services to small worker-owned companies and cooperatives. Finally, still other amendments to the new EDA bill, by congresspersons Dodd (Democrat-Connecticut) and McKenney (Republican-Connecticut), would require advanced notification of military contract cancellations by the Pentagon, and long-term income maintenance for workers displaced by such cancellations. As of January 1981, none of these bills had been passed.

CORPORATE OPPOSITION TO PLANT CLOSING LEGISLATION

Business executives, lobbyists, management consultants, and their elected supporters seem to be taking these legislative initiatives seriously. In the last two years, books, magazine articles, and public speeches have denounced the efforts of labor and community groups to—as business spokespeople put it—"hold industry for ransom."

Management argues that companies will stop expanding operations in states which pass legislation regulating the mobility of private capital. Moreover, they say, no new companies are likely to build in such places. For example, William McCarthy, an official of the corporate lobbying group Associate Industries of Massachusetts (AIM), warned at the time of the first plant closing legislative hearing in the Massachusetts State House, that even the *consideration* of such legislation "would be raising a sign on the borders of this state that investment isn't welcome here."[32]

In his American Enterprise Institute monograph, Clemson University Professor Richard McKensie views plant closing legislation as direct support of trade unions and local governments, against the interests of business. By inhibiting companies from shutting down, unions would (he argues) be able to "increase their demands on employers" for higher wages and fringe benefits, while local governments could increase business taxes without improving quality of services.[33]

In the same vein, the editors of the *Wall Street Journal* recently took the position that the new plant closing legislation would give politicians and unions "property rights in the existing distribution of jobs and business activity." Companies' assets could then be "pillaged" by the "featherbedding" and "antiquated work rules" imposed by the unions, and stuck with bills imposed by "vote-buying politicians." Eventually, said the *Journal*, such legislation might actually *increase* job loss, since "shareholders who can't run can be more quickly plundered into bankruptcy."[34]

Andrew Kramer, a partner in a Washington, D.C., labor relations management consulting firm, suggests that announcements of plant shutdowns may (1) lower productivity and lead to the loss of skilled and semiskilled workers and (2) increase the administrative burden on management, while posing a serious danger of protracted litigation. Firms would be tied up indefinitely in court proceedings, as has occurred with respect to the environmental impact statements mandated by the National Environmental Protection Act.[35]

Probably no measure in the proposed legislation is more violently opposed by business than the requirement for advanced notification of major cutbacks or total shutdowns. In a 1977 letter to the study group that subsequently drafted the first Massachusetts bill, the then Acting Commissioner of Commerce and Development asserted that he had "discussed this with several people" and concluded that it would be "impractical" for a firm to be asked to announce such a decision in advance. Besides, he told the group, for most businesses "the decision is often abrupt," so that anything like a six-month to two-year lead time wouldn't even be possible, let alone "practical."

But case studies of a number of plant closings in different industries and different regions make it very clear that a great many shutdowns are either explicitly planned far ahead, or are easily predictable in the light of the parent corporation's measurable disinvestment in the plant or store.[36] Peter Drucker, probably the country's foremost management consultant and analyst, has stated that "there is usually a two-year lead time between the identification of the need to close plants or make reductions and the actual closing."[37]

From our own field notes, we can offer two examples from the women's apparel industry in New England. Its own corporate reports reveal that the Nashville-based conglomerate Genesco underwent a major change of management (including its board chairman) in 1977, after which the new team announced that it would close down the entire women's apparel division—sixteen companies operating forty-seven plants. One of these was Girl Town, a sportswear operation in the Dorchester section of Boston, which had been acquired in 1967. Girl Town was not completely closed (the last of approximately 400 jobs eliminated) until mid-1979—two years after Genesco's managers publicly announced that the closing would take place.

One might also look at the even longer-term planned reorganization strategy of a major New England dress company, started in New Bedford in the 1930s. As our interviews with some of the managers disclosed, the firm maintained its headquarters and cutting room in the New Bedford area, and prior to the 1960s, had contract shops (for the sewing and stitching operations) in Rhode Island, Vermont, and upstate New York. In 1963, what had been a family business went public, and with the new infusion of capital that this brought, immediately acquired an industrial building in Tennessee, and another in North Carolina, a few years later. Once these factories were fully operational, the firm sold off its Rhode Island operation and shut down the New York plant. The major clothing conglomerate which acquired the firm in 1971 accelerated the regional shift, opening two more plants in Tennessee in 1972 and 1973, after which it shut down the last of the New England–based assembly plants in Vermont.

In both cases, as with the Lykes Corporation's conglomerate acquisition of the Campbell Works in Youngstown, there is simply no doubt that the disinvestment was planned, and the facilities phased out, over time. Moreover, as we reported earlier, a number of U.S. companies (including the Westinghouse Corporation) seem able to live with prior notification clauses in their labor contracts. And in Europe, virtually all firms have had to come to an accommodation with the principle of prenotification.

Furthermore, for large, often multiplant corporations, the proposition that advanced notice will reduce workers' productivity or lead to the premature loss of the most qualified workers does not seem to be supported by case studies of plant closings or by surveys conducted by the British Manpower Commission.[38] In fact, there is reason to believe that many workers often do hear of an impending closing, but do not know precisely *when* it will occur. As a result, if anything, companies' unwillingness to give advanced notification *induces* quitting because of the free-floating insecurity associated with rumors of a plant closing. Knowing the future date allows the worker to plan rather than merely act out of misinformed apprehension.

CONCLUSIONS

Will anything resembling the proposed plant closing and related legislation be passed into law in the foreseeable future? And even if it were, how much real progress toward more orderly economic planning, which necessarily means progress in the planning of investment and disinvestment, would be made without complementary and far-reaching changes in tax, tariff, antitrust, and *then* economic development policy? These are among the central economic policy issues for the 1980s. Certainly they are crucial to any serious—that is, non-rhetorical—discussion about reindustrialization.

In any case, with regard to all such reforms, it is clear that the business community is adopting a militant posture. In many ways, the clarion call was sounded publicly for the first time in a commentary that appeared in the October 12, 1974, issue of *Business Week:*

> Some people will obviously have to do with less, or with substitutes, so that the economy as a whole can get the most mileage out of available capital. . . .
>
> Indeed, cities and states, the home mortgage market, small business, and the consumer, will all get less than they want because the basic health of the U.S. is based on the basic health of its corporations and banks: the biggest borrowers and the biggest lenders. Compromises, in terms of who gets and who does without, that would have been unthinkable only a few years ago, will be made in coming years because the economic future not only of the U.S. but also of the whole world is on the line today.[39]

The magazine goes on to observe that the idea that income and resources will have to be redistributed to big business will be a "hard pill" to swallow. To get the American people to swallow it is, they predict, going to require a "selling job" beyond anything that any country has attempted in modern times, to make people accept the "new reality."

As we have seen, the "new reality" includes a high incidence of direct job loss due to shutdowns, in a wide range of industries, and in all regions of the country. Indeed, although the absolute and per capita levels of establishment closings have (predictably) been highest in the northeast, the odds of a pre-1969 large manufacturing plant shutting down sometime before the late 1970s were actually higher in the south than anywhere else. Overall, the country was losing an average of 3.2 million jobs a year to shutdowns (not counting multiplier effects) through the end of 1976. Since then, the incidence of job loss has almost surely increased, with the rapid pace of industry-wide restructuring schemes in autos, steel, and rubber, and with the growth of conglomerate-like behavior on the part of many corporations.

In all of this, corporate managers' use of industrial location to keep organized labor off guard has helped to destabilize (if not to altogether destroy) the consensus between big labor and big business that has formed the basis for more or less orderly private capital accumulation since the early 1950s. Concisely put, the trade unions are under explicit attack once again,[40] with capital "hypermobility" being the newest weapon in the management arsenal.[41]

To us, a key question is therefore whether the unions will respond to the very great need for leadership in the continuing struggle over strategic plant shutdowns, and what that response will be. Will they attempt to restore consensus with (now) global capital? Or will they become an agency for resisting and challenging unregulated capital mobility? The fate of legislation concerning plant closings, labor law reform, and much else may ultimately turn on how these conflicting tendencies within the labor movement work themselves out in the years ahead.

NOTES

The research upon which this chapter is based was sponsored by the Progressive Alliance, a Washington-based coalition of trade unions, community, feminist, environmental, and public interest groups led by the United Auto Workers. We are grateful to David Birch for making certain of the data available to us, to Maryellen Kelley for helpful criticism, and to Leona Morris and Virginia Richardson for preparing the manuscript.

1. For example, in its November 28, 1979, edition, the *New York Times* reported the closing of fifteen United States Steel Corporation plants and mills in eight states resulting in the loss of 13,000 white and blue collar jobs. This announcement was made in spite of the increased demand for steel.

    The near-collapse of the Chrysler Corporation, and major cutbacks in the domestic (but not in the overseas) operations of Ford, are by now too well-known to require documentation. On the other hand, there is still limited awareness of the extent to which the restructuring process has spread, even to non-manufacturing industries. For example, "Food Fair, Inc. [owes] $15 million . . . to . . . employees . . . who lost their jobs when the company closed 212 supermarkets and seventy-nine J. M. Fields department stores (including all its stores in Philadelphia)" (*Wall Street Journal*, September 18, 1979, p. 1).

2. Barry Bluestone and Bennett Harrison, *The Deindustrialization of America* (New York: Basic Books, 1982). Related research has been conducted by William F. Whyte and Robert Stern at Cornell University, by Belden Daniels at Harvard University, by Robert Cohen at Columbia University, by Charles Craypo at Notre Dame, by Doreen Massey at

the London School of Economics, and by the staff of the North American Congress on Latin America in New York City.

3. In this chapter our interest is mainly in private *dis*investment and its consequences, especially in older regions. But, of course, capital also moves into such areas all the time. It is incorrect to imagine the situation as one in which *everything* is leaving. However, the activities that still do business there, or the new ones that are starting up, may be growing too slowly to make up for those businesses that are cutting back, closing, or leaving. Or the new companies may not want to employ the people who were thrown out of work by the old closings. The jobs that make up the new economic base may pay lower wages and offer less steady or fewer hours of work than did the old base. We estimate, for example, that it takes at least two service sector jobs to make up in family income what is lost by the elimination of one manufacturing job. These larger questions about economic base transformation (in contrast with decline per se) are examined in detail for one region in Bennett Harrison, "Regional Restructuring and 'Good Business Climates': The Economic Transformation of New England Since World War II," ch. 3 in this volume.

4. See Carol Jusenius and Larry Ledebur, "A Myth in the Making: The Southern Economic Challenge and Northern Economic Decline," in E. Blaine Liner and Lawrence K. Lynch, eds., *The Economics of Southern Growth* (Durham, N.C.: The Southern Growth Policies Board, 1977); and Bernhard L. Weinstein and Robert E. Firestine, *Regional Growth and Decline in the United States: The Rise of the Sunbelt and the Decline of the Northeast* (New York: Praeger, 1978). In earlier published work, one of us also erroneously cited the 1.5 percent figure as evidence that there is relatively little short-term spatial movement of businesses in the United States (Bennett Harrison and Sandra Kanter, "The Political Economy of State Job-Creation Business Incentives," *Journal of the American Institute of Planners*, November 1978).

5. Richard B. McKenzie, *Restrictions on Business Mobility* (Washington, D.C.: American Enterprise Institute, 1979), p. 5. The basic data may be found in David Birch, *The Job Generation Process* (Cambridge, Mass.: MIT Program on Neighborhood and Regional Change, 1979). Birch's work has been quoted by the *Wall Street Journal* and by many southern researchers to counter the argument that southern growth is occurring at the expense of northern workers. Research papers by regional economists that have cited Birch's famous "one and a half percent" have been similarly used. For example, one study of plant migrations out of the state of Ohio over the period 1970–1974 found that "migrant firms were few in number and mostly small in size" (Jusenius and Ledebur, "The Migration of Firms and Workers in Ohio, 1970–1975," Academy for Contemporary Problems, Columbus, 1977). When this conclusion was announced in late 1977, it was quickly reported by daily newspapers all across the state. At the time, a coalition of trade unionists, community activists, and church leaders was trying to find a way to save the jobs of the 4,100 workers who had been laid off that September when the Campbell works of the Youngstown Sheet and Tube Steel mill was closed down by its conglomerate parent, the Lykes Corporation. In a study by two Harvard Business School economists (Robert A. Leone and John R. Meyer, "Can the Northeast Rise Again,"

Wharton Quarterly, Winter 1979), the authors report that "of the more than 1450 northeast manufacturing facilities that can be definitely identified as making a long distance move from 1971 to 1976 . . . only 128 emigrated to the sunbelt" (p. 23).

6. The fact that more and more large corporations and conglomerates deliberately milk profitable plants instead of reinvesting in them, or liquidate plants or subsidies that fail to meet arbitrarily set minimum profit targets, represents a culmination of tendencies in the development of modern management with literally epochal effects on the international capitalist system. We present numerous examples in our monograph. Striking confirmation of these developments has now appeared in a most unlikely place: the pages of *Business Week* itself. In a nearly 100-page editorial on the problem of reindustrialization, the editors explicitly accuse modern quantitatively trained managers of not keeping their plants modern; of establishing arbitrary target profit hurdles and then shutting down even relatively efficient facilities which fail to meet them; of pursuing growth for their firms by acquiring unrelated existing businesses rather than by building new plants or expanding existing capacity; and of generally adopting myopic behavior with respect to the investment decision. See "Reindustrialization: Special Issue," *Business Week,* June 30, 1980. See also Robert H. Hayes and William J. Abernathy, "Managing Our Way to Economic Decline," *Harvard Business Review,* July/August, 1980; and the series of case studies assembled by the Committee on Small Business, U.S. House of Representatives, *Conglomerate Mergers—Their Effects on Small Business and Local Communities* (Washington, D.C.: GPO, 1980).

7. This has not stopped business spokespersons from continually *threatening* to move out of town if they don't get their way. In an interview with the trade magazine *New England Business* (October 1, 1979, p. 14), Associated Industries of Massachusetts lobbyist Jim Sledd asserted that Massachusetts high-technology firms are "very mobile" and that "they can be on the back of a flatbed truck tomorrow and be in North Carolina if things don't go the way they want them to."

8. There also appears to be a systematic downward bias in D&B's counts of even what we are calling simultaneous or sequential relocations. That is, D&B almost surely undercounts "movers." Most users of the data seem to agree on this. For details, see Bluestone and Harrison, *The Deindustrialization of America,* ch. 2, and Birch, *The Job Generation Process.*

9. In this essay, we report only on job loss as an impact measure. There is a rich literature on the income, earnings, health, community, and labor relations effects of plant closings, which we review in chapter 3 of our monograph. See also Robert Aronson and Robert McKersie, *Economic Consequences of Plant Shutdowns in New York State* (Ithaca, N.Y.: N.Y. State School of Industrial and Labor Relations, Cornell University, 1980); Felician Foltman, *White and Blue Collars in a Mill Shutdown* (Ithaca, N.Y.: Cornell University Press, 1968); Arlene Holen, "Losses to Workers Displaced by Plant Closure or Layoff: A Survey of the Literature," The Public Research Institute of the Center for Naval Analyses, November 1976; Louis Jacobson, "Earnings Loss Due to Displacement," The Public Research Institute of the Center for Naval Analyses, Working Paper CRC-385, April 1979; Peter B. Meyer and Mark A. Phillips, *Worker Adaptation to Internationally Induced Job Loss: Final Report*

on a Pilot Study, Bureau of International Labor Affairs, U.S. Department of Labor, April 27, 1978; Stephen C. Mick, "Social and Personal Costs of Plant Shutdowns," *Industrial Relations*, Vol. 14, No. 2, May 1975, p. 205; James L. Stern, "Consequences of Plant Closure," *Journal of Human Resources*, Winter 1972; and Richard Wilcock and W. H. Franke, *Unwanted Workers: Permanent Layoffs and Long-Term Unemployment* (New York: Glencoe Free Press, 1963).

10. For example, companies now typically select depreciation schedules from a menu offered up by the Internal Revenue Service to fit the former's cash flow requirements. As a result, officially measured differences between gross and net private investment are becoming artifacts of the political process rather than an indicator of disinvestment.

   Moreover, the U.S. Bureau of Labor Statistics' and Census Bureau's regularly published figures on changes in employment, no matter how detailed (by industry, occupation, race, sex, age, location), cannot be used to make inferences about what is going on in terms of capital investment. Employment can change due to changing product demand, inventory build-ups (or shortages), seasonality, snowstorms, energy brown-outs, and even unofficial vacation practices traditional to some industries (New England women's apparel manufacturers, for instance, typically complete the production of their fall lines by late spring; some then "invite" their production workers to take off for the summer and return in September, to be supported in the interim by Welfare or Unemployment Insurance). In none of these instances has the facility itself or any of its machinery and equipment necessarily been expanded or contracted.

11. See Birch, *The Job Generation Process*, pp. 3–25 on some of the problems with the data, his own (sometimes controversial) methods for rearranging and editing the raw D&B records, and so forth.

12. For additional detail on establishment openings and closings in New England, and a more complete description of the methodology, see Bluestone and Harrison, *The Deindustrialization of America*, ch. 2.

13. Recall that these data refer to individual establishments, that is, stores and plants, *not* to firms. The failure rate of firms is presumably much lower. For some evidence on the latter, see Harrison, "Regional Restructuring," Fig. 1.

14. The criterion used to distinguish a multiestablishment "corporation" from a multiestablishment "conglomerate" is as follows. If the various establishments belonging to a central firm share the same DUNS number (and therefore the same credit rating), and if they do not have legal standing to be sued individually in court, then Birch assigns them to a category he calls "headquarters or branch." We call this the "corporate" sector. Otherwise, all of the establishments that make up the multiestablishment firm—each with its own individual DUNS number and court standing—are assigned by Birch to what he calls the "parent-subsidiary" category, which we label "conglomerate." This procedure unquestionably understates the degree of conglomerate-like *behavior* in the sample. For example, a corporation with a famous name may acquire a totally unrelated product or service line, yet treat it as a division rather than as a separate entity, perhaps in order to exploit its own famous name. Birch's and our procedure would classify these as corporate establishments, even though this would be a clear case of conglomerate behavior in the eyes of (say) the Federal Trade Commission. Future researchers will need to

develop a more market structure–oriented definition of conglomeration than the essentially legalistic definition used here. Such a definition should explicitly recognize conglomeration as a process of corporate expansion which involves both product (and service) diversity and acquisition of existing facilities as distinct from the construction of new ones. The history of the conglomerate movement in the United States is reviewed in Bluestone and Harrison, *The Deindustrialization of America,* ch. 6.

15. Cited in *Business Week*, p. 78.
16. Among the more recent entries are Robert Goodman, *The Last Entrepreneurs* (N.Y.: Simon and Schuster, 1979); Jerry Jacobs, *Bidding for Business: Corporate Auctions and the Fifty Disunited States* (Washington, D.C.: Public Interest Research Group, 1979); Roger Vaughan, *State Taxation and Economic Development* (Washington, D.C.: Council of State Planning Agencies, 1979); and Harrison and Kanter, "The Political Economy of State Job-Creation Business Incentives."
17. Direct financial assistance and tax subsidies are by no means the only major concessions being offered to business to influence their investment decisions. Relaxing business regulation and limiting social wage legislation are advocated as an additional means to create—or at least to advertise—a "good business climate." Because business lobbyists complain most about the compliance costs entailed in environmental protection laws, occupational health and safety regulations, zoning statutes, building codes, and anti-discrimination measures, these have become the prime targets for reform. For example, in Massachusetts, the defeat of a series of 1975 statewide referenda on progressive income taxation, public power, throwaway containers, and "lifeline" electric rates is credited by government officials with restoring business confidence in the Commonwealth. Restrictions on unemployment and workmen's compensation eligibility, labor law reform, minimum wage coverage, and corporate property tax classification are other measures that fall under this category.
18. U.S. Department of Labor, *Employment and Training Report of the President 1979* (Washington: U.S. Government Printing Office, 1979). Table F–10, p. 372.
19. Bluestone and Harrison, *The Deindustrialization of America*, ch. 3.
20. For a detailed history of TRA, see *Employment and Training Report of the President 1979*, pp. 243–46; and James E. McCarthy, *Trade Adjustment Assistance: A Case Study of the Shoe Industry in Massachusetts,* Federal Reserve Bank of Boston Research Report No. 58, June 1975.
21. *Wall Street Journal,* October 31, 1977, p. 6.
22. Reported in *American Labor,* December 1979, pp. 2–3.
23. Reported by Bob Baugh, Department of Research, Education and Collective Bargaining Coordination, International Woodworkers of America, "Shutdown: Mill Closures and Woodworkers," IWA, Portland, Oregon, December 3, 1979, p. 7.
24. Ibid., p. 9.
25. Bluestone and Harrison, *The Deindustrialization of America*, ch. 18.
26. Personal communication from David Blitzstein, United Food and Commercial Workers, International Headquarters, Washington, D.C., January 18, 1981.
27. Quoted in Baugh, "Shutdown," p. 32.
28. Labor Union Study Tour Participants, *Economic Dislocation: Plant*

Closings, Plant Relocations, and Plant Conversion, UAW, USA, IAM, Washington, D.C., May 1, 1979, pp. 7–8. On the same subject, see also C&R Associates, *Plant Location Legislation and Regulation in the United States and Western Europe: A Survey*, Federal Trade Commission, Washington, D.C., January 1979.

29. Labor Union Study Tour, *Economic Dislocation*.

30. Among the other states with legislation pending as of December 1980 are: Connecticut, Illinois, Maine, Massachusetts, Michigan, New Jersey, New York, Oregon, Pennsylvania, and Rhode Island. The following material is drawn from William Schweke, ed., *Plant Closing Strategy Packet* (Washington, D.C.: Progressive Alliance and Conference on Alternative State and Local Policies, January 1980). This document contains a detailed comparison of the provisions of each state's bill.

31. Labor Union Study Tour, *Economic Dislocation*, pp. 32–34.

32. Quoted by Liz Bass, "Runaway Plants Leave Workers Out in Cold," *The Citizen Advocate* (Massachusetts), March 1979, p. 3. This is hardly a new position for Mr. McCarthy's organization to be taking. As far back as the 1922–1923 legislative sessions in Massachusetts, AIM officials were making the same threats. For example: "By far the most serious menace which confronts the industries of our section today is that growing out of a public misconception of the proper obligation of business enterprise to society," Colonel Gow, President of AIM, July 1, 1922; "The community must see to it that legislation shall not unduly hamper business management," Frank Dresser, AIM staffer, December 29, 1923; "It cannot be hoped that, with these great industrial plants once driven out of New England, others would come in to replace them, when competing sections . . . offer such attractive advantages," AIM editorial, March 3, 1923. All three quotations come from AIM's official magazine, *Industry*. The Dresser statement was part of an article entitled: "What Can We Do to Prevent Unwise Social Legislation?" The "unwise social legislation" being debated on Beacon Hill that prompted these thinly veiled threats included revisions of the minimum wage law, workmen's compensation, and amendments to toughen the child labor laws.

33. McKenzie, *Restrictions on Business Mobility*, pp. 57, 60.

34. "Words and Deeds," *The Wall Street Journal*, November 23, 1979, p. 20. Incidentally, these quotes clearly imply that, precisely because capital mobility is *not* presently regulated, companies *do* run after all, something which McKenzie goes to great lengths to deny in the earlier chapters of his book.

35. Andrew M. Kramer, "Plant Locations (and Relocations) from a Labor Relations Perspective," *Industrial Development*, November–December 1979, p. 4.

36. Cf. the discussion of the shutdown of the Campbell Works of the Youngstown Sheet and Tube Company, in Belden Daniels et al., *The Impact of Acquisition on the Acquired Firm* (Cambridge: Dept. of City and Regional Planning, Harvard University, 1980), ch. 4.

37. Quoted in Pennsylvania Public Interest Coalition, *Public Interest News*, vol. 1, no. 2, July 1981, p. 7.

38. Harry J. Gilman, "The Economic Costs of Worker Dislocation: An Overview," prepared for the National Commission for Employment Policy, July 13, 1979. The research to which Gilman refers is by Arnold Weber and David P. Taylor, "Procedures for Employee Displacement: Advance Notice of Shutdown," *Journal of Business*, July 1963; and OECD,

Job Security and Industrial Relations. Report of the Working Party of Industrial Relations, Paris, May 1977.

39. *Business Week,* October 12, 1974. Copyright © 1974 by McGraw-Hill, Inc. Reprinted with permission.

40. Cf. Donald D. Cook, "Laws to Curb Plant Closings," *Industry Week,* February 4, 1980.

41. This challenge has been reiterated by representatives of the Business Roundtable and the U.S. Chamber of Commerce on several television news programs, for example, the "McNeil-Lehrer Report" of June 18, 1980. Arnold Weber agrees that the challenge to labor is to be understood as corporate *policy:* "Instead of working with unions to solve problems that might prevent plant closings," Weber is quoted by *Business Week,* "companies increasingly attempt to create a bona fide open shop movement . . . by shifting production overseas or to the Sunbelt" (*Business Week,* June 30, 1980, p. 82).

16

Economic Democracy and Regional Restructuring: An Internationalization Perspective

WILLIAM K. TABB

The U.S. political economy is undergoing a transition of historic proportions, comparable to the first merger wave at the turn of the century that created the structures of oligopolistic corporate dominance, and to the growth of state intervention in the New Deal period and the Great Society decade of the 1960s. The immediate transition is from the redistributive liberalism which has dominated for nearly fifty years. Its presuppositions were that an activist state can stimulate aggregate growth without detailed sectoral interventions and can redistribute part of the growth dividend to the less fortunate, incorporating them into the general prosperity which the Keynesian policy promises. This model of accumulation, based as it was on cheap raw materials, most notably oil, and on expanding world trade and record growth rates, has proven untenable amid the disarray of a world economy wracked by the impact of overcapacity in almost all basic industries—auto, steel, rubber, textiles—and by the need to adjust to higher energy costs. Equally profound is the growth of global transnational corporations that are able to play nation against nation, deriving tax advantages which inflict fiscal crises everywhere, and to set worker against worker, undermining unions and forcing down wages at the same time as technological innovations deskill a greater proportion of the labor force. The interchangeability and the cross-national practice of multisourcing—producing the same components in many plants around the world—both increase the bargaining power of capital.

The long postwar period of European recovery, rebuilding, and expansion has come to an end. World capacity has at least temporarily outrun demand, despite a vast creation of credit by national governments and international funding agencies. Private banks operating in an increasingly shaky Euro-currency market appear overextended in loans to corporate and government clients. In this world of capital mobility and global corporations, the conservative approach of letting market forces determine the state of the economy has a superficial plausibility. Just as within the United States the Northeast must "hold taxes and wages down" to discourage runaway shops (the alternative being to move to social control of investment and production decisions), so too nations must remain competitive or lose out internationally to more attractive sites for capitalist investment. The attack on social welfare spending is part of this phenomenon of removing impediments to market allocation.

What is unique about the present period of crisis (unlike the 1930s and earlier important crises) is the internationalization of production, which reduces the ability of any nation state to control its own economy. The qualitative change is that because capital is far more mobile across national frontiers, and product competition is worldwide, no capitalist government thinks it can do much except give corporations better terms and hope for a trickle-down effect. In the aggregate this does not work. It is like New Jersey lowering taxes to take business away from New York. Overall no new jobs are created, but the taxes from corporations go down everywhere.

The nation state is an important intervening agency in this process, mediating the desires of globally oriented capital and its conflicts with smaller local, regional, and national capital on the one hand, and the working class on the other. Struggles over tariff protection and state subsidies and restrictions on capital mobility must be seen in these terms. Foreign competition comes heavily from our own multinational corporations. A third of U.S. imports is from U.S. subsidiaries abroad. U.S. firms export more merchandise from subsidiaries abroad to markets around the world than they do from their U.S. operations. The largest U.S. firms typically receive over half their income from foreign affiliates and subsidiaries. For example, some U.S. television producers are against being protected from "foreign" TV sets—they are the foreign producers using cheaper labor to service the U.S. market from abroad.

For workers, too, the state is the level at which important struggles are waged. It is the state that institutes wage controls and cuts social services. The globalization in the arena of decision making by increasingly mobile multinationals affects the workers and smaller producers in ways that are mediated by national governments. The working-class movement is paradoxically forced to unite with workers of all nations, not because of stirring polemics but because of material needs in an era of monopoly capital. The national state is the jurisdiction through which capital disciplines labor and plays groups of workers against each other. By fighting cutbacks in social expenditures, efforts to limit the right to strike, and so on, workers make demands which make clearer the class position of the state apparatus. The political struggles and the class struggle become one.

There is a cycle of regional impoverishment which is affecting increasingly large parts of the United States in much the same way as it does poorer countries. The industrialization of agricultural nations and parts of nations, such as Puerto Rico and the Mexican side of the Rio Grande, is a process of capital penetration of a low-wage area, the establishment of infrastructure at government expense, and the building of plants and installation of machinery to exploit local labor. Over time, as the surplus labor of the area is absorbed, as workers organize and demand more of the surplus they produce, as the penetration of capitalist relations drives up the cost of living and so the wages required to produce more workers, as more and more goods and services must be bought in the money economy, the firms move on, leaving a depressed region no longer able to meet its needs. The disinvestment of much of the industrial Northeast is a process akin to the one we have been describing.

Decreasing transportation and information telecommunications costs shrink the world. The penetration of the cash market and the proletarianization of the peasantry expand the work force and integrate the smallest villages into international market social relations. Capital's expansion into South Korea and Brazil affects garment workers in New York and auto workers in Detroit and undercuts trade union strength in the advanced economies, leaving its mark on declining industrial cities and traumatizing previously secure and well-paid workers. This restructuring crisis changes the balance of forces between capital and labor in favor of the former. Increased internationalization also has undermined traditional liberal Keynesian economic programs.

INTERNATIONALIZATION, KEYNESIAN ECONOMICS
AND THE NEOCONSERVATIVE CRITIQUE

In a period of economic downturn, the continuous process of the internationalization of the law of value is felt with a vengeance. Competition for jobs puts downward pressure on the wages of all workers in enterprises tied to the international capitalist division of labor. As important, the dramatic pressures of increased international competition make it impossible for any one nation to successfully follow expansionary fiscal policies. The Keynesian model flounders on the closed nation-state premise, which implicitly argues that stimulating consumer demand will increase output, employment, and profit rates. In an open world economy, this need not be the case. One nation, for example the United States, by stimulating its own economy in the midst of a worldwide slowdown creates employment abroad, inflation at home, and balance of payments difficulties.

Interestingly enough, Keynes believed in import controls and economic nationalism. He was against an extensive international division of labor because it increased the vulnerability of a country to forces beyond its control. Believing in national self-sufficiency, he argued that national capital would support state intervention to protect itself. Those who have taken his name to describe their economics have in general been advocates of free trade and stress deficit spending as the central aspect of their policy prescription. While other factors are involved, the demise of Keynesianism is closely tied to the intensification of worldwide competition. It has heightened the instability of capitalism and increased the imbalances between investment and consumption.

Liberal Keynesianism has been dead for a long time in Washington. Even before Reagan's dramatic budget cuts, President Carter accepted the conservative, Nixon-Ford administration contention that increased government spending on "nonproductive" activities is inflationary. Fiscal conservatives have suggested that Keynesianism is a one-sided policy of constant overstimulation. In this view, good intentions must give way to "realism," for if we expand government spending and provide more and more for our citizens, two sorts of problems follow. To the extent that more flows through the public sector, less is available to private enterprise. To the degree that larger and larger deficits are funded through the money markets, private corporations are either forced to pay more (and this, of course, both discourages investment and is passed on to consumers in higher prices) or they are crowded out of financial markets by the government outbidding them. Thus, the private sector is weakened with the growth of the public sector, fiscal conservatives maintain.

A second argument is equally important to the conservatives. To the degree to which the federal government raises welfare benefits, extends unemployment compensation to cover longer periods of joblessness, and provides food stamps and similar programs, it undercuts the incentive to work. The "incentive to work" was, in earlier days, also called the "whip of hunger." By either name, it uses the threat of poverty to force U.S. workers to accept unsafe, unpleasant, or low-paid work. The effect of the welfare state on work incentives is a major concern. To the extent that jobs are stratified and pay scales hierarchical, an increase in the minimum wage for entry-level jobs has profound effects. In order to retain the original differentials in pay, other wages are forced up. Thus, if well-paying public sector jobs were made available in significant numbers, they would wreak havoc in the labor market for low-wage employment.

Conservatives point out that in periods of sustained full employment, labor discipline breaks down, worker productivity drops, and there is strong upward pressure on wages. Put otherwise: when a range of job choices exists, worker quit rates go up in the most oppressive and low-paying jobs, and all workers feel more confident in demanding promotion in pay grade and improved safety conditions. They collude more widely and more openly in slowing down the work pace, knowing that management has limited control over them. With a booming economy and a full orderbook, strikes are far more costly to management and less necesary for labor. By the same token, while long recessions are costly to capital, intermittent unemployment is less harmful and may perhaps be useful. The presence of Marx's reserve army of the unemployed and the threat of becoming an unwilling conscript in it improve worker attitudes in ways management finds congenial to higher profits. From a profit point of view, the idea is to be able to produce for less. Therefore, so long as markets exist, it is better for capital as a whole to keep wages low. The Keynesian logic was to cut taxes in order to build purchasing power; the conservatives prefer to hold down wages and increase profit margins.

The ideological reflex of rising corporate power is neoconservative reprivatization, scapegoating the government for whatever is wrong with the economy, along with calling for less government with more reliance on market forces. Neoconservatives believe that government is inefficient and that given proper incentives—lower taxes and less regulation—those with money will restore dynamism to the economy. Those who have been the designated beneficiaries of liberalism's good intentions, the victims of exploitation and discrimination, will find job opportunities in an expanding economy unleashed by supply-side incentives.

THE IMPACT ON LABOR

There is an implicit corporate restructuring strategy for the 1980s. It calls for the continued decline of manufacturing in the United States, especially in the Northeast and industrial Midwest, a disinvestment which has profound effects on the older cities. This restructuring of where and how production takes place involves a continued deskilling of the labor force due to new investment technologies which call for less and less creativity and initiative on the part of workers. They become increasingly interchangeable and easily replaced by labor which has no training and has less bargaining power as a result. The spatial incidence of this change is partially a Snowbelt-Sunbelt phenomenon, but the regional aspect is likely to become less important. The social restructuring has less to do with the advantages of particular regions which are temporary and more to do with wider corporate strategies made possible by changes in technology and the organization of production.

New plants are on the whole smaller. Equipment is designed to become economically obsolete sooner. These factors allow for two important bargaining strategies. The first is multisourcing. Should labor "trouble" develop in any one isolated facility, its output can be made up through slight increases in facilities elsewhere. Organizing efforts are made more difficult and union power eroded. The impact on unions has been devastating. A third of all U.S. workers were organized twenty years ago; today, less than a fifth belong to unions. The second advantage involves tax subsidies. Corporations can play off one jurisdiction against another just as they play off one group of workers against another. Modern plants can be closed up and moved at small expense to the owners because local governments competing for business can be induced to build the physical structures to house the equipment, levying no or low taxes as part of the bargain. Thus, the corporation maximizes its power and minimizes its tax burden.

The effect of this restructuring has been devastating for both U.S. workers and taxpayers (and of course the majority of us who are both). Real wages were lower in 1982 than they were a quarter of a century earlier for the average worker (the Bureau of Labor's non-supervisory production worker), adjusting for Social Security and all other taxes as well as decreases in income due to inflation. Corporate income tax payments were over a third of total federal revenues at the end of World War II. The corporate income tax share by 1980 was less than 12 percent, and under the 1981 Reagan law, it will fall still further, to less than 8 percent by 1986. The impact of these tax changes has been growing deficits and a loss of government services.

Since the great union organizing drives in basic industries succeeded in the 1930s, large capital has come to accept the inevitability of unions and has worked to turn them into institutions to control and discipline labor. In the post–World War II period, one of the central functions of the cold war was to expel the American Communists and other militants who had built the CIO from positions of leadership in the trade union movement, and to support class accommodationist business unionism and even gangsterism.

The productivity deal which supplanted class politics called for multiyear contracts to promote labor peace, and the security of seniority and retirement benefits to buy loyalty and give workers a stake in the company. Most importantly, an implicit deal was made. The company was given control of the production process and was more or less free to introduce new technologies which would hold down the need for labor. The workers who continued to have jobs with the company would share in part of the gains through higher wages. The consequence of this deal is that a smaller and smaller proportion of the work force is organized. The multidivisional corporations first subcontracted parts to nonunion shops and finally moved plants to nonunion areas and actively fought unionization efforts. The trade union movement today is paying the price of its earlier accommodations. Led by men more interested in the steady inflow of dues and labor peace than they are in the well-being of their members, unions are viewed as authoritarian by the workers, as arrogant and selfish by the general public. The AFL-CIO Executive Council pronouncements seem hardly a threat to a president bound on a policy of forcing down the real wages of American workers.

American trade unions, unlike many of their European counterparts, believe that the interests of labor and management are interdependent, that they both rely on the prosperity of the company, and that there is no contradiction between the groups. This has led some "responsible" union leaders to contain rank-and-file militancy and to protect the productivity of the firm by enforcing work rules or allowing the companies to do so even when workers feel that these rules violate traditional norms and impose hardship. After all, the position goes, higher wages come out of higher productivity. Sometimes union and industry leaders together lobby government to protect and extend profits and wages.

There are a number of problems with this strategy. First, tax incentives and other measures to pay U.S. corporations to modernize or build new plants result frequently in fewer production jobs in the new facility. Thus, when a major steel producer contemplates the construction of an eight-billion-dollar complex, labor needs are reduced by two-thirds compared to those in older facilities. Second, lower corporate profit taxes and other stimulants to investment may not lead to new domestic capacity. Mobil buys Montgomery Ward. U.S. Steel, helped by taxpayers, expands further into petrochemicals, seabed mining, real estate, and mining of zinc, copper, and cobalt. It outbids Mobil for control of Marathon Oil. Tax policies that redistribute the nation's income and wealth toward the corporate sector stimulate speculation, unnecessary mergers, and investment abroad.

Between 1970 and 1980, after adjusting for fringe benefits and exchange rate movements, the percentage rise in hourly compensation was far lower in the United States than in all other industrial nations. Adjusting for the slower rise in output per labor hour, the rise in unit labor costs in the United States was still dramatically below all other industrial nations. Despite this deterioration the U.S. labor movement has experienced a declining ability to organize American workers. Unions have been winning fewer National Labor Relations Board representation elections. Indeed, over the decade of the 1970s, unions lost more certification contests than they won. The number of decertification elections lost has also been increasing—unions in the early 1980s lost three out of four.

Without a substantial progressive movement within the unions, union leaders will try to protect their institution, members, and themselves on an industry-by-industry basis. Their concern for workers as taxpayers, consumers, and inhabitants of hazardous workplaces and deteriorating neighborhoods will be subservient to an accommodationist effort that they hope will keep them from losing a large part of their membership. To break out of its malaise, the labor movement must change its strategy.

The political movements of the 1970s, the ecology and antinuclear campaigns, the women's movement, and various community struggles over turf rights were in a profound way more fundamental challenges to capitalism than trade union struggles, which confine themselves to demanding "more." In a period of intensified economic competition, "more" is not possible, at least not very much more, because the boss must stay in business. While the 1970s movements wanted more also (more or equal pay for women and minorities), they wanted "different" as well. They called for a new way of thinking about personal, social, and communal development. They challenged the mode of thinking that accepts people only as instruments, ignoring feelings and personal growth needs, and that denies respect to the earth. The question is, Can traditional labor's concern for wages and narrow work issues be broadened and alliances developed with other progressive social movements? Organized labor needs to better deal with racism and sexism. It must also synthesize quality of life and corporate control issues.

Most Americans are skeptical of the ability of the government to control the corporations. They know that the corporations can buy public officials. They are not convinced that there is an alternative, even if it is long-range, outside the framework of corporate dominance. An alternative perspective must clarify the concept of the social nature of production, and the origin of the social surplus. This perspective is called *economic democracy*. It asserts that democratic control of investment and work relations is as much a right as being able to vote over who shall pay taxes and whether there shall be limits on corporations' ability to pollute the environment. The money to meet social needs is available in the surplus now being appropriated by capital. Since this is a social product, the exclusive right of capitalists to appropriate it should be challenged. Short of that, capitalists must be required to pay their "fair" share of taxes. The idea that decisions concerning production, investment, and other economic matters that are now left primarily to private managers should be subject to the democratic process seems very radical. Yet many European nations already accept the principle and debate only the proper extent and mechanisms of control. Further, the seriousness of our current economic situation argues for such a radical new departure.

ECONOMIC DEMOCRACY, THE ALTERNATIVE?

Elements of the American trade union movement have been considering such an approach. Some progressive elements of labor suggest the need for public corporations which would be directly productive, a yardstick energy corporation, for example. A second approach is worker-community ownership of cooperatives, whether to produce solar collectors or steel, as in the Youngstown attempt. Like strategies for public sector employment these approaches attempt an end run around corporate control. They can be contrasted with demands for social control of industry.

A number of arguments can be made for regulating capital flight and foreign investment. The most important is that the social costs of disinvestment to an older industrial area and its people, to laid-off workers, especially older ones, to local business, and to the tax base may outweigh the possible gains in lower cost of products or other more "efficient" allocation of resources as measured in private gains to the corporation. Internationally, investments which support repressive dictatorial regimes are also increasingly condemned both on moral grounds and as a matter of self-interest. Trade unions in the United States are beginning to see the connection between the use of their tax dollars to prop up brutal military governments and the transfer of union jobs from the United States to these same countries, where workers are not able to form free trade unions. The cold war has been used to justify repression of working people's rights and human rights generally among our "free world" Allies.

Capitalism on the European continent has been quicker to seize upon the nation state as an agency of economic planning. This is in part due to pressures from a strong labor movement and from parties on the left, but also to the desire on the part of policy makers to stimulate the formation of a strong national economy by encouraging concentration and centralization of capital. In these economies the scale of enterprise required, and relative capital scarcity stimulated government intervention. Where workers' movements were stronger, the government's infusion of investment funds tended to be in the form of equity, as in France, where the state owned about a quarter of the industrial sector in 1980 and nationalized the banks and other key sectors in 1982. Today, in Italy, the public sector accounts for between 35 and 40 percent of direct output. In Germany the contemporary pattern of state intervention involves management through a close working relation between state banks and large corporations. In Japan there is interpenetration of the giant conglomerate holding companies and the Ministry of Foreign Trade and Investment.

The issue for the United States is what kind of economic planning we shall have. At present, little public long-range planning goes on, with rather severe "side effects" on the society. Can democratic forms of planning do better?

The goal from a democratic standpoint is to decentralize planning, encourage popular participation, minimize bureaucratic controls, and, in every respect, to make planning more responsive to a progressive reorienting of goals and means. Planning politicizes economic decision making. It can involve those without significant ownership or positions of authority within the corporate world to participate in decisions which profoundly affect their lives. Thus, political pluralism is extended into the economic realm. In addition, the state becomes an arena for struggle over investment and production priorities.

The least frightening form of planning to consider is the Swedish social democratic version. Some elements of this approach have been introduced to America in modified forms. Social democrats seek a greater democratization of the investment function through using worker pension funds, putting worker representatives on corporate boards of directors, increasing workplace democracy, legislating social regulation controls on capital mobility, and intervening to provide better health care and other services, and better control over prices, especially energy. In the United States, such demands tend to take a populist flavor. Ralph Nader and his associates have proposed a Corporate Democracy Act which would provide for federal chartering of corporations, independent audits, community impact analyses of plant expansion or relocation, and the protection of the constitutional rights of workers and would stipulate that a majority of corporate directors be independent. The working people will then be in a position to share in controlling decisions on what is produced, where productive investment is to be located, how work is organized, and the quality of the product. This participation will surely transform the self-appreciation of working people, including their self-pride and pride in their work. Achieving these results must involve the progressive development of worker decision-making institutions, including the formulation and application of their own criteria with respect to all aspects of production work.

The involvement of consumers and other independent, public interest directors would ensure that production decisions, product design, and other matters would be in the interests of the wider community as well. Such a chartering proposal is the natural extension of the social regulation movements of the last two decades, of the emerging ecological consciousness, worker rights, and consumer protection movements. Could this populist approach be extended into a fully socialist program to challenge the logic of capitalist ownership and control more fundamentally? Or would such a development lead to a totalitarian nondemocratic form of government?

Gunnar Adler-Karlsson and other theorists of Swedish social democracy have developed the concept of functional socialism under which legislative and union action transfers power to the working class while property remains formally private. The Swedes have gone further than others in actualizing a redivision of property rights. Over the last hundred years, formal ownership has become increasingly circumscribed. While Sweden is not being put forward as a model for the United States (Sweden today is far from an economic democracy of the sort we have in mind), there is much we can learn from Swedish thought and practice.

In his address to a Eurosocialism and America Conference in December 1980, Olaf Palme set forward his view of the historic development of the workers' movement as a three-stage progression, with the struggle proceeding from political democracy to social democracy and now to economic democracy.[1] (Palme's comments are especially relevant in the light of his election in 1982 to head once again the Swedish government.)

The extension of political democracy into the economic realm is attractive to most people, who want to play a useful role in society, to make a difference. Personal development and self-actualization is tied to feeling valued in one's job. As Palme pointed out, "For the individual it is a very important part of economic democracy to be able to choose his job freely, to change his job, to receive support to get training for another employment" (Palme:35). The control of technology to safeguard the nature of work, not only the possibility of employment, the protection of our living environment, and the promotion of a fair distribution of income requires planning. In an implicit contrast to the Soviet style, Palme told his listeners, "Planning is no act of mindless machinery. It should be founded in people's participation. Its purpose is to serve people. Since all political decisions are based on value judgments, they should not be left to experts or professionals. They must be reachable for ordinary people" (ibid.:36). This contrast between participatory planning and top-down state-controlled planning deserves extended comment.

There is no reason to believe that economic planning in the United States would resemble Soviet-style centralized planning. Nor is there reason to expect that one could, or should, try to import Swedish economic democracy. It has its own problems. Among these is its acceptance of capitalist market allocation where social priorities might dictate other organizational logic. The point is to learn from the mistakes and achievements of others while building on one's own national strengths and traditions. In this regard there are a number of characteristics of the American situation which must be taken into account in designing any economic alternative. First, most transnational corporations still call the United States their home. For this reason the American people are able to legislate the control of international capital flows and investment patterns to a degree impossible for any other electorate in the world. Eventually, there will be international treaties and planning agencies to coordinate global economic policy, but this is far down the road. In the interim the backwardness of the U.S. political consciousness allows destructive behavior by U.S.–based corporations both at home and abroad. The crucial point is that the potential power of economic democracy to raise our living standards and provide economic security is unparalleled, and the direction the United States takes in the eighties is decisive.

A second crucial reality is the American heritage of individualism, localism, and the fear of centralized power. Our political tradition is subject to manipulation by those who advocate grass-roots government and freedom of choice in the marketplace as a way to obscure the enlarged power of transnational capital to deprive Americans of their freedom. The return to a full employment economy and a progressive welfare state that provides good public schools, health care, comfortable retirements, and peaceful, crime-free communities requires social control of collectively produced wealth. Key investment decisions cannot be left to the "free" market, as some ideologues advocate. Today the market is not free, and looking backward to our eighteenth-century past won't change twenty-first-century realities. Individualism is possible in our world only when democratic power controls concentrations of wealth.

Third, eighteenth-century America had its problems which, in modified form, are still with us: racism, sexism, and classism. The legacy of slavery continues in the separate and unequal existence forced on millions of Americans of color. Women can vote but receive fifty-nine cents for every dollar men earn because of continued job discrimination. Classism, the ownership and control of the U.S. corporate system by a small group of predominantly older white males, disenfranchises working people from equal access to resources and decision making on public policy. Not only should our economic decisions be made democratically, but our political practice should be made more inclusive. People of color and women are underrepresented in positions of power. Progressive white males must understand this priority if our society is to control its economy democratically. Racism and sexism are important barriers to unity.

A clear understanding of how ideology affects our views of ourselves and others, and how our internalized views of realities differ, is a crucial part of thinking about economic policy. Belief systems are complex. We need to sort out our own and to understand why our neighbor sees the world differently than we do. We have to develop a common language so that we can understand each other's dreams and fears. Different ethnic and racial groups, different professional strata, and different regional cultures have their own unique styles, and these reflect real world differences which must be seen as genuinely diverse and deserving of mutual respect. Only then are sound political alliances possible. Only then can a truly democratic culture be created.

NOTE

1. Olaf, Palme. "Address." Eurosocialism and America Conference. *Working Papers for a New Society*, January–February 1981.

Contributors

Barry Bluestone is a professor of economics at Boston College and director of the Social Welfare Research Institute. He has written a number of industry studies including *The Retail Revolution: Market Transformation, Investment, and Labor in the Modern Department Store Industry* and *Aircraft Industry Dynamics: An Analysis of Competition, Capital, and Labor.* He is co-author of *The Deindustrialization of America.* His work focuses on the impact of industrial transformation on workers and their communities.

Joe R. Feagin, a native of Texas, teaches sociology at the University of Texas. His current research is focused on the urban developer as a new capitalist and on Houston as a case study in frontier capitalism. His recent books include *School Desegregation* (Plenum, 1980) and *Social Problems: A Critical Power-Conflict Perspective* (Prentice-Hall, 1982).

William W. Goldsmith teaches city and regional planning at Cornell University and directs the Program on International Studies in Planning there. He is on the national steering committee of the Planners Network and divides his research time between urban policy in the U.S. and regional development in Latin America.

Bennett Harrison is associate professor of urban studies and economics at the Massachusetts Institute of Technology, where he teaches political economy, economic development, and labor economics. His most recent books are *The Deindustrialization of America* (co-authored with Barry Bluestone) and *The Economic Transformation of New England Since World War II.* He has been working with a number of

417

union locals and labor-community coalitions on the problems of runaway shops and company demands for wage givebacks.

Richard Child Hill teaches urban studies and political economy in the Department of Sociology at Michigan State University. He has published articles on urban theory, race-relations, employment policy, and the postwar history of Detroit. He is currently doing comparative research on the crisis and global reorganization of the automobile industry. He has given up an earlier addiction to pool hustling for squash and hatha yoga.

Robert Kraushaar teaches planning and environmental design at SUNY–Buffalo. His paper was the result of three years spent researching planning in declining industrial cities in England. Although a native of Los Angeles, he is currently in Buffalo exploring how the English experiences relate to the American context. His concern is that in a changing economic environment, the theories and styles of intervention must also change. He is in the process of developing a graduate planning program at SUNY–Buffalo which specifically addresses this issue.

Michael Luger has taught planning, public policy, and economics at Duke University since 1980. Before then, he studied at Princeton and Berkeley and worked in local government in England and his native Pennsylvania. He has written in the areas of urban and regional development, public finance, and national economic policy. He lives in Durham, North Carolina.

Dan Luria is on the research staff of the United Auto Workers in Detroit. He holds a Ph.D. in Economics from the University of Massachusetts. He is currently working politically to build the labor side of the quadripartite coalition needed to implement the proposals discussed in his paper in this volume and on a book with Matthew Edel and Elliott Sclar on suburbanization called *Shaky Palaces*.

Dorothy Remy is an Associate Professor in the Department of Urban Studies at the University of the District of Columbia in Washington, D.C. She is an anthropologist who has carried out field work in factories in both the United States and Africa. Her research interests focus on the interrelations between family, community, and work.

Jack Russell is a consultant to the Michigan State Committee on Corporation and Economic Development, where he recently wrote amendments and laws to help workers and investors secure financing to convert plants to new product lines, a key aspect of *Rational Reindustrialization*. From 1978–81, he was economic development aide to Detroit City Councilor Ken Cockrel.

Larry Sawers is a Professor of Economics at The American University in Washington, D.C., where he has taught Urban Economics since 1969. He was part of a group of faculty and students who in the early 1970s organized one of the first academic programs in the country in which one could specialize in Political Economy. His research interests have focused on urban transportation, labor markets, and suburbanization. He is co-editor (with William Tabb) of *Marxism and the Metropolis* (Oxford University Press, 1978 and 1983).

AnnaLee Saxenian (known to her friends as Anno) is currently living in Cambridge, Mass. and working on a Ph.D. in urban studies and planning at MIT. She is researching capital restructuring in the so-called high-tech industries and regional economic development, interests which she developed while working with the Western Urban and Regional Collective (WURC) in Berkeley. Between 1976 and 1978 she lived in Hong Kong, and hopes to return soon.

Michael Storper teaches urban planning at UCLA. He studied geography at Berkeley. He spent several years as a lobbyist for environmental groups, and has recently been a leader of a coalition in California that promoted a ballot initiative to stop agribusiness-promoted water projects.

Gregory D. Squires works for the Midwest Regional Office of the U.S. Commission on Civil Rights and teaches in the sociology department at Loyola University of Chicago. He also edits *The Journal of Intergroup Relations*. He received his Ph.D. in sociology from Michigan State University in 1976. His publications include *Education and Jobs: The Imbalancing of the Social Machinery; Insurance Redlining— Fact Not Fiction;* and *Shutdown: Economic Dislocation and Equal Opportunity.*

Bill Tabb is professor of economics at Queens College, City University of New York and is on the CUNY Graduate Center Faculty in

Sociology. He is author of *The Long Default: New York and the Urban Fiscal Crisis* (New York: Monthly Review Press, 1982) and is involved in economic education with church, community, and labor groups. For a number of years, he has had a monthly call-in program, "Behind the Economic News," on listener-sponsored WBAI in New York.

Dick Walker is assistant professor of geography at the University of California, Berkeley. His main work is in the areas of water resources, environmental pollution, urbanization, and industrial location. Some of it is not half bad, but most is buried in obscure journals. He has taught classes on *Capital* for many years at the Bay Area Socialist School; he serves as a national coordinator for the Faculty Committee for Human Rights in El Salvador; he worked hard to defeat California's notorious "Peripheral Canal"; and he is a gardener of some repute among the East Bay left. Walker and Mike Storper have enjoyed a fruitful collaboration that now spans five years and more articles.

David Wilmoth lives in Sydney, Australia, where he manages the central policy division of the state government's Department of Environment and Planning. Before that he was a Ph.D. student at the University of California, Berkeley, where he wrote a dissertation on U.S. national urban policy. He also enjoys regional economic policy, metropolitan planning, intergovernmental relations, and body surfing.

Goetz Wolff has taught political science at several universities and has worked with labor unions. He is currently pursuing a doctorate in urban planning at the University of California, Los Angeles.

Index

Page numbers followed by *t* indicate tables, and those set in italic indicate figures.